The Secret Feminist Cabal:
A Cultural History of Science Fiction Feminisms

The Secret Feminist Cabal:

A Cultural History of Science Fiction Feminisms

Helen Merrick

AQUEDUCT PRESS | SEATTLE

Aqueduct Press
PO Box 95787
Seattle WA 99145-2787
www.aqueductpress.com

The Secret Feminist Cabal:
A Cultural History of Science Fiction Feminisms

First Edition: December 2009
ISBN: 978-1-933500-33-1
Library of Congress Control Number: 2009940085
9 8 7 6 5 4 3 2 1

Cover and Book Design by Kathryn Wilham
Cover illustration © Lee Abuabara
Cover collage images:
Girl Reading, *Aurora* 23, 1983, by permission of Brad Foster
http://www.jabberwockygraphix.com
©iStockphoto.com/
Simfo: stock-photo-3508661-armillary-sphere
Prill: stock-photo-4842054-calligraphy-detail
gabor_h: stock-photo-3824453-handwritten-text-1

Text Illustrations by permission of Jeanne Gomoll
© Jeanne Gomoll:
"Will the Real James Tiptree, Jr. Please Stand Up," poster, 1978
"FIAWOL," poster, 1977

Printed in the USA by Thomson-Shore Inc.

Contents

PREFACE

Confessions of a feminist science fiction reader

I don't scorn science fiction, any more than I scorn Afghani-
stan; I'm just one of those types who prefer to stay at home
and mumble about the problems at hand... I believe that, if
we wish to make new fictions of our lives, adumbrate new pos-
sibilities for experience and awareness, we must do it in the
language life has given us... I think we must imagine, not a
fantastic world, but how we might speak and act differently in
this one... It is the utopian mode that separates science fiction
from the other categories of popular feminist fiction... But I
live here, where I must find the language to incarnate these
things: whether through weakness of intellect or paucity of
imagination, I am not content, nor even able, to dream them.

—∞ Carolyn Heilbrun (1984: 117-119)

Back in 1984, Carolyn Heilbrun explained why she didn't read science fiction (sf). This book is essentially a long and convoluted attempt to answer an apparently simple question. Why would feminists read sf? And more to the point, why do I read feminist sf?

The journey began (as it so often does with sf readers) with my adolescent self of the 1970s. I was your classic "square" kid: a bit of a geek who took maths and science subjects, always did my homework, liked *Omni* magazine, read all the sf and fantasy I could find, and argued about the existence of aliens with my friends (when we weren't trying to convince people they were just a construct of our imagination). Despite the signs, I didn't follow the science route, but with a short detour through music found myself eventually studying history at university. Up until this time I had still been avidly consuming the classics of sf, which came to an abrupt halt as I discovered feminist theory and, with growing horror, turned its lens on the Asimov, Clarke, and Heinlein I was reading. Henceforth I officially foreswore sf (despite occasionally indulging in guilty binges in semester breaks).

And then, in 1992 I was rescued from my self-enforced abstinence. I was taking a class on the history of technology in which we read Donna Haraway's "A Manifesto for Cyborgs." ([1985] 2004a). Here was a feminist theorist after my own heart. I must confess that on first reading, most of the theoretical revelations passed me by; I was too enthralled by the magic phrase Haraway conjured before me—the authors she called on to be her storytellers for cyborgs were writers of feminist science fiction. What wondrous beast was this? Was it possible that my politics and reading pleasures could be reconciled? Eagerly I set about tracking down and reading every author and story hidden in Haraway's footnotes and, as they say, the rest is history. Within a few years I had started a PhD on feminist SF, and more than fifteen years on from that "aha" moment, feminist sf is still my passion, my fiction of choice, the core around which most of my critical activities circulate.

From fairly early on, however, it became apparent that most other feminists and women I knew did not share this passion. Rather, they found it incomprehensible and more than a little strange. Increasingly in my research I was drawn to examine what to me was a conundrum. Others wondered why a feminist would read sf. I wondered, why wouldn't they?

For me, the pleasure I gained from reading women's and feminist sf was not just about a return to my own personal golden age of twelve, but was precisely animated by the particular archaeologies of feminism/s expressed in the texts. Various historical developments within feminist criticism and theory became much more vivid to me through my concurrent readings of sf texts. As I read more, including the critical work on feminist sf, the issue of why so many feminists were antagonistic towards, or ignorant of sf became ever more pressing. Why was this innovative and challenging body of feminist work so rarely acknowledged as a "legitimate" subject for feminist study? I was not the only feminist sf reader to ask such questions. Sf writer and editor Susanna Sturgis put it very neatly in the title of her essay "Why Does a Bright Feminist Like You Read That Stuff Anyway?" (1989, 1-9). Like me, Sturgis discovered feminist sf later in life, and perhaps for this reason she has also felt the proselytizing urge which generally produces amazement, indifference, or outright scorn (see also Cook, 1985, 133-45).

It is this quest(ion) which initiated my desire to consider in the broadest sense, all of the commentaries on feminist sf I could find. My search led me beyond the normal confines of sf criticism, to audiences and readers outside academe. I discovered fandom, fanzines, and conventions. I started attending the local West Australian convention, Swancon and even managed to attend the feminist sf convention, WisCon in Madison Wisconsin. WisCon 20 was a pivotal moment for me. Not only did it introduce me to the global feminist sf fan and writerly community, but also gave me a sense of the history of feminist fandom including access to copies of some of their increasingly rare fanzines.

My particular journeys through feminist sf texts, academe and fandom inevitably inflect my account, producing a very particular and invested story of sf feminisms. My immersion in the sf texts and fandom together have led to a concern with the sf "field" as it is broadly constituted and thus I focus on fan writings as much as academic texts in telling this story. It is no accident that my narrative heads inexorably towards science studies, as this is what founded my engagement with feminist sf, and to me always appeared to be a part of the sf "field" as I encountered it.

Thus my opening confessions, intended to contextualize what is a necessarily partial, situated and invested account of the nexus of feminism and sf. If nothing else, this book might provide an answer to why I have found feminist sf so engaging. Hopefully it does much more, and reveals what all kinds of feminist readers might find illuminating, challenging and inspiring about the production of sf feminisms.

ACKNOWLEDGMENTS

Portions of some chapters have appeared elsewhere in earlier versions, including articles in the journals *Refractory* and *Women's Studies International Forum*, and as chapters in Helen Merrick and Tess Williams (eds), *Women of Other Worlds: Excursions through science fiction and feminism* (UWA Press, 1999); Andy Sawyer, et al. (eds), *Speaking Science Fiction* (Liverpool University Press, 2000); Margret Grebowicz (ed), *Sci-Fi in the Mind's Eye: Essays in science and technology studies* (Open Court, 2007); and Farah Mendlesohn (ed), *On Joanna Russ*, (Wesleyan University Press 2009).

Given the very long gestation period of this book, there are a lot of people I want to thank. From the beginning, the advice and friendship of Justine Larbalestier, Sylvia Kelso, Tess Williams and Joan Haran kept me sane and contributed immeasurably to the ways I thought and wrote about feminist sf. For their help in the very earliest stages of this project, I am indebted to Rob Stuart, Philippa Maddern, Charlie Fox, Maureen Perkins and Esta Ungar. Thanks also to Grant Stone, the Murdoch University Library, and Graham Stone. Thanks to Veronica Hollinger, Katie King and Terry Threadgold for their advice, comments, and ongoing support of my work.

None of this would have been possible without the help and enthusiasm of so many people in the sf community, in particular, those involved in Fem-SF and WisCon as well as many members of the UK fan community who helped me out through interviews, chats, provision of rare fan material or permission to cite their words; so thanks (in no particular order) to: Jeanne Gomoll, Amanda Bankier, Susanna Sturgis, Candas Jane Dorsey, Nicola Griffith, Karen Joy Fowler, Pat Murphy, Melissa Scott, Nalo Hopkinson, Rebecca Holden, Jane Donawerth, Sherryl Vint, Lisa Yaszek, Edward James, Farah Mendlesohn, Elizabeth Sourbut, Jenny Wolmark, Andy Sawyer, Maureen Kincaid Speller, Carol Anne Green, Elizabeth Billinger, Avedon Carol, Rob Hansen, Caroline Mullan, Brian Ameringen, and Mark Bould. And my thanks are due to the late Vincent (Vin¢) Clark who so kindly answered all my questions, served me tea and gave me photocopies of rare UK fanzines. Many other people along the way have provided various kinds of support or feedback including Catherine Macdonald, Jane Long, Matthew Allen, Sara Buttsworth, Emma Hawkes, Darren Jorgensen, and Peter Fletcher. My wonderful doctoral student Kandace Mavrick not only provided lots of opportunities to chat about all things sf, but was the best research assistant and endnote wrangler anyone could hope for.

In recent years, I have been inspired and encouraged by the many wonderful women active in West Australian fandom and the fabulous institutions of Gynacon (the feminist guerilla programming track of our local convention, Swancon) and Femmecon. In particular, thanks to Sarah Parker and Sarah Xu for reminding me what feminist activism, community, and consciousness-raising is all about.

I feel very privileged to be publishing this book through Aqueduct Press, home to so many wonderful authors from the feminist sf community. An enormous thank you to Timmi Duchamp for your encouragement, insightful comments, and sharp editing, which helped me improve the book in so many ways. I am indebted to Kathryn Wilham for her eagle eye in copyediting and her wonderfully enthusiastic attitude throughout the proofing process. Thanks also to the readers of the manuscript and to the fabulous, Tiptree-award winning Nisi Shawl who so kindly made me an index!

And of course, my long-suffering family—to Anne, Geoff, Stephen, and Kathryn Merrick, thank you for the hours of childcare, fun, distraction, and belief. And for making sure it all means something in the end, my thanks and love to Stewart for the house-husbanding and everything else, to Louis, and especially to Alisdair who was there right from the beginning, and to Julia for putting up with a mummy who spends way too much time in front of the computer.

1

INTRODUCTION: THE GENRE FEMINISM DOESN'T SEE

*Who roams the galaxy, single-handedly fighting injustice, op-
pression, and outdated portrayals of gender roles in speculative
fiction? Space Babe! Join her in her quest, and be recognized by
her allies everywhere when you wear the sign of The Secret
Feminist Cabal.*

⤞ http://www.tiptree.org/?see=spacebabe

This book is a journey through the rich history of feminist activity
within the literary genre of science fiction (sf). The title deliberately
invokes a recent phase in this history: the not-so secret establishment
of a self-proclaimed "feminist cabal" to promote feminism through
sf awards, conventions, and publications. Borrowed (with kind permission) from the James Tiptree Jr. Award, the title seemed apt for a
number of reasons. First, it serves to highlight the fact that a feminist
presence within sf has often been considered unusual, if not unnatu-
ral. The phrase also hints at an unacknowledged or suppressed history,
a secret record of deliberate, conspiratorial, and political action. The
use of the term "cabal" to describe the diverse and shifting alliances
of the feminist sf community is an ironic, performative move. In both
this book and the community itself, the cabal is not meant to be taken
literally. After all, what kind of self-respecting cabal would openly ad-
vertise its "secret" existence through websites and conventions, identify its members through the wearing of garish temporary tattoos,
and fund itself by the sale of home-baked chocolate chip cookies? In
other words, the secret feminist cabal is a joke. But a very serious joke.
It is this particular understanding that makes the phrase so appropriate for my purposes. For, despite the seriousness of the issues at stake
in this history, one of the most appealing yet overlooked aspects of sf
feminisms is the humor and wit of its writers, critics, and fans. Science fiction may be a place where feminists go to dream of utopia or
plot revolution, but it is also a source of *pleasure*—of individual reading pleasure, of emotional connection with like-minded folk—and at
times a place to make life-long friends and allies.

Yet sf is often assumed to be an inappropriate or unlikely place to find feminist visions, debate, and theory. Many assumptions persist about the genre—including its exclusively adolescent (white) male appeal; its trashy, escapist nature; and its adherence to a technophile, gadget-oriented, scientific world view. Some of these assumptions hold true, at least in part, for at least some proportion of sf. But such a picture does not acknowledge the discursive and creative spaces that many feminist authors and readers have created within sf. In pursuing a history of sf feminisms, this book examines the cultural work that has been performed by and around "feminist sf." That is, the sorts of feminist knowledge production and cultural activity that have taken place within sf, and the ways certain texts become collectively figured and represented in feminist critical and fan activity. I focus on a number of key discursive communities that have been central to the construction and reception of feminist sf from the 1930s to the present: namely, the early sf community of writers, fans, and readers; pre-feminist fandom; feminist fandom; academic feminist sf criticism; and feminist techno-science studies.

Borrowing from theorists Donna Haraway and Katie King, I situate feminist sf as an "object of knowledge" that functions as an "apparatus for the production of feminist culture" (Haraway 1991a: 162-3; see also K. King 1994: xv-xvi, 92). In particular, I am interested in the sociocultural, historically specific contexts that enable and inflect this process of "production." My focus is on how feminist sf texts function not only as popular fiction but also as examples of feminist knowledge, as discourses of science and technology, and as the commerce for sociopolitical engagements between communities of readers, writers, fans, critics, and editors. Thus, unlike in many previous studies of feminist sf, I am not so much concerned with providing interpretations of fictional texts as with providing a cultural history of the readings and stories generated by the "object" feminist sf and the ways in which this object becomes a locus for feminist cultural production in sf.

Despite their culturally marginalized location, the feminist histories played out in the sf field are fascinating both for the insights they offer on sf historiography and for feminist theory and praxis more generally. The dialogues I examine (re)produce in microcosm the processes and trends of feminist knowledges and debate of the last four decades, and indeed sometimes predate nascent feminist concerns in the "mainstream." Whilst feminist sf in many ways reflects and parallels broader feminist theoretical and cultural journeys, there are marked specificities in the feminist engagements with the discourses and cultures of sf. An important and distinguishing context for this engagement is the nature of sf communities. In contrast to the production of feminist knowledge in the academy, which from the 1980s on has been criticized for becoming isolated and disengaged from non-academic discourse, the feminist sf community encompasses academics, authors, fans, and editors/publishers. The dialogues and interactions of these community participants actively contribute to the discursive formation and mediation of "feminist sf" and indeed "feminisms" in general.

Learning to tell stories

My approach in this book is indebted to the work of Haraway, the most obvious influence being my concern with science studies as an arena in which stories about feminist sf are re-told. Haraway's insistence on the power of telling stories and emphasis on the "narrativity" of many modes of knowledge have influenced the ways I have thought about and tried to represent the conversations traced here. I also try to keep in mind her insistence on the power of evolutionary—especially Darwinian—stories that unconsciously inform any history we construct, especially when science, knowledge, nature, and gender are the major characters of our narrative. Following Haraway and King, I think about feminist sf—and feminist sf criticism—as "objects of knowledge"—that is, the end points of complicated historical processes and discursive battles rather than something obvious, static, and known—that are best fashioned as practices not things, as verbs not nouns.

I owe much to King's approach to narrating a history of feminist theory. In the opening "story" of her *Theory in Its Feminist Travels* she comments: "I want to describe feminist theory as a politics of knowledge making. The kind of object I mean might be called an 'object of knowledge.' Theory too is such an object... We produce the things we know" (K. King 1994: xv). Acknowledging Haraway's formulation of "objects of knowledge," King employs this tool from science studies to shape her enquiry into what counts as feminist theory—one motivated by clashes between her personal experiences as an activist and feminist academic with "canonical versions" of feminist theory (95). King's description of her approach in looking for the object feminist theory resonates with my constructions of feminist sf:

> What I look to, in considering what an object [of knowledge] is, are especially the moments and histories of its production over time, the contests for meanings within which it is embedded, the political contours that are the circumstances out of which it is fabricated, and the resources and costs of its making, contesting, and stabilizations, some lasting, some ephemeral. (xvi)

My story is inspired, too, by King's approach to reconstructing and rehistoricizing feminist theory through the adoption of what she calls "writing technologies" such as "poem," "story," and "song" to construct an alternative to dominant notions of "cultural" and "radical feminism" as a site called "the apparatus for the production of feminist culture" (1994: 92). Finally I admire King's admission of the historicity and thus "messiness" of her book, which does not try to smooth out inconsistencies (xiii). My book too has bumps and unresolved tensions, particularly obvious in my struggle to resist the pull of the singular object "feminist sf"—such a useful tool to smooth messy stories with; seductive, as its fashioning required so much effort, and tempting, because it signals an apparently clear identity, a way of thinking and being a (sf) feminist. A different perspective on the ways we have constructed stories of feminist theory is provided by Clare Hemmings; in a historiographical review she notes the importance of emotion in such constructions:

> Feminist emotion...is central to the feminist stories we tell, and the way that we tell them...as a result, an account of ways of telling feminist stories needs to be attentive to the affective as well as technical ways in which our stories about the recent feminist past work. It hurts because it matters... (2005: 120)

In thinking about the sometimes challenging conversations that inform the making of feminist sf, I have found it useful to keep in mind the emotional investment of the various participants in these dialogues.

The importance of stories is also key to other works that have influenced my approach. L. Timmel Duchamp highlights the way readers of feminist sf imagine themselves into an ongoing dialogue and community, encapsulated by her notion of the "grand conversation" (2004b). My story is engaged in such a conversation with many academic and non-academic critics, from those pioneers who from the 1970s through to the '90s defined and consolidated feminist sf, as well as more recent work by critics like Brian Attebery, Justine Larbalestier, and Lisa Yaszek, which has expanded the texts and subjects of feminist sf criticism. Finally, I aspire to the kinds of interdisciplinary and historically situated studies that critics such as Roger Luckhurst call for. Luckhurst's study *Science Fiction* aims to present a model of a cultural history of sf: one that "situates SF texts in a broad network of contexts and disciplinary knowledges" that "necessitates an ambitious stretch of contextual material, ranging from the history of science and technology, via the softer social sciences, to the rarefied world of aesthetic and critical theory" (2005: 3). While my scope here is much less ambitious in its contextual material, this book is intended as a contribution to the growing body of work that attempts such multidisciplinary and historical approaches to the field.

All these influences help me to view my story of feminist sf as a necessarily partial, indebted, and very personal one. Like many other accounts of feminist sf, mine is very much focused on the North American community and almost entirely on Anglophone texts. This bias emerges partially from the fact that the majority of feminist activity in sf has emerged in the US as well as my inability to locate or read sources not written in English. There remain many stories to tell of the experiences of feminists engaged in sf in the UK, Australia, and other sites of significant feminist activity such as Eastern Europe, Japan, and South America (see for example, Agosin 1992: 5; Ginway 2004; Hauser 1997; Kotani 2007). I have been particularly drawn to charting the details of early conversations eddying around the emergence of feminist sf and its pre-history. Most intriguing for me are those moments where the meaning/s of feminist sf were emerging or contested. For, as King notes of her "object" feminist theory, the point is,

> to heighten the local aspects of discourse, very much historically—at times almost "momentarily"—located, continually

rewritten or reinscribed with new meanings by feminist
practitioners and to foreground how the terms, constituen-
cies, and strategies of feminists shift and travel. (1994: xi)

Given the wealth of these details, I have also remained for the
most part focused on the sf community—that is, the writers, readers,
and critics who are located in and publish within the sf field. In consequence, there is an obvious omission of those dialogues carried out
under the aegis of utopian studies. Initially, my aim was to chart the
various feminist sf objects produced by different critical and popular
communities, including utopian studies, mainstream literary criticism,
and genre and cultural studies. I finally chose only to give a brief overview of these critical sites because although many texts recognized as
feminist sf are discussed in these fields, the impetus of such discussion
is not toward the construction of "feminist sf," but the production
of different kinds of objects—feminist utopias, feminist literature,
or feminist popular fiction, for example. Utopian studies in particular
is now such an enormous field, and the historical and formal relation
between utopia and sf so complex, that to deal adequately with the
topic would have required another book. Therefore, apart from a brief
overview of such critical commentaries later in this chapter, the rest
of this present book concentrates on those dialogues that are clearly
about sf as a field and (eventually) feminist sf as its subject.

I trace a number of discursive communities that have contributed
to the production of feminist sf: the sf field generally, proto-feminist
and feminist fan communities, feminist sf critics, and feminist scholars of science and technology. With the exception of the latter, each
of these communities overlaps with the others and with the broader
sf field. The book is arranged roughly chronologically, with the early chapters providing a "pre-history" of sf feminisms, whereas later
chapters trace various developments of sf feminisms from the 1970s
onwards. Chapter Two, "Resistance Is Useless!: The Sex/Woman/Femi-
nist Invasion" provides a context for the "arrival" of women in the
field, as subjects, writers, and readers. Beginning with the letters and
editorials of the pulp magazines from the 1920s and 1930s, I trace the
overt and covert narratives around women, sex, and gender in the sf
field prior to the emergence of feminist activity in the 1970s. Chapter
Three offers a different kind of prehistory, attempting to uncover stories of women's involvement in sf as readers and fans from the 1920s

to the 1960s. Entitled "Mothers of the Revolution: Femmefans Unite!" the chapter not only uncovers women's presence in this period, but identifies moments of woman-identified and proto-feminist activity.

Starting with 1970s, my analysis becomes necessarily more synchronic and dialogic, as the sf field becomes larger, encompassing both expanded fan communities and the growing numbers of academic sf critics, who have increasingly become a distinct and often separate community themselves. "Birth of a Sub-Genre: Feminist SF and Its Criticism" (Chapter Four) traces the emergence of feminist sf criticism, from its beginnings in critiques by writers and fans to its establishment as an identifiable body of criticism. The same period is covered in Chapter Five, "FIAWOL: The Making of Fannish Feminisms." As the title suggests, the focus here is on how sf feminisms developed in fandom. Chapters Six and Seven concentrate on two key issues that surfaced in feminist sf criticism from the mid-1980s through the 1990s and overlapped with the field of cultural studies of science and technology. "Cyborg Theorists: Feminist SF Criticism Meets Cybercultural Studies" traces the impact of cyberpunk and the cyborg on sf feminisms and the emergence of the body and the posthuman as central concerns. Covering roughly the same period, a related but distinct cross-disciplinary dialogue is the subject of "Another Science 'Fiction'? Feminist Stories of Science." Concluding the book is "Beyond Gender?: Twenty-first Century SF Feminisms," which summarizes some of the directions and contests that characterize contemporary sf feminisms. Fittingly, it also returns to a more holistic overview encompassing the stories of critics, writers, and fans, which together produce and re-produce a variety of feminisms within sf.

The remainder of this introductory chapter contextualizes the various elements of the sf field and bodies of criticism I survey in this book. Crucially, I begin by outlining what it is I mean by feminist sf. I then briefly introduce key moments in the establishment of the sf fan community, academic sf criticism, and feminist sf criticism. Finally, I address the often fraught relation of sf to mainstream literature and criticism and chart developments in feminist literary and genre criticism in the period when "feminist sf" was being formulated by sf fans, authors, and critics.

What does "feminist sf" stand for?

Integral to the feminist theorizing played out in engagements with feminist sf is a struggle over definitions—what *is* feminist science fiction? (Or sf? Or feminism?) My concern with multiple constructions means that the object feminist sf cannot be neatly pinned down, even if some consensus on feminism and sf could be reached.

A multiplicity of feminist theories, existing synchronously and diachronously, can be traced through the variety of objects classified as feminist sf. Indeed, the competing taxonomies of feminist sf now available reveal the escalating growth of feminist critical narratives in microcosm. Within the field, analysis of feminist sf has developed into a specialized feminist sf criticism, whose critical project, like its object of study, has now became large and diffuse enough not to be considered a singular, unified venture. As Veronica Hollinger observed as far back as 1990, the project of feminist sf criticism had concentrated on "the construction of the subject, whether this is the female subject/ character at the center of feminist science fiction or feminist science fiction as a 'subject,' i.e., a unified body or field of study" (1990b: 235). Hollinger argues, however, that,

> the large number of feminist science fiction texts produced over the last twenty years or so now comprises a body of work no longer well served by criticism that reads it as a unified undertaking, i.e., individual texts all grounded upon the same ideological foundations and all working together for the promotion of a single coherent feminism. (229)

My approach works to unravel this monolithic subject by paying attention to the multiplicity of historical and political positionings subsumed under the label "feminism/s." The book also challenges unitary conceptions of feminist criticism by acknowledging critical commentary and productions outside institutional academic publishing. Much influential work on women, sf, and feminism is found not in journal articles, but in those paratextual spaces that have traditionally served in sf as forums for critical commentary and review: forewords, editorial columns, introductions to collections, and letters to fanzines. Such spaces are evidence and markers of the discursive communities that may overlap, but also exist independently of the academic field of sf criticism. In order to acknowledge such complexities, I refer often to the term "sf feminisms" rather than "feminist sf" since the former does a more inclusive job of indicating a variety of communities and generations expressed through different kinds of cultural activity.

Talking of sf feminisms also avoids the tricky definitional problems that a term such as "feminist sf" immediately provokes. At the simplest level, feminist sf conjures up the problems noted by Paulina Palmer in relation to "lesbian writing": "Does it denote writing by lesbians, for lesbians, or about lesbians?...none of these definitions is entirely satisfactory or foolproof" (Palmer 1993: 4). Feminist sf is most commonly used to denote "sf for feminists," and (increasingly from the 1980s on) "sf by feminists," but also sf by, or for, women. The slippage between women's sf and feminist sf (also characteristic of feminist literary criticism) is a common occurrence in the narratives I trace. Despite the trend to deconstruct a unitary and universalizing category of "Woman," a continuing and longstanding thread of criticism continues to oscillate freely between "women" and "feminism" as the definitional category.

Early criticism by feminists focused on women's portrayal in sf and the neglect of female authors to support a critique of androcentric sf and its masculinist culture. Academic feminist sf criticism then developed from the championing of female authors and strong female characters (women's sf) to a focus on overtly feminist texts and authors. In the process, what Sarah Lefanu termed "feminized sf" was, until very recently, increasingly abandoned by feminist sf critics (Lefanu 1988: 93). Authors whose work does not sit easily within a feminist framework, such as Marion Zimmer Bradley and Kate Wilhelm, have been neglected by academic critics despite their influence on later feminist readers. Many feminist sf authors have acknowledged the influence of writers such as C.L. Moore, Andre Norton, and Leigh Brackett on their early reading and writing of sf. Joan Vinge has written of the deep impression left on her by the discovery that Andre Norton was female:

> In the early mid-Sixties, well before the women's movement became widespread, I read her *Ordeal in Otherwhere*, the first book I'd ever read with an honest-to-God liberated woman as the protagonist. Not only were female protagonists extremely unusual at the time, but this character came from a world on which sexual equality was the norm. I never

forgot that, and in the late Sixties, when I began to see articles on feminism, something fell into place for me in a very
profound way. (Vinge, quoted in Lefanu 1988: 93)

Thus, attempts to construct a female subject in sf were important
predecessors to the more direct constructions of a *feminist* subject in
sf. As Justine Larbalestier has observed:

> While not all of the women who have been part of the field
> of science fiction would identify as feminists, the fact of
> their participation has become a feminist issue. The mere
> fact of their presence created a tradition that other women
> could then become a part of. (Larbalestier 2002: 2-3; see also
> Yaszek 2008)

Nevertheless, when considering a "pre-history" of feminisms in
sf, it is important to be sensitive to generational differences, and indeed, the layering of different generations and histories present in
any conversation about feminism. Texts that critics may identify (and
thus judge and perhaps neglect) as representing humanist or liberal
forms of feminism continue to have purchase in the exchanges between feminism and sf. These ideas not only juxtapose and interact
with other developments in feminist thought, but are also part of
the very development of other forms of feminist thought—both in
theory and in fiction. In addition, every lineage of texts is produced
to a certain extent through an individual's reading experience, which
rarely corresponds to their chronological production. Personal reading histories are central to the individual construction of feminisms;
many younger readers will not have come across 1970s texts until decades after they were written, and thus may read them within a very
different contextual sense of feminism. My reading of Joanna Russ's
The Female Man in the 1990s, for example, provided a very different
sense of the feminism of that time than did my readings of feminist
history and theory, and brought the movement alive to me in a way no
other text had done.

But one must be careful in these readings across time (and generation and geographical location), especially when trying to excavate
marginalized or non-dominant stories. Duchamp points to the insta-
bility of discursive shifts in terms and their impact on our conversations. In particular she identifies the way that attempts by younger

critics (including myself) to "recover" certain texts variously labeled as "housewife" or "domestic" sf have underestimated the importance of the cultural context within which some feminists denigrated the sub-genre. In understanding this position, she argues, it is crucial to realize the extent to which the "feminine mystique" informs the figure of the housewife and the "ideological regime" it represented (Duchamp 2004b: 52-3). This is a telling point for, although I was theoretically aware of this history, it did not—could not—have the emotive or affective "truth" for me that it did for Duchamp (or Joanna Russ or Pamela Sargent). Thus, although I endeavor to foreground the affective as well as technical contexts in which discursive meanings shift and evolve, my account is always colored by my particular generational, geographic, and political locations. Part of this positioning also involves the ways in which I locate myself within the various discursive fields and communities that constitute both sf and feminism/s.

Introducing the sf field

The sf community is made up of sf writers, fans, editors, and publishers, who interact most visibly at sf conventions ("cons"), but also in various organizations, clubs, and through fanzines (amateur fan publications) and prozines (such as *Locus*, which began as a fanzine, and the *New York Review of Science Fiction*). As Edward James writes:

> Since the late 1920s sf fandom—the body of enthusiastic and committed readers of sf—has had an appreciable and unique, if unmeasurable, impact on the evolution of sf, influencing writers, producing the genre's historians, bibliographers, and many of its best critics, and, above all, producing many of the writers themselves. (1994: 130)

Although fans have been a vital part of the sf community,[1] their influence and even presence in sf has until recently been absent from many critical and feminist accounts of sf. A vast amount of research, documentation, and bibliographical work, however, has been carried out by fans themselves, for the most part focusing on the activities of "Big Name Fans" (BNFs) (Moskowitz 1954; Warner Jr. 1969). Since

---

1 Indeed, Edward James suggests that fans predated sf as a genre and helped bring it into being: "Sf fans existed before sf itself was named: in a sense readers had created a genre before publishers, or even writers, were clear what that genre was" (James 1994: 52; see also Hartwell 1984: 158).

the late '80s, very different accounts of "fandom" have also emerged from the growing body of academic work on media fandom (Bacon-Smith 1992; Hellekson and Busse 2006; Jenkins 1992; Penley 1990: 135-61; 1992: 479-500). And more recently works, such as those by Larbalestier (2002) and Camille Bacon-Smith (2000), have looked to fandom for more complete histories of the sf field.

From the beginnings of fandom in the 1920s and '30s (well before critical interest in popular culture and readers), fans proclaimed their own importance and influence in the field of sf (for example, signaling their superior knowledge and intelligence in the slogan "fans are slans")[2] and, in some cases, saw sf as incidental, rather than central, to fandom as a community. A great deal of "Fanac" (fan activity) revolved around fandom itself—this interest in the community itself being dubbed "faandom." Personalzines, APAs,[3] and the partying interactions with friends at conventions (which for "faans" often takes precedence over the more "sercon" attendance of official programming) demonstrate the importance of the community in and of itself as a network of people who have an interest in sf but do not necessarily base all their communication around it or, indeed, even read sf texts any longer.[4]

It is hardly surprising, then, that a significant part of fanac has been the chronicling of fannish history and activity: the feuds, the hoaxes, the careers of BNFs, the fortunes of numerous fanzines and prozines, and of course, Conventions. Fan-authored books, articles in prozines and fanzines, encyclopedias, dictionaries, indexes, and bibliographies all attest to the vigor and diversity of fan culture, and these sources have established a sense of fannish history (marked by "epochs" of fandom, from "First fandom" through to the "phony

---

2   *Slan* (1940) was A.E. van Vogt's first novel, in which a superhuman mutant race is forced into hiding by the animosity of "normals." Fans leapt on this image as an emblem of their own position within "mundane" society.

3   An APA (Amateur Publishing Association) is a compilation of mini-fanzines, each assembled by individuals, then collated and sent to all members of the APA group. It resembles a "paper version" of online communities such as blogs or LiveJournal. Personalzines are fanzines that are usually diary-like, relating to the writers' personal lives, and often with little reference to sf.

4   For a wonderful explication of fan culture (and the rather incidental role of sf texts in some portions of it), see Warren 1974.

Seventh").[5] While the sense of a long and significant history is well established in the fan community, debate continues over issues such as the first "real" fanzine, or whether the US or the UK held the first "official" convention. Many of these debates reveal tensions between various factions of fandom—or, more correctly, various communities, separated by generation, nation, politics, sexuality, and purpose (see for example, r. brown 1994; Warner Jr. 1994b).

Fans have constituted a vital reception community for feminist sf and have engaged in dialogues about feminism and sf amongst themselves in fanzines and letters as well as within the broader sf community, through convention programming. Alongside the development of feminist sf, fan responses and debates about texts and feminist issues played a key role in the recognition of sf as a legitimate arena for feminist thought and expression. From the 1970s on, feminist fandom has not only produced some of the earliest feminist sf criticism, but has also actively set out to change the environment in which sf was produced.

Critical attention to popular culture fans highlights the congruence between the "excessive" consumption of both the fan and critic. As Laura Stempel Mumford comments in her work on TV soap operas: "I am a fan, but not merely a fan; a critic, but never simply a critic" (1995: 5). Paying attention to fans involves recognizing and legitimating a source of knowledge and competency outside the domain of academic criticism. In feminist sf fandom, in particular, fans have from the outset engaged with readings that are informed by feminist theory. Feminist fanzines offered critical writings that placed sf texts in the context of feminist praxis and theorizing, and used sf as the starting point for political and theoretical arguments that roamed far from this culturally "debased" set of texts.

The transformation of critical writings on sf into a "scholarly" or academic pursuit began in the 1960s, when courses began to appear at US universities, a series of critical monographs were published,

---

5   Jack Speer, editor of the first *Fancyclopedia* and an early fan historian, divided fandom into eras. His periodization was modified by Bob Silverberg, resulting in six periods, with a "seventh" added by a "group of brash young fans [who]...announced that Sixth fandom was dead, and that *they* were the new and magnificent Seventh" (Tucker 1976: 5). The eras are First Fandom, 1930-1936 (also known as "Eofandom"); Second Fandom, 1937-1938; Third Fandom, 1940-1944; Fourth Fandom, 1945-1947; Fifth Fandom, 1947-1949; Sixth Fandom, 1950-1953; The Phony Seventh, 1953. As Tucker notes, "Partly because of disinterest, no one has seriously attempted a continuation of the numbering system" (1976: 5).

and an academic sf journal (*Extrapolation*) dedicated to criticism was established. The institutionalization (or professionalization) of sf critique saw a shift in the locus of the production of sf criticism in terms of what Pierre Bourdieu calls "symbolic capital" (Bourdieu 1984)—a move from the "shadow economy" of the sf community of fans and authors to an (admittedly marginal) place in academe. However, the origins of sf criticism are to be found much earlier in the fan community. Fan commentary, reviews, and criticism of sf were a staple of sf fanzines, while the sf magazines contained critical commentary in editorials and review columns (James 1994: 136-7).[6] The first sf course was taught by fan Sam Moskowitz at The City College of New York in 1953 (Parrinder 1979: xv-xvi). Author and anthologist Reginald Bretnor edited a collection of articles by sf authors in 1953 (*Modern Science Fiction, Its Meaning and Its Future*); author/critic Damon Knight's critical essays appeared in book form in 1956 (*In Search of Wonder*); and in the 1960s, more books of critical writing followed from Moskowitz and William Atheling Jr. (pseudonym for the critical writings of Damon Knight and James Blish) (Atheling 1964; Bretnor 1953; Moskowitz 1966; Nicholls 1979: 146-7).[7] *Extrapolation*, launched in 1959 by Thomas D. Clareson, was initially very much like a fanzine in appearance but, according to Patrick Parrinder, signified the appearance of a body of sf scholars (Parrinder 1979: xv-xvi).[8]

Feminist criticism of sf was first published in sf (and some women's movement) academic journals in the 1970s by authors such as Joanna Russ and fans such as Beverly Friend (Friend 1972; Badami 1978; Le Guin 1975; Russ 1974b). Feminist criticism did not become an established presence in sf scholarship, however, until the 1980s, when it became more common in the sf journals, the first edited col-

---

6   James cites the fanzine by (male) Claire P. Beck, *Science Fiction Critic*, 1935-8, as a particularly serious critical review. Fans also provided an invaluable basis for later academic work through the compilation of bibliographical and reference works.

7   James considers Knight's book as the first book of criticism of sf—"a milestone in the evolution of the serious evaluation of the genre, and an important lesson to fan reviewers of the then prevalent 'gosh-wow' school of criticism" (James 1994: 137).

8   In 1970 the Science Fiction Research Association (SFRA) was founded in the US, and in 1973 R.D. Mullen and Darko Suvin co-founded *Science Fiction Studies*. In 1971 the British Science Fiction Foundation was formed, and its journal *Foundation* appeared in 1972. (See also James 1994: 88.)

lections on women in sf appeared, and the first two monographs on feminism and science fiction were published.[9] As the following chapters suggest, within the "informal" publishing institutions of the sf fan community, there were more immediate responses to feminist critiques in the 1970s (and earlier) that constitute a crucial element in a history of feminist criticism within sf.

Although obviously part of the same critical impulse to challenge the literary malestream that marks the beginnings of feminist literary criticism, with common origins, critical approaches, and tools, feminist sf criticism developed apart from its mainstream sister, as a subgenre of sf studies, rather than a branch of feminist criticism.

But is it literature?

Indeed, a central tension haunting all critical studies of sf is its relation to the mainstream of literature and criticism. As Luckhurst points out, "[t]he complaint of those who read and study popular genres is that they are always regarded as inferior because a singular, high cultural definition of aesthetic value is used to judge them" (2005: 2).

Sf has a problematic profile for mainstream critics for a number of reasons, the most obvious being the persistent view of sf as mere technophilic fantasy. Sf, as an example of "genre" fiction, continues to be constructed within literary criticism as a conservative mode, a form of fiction somehow intrinsically more escapist than its elevated counterpart, "literature" or literary fiction. Not surprisingly, sf proves even more troublesome for feminist literary criticism, which rests on political as well as aesthetic judgments in crafting an appropriate canon of texts. And generally, the technophilic, masculinist stereotype of sf (in terms of both theme and authorship) has meant the genre is assumed to be antagonistic, rather than welcoming, to the expression of feminist politics.

---

9 Apart from those cited above, few feminist or woman-centered critiques were published in the journals in the 1970s. There were special issues on women and sf in *SFS* in 1980 and *Extrapolation* in 1982. The first edited collections were *Future Females* (1981), Barr (ed.), *The Feminine Eye: Science Fiction and the Women Who Write It* (1982), Tom Staicar (ed.), and *Women Worldwalkers: New Dimensions of Science Fiction and Fantasy,* (1985), Jane B. Weedman (ed.). Single-author studies included Marleen S. Barr's *Alien To Femininity: Speculative Fiction and Feminist Theory* (1987), and the first to examine feminist sf, Lefanu's *In the Chinks of the World Machine* (1988).

Thus, despite the increased interest in women's popular and contemporary fiction in the last couple of decades (see, for example, Hogeland 1998; Makinen 2001; Whelehan 2005), feminist sf texts have not been well represented in feminist literary studies, and indeed their very existence is often marginalized or obscured. Sf critics such as Marleen Barr and Robin Roberts have confronted what they see as mainstream feminist critics' neglect of sf. When critics from outside the field *do* examine feminist sf, it is usually re-situated as part of a different tradition (such as feminist, lesbian, or utopian fiction) as a way of making sf, in Roberts' words, "palatable to the academy" (1995: 186-7). Such readings detach the texts from the very community within which their feminist intervention generated specific political and aesthetic consequences, and thus obscure the political and historical import of writing within, against, or beyond the sf tradition.

It is clear why feminist critics like Roberts and Barr would protest this exclusion. Not only are they protesting the implied inferiority Luckhurst notes, but also what might be construed as a lack of political solidarity: why devalue or ignore texts that are clearly a product of feminist critique, written and read by feminists? For my purposes, this exclusion is also worth exploring for the insight it provides into the operation and constitution of feminist criticism—particularly in terms of the ways feminist literary studies, as a discipline, has negotiated and reproduced the hierarchies and legitimating practices inherent in the very critical tradition it emerged to contest. Thus from a broader perspective, the exclusion of sf is significant not for what it implies about the genre, but rather for what it might reveal about feminist criticism—in particular, about the processes of canon formation and how and why certain texts, forms, and ideas come to be valued over others.

Since the 1970s feminist critics, in their challenges to traditional disciplinary ideas about literature, have constructed canons counter to that of the androcentric tradition of great (white, male) literature. In most cases these new counter canons did not encompass sf, for despite their re-evaluation of texts previously excluded from literature, feminist literary criticism has confirmed some boundaries even as it transgresses others, and often fails to fulfill its potential to "speak from the border." Like sf criticism itself, although focused on an object traditionally outside the respectable hierarchies of literature, the urge to argue for recognition of feminist texts often re-institutes the critical tools, hierarchies, and judgments that have arisen from the analysis of high culture. The operations of feminist criticism within the Anglo-American academy are marked by the hegemony of white, heterosexist texts, and the figuration of popular and genre texts as inherently conservative—characteristics that clearly point to the hierarchies of power and cultural values invested in critical processes. Some of the most trenchant critiques of the resulting lacuna in feminist critical canons and taxonomies have come from women of color and lesbian/queer critics.

The political implications of using a model of literary criticism and canon-making inherited from a white, androcentric, heterosexist critical and literary tradition have been most clearly pointed out by feminists of color (Holloway 1992; Hull, Scott, and Smith 1981; Moraga and Anzaldúa 1983; Pryse and Spillers 1985; Smith 1985).[10] Since the 1970s, critics such as Barbara Christian have challenged Anglo-American feminists to reconsider their theoretical practices, and pointed to tensions in "criticism as usual," which need to be confronted by all feminists:[11]

> Canon Formation has become one of the thorny dilemmas for the black feminist critic. Even as white women, blacks, people of color attempt to reconstruct that body of American literature considered to [be] *the* literature, we find ourselves confronted with the realization that we may be imitating the very structure that shut our literatures out in the first place. And that judgments we make about, for example, the BBBs (Big Black Books) are determined not only by "quality," that elusive term, but by what we academicians value, what points of view, what genres and forms we privilege. (Christian 1990: 69-70)

Similarly, Katie King argues that feminist critics "themselves participate in valuing some forms of writing over others. Genres of writing

---

10 See also Paul Lauter, "Caste, Class, and Canon" (1991: 228-30): who describes literary canons as the product of training in a "male, white, bourgeois, cultural tradition" and, in particular, the "formal techniques of literary analysis."

11 See also K. King (1994: 12-25) on the ways some white feminist stories obscure the history of black feminist critics and women's movements.

are highly important in these debates, as objects of knowledge, as producers of knowledge, as the very kinds of knowledge themselves" (1994: 182n30). These genres include, of course, critical and theoretical writings, which through re-telling, circulation, and citation can come to stand in for feminist knowledge and arbitrate what King terms the "apparatus for the production of feminist culture" (92).

The values and canons thus constructed in feminist criticism emerge not only from this system of literary and critical values, but also from the historical inheritance of the Women's Liberation Movement. From its beginnings, feminist literary criticism has had an uneasy relation with popular fiction. As a number of studies suggest, feminists at the time (and since) were often caustic in their appraisals of the success of what Lisa Hogeland terms the "consciousness-raising" novels of the 1970s such as Erica Jong's *Fear of Flying* (1973) and Marilyn French's *The Women's Room* (1977) (Hogeland 1998; Lauret 1994; Whelehan 2005). These texts were problematic on two fronts. First, their commercial success could be seen as "selling out to the capitalist 'malestream'" (Whelehan 2005: 13). Second, the focus on individual well-known authors worked counter to the ethic of collective action and authorship characterizing the more radical arm of the movement:

> Authors of successful books will necessarily be individuated from other feminists and their alienation from the Movement became a self-fulfilling prophecy. Their stardom was going to be unpalatable to other feminists and their feminist credentials, fairly or not, criticized. (Whelehan 2005: 14)

This mistrust of media success would meet with the distaste for popular culture in the high aesthetics of traditional literary criticism to become a continuing avoidance of popular women's writing in feminist criticism. As Imelda Whelehan notes, "feminist criticism was developing a methodology of reading women's literature from the past and rescuing it from patriarchal obscurity, but it had no real interest in popular fiction and very little in contemporary literary fiction" (2005: 3). Thus, these popular, widely read texts "did not fit in with the broader project of literary rediscovery," even as they evidenced "the contemporary health of feminist debate" (13). And if popular fiction was to be avoided, then it is not very surprising that genre fiction such as sf would be ignored. As I detail below, even when feminist criticism comes to acknowledge or occasionally embrace more popular fiction and genres, sf still occupies an ambivalent position at best.

What counts as feminist fiction?

The influence of postmodernist and "French Feminist" critiques on the mainstream of feminist criticism brought a new focus on contemporary fiction (though, according to Rita Felski, only in the context of an "anti-realist aesthetics of textuality") and more rigorous (and exclusionary) ideas about what constituted feminist fictions (1989: 2). For Maria Lauret, there is a key disjuncture in the history of feminist criticism, "between an early and rather unreflective celebration of women's writing in general on the one hand, and subsequently a stringent and often dismissive critique of the literature of the Women's Movement on the other" (1994: 3).[12] A similar disjuncture is not evident in feminist sf criticism, where the texts that are seen to have arisen most directly from the women's liberation movement continue to be central to most feminist sf canons; indeed a number of texts such as Russ's *The Female Man* and Wittig's *Les Guérillères* are also central to canons constructed in the light of poststructuralist influences on feminist theory.[13] Enmeshed in the contending critical narratives about which fictions embody "feminist politics" are judgments about what literary *forms* in themselves can express or explore feminist ideologies, with much debate centering on feminism's relation to an aesthetics of "realism."

Writing in 1992, Laura Marcus argued that feminist appraisals of literature assumed an "alleged opposition between 'experimental writing' and 'realism'" (1992: 11). Reacting against this trend, a number of critics since the late 1980s have mounted a defense of the place of realist literature in feminist criticism. Distinguishing between an academic and "popular" form of feminism, Paulina Palmer champions a reader-identified realist fiction against a poststructuralist

---

12 More recent studies have begun to move beyond such a disjuncture by re-evaluating popular feminist fiction and contemporary third wave or "chick lit" forms (see Makinen 2001 and Whelehan 2005).

13 One aspect in which feminist sf criticism departs from the developmental model of mainstream criticism is that (apart from initial early critiques of masculinist sf) critics have always been concerned with contemporary fiction, since in most critical stories, "women's sf" began with the women's lib movement and texts from the late 1960s and early 1970s.

academic defense of anti-realist texts (1989: 7). Palmer stresses the importance for many women of identifying with a "women's community" in reading, which she sees as "chiefly associated with the realist text" (7). But defenders of realist forms assume too easy a relation between realist texts and popular fiction, ignoring the appeal for at least some women of sf texts and the highly active community of feminist readers and authors that has formed the context for the development of feminist sf since the 1970s.

"Realism" figures in this debate in a slippery fashion. Bringing feminist sf into the debate reveals that the terms "realist" and "anti-realist" here have quite specific configurations, not necessarily related to generic form. In this particular opposition, from which sf seems to be excluded, "anti-realist" corresponds to a politically charged spectrum of avant-garde practices, "metafictions," and poststructuralist and postmodernist forms (see for example, E. Rose 1993: 355; Watts 1992: 88). The terms of the struggle over the function of "realism" in feminist texts suggests a reductive relationship between literary form and social order/experience—an assumption highlighted by the case of sf, which, while "anti-realist" and thus free of many of the conservative confinements of the realist or mimetic text, does in fact employ a range of "realist" devices in its world construction and cognitive estrangement. The anti-realism of sf can in fact contain a range of political positions from the most reactionary to the most radical of feminist positions. As Penny Florence indicates, there is a closer relationship between mimetic fiction and feminist sf than might be supposed for a "non-realist" form. But to argue that sf is "closer to realism or to naturalism than to fantasy" for example, is, as Florence has argued, distracting: "The point is to move towards reconstructing the basis of these classifications. Thus though what may be termed 'realist' elements are appropriated [in sf], they are used to different ends" (1990: 70). As Lauret argues, "particular literary forms are not in and of themselves radical in the political sense" (1994: 9-10; see also Watts 1992: 88).

What is at stake here is, as Felski puts it, the "social function" of literature, the significance of which is obscured by "the assertion that experimental writing constitutes the only truly 'subversive'...textual practice, and that more conventional forms such as realism are complicit with patriarchal systems of representation" (Felski, 1989:

7).[14] For Rose, feminist critics were slow to adequately theorize this social function of literature, that is, "the relation of fiction to experience and social change" (E. Rose, 1993: 361). The view that radical style and politics must go together implies an ahistorical approach that ignores the motility of both critical trends and the forms and genres they study.

An invisible fiction?
Mainstream constitutions of feminist sf

The field of feminist criticism is not, of course, a monolith. There have been mainstream studies that acknowledge and even celebrate the potential of sf. Sandra Gilbert and Susan Gubar's *No Man's Land*, for example, avoids concentrating on a restrictive canon mainly because it provides a broad survey of the history of *women's* writing (rather than "feminist fiction") in the twentieth century (1988).[15] It discusses sf texts by Joanna Russ, C.L. Moore, Marion Zimmer Bradley, and James Tiptree Jr. (Alice Sheldon), albeit briefly (116),[16] as well as a number of masculinist "war between the sexes" novels, which are seen as being in dialogue with feminism (18).[17] Gilbert and Gubar's study situates sf along with writing by women of color as,

> the most uncanonical of female-authored mid-century texts.
> Specifically, both in the science fiction tradition and in the
> black tradition women writers seem to feel freest to express

---

14 Felski also argues against abstract conceptions of a feminine text, which "cannot cope with the heterogeneity and specificity of women's cultural needs, including, for example, the development of a sustained analysis of black women's or lesbian writing, which is necessarily linked to issues of representation and cannot be adequately addressed by simply arguing the 'subversive' nature of formal self-reflexivity" (6).

15 Their view of sf is probably influenced by the fact that Gubar has published a number of articles on C.L. Moore, such as "C.L. Moore and the Conventions of Women's Science Fiction" (*SFS*, # 20, 1980, 16-27). Considering the length of *No Man's Land*, however, the main discussion of sf is negligible, consisting of only five pages out of almost 300: pp. 116-7, 119-20, 245.

16 Briefly mentioned are Tiptree's "Mama Come Home" and "The Women Men Don't See," Bradley's *The Shattered Chain*, and Russ's *The Female Man* (116-17).

17 Their argument here is similar to that of Robin Roberts in *A New Species* (1993: 40-65).

their fantasies about the inexorability of sexual battle as well
as their fears of female defeat in that conflict. (1988: 101)[18]

Gilbert and Gubar also offer an alternative to the common narrative
that plots a feminist movement from a '70s utopian to an '80s dystopian mode, through reference to Tiptree's often bleak and dark "fictions
about female defeat," which they read as signs of "feminist rebellion"
(119-20).[19]

Another unusual study is Olga Kenyon's *Writing Women: Contemporary Women Novelists*, which deviates from the canonical norm
both through its reference to sf and its concentration on British writers, including marginalized groups such as Jewish women, Caribbean
women, and Black British immigrants (1991).[20] Kenyon's chapter on
Angela Carter's work is unambiguous about its connections with sf:

> Carter breaks down academic (male) divisions between "good"
> and "bad" literature; popular forms of writing such as science
> fiction and detective stories are treated seriously. Both Carter
> and Lessing use science fiction, though in differing ways, to
> explore possible futures. (12)[21]

Kenyon also provides a useful way of conceptualizing Carter's eclectic and irreverent refusal of generic boundaries that confounds attempts
to classify and "fix" her fiction into one form, by referring to readers—an absent factor in the majority of feminist literary criticism.

18 The examples given are Moore's *Shambleau* and Ann Petry's *The Street* (1946). This
is an interesting view of possible similarities between marginalized but "freer" forms
of literature, similar to Lefanu's statements about the freedoms offered by the doubly marginalized genre of sf. However, there are, I feel, dangers in too easily drawing commonalities between two very different experiences of marginalization.

19 A later chapter also mentions Elgin's "sequence of sf novels," *Native Tongue* and
Judas Rose (245); this chapter (and the book) ends with analysis of Le Guin's "She
Unnames Them," describing Le Guin as a speculative fiction writer (270-1). On
the periodization of feminism from a utopian to dystopian mode (see E. Rose
1993: 358; Greene 1991; and Lauret 1994: 9-10).

20 There is a chapter each on Angela Carter, Jewish women writing in Britain, an
introduction to Black Women novelists, Alice Walker, Toni Morrison, Caribbean
women writers, and Buchi Emechta and Black immigrant experience in Britain.

21 While Kenyon does not discuss any other writers of sf, her chapter on Jewish
writers considers the eclectic range of Elaine Feinstein's novels, observing that
Feinstein "values her science fiction novel, *The Ecstasy of Dr. Miriam Garner* (1976)"
(40). Her chapter on Buchi Emecheta compares *The Rape of Shavi* (1983) ("a dis-
quisition on the near future") with Piercy's *Woman on the Edge of Time* (121).

Her narrative tends to allow bizarre extravagances of plot. While this may alienate the more traditionally-minded reader, her work appeals to science fiction devotees who are accustomed to the extravagant as a means to study possible futures or to illuminate the complexities of the present. Many academic critics still fail to take science fiction seriously enough. Yet, as a genre, it allows writers the structural freedom to explore new concepts. Carter's best novels add elements of science fiction to a range of sources from the phantasmagoric to the naturalistic, to project both the inner life of her characters, and a critique of the social world. (15)[22]

Such acknowledgment of sf as a genre open to feminist writers is not a characteristic of the majority of feminist literary studies, where, if sf texts (or more usually sf texts by mainstream authors) *are* discussed, they are not placed in the context of the genre, but instead firmly within the boundaries of a *feminist* fiction.

The most obvious way to draw the "unruly" texts of sf into feminist traditions is to link (and subordinate) them to "mainstream" authors.[23] The only genre sf writer to appear in feminist literary studies with any frequency is Joanna Russ. However, critics undertake some interesting negotiations to draw her work—more specifically *The Female Man*—out of the entanglement of genre and into the mainstream of feminist fiction. Many critics also cite Russ's criticism, especially "What Can a Heroine Do? Or Why Women Can't Write," even those who discuss no sf texts. In this essay, Russ outlined three options for feminist writers who do not want to follow traditional "female narratives": non-narrative texts, a lyrical mode, *or*—Russ's favored

---

22 Sf readers are referred to again: "[s]cience fiction fans praised *The Infernal Desire Machines of Doctor Hoffman*" (17). Carter herself recognized that sf readers would form part of the audience for her works: "I'm not worried about alienating readers by all my allusions, as science fiction addicts are quite prepared to look up things they don't know." Kenyon's private conversation with Carter, 3 Aug. 1985 (16).

23 Most of the studies I discuss here were published in the 1980s and 1990s, mainly because there remain, as Whelehan notes, surprisingly few studies of feminist popular fiction. Apart from Whelehan's own *The Feminist Bestseller* (2005), only a few texts have appeared since Lauret's 1994 study, including Hogeland's 1998 *Feminism and Its Fictions* (looking at consciousness-raising novels in particular, including feminist sf of the time) and Makinen's study, *Feminist Popular Fiction* (2001), which surveys feminist work within a number of genres, including sf along with detective fiction, romance, and the fairy tale.

approach—a turn to genre. Many feminist literary critics who approvingly cite Russ's model, however, omit the third option of genre (Rubenstein 1987: 165). (Other writers of "canonical" status in feminist sf criticism, such as Tiptree and Charnas, rarely rate a mention, and, despite the common assumption that she is one of the few sf writers to receive critical appraisal outside the genre, Le Guin also receives very little attention in feminist literary studies.)[24]

Attempts to co-opt sf texts for mainstream traditions often downplay the undesirable "genre" connections by situating sf as "elements" or "devices" of feminist literature, thus not condemning the whole work to a sub-literary genre. In Nancy Walker's *Feminist Alternatives*, sf texts are discussed in the guise of "fantasy" or "speculative fiction."[25] Situating "fantasy" in its broadest, rather than generic, sense, Walker's emphasis on "realism" renders "fantasy" as a literary device.[26] Walker's distinctions between fantasy "as an element in the plot" and as "fictions wholly constructed of fantasies" potentially blur the boundaries between genre and mainstream, but her reading of *The Female Man* in conjunction with texts such as Atwood's *Handmaid's Tale*, Erica Jong's *Serenissima*, and Fay Weldon's *The Rules of Life* in the absence of other genre writing firmly occludes genre in favor of the mainstream, Russ having been elevated from the ghetto to become part of this "fantastic" tradition.

Rachel Blau DuPlessis's "writing beyond the ending" provides a unifying motif for a tradition of women's writing that encompasses novels dealing with "the issue of the future" that "may have speculative, fantasy, or 'science fiction' elements" (1985: 178-9). However, DuPlessis also extricates Russ from the genre, arguing that Whileaway (the "eutopia" of *The Female Man* and "When It Changed") is presented "*as if* it were science fiction" (my emphases) (183). This com-

---

24 Out of a sample of over twenty book-length studies of contemporary women's writing, only two mention Le Guin as an sf writer, but they do not discuss her work; Tiptree is discussed by Gilbert and Gubar, while both Tiptree's and Charnas's work are discussed in some studies of feminist utopias.

25 Walker writes of the "overwhelming need for fantasy" in women's lives and notes that "[u]ltimately, the impulse towards alternative worlds takes some novelists into the realm of speculative fiction" (N. Walker 1990: 7, 8).

26 "The contemporary women's novel employs fantasy in a number of ways to accomplish this subversion [of the social order] while at the same time maintaining an atmosphere of reality that speaks to women's actual lives" (N. Walker 1990: 29).

ment appears directly after DuPlessis's discussion of Russ's "What Can a Heroine Do," outlining the options open to women writers (182). Sf becomes just a bit of decoration in *The Female Man*: "The sci-fi material, written as if on Russ's dare to herself, is presented to dress up...to camp up—the essential truth about Whileaway" (6).[27]

Other critics refer obliquely to sf through the more palatable notion of "fantasy" as a mode of expression. One such critic is Patricia Waugh:

> Given the acute contradictoriness [sic] of women's lives and sense of subjectivity, it is not surprising that many contemporary women writers have sought to "displace" their desires, seeking articulation not through the rational and metonymic structures of realism but through the associative and metaphorical modes of fantasy: romance, science fiction, gothic, utopia, horror. (1989: 171)[28]

Like many other critics, Waugh admits the existence of sf but marginalizes it, chiefly by assimilating sf within a (largely psychoanalytic) general category of "fantasy," which then becomes just another mode used by mainstream authors, here figured as "anti-realist" and thus "postmodern." The use of umbrella terms such as "fantasy" or "the fantastic" not only obscures the specificity of writing within the sf genre, but also allows the juxtaposition of writers from widely divergent backgrounds, decontextualizing their cultural, historical, and social positioning. Continuities and links are created between writers who seem to have little more than their biological sex in common, regardless of whether the tradition under construction is "feminine," "female," or "feminist."

Supplementing (and often contradicting) the critical traditions of feminist or women's writing are competing narratives, such as those produced by lesbian critics. Most lesbian criticism of contemporary writing that deals with sf texts frames them in the context of utopian writing. In the 1990s, a few general surveys of lesbian fiction mentioned sf, such as Paulina Palmer's *Contemporary Lesbian Writing*.

---

27 In her 1985 book, DuPlessis is less dismissive of sf, commenting of *The Female Man* that "the sci-fi material is used to cover up the essential truth about Whileaway," that it is not about the future but the present (DuPlessis 1985: 183).

28 This is her only reference to sf; none of the texts are analyzed in terms of sf, but of fantasy and "utopian desire."

Unlike her first book (*Contemporary Women's Fiction*), which focuses on mainstream authors and does not mention genre writing, Palmer here casts her net much wider in order to argue for the strength and diversity of lesbian fiction. Her survey includes writers like Russ who, in Palmer's words, are "appropriating and reworking the popular genres of the thriller, science fiction and gothic [which are] widely read" (1989: 1). Palmer's chapters on genre fiction provide an overview of the mixed critical response to feminist and lesbian genre fiction. Alongside critics such as Maggie Humm and Sally Munt, Palmer situates lesbian experimentation with genre as a positive development, one which "promotes the recognition that, rather than there being a single text or canon of texts which reigns supreme and represents the pinnacle of lesbian writing, there is a variety of different kinds" (64).[29] Whilst positive about the value of genre fiction, including sf, Palmer's study does not directly address lesbian sf; the only sf text Palmer discusses is *The Wanderground*, which is referred to as a "utopian fantasy" in a chapter on "political fiction."[30]

---

29 On feminist genre fiction in general, Palmer comments that "champions of post-modern developments in literature, such as Helen Carr, welcome it on the grounds that a focus on genre results in a recognition of the diversity of women's fiction and an emphasis on the contract between reader and writer" (H. Carr 1989: 5-10). For examples of positive treatments of lesbian genre fiction see Maggie Humm, *Border Traffic: Strategies of Contemporary Women's Fiction* (1991: 194-200) and Sally Munt, "The Investigators: Lesbian Crime Fiction" (1988). For an example of a critic who expresses reservations about lesbian genre fiction, see Bonnie Zimmerman, *The Safe Sea of Women: Lesbian Fiction 1969-1989* (1992: 211-12).

30 Along with Gearhart, Palmer cites other writers who have chosen to use the "utopian mode as a vehicle for ideas of lesbian feminist community" (54): Katherine V. Forrest, *Daughters of a Coral Dawn*, Russ, *Female Man,* and Anna Livia, *Bulldozer Rising*; (62n4)—not the usual list of utopian novels, with Livia's consisting more of a possible utopian community within a rather dystopian world, while Forrest's work is more a comic novel than utopia. Palmer divides her discussion of genre fiction into two chapters—the thriller and the comic novel, which has "unlike other forms of lesbian genre fiction such as the thriller and science fiction" received little critical attention (65). As well as Russ, this chapter discusses Suniti Namjoshi, *The Conversations of Cow* (London: Women's Press, 1985), which has been "claimed" as feminist sf by Penny Florence in "The Liberation of Utopia or Is Science Fiction the Ideal Contemporary Women's Form" (1990). At the end of this chapter Palmer also mentions the reworked images of vampires in the novels of Jody Scott (whose *I Vampire* and *Passing for Human* were published under the Women's Press sf imprint) and the stories of Jewelle Gomez (fantasy writer) (91). Interestingly, Palmer also points out the neglect of 1970s and 1980s lesbian fiction by Lesbian and Gay studies, arguing for a reclamation of the positive images

A much more detailed discussion of lesbian sf appears in Patricia Duncker's *Sisters and Strangers* in a chapter on genre fiction (1992: 89-131).[31] This chapter covers a greater range of lesbian sf texts, though as Palmer observes, Duncker doubts the value of feminist appropriations of genre conventions (Palmer 1993: 63).[32] Duncker does seem to be slightly more approving of lesbian appropriations of genre conventions, noting, with respect to feminist use of the thriller genre, that "[l]esbian crime fiction, is, necessarily more subversive, because the insertion of Lesbian meanings into any kind of genre fiction disrupts the heterosexist codes of desire" (1992: 99). For both Duncker and Palmer, then, the expression of lesbian politics immediately confers on the text—even if it is sf—a more "radical" political charge. And despite Duncker's underlying assumptions about the conservative nature of genre and sf (discussed further below), she does admit the potential freedom sf affords lesbian writers:

> The great advantage of science-fiction writing is, of course, that some things—in Livia's case the passionate and erotic connection between women—can simply be taken for granted. That Lesbianism should be primary is neither argued for nor constrained by realism. (109)

Feminist genre writing

The emergence of the field of genre studies, with its focus on popular texts and audiences, appeared to provide a more appropriate critical approach to sf than that of mainstream literary studies. Feminist writing in genres from sf and romance to crime fiction attracted increasing interest from feminist critics from the 1980s on, coinciding with the legitimation of popular fictions as a focus for cultural study. Unlike most literary criticism, genre studies usually entail an awareness and analysis of the production, publication, and reception of, or audience for, texts. As Carr notes:

---

created by writers such as Piercy and other "utopian fantasists" such as Gearhart (39-40).

31 Duncker's analysis provides a particularly useful and more forgiving reading of *The Wanderground* than do many other analyses.

32 See also below for further discussion on Duncker's rather negative conclusions about feminist genre fiction.

> Genres represent a set of conventions whose parameters are redrawn with each new book and each new reading. The concept involves a contract between reader and writer. Once we think of a text as an example of genre, we can no longer approach it only as an artefact to be analysed in some contextless critical purity. We need to ask who reads such books why and in what way, seeing them as...texts-in-use. (1989: 7)[33]

In this framework, the significant context of the work becomes not the "relation to the 'Great Tradition,'" but the consequences (both potential and actual) of the insertion of...[the text] into the domain of popular culture."[34]

A number of genre critics have challenged the more traditional literary and sociological approaches to popular fiction, approaches that adhere to formalist literary values, situate texts as commodities (and readers as consumers), and have often been based on "rescuing *other*, less enlightened readers from the predatory tentacles of the pleasures of popular fiction" (Longhurst 1989: 1).[35] In contrast, genre studies aim to challenge the literary canon as "given" and thus undermine the dichotomy of major and minor literature (3). Carr, for example, argues that "[l]ooking at genre is a way of escaping the pressure to construct an alternative canon of great women writers" (1989: 5-6).

The privileging of the popular, which would seem to be a central function of genre studies, is not, however, necessarily accompanied by disruption of traditional critical hierarchies of literary value (or of the critic's "authority").[36] A number of feminist critics who focus on genre revert to the argument that genre writing is essentially conser-

---

33 The term "texts-in-use" is from Helen Taylor's essay in this collection, "Romantic Readers" (66; see also Cranny-Francis 1990: 21).

34 I have appropriated this quote, which specifically refers to *Lady Chatterley's Lover*, from Stuart Laing, "Authenticating Romantic Fiction: *Lady Chatterley's Daughter*" in Gina Wisker (1994: 13).

35 An example of what Longhurst termed the "English Literature" approach is found in Maggie Humm's statement that feminist work on genre "has too often refused any framework of 'good' or 'bad' representation aesthetically...[and] ignores the whole issue of literary value" (Humm 1986: 100).

36 This is due to the fact that the studies under consideration here remain focused on texts, reading popular fiction in the framework of literary criticism rather than a "cultural studies" approach. A more complex analysis of genre necessitates an examination of audience.

vative and automatically presents obstacles to feminists attempting to appropriate the form (see for example, Cranny-Francis 1990: 89-131). Often, it is assumed that a *successful* feminist subversion means that the genre form itself has been transcended—in other words, that it is no longer "genre fiction" but *feminist* fiction. In this formulation, genre fiction such as sf remains outside the sphere of feminist influence and transformation: you cannot have good feminist literature that is also sf; a truly feminist text will break the confines of genre conventions and pass over the literary border into the realm of "real" literature (see, for example, Duncker 1992: 99).

Just as the blockbuster consciousness-raising novels of the early 1970s were troubling to some in the Women's Liberation Movement, the popularity of feminist genre fiction in the late 1980s and early '90s obviously caused critics some misgivings.[37] As the cover blurb of Nicci Gerrard's 1989 *Into the Mainstream* asked: "it is selling, but is it 'selling out'?" (1989). According to Gerrard, genre forms were "eagerly" taken up by feminist publishers, writers, and readers and "heralded by some as the way out of a literary cul-de-sac" (115). But in Gerrard's analysis, "accessibility slither[s] towards compromise," and popularity is synonymous with conservatism and incompatible with "cutting edge" feminist theory and politics:

> [C]an a novel that is popular entertainment and therefore confined by intrinsically conservative rules be converted to political ends?—if not, does that imply that radical ideas are the preserve of the elite, only to be diluted down into accessibility? (119)[38]

Writing specifically of feminist sf, Gerrard argues that despite opportunities offered by the form, it lays a potential "trap for more dogmatic writers who become locked into empty rhetoric, banal theory

---

37 See Palmer (1989: 5), who notes the disagreement between those who believe the "boom" in women's fiction popularizes feminist attitudes and those who see it as a "cashing-in" on feminism that produces books that are not really feminist.

38 She goes on: "in themselves, detective novels, science fictions, romances and sagas are not intellectual or literary developments. They are not usually on literature's or feminism's front line of change. They are the products and stimulants of clever packaging as well as the consequences of relieved acceptance by feminists of attitudes and pleasures previously policed by a sterner feminist ideology" (147).

and feminist cliché (142).[39] In other words, conservatism is inherent in the very form of "genre fiction," which is distinguished from feminist-appropriate fiction by its popularity. Similarly, Anne Cranny-Francis, whilst generally positive about the feminist use of genre, warns that "the feminist text may be recovered for patriarchy by a narrative which contradicts discursively the story told by the narrative" (1990: 3, 195). And Duncker is even more overtly dismissive of popular genres:

> All the women's presses, in the last days of the 1980s and on into the 1990s, have been engaged in promoting women's genre fiction because the combination of feminist textual noises and a brisk escapist read sells extremely well. It is clear…that I am not a convert to this kind of writing. (1992: 99)

Duncker's interest is in more subversive fiction, which in her view can only occur in genre writing when the "form of the genre breaks down. And we are reading a new kind of political fiction: feminist fiction" (99).[40] Again, the "popular" is positioned as "apolitical" (as if conservatism is not "political"). For Duncker, feminist fiction and genre fiction constitute mutually exclusive categories, rendering "feminist genre fiction" an impossibility. A number of critics echo such views, which rest on unquestioned assumptions inherent in much literary criticism: that the popular is necessarily and intrinsically conservative,[41] that genre "conventions" and codes are more constricting (and phallocentric) than the codes of "literature,"[42] that genre fiction is predictable, and that the market for genre targets "consumers"

---

39 Gerrard goes on to describe sf as an arena for "hypothesising imagination" and hence "the quality of feminist science fiction is a useful if crude barometer for the current climate of feminist thought" and concludes that it points to "patchy weather." There is also some discussion of "ghastly feminist utopias" that indulge in "wishful thinking," biological determinism, and are "pious feminist fables" (144).

40 Additionally, Duncker argues that "all genre fiction must operate within textual expectations that are indeed clichés. To write well within a particular genre without disrupting or subverting the form is, I believe, impossible" (125).

41 Cranny-Francis observes that feminist genre texts sometimes "do not seem to function at all—as traditional generic texts; sometimes they exhibit a complexity supposedly inconsistent with popular fictional forms" (1990: 1).

42 Gerrard argues that "feminist novels that most rigidly adhere to the conventions of their genre face grave difficulties... It is when they are ruptured that genres become fascinating and challenging" (1989: 147-8).

rather than "readers." To quote Duncker again: "Most of the consumers of genre fiction eat the novels like a favorite meal. They want to know what they are buying, even if it is junk food. Feminism, on the other hand, should always be disruptive, unsettling" (1992: 125). The message is clear: "Good" feminists don't like junk food!

Even those who are more enthusiastic about feminist genre writing, such as Cranny-Francis, emphasize the "dangers" of conservatism and phallocentrism that lie "embedded" in the very forms and codes of genre. This is a familiar feminist dilemma, of course: the question of whether feminist discourse is constricted or even undermined by the very structures of the literary forms and language inherited from an androcentric tradition. It is not, however, a problem specific only to genre or "popular" fiction, but to *all* forms of writing. The tendency in mainstream feminist literary criticism of genre is to see such forms, including sf, as inherently restricting feminist deconstruction and re-visioning of narrative. Of course, there are significant differences between the ways, for example, Joanna Russ and Anne McCaffrey each utilize sf, and some feminist interventions are more successful or destabilizing than others. The codes and conventions of genre, indeed of all writing, are not static. To ignore the fluidity of genre over time and cultures is to deny that feminist interventions have significantly transformed sf.

What's a nice feminist text doing in a genre like sf?

Despite the resistance to sf from many feminists, a number of critics have, nevertheless, seen sf as a particularly suitable medium for feminist theorizing and revisioning. Teresa de Lauretis, for example, privileges sf's "capacity to deal with this historical reality of our age":

> In tracing cognitive paths through the physical and material reality of the contemporary technological landscape and designing new maps of social reality, sf is perhaps the most innovative fictional mode of our historical creativity. (1990: 168-9)

Similarly, the potential of sf to serve feminist needs has been outlined by Mary Catherine Harper:

> [B]ecause sf is about a whole range of Subject/Other encounters, because sf often simultaneously exploits and critiques an

already gendered mind/body dichotomy, because sf marks
technology and subjectivity with separate genders, the genre
is easily adapted to the study of gender. (1995: 402)

And, in contrast to many of the general studies of feminist fiction or women's writing noted above, Lisa Maria Hogeland situates
feminist sf as a key literary expression of consciousness-raising (CR)
activity in the women's liberation movement (1998). Hogeland's study
shows the benefit of taking an historical approach, situating the texts
of feminist sf writers such as Russ and Charnas alongside other CR
novels of the 1970s. Indeed, she privileges sf as the form better able
to perform the "hard" or more radical aspects of CR—"in depicting both radical political analysis and substantive political change"
(50). Ultimately, Hogeland argues that feminist sf and the CR novel
"perform the same (counter) cultural work...both have 'designs' on
their readers" (110). Drawing on Russ (1974b) Hogeland avers that
"extrapolation itself is a fundamental part of the CR process...That
is, asking 'what if?' is a central project for consciousness-raising," just
as it is of feminist sf (110).

Despite the difficulties of operating within a traditionally masculinist genre, largely isolated from the feminist literary and critical
establishment, feminist sf writers have produced a substantial body of
innovative writing. Indeed, the very nature of this "doubly marginalized" fiction—on the periphery of both mainstream literature and
the sf field—has allowed female authors more freedom to experiment, enhancing the play of their feminist imaginings (Lefanu 1988:
99). Other factors inherent in the genre lend themselves to feminist
reworkings, in particular the convention of "estrangement," which
allows feminist writers to construct a narrative that "denaturalises
institutionalized modes of behavior, representation and self-represen-
tation in contemporary western society" (Cranny-Francis 1990: 74).
In Sarah Lefanu's words, feminist sf can "defamiliarise the familiar
and make familiar the new and strange...thus challenging normative ideas of gender roles" (1988: 21-2). Similarly, for science studies
scholar Hilary Rose, feminist sf functions as "a sort of dream laboratory—where feminisms may try out wonderful and/or terrifying
social projects" (1994: 228).

As Rose suggests, feminist sf not only reflects contemporary feminist concerns, but is also a site for the development and configuration

of feminist debates. Within the "male bastion" of the sf community, fans, authors, and critics have struggled over the meaning and manifestations of feminism—and in many ways kept alive a more fruitful atmosphere for CR activity than in other, more academic feminist communities. Arguments for "equi-sexism" can be found from the earliest issues of sf "pulp" magazines, and overt struggles over the meaning of feminism were played out between fans and authors in the prozines and fanzines of the 1970s. Debates about gender, sexuality, and (less often) race continue to engage different generations of authors, fans, and academics. The variety of forums in which these debates take place indicates feminist sf's potential to "reach beyond the restricted public of the already politicized and speak to a wider audience" (Fitting 1985: 156). The feminist interventions into the traditionally masculinist areas of sf and science that feminist sf represents are not played out solely on a textual level but reach beyond the text, to the cultural ramifications of female readers gaining access to the ideas and language of science and technology and drawing from (and providing) the impetus for creating a feminist space within sf fandom, and so changing their community through feminist activity.

2

RESISTANCE IS USELESS?
THE SEX/WOMAN/FEMINIST "INVASION"

*In the last six or seven publications females have been dragged
into the narratives and as a result the stories have become those
of love which have no place in science-fiction...*

*A woman's place is not in anything scientific. Of course the
odd female now and then invents something useful in the way
that every now and then amongst the millions of black crows a
white one is found.*

*I believe, and I think many others are with me, that sentimen-
tality and sex should be disregarded in scientific stories. Yours
for more science and less females.*

~ Donald G. Turnball (1938: 162)

The growth of feminist activity within sf was a direct reflection
of sociopolitical debates of the '60s and '70s, and of the impact of the
women's liberation movement, as well as a result of trends within the
field itself. Integral to the development of sf feminisms were debates
about the role of women and the representation of female characters in sf, debates that have been present from the genre's beginnings
in the pulp magazines. In contrast to earlier stories that situated sf's
maturation (in terms of issues such as sex, women, and literary value) in the 1960s, a number of recent works find evidence for such
engagements much earlier. Justine Larbalestier's study of early sf
magazines and fanzines demonstrates that issues of sex and gender
were not sudden arrivals in the 1960s but have always preoccupied
the sf community in both its fictions and discussions about the field
(2002). Tackling that preoccupation, Brian Attebery's *Decoding Gender in Science Fiction* examines the gendered nature of much of the
"sf code" throughout its history (2002). Concerns about women in sf
developed from the "sex in sf" question, which loomed large in the sf
(un)consciousness from the late 1920s through the sexual liberation
of the 1960s, to intersect with (and be partially absorbed by) feminist

34

narratives from the 1970s to the present. In this chapter I highlight key moments in which discussions of sex, gender, and women came to the fore, reinforcing the recent critical perception that such concerns were not merely triggered by an invasion of women's libbers, but are indeed central to sf history. As Larbalestier argues, "acceptance of an 'unexpressed,' invisible, absent body of women until the 'revolution' of the 1970s serves to rewrite and gloss over the complexities of the period prior to this 'influx' or 'explosion' of women in the late 1960s and early 1970s" (2002: 168).

Statements about the overwhelmingly masculine character of sf—particularly in the early days of sf pulp magazines—are a commonplace of both malestream and feminist histories. As Jane Donawerth notes, "[b]oth traditional historians of science fiction and also feminist ones have expected women not to appear in the pulps, and have invented reasons for their absence" (1994: 137). Whilst some sources estimate that men made up to 90 percent of the audience for magazines such as *Astounding SF*, the continual (re)construction of sf as a masculine domain has concealed women's interaction with sf, as readers, as authors, and as subjects represented through female characters. Writers like Connie Willis and Pamela Sargent have reminded later generations of the existence of women sf writers from the 1920s onwards (Sargent 1978b, 1978c, 1979; Willis 1992). Sargent's anthologies and others, like *New Eves: Science Fiction About the Extraordinary Women of Today and Tomorrow* (Frank, Stine, and Ackerman 1994) and *Daughters of Earth* (Larbalestier 2006), document the contributions of earlier women writers and editors. Research on the activities of women writers and readers has slowly emerged over the last few decades. Donawerth (1990, 1994, 1997) has examined women's writing for the early pulps, providing more than occasional evidence of the presence of women as authors in sf from the 1920s, and Robin Roberts (1993) analyzed representations of women in pulp cover art. Larbalestier's *Battle of the Sexes* (2002) provides the first detailed feminist analysis of the letter columns and editorials of early magazines such as *Astounding*, providing evidence of the presence of women as readers, and of Woman as the subject of sf debate.

The sex question in sf:
The early years of the pulps, 1920s–1930s

Debate about the stories that were forming the core of a nascent sf began as conversations between readers and editors in the pulp magazines, which printed readers' addresses to enable communication between them. Clubs such as the Science Correspondence Club and Sciences Club (both formed in 1929) began producing amateur publications (first known as "fanmags") such as *The Planet* (1930), *The Time Traveller* (1932), and what is generally considered the first fanzine, *The Comet* (1930) (Madle 1994: 37; Warner Jr. 1994a: 175). Hugo Gernsback (editor of *Amazing Stories* and *Wonder Stories*) was the first to identify these more active readers as "fans" (Larbalestier 2002: 23), and in 1934, through his magazine *Wonder Stories*, he created the SFL (Science Fiction League), which soon had chapters in many of the major cities of the US.

Larbalestier's reading of letters and editorials from 1927-1939 in magazines such as *Amazing Stories* (1926-2005) and *Astounding* reveals that a number of women readers wrote to the magazines and participated in overt struggles over the ownership of sf and whether or not women could be considered "fit" subjects for sf. A debate in the letter column of *Astounding* from 1938-39 illustrates, in Larbalestier's words, "that science fiction is a masculine space whose borders must be carefully patrolled to keep the pollution of women out" (2002: 117). Larbalestier's conclusion that the "battle of the sexes" has been a constant theme in sf since the genre's beginnings in the 1920s provides a very different historiographical view than the truism that, in the pre-1960s era, women signified in sf only through their absence. As her analysis demonstrates, debates about the appropriateness of sex in sf stories (or on the cover of the magazines in the form of scantily clad women) were always intimately connected with notions about women's place in sf.

While traditional histories of sf have emphasized the active rejection of sex as a topic suitable for sf, they have only rarely noted the slippage between sex and women (Carter 1977: 174). Although critics from the 1960s on would be virtually unanimous in their construction of earlier sf as a "sexless" space, again, reader's letters show that this was not a given. Paul Carter cites a series of letters provoked by the use of female nudes in the cover art of *Weird Tales* in the 1930s (most of them by one of the first female cover artists, Margaret Brundage). While many readers, male and female, expressed outrage and disapproval, others were enthusiastic: "By all means let her continue with her nudes offending the prudes" (E.L. Mengshoel 1936, cited in Carter 1977: 177).

Later critical assumptions about the lack of sex in sf overlooked the sexualized (and gendered) nature of many sf tropes, such as the alien, the rocketship, and even the (masculine) scientific colonization of the "feminine" Mother Earth, and space. The alien or BEM (Bug Eyed Monster) could signify everything that was "other" to the dominant audience of middle-class, young white western males—including women, people of color, other nationalities, classes, and sexualities (Le Guin 1975). The interactions between aliens and human men were often inherently, if covertly, sexual in nature.

Further, as Larbalestier argues, in the name of keeping sf pure of "romance," "puerile love interests," and "sex," male fans, authors, and editors pursued exclusionary tactics in their efforts to situate women characters outside the masculine domain of science and sf. In discussions of sf, as in the sf texts themselves, women were conflated with sex, such that they could only signify in sf if "sex" or "romantic interest" were allowed in. The term "love interest" in the letters examined by Larbalestier "frequently functions…as a synonym for 'women'" (2002: 117). Although some readers contested the exclusion of this "natural human relationship," the majority argued that sex had no place in the logical, scientific, cerebral topos of sf, and, ipso facto, there was no place for woman. A particularly telling example of such conflation occurs in a 1953 letter that asked "What's wrong with sex inside or outside [the covers] as long as the gal shows expression in her eyes?" As Larbalestier notes, "This inadvertently funny comment is revealing. Sex is a gal" (117).

The contest over women's position was not always so covert. The letter by Donald Turnball (see preface quote) that sparked the 1938/9 debate in *Astounding* addressed the "woman issue" directly: "A woman's place is not in anything scientific… Yours for more science and less females" (Turnball 1938: 162). Another participant was the 19-year-old Isaac Asimov, who was one of the most vociferous opponents of women in sf in the late 1930s (Larbalestier 2002: 117-18).

He also, notes Larbalestier, assumes "the position of the male under attack, when in fact the debate began with Turnball's attack on women in science fiction" (123). An attempt by a female reader to separate "that which is represented from the manner of their representation [was] to Asimov absurd and impossible to enforce" (125). Criticizing the usual stereotypes of "swooning damsels" that figure for "women" in sf, Asimov placed responsibility not on the (male) writers, but on women themselves: "Which is another complaint I have against women. They're always getting into trouble and having to be rescued. It's very boring indeed for us men" (Asimov 1939: 160). In Larbalestier's words, "Asimov conflates women with the way they are represented in science fiction and then makes them responsible for that representation" (126).

Larbalestier notes connections between the issues raised in this debate and later feminist analyses, for example in a letter from Mary Byers countering Asimov's arguments:

> To begin, he [Asimov] has made the grave error of confusing the feminine interest with the sex theme... He probably still cherishes the outdated theory that a girl's brain is used expressly to fill up what would otherwise be a vacuum in the cranium.
>
> To his plea for less hooey I give my wholehearted support, but less hooey does not mean less women; it means a difference in the way they are introduced into the story and the part they play. (Byers 1939: 160)[1]

As Larbalestier comments, "Byers' argument here is almost identical to some of those of Russ, Badami and Wood more than thirty years later" (122).

The resistance of female readers to the notion that women were incompatible with "anything scientific" (and thus with sf) did not just express the attitude of a few enlightened, brave individuals, but actually reflected cultural shifts evident, if not dominant, in US society of the 1930s-40s. During and post-WWII women had, of course, moved in significant numbers into various technical and engineering roles, and some had begun to make visible careers in science. As Eric Drown reminds us, successful female scientists such as Marie Curie and

---

1 Reproduced in Larbalestier (2002: facing 121).

Barbara McClintock "were prominent in the Sunday-supplements" in the 1920s and '30s (Drown 2006: 6). Male fans' expressions of resistance to women in science were thus not so much reflections of "real world" science but evidence of the anxieties of "a particularly beset group of would-be wage earners...and in particular how young middle-class women's move out of the home and into self-supporting occupations affected [their] prospects" (8).

Complicating the absence/presence of women

Intimately connected to these debates over the suitability of females as a fit subject for or presence in sf were complex reactions to the bodies of the real women reading the magazines, writing letters, and becoming fans. The varied explanations and justifications for women's arrival in the field offers a measure of this complexity, for, as Larbalestier demonstrates, male fans repeatedly made claims of an "invasion" of women, beginning as early as 1926. Editors such as Hugo Gernsback, Sam Merwin Jr., Charles Hornig, and Sam Mines all at various times expressed surprise that their magazines (in the 1920s, '30s, and '50s) received so many letters from women. In the sixth issue of *Amazing Stories*, in September 1926, Gernsback's editorial mentioned the "encouraging" fact that "a great many women are already reading the new magazine." Gernsback attributed this "totally unforeseen result" to the name of the magazine—"we are certain that if the name of the magazine had been 'Scientifiction' they would not have been attracted to it at a newsstand" (Gernsback 1926a: 23).[2] Despite his rather patronizing tone (adopted by all of the editors discussed here), Gernsback highlighted an important factor in women's actual and supposed lack of interest in science, one well documented by feminist historians of medicine and science (see for example, Schiebinger 2001). The "feminine" character necessary for fulfilling one's socialization as a woman supposedly entailed a mind and character in opposition to the logic, rigor, and rationality required

---

2 By 1930, Gernsback was far from surprised at the number of female readers. In response to a letter from a woman who presumed her letter would not be published, Gernsback wrote: "We have no discrimination against women. Perish the thought—we want them! As a matter of fact, there are almost as many women among our readers as there are men... We are always glad to hear from our feminine readers" (Gernsback 1930: 765).

and epitomized by "Science." For many women, the association of sf with science was enough to deter them from looking at such stories, or from at least admitting that they did so—an association of ideas that, World War II notwithstanding, continued into the atmosphere of "professional housewifery" of the 1950s and of course continues in an attenuated but still effective way to the present.

A number of women still managed to read and enjoy this most "unfeminine" of subjects. Over a decade later, in 1939, Charles Hornig, editor of the unambiguously-titled *Science Fiction* was also surprised to receive mail from female readers:

> I have received so many letters from women who read science fiction lately, that I must confess many of the fair sex have well-developed imaginations. Their group has grown to such proportions that they must certainly be taken into consideration by the male adherents. (Hornig 1939: 119)

Intriguingly, in this narrative, readers of the "fair sex" must possess "well-developed" imaginations to read sf, while presumably their male counterparts read it as an extension of their serious and rational interest in science and its future potentiality.

Another editor, Sam Merwin, also perceived a change during the pre-WWII years, noting the arrival of women writers and readers "at some indeterminate point in the nineteen thirties" (1950: 6). Merwin's editorial for the December 1950 issue of *Thrilling Wonder Stories* is worth citing at length:

> This metamorphosis—called either the Great Invasion or the Great Erosion depending upon the point of view—is too well and too long established to be regarded as any mere passing trend. The girls are in and in to stay.
>
> A number of women writers, ranging from adequate to brilliant, began to turn out science fiction stories of such excellence that in magazine after magazine they grabbed their share not only of inside short stories but of lead novelets and novels, hitherto an exclusively masculine prerogative.
>
> Certainly the fantasies of C. L. Moore were and are as fine as any in the field. And right up alongside her work we have today that of E. Mayne Hull, Leigh Brackett, Margaret

St Clair, Judith Merril, Catherine [sic] MacLean, Betsy Curtis, and Miriam Allen Deford [sic]...

Naturally, with such a group of talented women writers practicing successfully for more than a dozen years, the entire story-perspective on women in science fiction has changed. (6)

Before this period of "invasion," however, Merwin (like other commentators well into the '70s) depicted sf as "a world for men and men only" (6). In Merwin's narrative, previous to the "invasion," a female reader was a "space-minded Tomboy Taylor" who had to "keep her hair short and her mind on the refreshments rather than the boys" if she wanted to "crash" the "primeval" sf clubs. Following "the invasion,"

young women began to make their presence felt in the reader's columns of this and other stf magazines. They leaped recklessly into hitherto stag fan-controversies, thereby livening up same not only through the freshness of their approach but through the rebuttals they drew from resenting males. (7)

Merwin's comments make it quite clear that female intervention was met with less than approval on some sides, with one "school" withdrawing into "crusty male resentment toward feminine invasion of yet another masculine sanctum sanctorum." In contrast, Merwin situates himself in the "other camp," which believed "this female uprising, inrush or whatever it may be termed is entirely in line with the world-trend toward woman's emancipation and equality that has ensued at least since the fiery pronunciations of Mary Wollstonecraft and her companions" (140). Thus, unlike many of the narratives surrounding women's "invasion" of sf, women's entry into sf is characterized by Merwin as a natural development of equal rights activism.

The cycle of presumed absence followed by surprised discovery occurs again in the 1950s magazine *Startling Stories*. Writing only a few years after Merwin, editor Sam Mines locates the arrival of women at a later date: "[t]en years ago stf fans were practically all male," whereas by 1953,

a lot of girls and housewives and other members of the sex are quietly reading science fiction and beginning to add their voices [to the letter column of SS]... We confess this came as something of a surprise to us. We honestly never expected such a surge of female women [sic] into science fiction." (Mines 1953: 136)[3]

In the British magazine *Authentic Science Fiction*, a response to a female reader also notes the existence of female fans in the '50s and rather than expressing surprise, invites participation in fan activity: "We've had letters from several female fans...and we're convinced that there are many of them. We keep trying to get them to form a club...why don't you come along to the Globe in Hatton Garden one Thursday evening? You'll meet other girl fans there" (Campbell 1955: 126).

Big Name Fandom: Females need not apply

These letters and editorials demonstrate without doubt the existence of female readers of sf. The question of women's status or role in fandom, however, is another matter. Since its beginnings in the 1920s, sf fandom has been characterized as being almost exclusively composed of adolescent males. Fan histories of the 1930s and 1940s reinforce the assumption that sf was almost totally male dominated, with only the occasional exceptional female writer and even fewer female readers before the 1960s. Although opinions vary as to when female fans became numerous enough to be visible, the earliest fans or "First fandom" are usually tacitly assumed to have been all male. David Hartwell, for example, states that "until the 1940s, there just weren't any women in fandom to speak of" (1984: 161). Others suggest that those who did exist should be discounted because they were often the wives, girlfriends, or female relatives of male fans. Harry Warner Jr. comments that in the 1940s there was "no such thing as an independent honest-to-goodness girl-type fan, because virtually all the females in fandom had a fannish boy friend, brother, husband, or some other masculine link" (Warner Jr. 1969: 26). The key word here is *independent*, the implication being that connection with a male delegitimated the female fan identity—that her interest and presence was dependent solely on male influence. In retrospect, this is a particularly fallacious argument—now that there are numerous women involved in fandom, many still make significant partnerships within

---

3 Cited in Larbalestier, *Battle of the Sexes* (159). The abbreviation "stf" stood for "scientifiction" a name used earlier for sf.

the community precisely because of the shared interests and commitments, and indeed many early female fans were independently involved before they found partners within the fan community. Considering the fact that the "lack" of female fans was "oft lamented by males active in fandom" (r. brown 1994: 90), the desire for "honest-to-goodness girl-type" fans may have been attributable to young men's desire for single women to be available within their own, rather isolated community. Even in the 1990s, accounts claiming a lack of "femmefans" (female fans) rest on the same erasure of the few women present: "Most female fans involved between the 1930s and 1950s were male fan's wives, girlfriends, or sisters" (Luttrell 1994: 158n3).

The discounting of "secondary" female fans obscures the fact that, whatever their connections, these women were not necessarily passive hangers-on, as such statements imply, but were sincerely interested in sf, writing letters, editing fanzines, and attending conventions. The contradictory nature of accounts that recognize the presence of women while simultaneously undermining the significance of their participation is evident in the fan publication *Fancyclopedia*, first published in 1944.[4] Two entries in a later version refer directly to female fans:

> FANNE (pronounced "fan"). A female fan; also femme-fan.... Feminine objection to this term is caused by clods giving the silent E full value.

> FEMMEFANS. Explaining everything is contrary to our philosophy of education. (Eney and Speer 1959)

Reflecting the earlier conflations of females and "sex" discussed above, most of the information on female fans is found elsewhere. The entry on "Sex" states that "the great majority of fans are male, and it has been asserted that females cannot be the psychological type of the SF fan," but adds "tho there are many femmefans to refute this" (147).[5] In contrast to the examples above, this female presence is not counteracted; the entry continues: "*in addition* there are sweethearts, wives, daughters, sisters etc. of male fans" (my emphases). Thus the existence of "many

---

4 John Bristol (Jack) Speer, *Fancyclopedia*, Los Angeles: Forrest J. Ackerman, 1944. This was later revised and expanded as Richard H. Eney and Jack Speer, *Fancyclopedia II*, Alexandria, VA: Operation Crifanac, 1959.

5 This entry is the same in both issues, Speer, *Fancyclopedia* (78); Eney and Speer, *Fancyclopedia II* (147).

femme fans" who are not attached to males is implied; at the same time, even those "secondary" wives and girlfriends of fans seem to participate: they "*tag along* at fan gatherings, make some appearance in the fanzines, and assist in *dirty work* like mimeoing" (my emphases) (147). It would seem that assisting in compilation of a fanzine was not fanac in this case, but an accepted duty of the wife/girlfriend/sister; presumably women had to edit fanzines themselves to be considered a "true" fan. Since most fan histories concern those fen (plural of *fan*) who became well-known through their fan publications, fan editors, rather than the less active letter-writers or club and con attendees, are their main focus.[6] Correspondingly minimal attention is given to female fans, few of whom became well-known as editors until the 1950s.

The "liberation" of sf?: The 1950s and 1960s

The revolutionary decade of the 1960s seems the natural site to locate a radical shift in sf's relation to sex, women, and liberation. This was the period marked by the upheavals and turf wars of the New Wave with its turn to inner space and championing of the cultural and literary avant garde. It is in this period that most critics locate the new maturity of the genre and the "arrival" (again) of women writers and readers. Such stories obscure the extent to which a variety of social, political, and economic changes had impacted the field earlier. Recently, more nuanced accounts of the 1950s have emerged in works such as Lisa Yaszek's book on postwar women's sf (2008), Rob Latham's studies of the New Wave (2005, 2006), and Roger Luckhurst's cultural history of the genre (2005).

It is becoming increasingly apparent that the supposed invasion of women in the 1970s built on a significant legacy of female involvement in sf in the 1950s and '60s. Yaszek claims that almost 300 women began writing in the (US) sf field in the post-war, pre-Women's Lib period (2008: 3). A smaller, but still significant number is documented in Eric Davin's bibliography of sf writers, with 154 women identified as writing sf in the period 1950-60 (Davin 2003: 342). Women also had a visible impact in the field as editors: Judith Merril began her "Year's Best" series in 1956, and several women worked as editors for sf magazines, for example Cele Goldsmith (*Amazing* and *Fantastic*

---

6   In the early stages, fans who ran and organized conventions were likely to be those who were also most active in fan publishing.

Stories), Lila E. Shaffer (*Amazing, Fantastic*), Gloria Levitas (*F&SF*), Fanny Ellsworth (*Startling Stories, Thrilling Wonder Stories*), and Evelyn Paige (*Galaxy*) (Davin 2003: 345-6; see also, Frank, Stine, and Ackerman 1994). Moreover, opportunities for women writers were enhanced by the establishment of magazines such as *F&SF* (1949) and *Galaxy Science Fiction* (1950), founded by Horace L. Gold, who tried to include "at least one story that appealed to women" in each issue (Attebery 2003: 42). The rise of *F&*SF and *Galaxy Science Fiction* marked the waning of the significant editorial power of figures like Campbell, whose control had been "particularly inhibiting for authors whose work was in any way idiosyncratic or stylistically ambitious" (Latham 2005: 204). As Latham points out, the '50s also saw some significant explorations of sexuality that prefigured the avant garde innovations of the New Wave. Accounts that emphasize the New Wave's "'liberated' outburst of erotic expression" as a counter to the "priggish Puritanism of the Golden Age" obscure important continuities (Latham 2006: 252). Both New Wave advocates and later critics thus obscured significant developments in the 1950s by contrasting their calls for a more "mature" sf to a "caricatured portrait of the genre as naively juvenile prior to the advent of their fearless avant-garde" (253).

Indeed, by the early 1960s, it had become commonplace for sf critics, whether champions of the New Wave or not, to bemoan the field's avoidance of sex and sexuality on the grounds that it was inappropriate for an otherwise "progressive" and innovative genre.[7] Academic attention in concert with New Wave-type sensibilities resulted in a new focus on the literary qualities of sf. Criticism was leveled at the lack of characterization in sf—a problem that was seen to be at the root of sf's failure to portray (or even include) women and sex. As Larbalestier observes, critics promoted "the idea that science fiction had always ignored sex and that this had retarded its growth" (Larbalestier 2002: 137).

Additionally, as the sf paperback market continued to expand, authors were seen to be less constrained in their subject matter than they had been when the pulps provided virtually the only arena for sf. Publishers and editors of the pulps supposedly had to patrol their borders to ensure protection for younger readers, and many letters to the

7   See discussion in Nicholls (1979: 538-9).

pulps mentioned the possibility of "corrupting" younger readers (or sons) through unsuitable stories (Frank, Stine, and Ackerman 1994: ix-x; Nicholls 1979: 538).[8] However, as Eric Drown notes, the notion of the sf reader as a young adolescent may well be another truism not supported by historical research. On the contrary, Drown claims that "[w]hile there was a significantly visible contingent of precocious mostly middle-class boys among the letter-writers, most readers were the adults who provided the routine intellectual, clerical, mechanical and physical labor that made the new mass production economy function" (Drown 2006: 8). The idea that, no matter their age, sf was patrolled by "puritanical readers" as much as by editors is questioned by Latham who found mostly enthusiasm, rather than censure in the letter pages of magazines that had published sexually explicit stories such as Philip José Farmer's 1952 "The Lovers" (Latham 2006: 253).

The history of sf before 1960 was marked as an "innocent" and "naive" period, predicated on the notion that, in Larbalestier's words, "the intellectuality of science fiction perforce [kept] sex and the body out of the picture" (2002: 138). The earlier struggles over the subjects of "sex," "love interests," and "women" were not acknowledged in critical stories from the 1960s. Now the critical consensus decreed that "sex" was a "good thing" for sf, a sign of its maturity and a topic that did not automatically require consideration of the function of women in sf. And yet the slippage between sex and women had not disappeared. When the feminist critiques of Russ and others forced the community into consideration of the images of women in sf, many responses rested on the same assumptions displayed by Asimov and others in the 1930s. Indeed, the text that continues to be constantly valorized by critics as representing a watershed in sf's "maturity" in terms of sex is one that has attracted much feminist critique. Philip

---

8 While Frank et al. emphasize the power exerted by the owners of the publishing companies, Nicholls focuses on John Campbell's assistant Kay Tarrant commenting that she "was famous for her prudishness, and persuaded many writers to remove 'offensive' scenes and 'bad language' from their stories" (1979: 538). (This was, Latham tells us, a game amongst some authors known as "slipping one past Kay.") However, Latham counters this story, commenting that "Some of Campbell's admirers in the field...have attempted to absolve the editor of culpability for the excessive chasteness of his magazine, blaming it instead on the priggish Ms. Tarrant...but there can be little doubt that Campbell himself had, in this area as in so many others, quite firm and eccentric views of what was acceptable and what was not" (Latham 2006: 53).

José Farmer's "The Lovers" was identified by many critics in the 1960s and '70s as being one of the earliest stories to break sexual taboos and cited as evidence of sf's progression (Moskowitz 1966: 393; Scholes and Rabkin 1977: 185-6). It was left to later feminist critics to point out the misogyny of this graphic picture of interspecies miscegenation ending in the destruction of the *female* alien.[9] Indeed, Latham draws explicit connections between the emergence of feminist sf and the atmosphere of "sexual openness" of the '60s, arguing that "feminist sf served as a kind of conscience for the New Wave movement" with stories by the likes of Tiptree providing "corrective extensions of Farmer's pioneering tales of interspecies desire" and serving as "a counterweight to the more or less explicit misogyny of the sexual revolution" (2006: 262-3).

The "sexual revolution," in sf as elsewhere in society, did not by any means go hand in hand with gender equality. As Paul Carter (1977: 192) observes, "if the sexual behavior in the stories became more explicit, the conventions surrounding it remained archaic."[10] Even the slightest signs of women's increasing social independence could provoke defensive attitudes. In 1960, *Amazing Stories* published an article by sf writer Lester del Rey entitled "Polygamy, Polyandry, and the Future." Here the sexual revolution is figured as a way of *escaping* the possible revolution in sexual roles. The article opens:

> In a world where men do housework and women run offices, the old balance of the sexes is coming apart at the seams. Is a revolution in sexual mores the answer for the future, both here on Earth and outward in the new worlds of space? (del Rey 1960: 99)

Despite the classification of his piece under the "fact" heading, del Rey's hypothetical exploration of "the future of man's social patterns" is comparable to the misogynist "women dominant" sf stories that refigured and recontained the "threat" of women's independence

---

9   See for example, Roberts, *A New Species* (1993: 152). One critic who remained skeptical of the "breakthrough" begun by Farmer's example was Anthony Boucher: "one can complain no longer of the sexlessness of s-f after 1960's rash of novels which attempted to combine prognostication and pornography and achieved only boredom" (Boucher 1963: 379).

10 He recognized this as a trait not specific to sf: "many a supposedly avant-garde writer out in the literary 'mainstream' also commonly confuses freely available sex with genuine human liberation" (192).

and the "new woman" ideal of the 1920s.[11] Del Rey argues that the future demands of space travel would necessitate a complete restructuring of the family unit and sexual behavior, particularly the "western custom" of monogamy. He declares that there are "rather ugly factors already at work today" that augured against monogamous marriage, including the reduction of men's life spans due to marriage to the "modern" consumer-mad work-shy woman (102-3). This overtly misogynistic article expresses deep-seated contemporary fears concerning what were seen as unsettling social developments in "modern" culture, associated with the emerging "equality" of women. The article ends with del Rey's painting a picture of the rather "distasteful" but probable result of "man's desire to spread his seed to the stars" — the use of all-female crews and frozen sperm to colonize worlds. Del Rey hypothesizes that such a society would see men as a "necessary evil at first" then evolve into a specific form of polygamy rigorously controlled by women—a world that del Rey obviously "would keep far away from!" (106). Del Rey connects his vision with earlier sf texts positing "worlds of women without men," but cites only Poul Anderson (presumably referring to his 1957 *Virgin Planet*). In fact there were innumerable examples of this theme that together form a recognizable tradition, appearing first in the nineteenth century, and then in many pulp stories, through to the 1970s, where exploitation of the theme culminated in its radical reformation at the hands of feminist authors. The "world of women" — or what Russ and Larbalestier term "the battle of the sexes" story—is in fact one of the primary sites of female activity in sf and is a recurring concern in later critical works (Larbalestier 2002; Moskowitz 1976; Russ 1980).

---

11 Sam Moskowitz (1976) uses this term to describe role-reversal stories, where women rule and men are subjugated, functioning most often as a warning against increases in women's social and political power. Examples include Wallace West, "The Last Man," *Amazing Stories*, Feb. 1929, and E. Charles Vivian, *Woman Dominant*, London, Ward, Lock and Co., 1930. One of the few critics to recognize that women and sex had been subject to debate in sf, Moskowitz noted that "Woman Dominant" stories had "since the beginning" been an sf theme "spotlighting the female sex" (70). Moskowitz acknowledged that many stories contained "snide digs at women" and commented that male authors "in every case, seem uneasy about this 'equality' (of women), claiming that it will end in domination" (90). One of the few such early stories written by a woman was M.F. Rupert's "Via the Hewitt Ray," *Wonder Stories Quarterly*, Spring, 1930, discussed by Moskowitz (80).

In 1961, Kingsley Amis provided a view of sf that better characterized the critical approach developing through the 1960s, especially concerning the "oppressively normal" nature of sexual interest in sf, which in his view was "rare, conventional and thin." He rather patronizingly added that: "No wife who finds her husband addicting himself to science fiction need fear that he is in search of an erotic outlet" (Amis 1962: 66, 87).[12] One of sf's "earliest advocates in the literary mainstream" (Parrinder 1979: xv),[13] Amis argues, in *New Maps of Hell*, that representations of both "sex" and women in sf were outdated.

> Amid the most elaborate technological innovations, the most outré political or economic shifts, involving changes in the general conduct of life as extreme as the gulf dividing us from the Middle Ages, man and woman, husband and wife, lover and mistress go on doing their stuff in the mid-twentieth-century way... The sentimental consensus that this is perhaps the only part of human nature that can never be changed...is a disappointing trait in science fiction writers. (1962: 114-15)

This statement resonates with later feminist critiques, yet Amis's emphasis here is still on sex and sexual behavior, rather than sexual identity and gendered roles, although he did consider the ramifications of such conservatism for the representation of women in sf.[14] With an ironic (and not wholly convincing) nod towards the desirability of female emancipation—"one of those interesting ideas that have never actually been tried out"—Amis noted that few authors had seriously attempted to reconsider normative sexual roles. He cites two exceptional examples, namely Philip Wylie's "The Disappearance" and John Wyndham's "Consider Her Ways," but argues that "the female emancipationism of a Wylie or a Wyndham is too uncommon to be significant" (1962: 99).

---

12 He also distinguishes sf from fantasy in this aspect; commenting on a fantasy story "The sound of His Horn," he quips that an sf story would have "wrapped up the young ladies in veils of abstractions and outraged modesty" (102).

13 For Amis's influence on the field of sf criticism, see Parrinder (1979: 156). (See also Scholes and Rabkin 1977: 237.)

14 Cf. Joanna Russ: "In general, the authors who write reasonably sophisticated and literate science fiction...see the relations between the sexes as those of present-day, white middle-class suburbia" (Russ 1974b: 54).

Amis's direct, albeit brief, critique of gender roles in sf presaged an increasing societal acceptance of equi-sexist beliefs. Amis explicitly notes the "anti-feminist prejudice on the part of selection boards for planetary survey teams," an observation much more amenable to feminist sensibilities than assumptions that scientific rigor precludes the inclusion of mere "love-interests." Amis concludes that sf should "go easy" on the puritanism, but also suggests that sex should be excluded altogether when functioning as no more than a "perfunctory love interest," thus conflating "love interest" and women and intimating that women were better absent than functioning only as an excuse for providing sex. His rather limited view of the ways women could enter sf was emphasized by his critique of writers' attempts to "introduce a women's angle" (an effort "perhaps harmless in intention but unspeakable in execution") (Amis 1962: 144). It is not clear exactly which writer he was referring to, but his objections concerned the portrayal of "gallant little" wives and mothers. Feminists could (and did) also object to such characters, but the implication of Amis's stance is that women can really only function in boring domestic roles (undesirable in sf) or as sex objects/love interests (all right in their place). Amis's contradictory view of sexuality in sf—at times pro-feminist and at others reactionary—is reflected in similar debates well into the 1970s and beyond, when feminist criticism began to have an impact on sf studies.

1970s: Incorporation

By the mid-1970s, the critiques of women's position in sf had achieved a much more visible presence in sf scholarship and were frequently framed in overtly feminist terms. General works of sf criticism and history responded to this development. Increasingly, critics recognized the contribution of women writers (especially from the 1960s on) and saw a trend towards the "softer sciences" and better characterization resulting from their influence (a judgment that could be either welcomed or lamented). Reflecting gynocentric analyses, many established (male) critics and fans acknowledged the appalling limitations of stereotyped female characterization in sf, but often attributed this fault to causes such as a deficiency in characterization generally, or to sf's "natural" concentration on technology. Usually only feminist critics were prepared to admit the full extent of misogyny or sexism inherent in these problems of representation.

First published in Sweden in 1969, Sam Lundwall's *Science Fiction: What It's All About* presented a clear statement of sf's deficiencies when it came to representations of women. Obviously influenced by the insights of the Women's Liberation Movement (but without the benefits of the feminist critiques of sf that other commentators were soon able to draw upon), Lundwall argued: "In a world where women at last are beginning to be recognized as human beings, science fiction still clings to the views of last century" (Lundwall 1971: 145). Lundwall was also one of the few commentators on sf to recognize the explicit continuity between attitudes to women from the 1930s to the 1960s. Citing a 1939 letter from Asimov in *Startling Stories* (written in the same tone as his letters discussed above), Lundwall noted that little had changed in sf:

> [T]he woman is the same now as she was then. She shouldn't be in sf in the first place. If she nevertheless manages to get into it, she shall know her place. Period. (148-9)

In Peter Nicholl's *Encyclopedia of Sf*, the entry "Women" (dealing both with women who write sf and depictions of women in sf) states that "one of the more shameful facets of genre sf is the stereotyped and patronizing roles which are usually...assigned to women" (1979: 661).[15] Recognition of this problem, Nicholls notes, "began to filter, very slowly, into sf" with the rise of the feminist movement and its eventual influence in the sf world.[16] Citing several female critics who had "naturally been incensed at this chauvinism," he lists critical articles by Joanna Russ, Beverley Friend, Mary Kenny Badami, and also the special issue of the fanzine *Khatru* on women in sf (661).[17]

15 In the second edition of the *Encyclopedia*, the influence of the consolidation of feminist criticism over the next decade is obvious. The section "Women" is replaced by two: "Women as portrayed in science fiction" and "Women SF writers," and there is also a separate entry for "feminism": all of these entries are written by feminist sf author Lisa Tuttle (Clute and Nicholls 1993).

16 Nicholls noted that mainstream fiction had not had "this dishonourable history" to the same extent. He also made the interesting observation that the rise of feminism in the late '60s did not really have any repercussions in publishing until around 1974.

17 Nicholls lists a number of feminist sf works, including Sargent's *Women of Wonder* anthologies and Vonda N. McIntyre and Susan Janice Anderson's (eds), *Aurora:*

A number of male critics also (unwittingly) contributed to the recovery of herstory by situating Mary Shelley as the "mother" of the sf genre with *Frankenstein*. Although many critics had written of links between Shelley's Gothic novel and the sf genre previously, Brian Aldiss claimed he was the first to situate *Frankenstein* as the beginning of the sf genre (and commented in a later edition that most in the community found the idea that sf "was a Gothic offshoot" totally unacceptable) (Aldiss 1975; Aldiss and Wingrove 1988; Scholes and Rabkin 1977).[18] Another early female author who had been fairly consistently recognized was C.L. Moore. In his 1966 study, Moskowitz observes that Moore was the "most important woman to contribute to sf since Mary Shelley," and was additionally "one of the most perceptive literary artists in sf," who enriched the genre with her "rare feminine insight" (Moskowitz 1966: 305, 318). In a mostly biographical essay (that predictably focuses on her relationship with Henry Kuttner) Moskowitz raises some interesting points about the effect of Moore's gender on her career, including the way editors attempted to conceal her gender (until it was "discovered" by fans) and how the use of a pseudonym for her writing partnership with Kuttner largely detracted from and concealed Moore's influence and standing in the sf community (314).[19]

By the 1970s male critics at least recognized the existence of the increased number of female writers, even if they still gave little space to analyzing their works. Nicholl's *Encyclopedia*, for example, listed over sixty female writers in a special entry on "women," usefully in-

---

Beyond Equality, and is one of the few critics (along with Aldiss) to mention Mitchison's *Memoirs of a Spacewoman*, a very early example of feminist sf from 1962.

18 By the 1990s critical opinion had changed to the extent that few critics would now argue the import of *Frankenstein* for the development of sf (see for example Freedman, 2000). Nevertheless, as noted in the Introduction, moves to connect sf to earlier literary forebears (including in gynohistories of sf) often proceed from the impulse to recraft sf as a more respectable and literary field (see also Duchamp, 2006b).

19 Indeed, much of the basis for recovering "herstory" was initially provided by fan historians such as Moskowitz, whose collections and knowledge of the early period of sf provided evidence of female writers (see Moskowitz 1976). Moskowitz's collection of "women dominant" stories, *When Women Rule*, was also important for preserving examples of what Russ terms "battle of the sexes" texts or "flasher" stories that demonstrate the long history of anxiety about gendered relations and the heterosexual economy in sf.

cluding those who used male or ambiguous pen names, such as Rosel George Brown, Murray Constantine (Katherine Burdekin), Lee Hoffman, J. Hunter Holly, A.M. Lightner, Wilmar H. Shiras, Francis Stevens, and Leslie F. Stone. Many of the women on his list have still received little if any critical attention: for example, Hilary Bailey, Christine Brooke-Rose, Mildred Clingerman, Miriam Allen deFord, Sonya Dorman, Carol Emshwiller, Phyllis Gotlieb, Zenna Henderson, Anna Kavan, Katherine MacLean, Naomi Mitchison, Doris Piserchia, Margaret St. Clair, and Josephine Saxton (Nicholls 1979: 662). Aldiss implicitly acknowledged the neglect of female writers' contributions to sf—whilst repeating that neglect himself. After a fairly detailed discussion of influential male writers of the 1960s, Aldiss adds, "[n]or have I mentioned the women writers of this period," giving a brief list of names followed by a few sentences on Ursula K. Le Guin and a long quote from *The Left Hand of Darkness* (Aldiss 1975: 349-50). Nevertheless it is interesting to note the authors he includes: "Even a brief list must contain the names of Angela Carter... Jane Gaskell; Hilary Bailey; Sonya Dorman; Carol Emshwiller; Ursula Le Guin; Anne McCaffrey; Naomi Mitchison; Kit Reed; Joanna Russ; Josephine Saxton; Kate Wilhelm; and Pamela Zoline." Like Nicholls, Aldiss brings attention to a number of writers who disappear from view in later feminist critical work. He is, however, overly optimistic about the circumstances that had "allowed" these women to appear.

> What has made the difference is the disappearance of the Philistine-male chauvinist-pig attitude, pretty well dissipated by the revolutions of the mid-sixties; and the slow fade of the Gernsbackian notion that sf is all hardware... Science Fiction has returned from the Ghetto of Retarded Boyhood. (350-51)

Indeed, in a number of accounts, female writers—in particular Le Guin—were given credit for "saving" sf from its "retarded" past (Scholes and Rabkin 1977: 75-88). Women writers were perceived to be addressing a previous weakness in sf: the poor quality of its characterization, or as Philip K. Dick put it, a failure to deal adequately with "the man-woman aspect of life" (1974: 106). Aldiss, for example enthusiastically concurs with Harlan Ellison's sentiment in *Again, Dangerous Visions* that "much of the best writing in science fiction today is being done by women. (And he didn't even mention Christine

Brooke-Rose...)" (Aldiss 1975: 349-50; Ellison 1972: 230). Robert Silverberg was another author to espouse such statements: "about two thirds of the best SF these days is being written by women" (Silverberg 1979: 82). Even some older authors who had previously appeared extremely resistant to the "intrusion" of women (as people or characters) into sf proselytized for women's beneficial influence. Lester del Rey welcomed the "emergence" of new women writers in the 1970s; he comments, "this evolution was probably the healthiest and most promising for the future" (del Rey 1980: 262). Asimov was another to proclaim the arrival of women in the mid-1960s, a development which, he argued, induced enormous changes in the writing of sf. Writing in 1982, he argues: "It is the feminization of science fiction that has broadened and deepened the field to the point where science-fiction novels can now appear on the bestseller lists." Asimov claims that this development was a "good thing"—incidentally reinventing himself from the adolescent letterhack who vehemently argued that women equaled sex, to someone who had "always said: Liberate women—and men will be liberated as well" (Asimov 1982: 608).[20] Asimov's explanation for the influx of women is a common and generally accepted one: he attributes it to the influence of mass-media sf, specifically *Star Trek*. Nearly every commentator on the 1970s arrival of women mentions the influence of this TV series. Women's attraction to *Star Trek* is figured in accounts such as Asimov's in a way that recalls earlier ideas displayed in the pulps that women's interest is dependent on emotional response (rather than scientific interest). *Star Trek*'s appeal, according to Asimov, lay in the "human interest" of the stories, and of course, "they had Mr. Spock... What's more, Mr. Spock had pointed ears and, for some reason, this, too, seemed to appeal to women" (608).

By the late 1970s, critics such as Carter, Robert Scholes, and Eric Rabkin went beyond welcoming the "feminine influence," to draw-

---

20 However, his view could be seen as contributing to an analysis situating the mass market novel as a "feminized" arena and thus a devalued element of culture. This opens up possibilities for rather more negative interpretations, not just in terms of preventing sf from being considered serious literature, but also, in sf terms, the "pollution" of the hard core or golden age of masculine-type sf, which has been threatened by literary experiments from the New Wave, by feminist propaganda, by the softening influence of women's fantasy, and by the diluted and contaminated Hollywood versions of sf in the movies. Such a tack is taken by Charles Platt in "The Rape of Science Fiction," *Science Fiction Eye*, vol. 1, no. 5, July 1989, 45-9.

ing on feminist critiques (particularly by Russ) in their analyses of women in sf. Scholes and Rabkin even drew on feminist criticism to minimize the influence of earlier female writers; Merril, they argue "introduced feminist themes in her fiction but in her form and content she could hardly be called radical" (Scholes and Rabkin 1977: 89). This is in contrast with an author they portray as the "leading edge of the American New Wave"—Joanna Russ, typified by her "alive, vigorous and daring" language and her commitment to radical feminism, which they say is "typical of the social consciousness of this movement" (89). Such enthusiastic approval of Russ's style and content was, however, far from the norm, as demonstrated by the many vitriolic reviews of *The Female Man* appearing only a few years earlier (discussed below).

While also drawing on Russ to validate his reading of the chauvinism of sf, Carter was unusual for his defense of the "domesticated" fiction of the '50s, dismissed by Russ as "'ladies' magazine fiction" (Russ 1974b: 56). There is some truth in his comment that,

> it was something to have persuaded male readers brought up on boom-boom pulp action and an engineering mystique to read and enjoy stories which told them that gentleness, intuition and domesticity are as legitimately part of the scheme of things as aggressiveness, logic and high adventure. (Carter 1977: 196)[21]

Although Carter's suggestion that these qualities were gender specific is problematic, his suggestion of the impact such stories may have had in the "thud and blunder" atmosphere of 1940s and '50s sf is worth considering, as is their contribution to the development of feminist science fiction (see Yaszek 2008, for example).

If many critics had, to a certain extent, "incorporated" feminism as far as accepting the contributions of female and even feminist writers, there were still limitations on the extent to which feminist analyses were seen as appropriate, or on considerations of the more subtle processes by which sexist and androcentric attitudes could persist in texts (and amongst readers, authors, and critics). Often critics who praised the influence of female writers still spent very little time analyzing their texts. A broader knowledge of feminist and female writers

---

21 Carter mentions Margaret St. Clair, Judith Merril, Wilmar H. Shiras, Miriam Allen deFord, Zenna Henderson, and Andre Norton (194-6).

was not seen as integral to the history of sf—an assumption still common today. For example, Scholes and Rabkin argued that while the scientific possibilities for genetic engineering came into existence in about 1970, such possibilities had (in 1977) "not yet made their way into science fiction stories" (Scholes and Rabkin 1977: 144). Against this statement could be laid a number of examples by women writers. Le Guin's "Nine Lives" (first published in 1968) was about groups of male and female clones from human cells, and Pamela Sargent's *Cloned Lives (1976)* and Kate Wilhelm's *When Late the Sweet Birds Sang* (1976) both dealt with cloning.[22] The Scottish author Naomi Mitchison had also written a novel describing a world ordered by cloning and human genetic manipulation in the 1970 *Solution Three* (although it was not published till 1975) (Mitchison 1995).[23]

Feminist critiques thus remained a partial and inconsistent influence in "malestream" studies of sf. While a survey like Sam Lundwall's was generally extremely critical of the representation of women in past sf (indeed earning him criticism from male fans in reviews), he still "naturally" combined the consideration of women with the subject of sex in his ironically titled chapter, "Women, Robots and Other Peculiarities." A review by Jeffrey Anderson gleefully pointed out that Lundwall's conflation of sex and women in the same chapter was somewhat problematic: "how ironic, says the Liberationist, that Lundwall should link women with sex while trying to be liberal about it all" (J. Anderson 1973: 232).[24] Even more tellingly, Lundwall concludes his indictment of sf's chauvinism with the rejoinder:

22 My thanks to Sylvia Kelso for reminding me of the Le Guin story. This is the only story Le Guin has published under the pen name U.K. Le Guin. In the introduction to the story in this collection, she noted "The editors [of *Playboy*] politely asked if they could use the first initial only, and I agreed... It was the first (and is the only) time I met with anything I understood as sexual prejudice, prejudice against me as a woman writer, from any editor or publisher; and it seemed so silly, so grotesque, that I failed to see that it was also important" (119). Portions of the Sargent novel were first published in 1972, 1973, and 1974.

23 The book was not originally published in the US and was out of print in Britain by 1980 until republished by the Feminist Press in 1995 (see Benton 1992; L. Hall, 2007; Squier 1995a).

24 This two-pronged attack did not go unnoticed; Adrienne Fein was one who replied with misgivings about both Lundwall's and Anderson's approaches (Fein 1973: 337-9).

Of course, I am not demanding that all science fiction should contain women or even treat them as human beings—I am decidedly against stock characters, and those sf writers who think that women should be kept in the harem should of course be allowed to keep them there—in their fiction. (Lundwall 1971: 149)[25]

The notion that at least some sf texts were justified in omitting women was a common argument against feminist innovations throughout the 1970s. Such arguments were still predicated on the notion that science and thus sf involving scientists or space ships were and would remain masculine endeavors; therefore, the only mechanism for introducing a female character was as a love/sex interest. Interestingly, few, if any, sf texts set out to be all-male worlds in a conscious way similar to the feminist all-female utopias (or misogynist male-authored all-female dystopias)—women are not absent from the world necessarily: they just do not appear as actors.[26] Carter also contributed to the notion that women were not always "relevant" to sf topoi.[27] He attributed the

---

25 Lundwall also used Anne McCaffrey's "A Womanly Talent" as one of his pointed examples of appalling representations of "woman as appendage." McCaffrey took him to task for this criticism, claiming that originally writing the heroine Ruth as a "liberated woman," she was asked by John Campbell to "define Ruth in terms of a customary womanly role to cater to his readership." She went along with this—in her "inimitable fashion," which was an underlying "facetiousness"—a treatment Lundwall failed to appreciate:

> Because Ruth did, during the course of the story, what the men could never have done, and she did it in the traditional role of mother-mistress-healer. Actually, I was two up on the *Analog* readership: the woman not only bests the men in the story *but* there was an explicit sex scene in *Analog*'s virtuous pages. (A. McCaffrey 1974: 282-3)

26 Russ's survey of "flasher" or battle of the sexes novels found no book that "envisioned a womanless world," "Amor Vincit Foeminam" (1980: 14). One recent example of a womanless world is by Lois McMaster Bujold: her *Ethan of Athos* concerns an all-male world that relies on uterine replicators for reproduction.

27 Although Lester Del Rey presented the most overt example, arguing that sf should deal with "human values" that would "always remain relevant," rather than "current fads and ideas":

> Even such issues as the women's movement for equality should not normally be an issue in a story taking place in the year 2250; by that time, the matter will have been resolved, one way or another... Of course, there's nothing wrong with assuming that women do gain equality and trying to show a future society where that is taken for granted. But no

lack of "sexuality" (and women) in the pulp magazines to the masculinism of Science in general, and concluded, therefore, that "the Gernsback-Campbell engineering gadget kind of story—regrettably but realistically—required no female characters at all" (Carter 1977: 177). Putting aside the rejoinder that if these stories were being "realistic" about science they might have reflected women's entry into the sciences that began in the nineteenth century, such statements reflect resistance to feminist re-writings of history beyond the admission of absence. Such "sympathetic" critiques are thus distanced from Larbalestier's observations of the *active* patrolling against feminine invasion, and from feminist critiques of science, which provide more sophisticated analyses of the maintenance of the masculine culture of the sciences.

Yet for others in the sf field, even these "fellow-travelers" of feminism went too far. Jeffrey Anderson's review of Lundwall's book criticized him for mouthing "the rhetoric of the modern liberal outrage" as he "takes s-f to task for the sorry role it has relegated to women characters" (J. Anderson 1973: 232). Anderson clearly illustrates the "halfway" mark reached by the 1970s: feminist analyses had had enough impact for their initial point about the image of women in sf to have been incorporated into the critical view. There remained, however, a measure of defensiveness, expressed through critiques of "anachronistic" feminist historiography, and claims that sf as a field was no worse, and in many cases better, than other bodies of fiction. Thus Anderson argued:

> Admittedly, women haven't progressed far beyond the dependent-housewife image in s-f. But I think Lundwall comes down on s-f a bit harshly here. One must consider the culture from which it came; it is no worse than anything else written between 1920 (say) and 1970. (232)

Resistance...

The appearance of feminist sensibilities and awareness of feminist critiques in malestream sf criticism in the 1970s suggests some of

---

great point should be made of that—because readers ten years from now, particularly younger ones, may also take it for granted and wonder what all the fuss is about. (del Rey 1980: 368-9) the impact of feminist critiques on the field. A more immediate context for the reception of feminist critiques is found in the fanzines and magazine letter columns of the time, which responded to statements and fiction by feminist authors and critics. Indeed, the intense nature of debates around feminism and women in sf is suggested by repeated statements from fans and authors that, by the late 1970s, the whole issue was "old-hat." This is certainly not the impression gained from academic criticism in book-length studies and journal articles. In the more rarefied atmosphere of the academy and "sf scholarship," feminist sf criticism was by no means a constant, let alone "overdone," theme.

A wonderful example of the complex responses to feminist critique within the sf community is provided by the re-publication of Joanna Russ's article, "The Image of Women in Science Fiction" (Russ 1974b: 53-7).[28] The first critique of sf's representation of women consciously informed by the women's movement, "Image of Women" was initially published in a small literary magazine, *The Red Clay Reader*, in 1970, but the article did not appear to attract much attention in sf commentary until its second re-publication in the sf magazine *Vertex* in 1974. Subsequent issues of *Vertex* contained replies to Russ from two prominent male authors. The first reply was a rebuttal from Poul Anderson, whose tone of patronizing correction from a kindly, better-informed patriarch is signaled by his title "Reply to a Lady" (P. Anderson 1974). Beginning by situating Russ as a knowledgeable figure, "one of the perhaps half a dozen science fiction critics worth anybody's attention," he proceeded to recast her as a biased female (or worse, "lady") who had "let her fervor in a cause run away with her" and "let her political convictions influence her literary judgment to the detriment of the latter" (8).[29] Like a number of his contemporaries, Anderson believes that women simply are not relevant to much sf: "the frequent absence of women characters has no great significance, perhaps none

---

28 Joanna Russ, "The Image of Women in Science Fiction," *Red Clay Reader*, 1970; reprinted in Susan Koppelman Cornillon (ed.) *Images of Women in Fiction: Feminist Perspectives*, Bowling Green, OH, Bowling Green University Popular Press, 1972; reprinted in *Vertex*, vol. 1, no. 6, Feb. 1974, 53-7. All page numbers cited refer to this issue. Russ's article is discussed in Chapter Four.

29 Russ wrote a number of reviews for *F&SF* in the 1960s and 1970s including reviews of Anderson's work, as well as a piece that pointedly confronted those who believed "politics" had no place in such reviews (November 1979, 107 in Russ, 2007). For more on Russ' reviews see James (2009).

whatsoever" (99). Anderson's defense of sf recalls earlier arguments conflating women and sex; he argues that in many works there was no need to introduce women or to "bring in a love interest."

> Certain writers, Isaac Asimov and Arthur Clarke doubtless the most distinguished, seldom pick themes which inherently call for women to take a lead role. This merely shows they prefer cerebral plots, not that they are antifeminist.

> ...Ms. Russ' charge of sexism, like her charge of ethnocentrism, will not stand up unless one deliberately sifts the evidence... I think she simply let her fervor in a cause run away with her. (99)

After establishing women's irrelevance to the genre, Anderson claims that sf had never in fact been anti-feminist, but indeed was "more favorable to women than any other pulp writing." Amongst the writers he brought to his defense were Moore, Brackett, and Zenna Henderson, while additionally citing examples of sympathetic portrayals of female characters by male sf writers—including those of Heinlein and Asimov's "brilliant protagonist" Susan Calvin (99). These examples of course would not have appealed to feminists; even Lundwall had criticized Heinlein's "harem" and Asimov's Calvin (Lundwall 1971: 145, 148-9). (Incidentally, it may well have been the use of earlier female writers as "evidence for the defense" by male critics and authors who refused to acknowledge the validity of feminist critiques that led to their rather tenuous position in later feminist criticism.)

A couple of issues later, there followed a rather ambiguous response to both Russ and Anderson, ostensibly supporting Russ, from writer Philip K. Dick. Dick's "An Open letter to Joanna Russ" illustrates the very complex reaction to feminist critiques from sf authors and critics accustomed to viewing themselves as "liberals."

> Ms. Russ has in the most polemical manner, familiar now to most of us, hit where it hurts...to make her point, even at the cost of strewing the landscape with the wounded and puzzled corpses of otherwise reputable sf writers unaccustomed to such unfair attacks...

> And yet...I suddenly realized that beneath the anger and polemics and unfair tactics, which remind me of my old Left

Wing girlfriends when they were mad at me for whatever reason—under all her manner of expressing her views, Joanna
Russ is right. And Poul and I and the rest of us are wrong…

So Joanna is right—in what she believes, not how she puts
it forth. Lady militants are always like Joanna, hitting you
with their umbrella, smashing your bottle of whiskey—they
are angry because if they are not, WE WILL NOT LISTEN.
(Dick 1974: 99)

Dick's letter begins by positioning himself firmly in the camp of
"male sf writers": he acknowledges Anderson as a personal friend and
praises his article profusely, saying it is "superb" and "could not be
bettered"—but for the fact that it is "wrong." In contrast to Russ's polemical tactics Anderson's article, although "reasonable and moderate
and respectable" is, Dick concludes, nevertheless "meaningless":

It was like telling the blacks that they only "imagined" that
somehow things in the world were different for them, that
they only somehow "imagined" that their needs, its articulations in our writing, were being ignored. *It is a conspiracy
of silence*, and Joanna, despite the fact that she seemed to feel
the need of attacking us on a personal level, shattered that
silence, for the good of us all. (99)[30]

Unlike Anderson, the problem for Dick is not the substance of
Russ's article, but the *manner* of its writing. However, he traverses
a fine line between acknowledgment of the necessity of "Joanna's"
anger and resentment toward what he perceives as a "personal" attack. A typical response to feminism(s), then as now, is that it inherently consists of attacks on individual men—on *their* sexism, *their*
particular acts of power, discrimination, and so on. This problem was
if anything highlighted in the sf community, where so many people
did indeed know each other personally, so that when examples were
brought forth to display sexism in sf, they had often been written by
contemporaries—even friends—of the (feminist) critic.[31] Certainly

30 This comparison to the Black civil rights movement appears in a number of other
    instances as a comparative point for the women's movement and is used to argue
    both for and against the "justice" of women's liberation.

31 It is worth noting that not nearly as much personal invective was aimed at Samuel
    R. Delany's feminist critiques of the field.

the letters in *Vertex* suggest that Dick's and Anderson's perceptions of Russ's "anger," "militancy," and charges of "sexism" are derived from more than just this one article; perhaps influenced by personal interactions with Russ, her reviews of their work, or awareness of her fictional texts, such as "When it Changed" or *The Female Man*.[32]

This tension between feminist, anti-feminist, and more ambivalent positions was continued in a debate responding to Russ and Anderson's exchange in the fanzine *Notes From the Chemistry Department*. The conversation opens not with a direct reference to Russ, but a rebuttal of Anderson's article by Loren MacGregor entitled "A reply to a Chauvinist" (MacGregor 1974).[33] MacGregor's "A reply to a Chauvinist" refutes Anderson's article in much more decisive terms than Dick's reply. While MacGregor also initially aligns himself with the "cohort" of male writers (and in this case male sf fans), unlike Dick, he accepted Russ's "charges" without qualification. Initially expecting, and indeed wanting to agree with Anderson (as many of Russ's points "hit uncomfortably close to home"), MacGregor points out that "Mr. Anderson had managed to ignore, or misinterpret virtually all of [Russ's] assessments" (2). Most importantly, MacGregor notes that in Russs's article, "the charge was not one of antifeminism, but of male chauvinism." Further, in MacGregor's eyes, Anderson's attempt to defend sf from the accusation of "anti-feminism," by referring to "sympathetic" portraits of women, was ultimately stereotypical and chauvinist.[34]

A number of responses to MacGregor's article appeared in the following issues of *Notes*. As with other similar debates, many fans and authors who did not accept feminist characterizations of sexism and chauvinism in sf still claimed that they supported "equal rights" generally. These exchanges clearly display representational contests over the meaning of equality and whether feminists should control the

---

32 Although not published until 1975, *The Female Man* was in circulation in the sf community for a number of years previously, according to Samuel Delany (Moylan 1986: 57). See also the collection of Russ's reviews in *The Country You Have Never Seen* (2007).

33 MacGregor was commenting as a fan; he later went on to become an sf novelist himself.

34 The impact of MacGregor's reasonable assessment is somewhat marred by the fact that his title is illustrated by a three-cup brassiere (presumably for some "alien" female) hanging from the word "chauvinist"—a fact bemoaned by Russ in the next issue (see below).

delineation of what "equal rights" might encompass. The responses from fans and authors in the March 1975 issue of *Notes* present an interesting range of political positions that all to some extent agree with Russ's or MacGregor's conclusions about the limited portrayals of women in sf, even whilst some explicitly express opposition to "feminism" as a movement or theory. In many of these examples, Russ is positioned (often almost metonymically) as representative of a stereotypical notion of feminism that is anti-male, "rabid," and blindly judgmental.

The article "Sexual Stereotypes" by Paul Walker begins by stating that "in general" Russ and MacGregor are right, and Anderson is wrong, but goes on to argue that women are just as guilty as men are for promoting sexist stereotypes, and indeed are "*far more* to blame for the inequalities that exist" (italics in original) (P. Walker 1975: 9-10). Like many other commentators (including Dick), Walker evokes the "danger"—and ease—of inciting Russ's anger: "I'm sorry, but at the risk of bringing down the wrath of Ms. Russ, I do not beleive [sic] men and women are identical" (11). In a similar vein, a letter from Victoria Vayne expresses support for "a certain amount of equality in law, and justice, and working remuneration," but sharply delineates these issues from the arguments of feminists, who she refers to as "rabid" and a "paranoid bunch." Referring implicitly to Russ, Vayne observes that "Feminists seem to me to be a touchy lot; they get so caught up in their cause they seem to have a vendetta against men in general. They are generally too ready to boil over in anger over some slight" (Vayne 1975: 37). Jerry Pournelle also contributes, in a fashion very similar to Anderson, concluding (after a lengthy discussion of philosophy and biological determinism) that "a writer is no more compelled to accept the [sexual] equivalence argument, or its negation, than he is to accept or reject the possibility of faster than light travel" (Pournelle 1975: 9).

The issue also includes letters supportive of MacGregor and Russ. In contrast to the anti-feminist arguments of Walker and others who situated physical and biological difference as justification of sexual inequality, one letter emphasizes the sociocultural context of gendered assumptions: "The fault...does not lie with the fiction or its creators, however. It lies in the culture that produced the creators and those who appreciate their works" (Franke 1975: 37). In her own letter to this issue, Russ also re-asserts the cultural, political, and economic elements of sexism: "sexism isn't a personal failing, it's institutionalized oppression" (Russ 1975b: 39).

The tone of Russ's letter is interesting to note; in the year that the *Female Man* was published, already a certain weariness in having to explain sexism and defend her theoretical position is more than evident. After opening with thanks to the editor for sending her a copy of the previous issue, she comments "I'm glad the exchange in *Vertex* has sparked something, though I sometimes wish someone else had done it. Because, you see, I must answer..." (38). Russ answers, presumably, because she cannot resist the pull to try and explain—once more—that sexism is not always conscious, or personal, but can inhere in "small things" like the ratio of female contributors to male in the fanzine index, or the use of hearts and a (three-cup) brassiere in illustrating an essay on women in science fiction.

Contesting the texts of feminist sf

The clash of invested narratives about sf occurred in response not only to feminist critiques of the field, but also to the overt feminist sf appearing in the 1970s. A good example is the reception of Russ's works "When It Changed" and *The Female Man*, which rewrote and challenged sf tropes and disrupted conventional narrative structures.[35] Many of the reviews and responses to her works in magazines and fanzines rehearsed the criticisms she predicted in the interjection in *The Female Man*:

> We would gladly have listened to her (they said) *if only she had spoke like a lady*. But they are liars and the truth is not in them.

> Shrill...vituperative...[...]this shapeless book...of course a calm and objective discussion is beyond...[...]no characterization, no plot...[...]this pretense at a novel...trying to shock...[...]a warped clinical protest against...violently waspish attack...[...]we "dear ladies," whom Russ would do way with, unfortunately just don't *feel*...ephemeral trash,

---

35 "When It Changed" was first published in Harlan Ellison (ed.), *Again, Dangerous Visions*, New York, Doubleday, 1972; *The Female Man* (1975), Boston, MA: Beacon, 1986.

missiles of the sex war...a female lack of experience which...
Q.E.D. Quod erat demonstrandum. It has been proved.

(Russ 1986: 140-1)

Over a number of issues from 1973-74, an often heated round of
letters graced the pages of the fanzine *The Alien Critic*, edited by fan
and writer Richard E. Geis.[36] SF author Michael G. Coney led the
attack, in a letter describing "When It Changed" as a "horrible, sick-
ening story." According to Coney, Women's Liberation was a topical
"bandwagon," whose oppositional stance could be distilled to the view
that "the-majority-is-a-bastard," a critique he suggests could be better represented through "blacks" versus "whites," or Catholics versus Protestants (Coney 1973). The source of Coney's displeasure was
made clear when he situated himself as part of that majority ("quite
the opposite of a crank") attacked by Russ: "I'm a white non-religious
male of heterosexual leanings, a member of a vast and passive majority which seems to be the target of every crank group under the sun"
(53). Coney here sets himself up perfectly as part of the dominant
group controlling the production of science and fictional meanings
that is, and indeed continues to be, the target of feminist (and later
postcolonial and queer) interventions. It is worth quoting Coney at
length to indicate the depth of passion that feminist positions—via
Russ—could inspire in some sections of the sf community.

> The hatred, the destructiveness that comes out in the sto-
> ry makes me sick for humanity and I have to remember, I
> have to tell myself that it isn't humanity speaking—it's just
> one bigot. Now I've just come from the West Indies, where
> I spent three years being hated merely because my skin was
> white—and for <u>no other reason</u>. Now I pick up A, DV [*Again,
> Dangerous Visions*] and find that I am hated for another rea-
> son—because Joanna Russ hasn't got a prick. (53)[37]

In narratives like Coney's, the sociopolitical basis of feminist and black
critiques are refigured as biologically determined, direct attacks on his

---

36 Geis was the author of a number of "sf-and-sex novels" with titles such as *The
Endless Orgy* and *Raw Meat*, which were described by Richard Delap as a "messy
bit of sex-drenched but puerile humor" (Delap 1974: 5).

37 Not surprisingly, such reviews and responses to Russ's work rehearsed the criticisms she predicted in an interjection in *The Female Man* (Russ 1986: 140-1).

white, male person—who, because of his body marked by its color and penis, is vulnerable to (but not responsible for) such "bigoted," "unhuman" challenges.

Not surprisingly, a number of women responded, including Russ and Vonda McIntyre. McIntyre's letter expresses her discomfort with the sexist tone of the fanzine, including Coney's dismissal of women's anger "as penis envy (penis envy! In 1973 he talks about penis envy)" (McIntyre 1973: 47). Another letter from a female reader also ridicules the notion of penis envy and asks if Coney was suffering instead from "vagina envy" (Aab 1973: 47-8).[38] In contrast, a letter from a female reader describes herself as "one of the demon Women Libbers," but directs the brunt of her disapproval at McIntyre:

> I was goddamned mad to hear Ms. McIntyre refer to "the anger and hostility of women" because women includes *me*—and I love my husband. All I want is equality Mr. Geis [the editor]. I don't want to hate anyone. Why does Ms. McIntyre? (Plinlimmon 1974: 18)

In the following issue is a letter from Russ (who ironically only looked at the 'zine because it had a letter from McIntyre), which opens: "Please don't send me any more copies of *The Alien Critic*...You are certainly free to turn your fanzine into a men's house miniature world, but why you think I would like it or be interested in it—a mystery" (Russ 1974a: 36). Her letter focuses not on Coney's critique, but the editorial comments appended to McIntyre's letter. In a "one-man" fanzine like this, much overt sexism could reside in the "conversation" set up by the editor with other contributions. As in many of the letter columns of the pulps and other fanzines, Geis added his view to virtually every piece and letter he published. In his comments following McIntyre's letter, Geis argues that women's status as "sex objects" and "cultural victims" is due to men's capacity to commit physical violence upon women on a one-to-one basis. Russ in turn, feels compelled to once more adumbrate the argument that sexism is, rather, "enforced by ideology and economics" (37). Evidence of Russ's

---

38 In a letter to the following issue, Coney separates Aab from Russ and McIntyre, describing her as "young and nice and genuinely upset about my remark," but calling her reading of Russ's story "naïve." His tone of paternalistic tolerance reaches its peak in the final response to Aab's letter: "I find my penis just great and hope you are enjoying your vagina" (Coney 1974: 38).

frustration at having to explain "feminism 101" again appears in her letter's postscript:

> P.S. Apologies will be cheerfully read, but nothing else. No explanations of how wrong I am, or oversensitive, etc. etc. (the usual stuff). After all, you don't have to print this. And I'm damned if I will get into another long-drawn-out argument. (The first was with—via Harlan Ellison and *Last Dangerous Visions*—guess who? Michael G. Coney.) (37)

Not surprisingly, Geis ignored Russ's plea, and filled a whole page (twice the length of Russ's letter) with his rebuttals (Geis 1974: 37).

The reduction of feminist interventions to a "battle of the sex organs" was still prevalent two years later, when Richard Geis reviewed Russ's *The Female Man*, which, directly evoking the previous debate, was entitled "Pardon Me, But Your Vagina Just Bit My Penis" (Geis 1975: 64-5). Almost despite the title, the review attempts to be a "serious" consideration of Russ's book. Geis, like a number of more respected sf critics, focuses on Russ's failure to "resolve" the problems highlighted by feminism, rather than attacking her political stance per se. Geis accused her of writing nothing more than a "revenge fantasy" (1975: 64). And when Alexei and Cory Panshin refer to Russ's calls (in her role as sf critic) for representations of "whole women," they conclude that "the answer is not *The Female Man*" (Panshin and Panshin 1975: 52). In both of these reviews, the critics outline what kind of text they think would best serve the women's movement. Geis argues that Russ does not address the opposition of other women (64), while the Panshins believed she should have constructed a picture of "whole women" (51). As Russ's text does not meet these agendas, it is castigated for being a "tract" and "an exercise in self-indulgence" (Panshin and Panshin 1975: 51). Thus Russ's devastating critique of female stereotypes and masculinist sf tropes, her deconstruction of the drive for an acceptable, liberal "whole" woman, and her movement toward a multiple, shifting postmodernist sense of self was bypassed. Indeed, these critics place *The Female Man* outside of sf and even the novel form itself;Geis terms it "a non-novel...more vehicle than story," an example of Russ using sf "to grind her axe" (1975: 64). Similarly, the Panshins' review states, "*The Female Man* is advertised as a science fiction novel, but it is not one. It is not a story. It is not an action. There is no narrative thread" (1975: 51). Again, Russ satirized exactly such critical responses to her work in *The Female Man* itself: "We would gladly have listened to her (they said) *if only she had spoken like a lady*...no characterization, no plot...really important issues are neglected while...this pretense at a novel..." (Russ 1986: 140-1).

So, by the mid-'70s, sympathetic and even chauvinist sf critics had incorporated feminist threads to the extent that they enacted a "colonization" of certain feminist critical insights and attempted to (re)direct a "Women's Lib" agenda.[39] In contrast to "official" sf scholarship (represented by monographs, collected essays, and the sf journals) where feminist criticism was still a novelty, by the close of the 1970s, feminist narratives within the "unofficial" field of magazine letter columns and fanzines were rendered banal. Some of the most blatant statements of the dissolution of feminist critiques occurred in response to fan Susan Wood's article on "Women in SF" in the semi-prozine *Algol/Starship* published in 1979 (Wood 1978/1979: 9-18). Ironically, Wood's article, which was so well known in the sf community and whose themes were supposedly "assimilated" with little difficulty, remains absent from the majority of feminist critical narratives of sf. Because it was published in a semi-prozine rather than a critical journal, Wood's work has rarely been acknowledged as part of the critical conversations producing feminist sf criticism. Amongst enthusiastic and receptive letters were a number that cast Wood's critique as unnecessary or overdone, such as the anonymous reader who commented "Talk about using an atom bomb to kill a flea!" (Anon. 1979: 66).[40] Such responses attempted to dilute the impact of Wood's feminist analysis by denying its radical or disruptive potential. According to one reader, Wood's article was a "bit trite" as it "belabor[ed] a point which is...chewed to death in the fannish literature" (Antell 1979: 67), while Gregory Benford claimed that Wood's thesis had been "conventional wisdom for years" (Benford 1979: 65).[41]

---

39 I am indebted to Sylvia Kelso's thoughts on the "synergy" of feminism and popular fiction: Kelso, "Singularities," PhD Thesis, James Cook University, Townsville, 1996. I have borrowed her use of the term "colonization," which she uses to refer to Marion Zimmer Bradley's partial engagement with "the areas feminism(s) opened for SF writers" (165).

40 "Anon" also bemoaned women authors' concentration on the "injustice of the past and near-present" rather than opportunities of the future.

41 Similar responses appeared in the next issue, when Dan Davidson asked "is it necessary to keep going over all this old ground?" (Davidson 1979: 89)

Robert Bloch (like the Panshins and Geis) attempted to redefine and guide the feminist critical agenda, arguing that Wood (and McIntyre) should "stop worrying about how many females can be counted in *Star Wars*...and address themselves to some of the more pressing ERA problems—rape, battered wives, child support and welfare, abortion legislation, etc." (Bloch 1979: 81).[42] Bloch's statement reflects a common stance concerning political activism in sf: that oppositional ideologies are "best" or properly expressed through direct sociopolitical action (and not, by implication, in the "pure" non-political space of sf and its fandom). Yet for many sf authors and fans, sf was figured as a site of cultural praxis or, to modify Katie King's term, as an apparatus for the production of scientific culture (K. King 1994: 92),[43] when it came to the future of scientific and technological developments and their effect on human society.

---

42 A good response came from Alexander Strachan, who claimed he was "mystified" by Bloch's statements: "Of course equal representation in *Star Wars* isn't the issue, but it's a symptom none the less" (Strachan 1979: 65). Strachan's letters are a good illustration of the complex responses to feminisms: he rebutted Bloch's attack on McIntyre and Wood (for not being feminist enough) and commended Wood's analysis of a "sorely neglected" topic, but comments in another letter: "As for the back biting between the 'feminists' and the 'chauvinists,' we can all do without it" (67).

43 Here King is referring to her analysis of various cultural or "writing" technologies (such as "poem," "story," and "song") as part of "the apparatus for the production of feminist culture."

3

MOTHERS OF THE REVOLUTION: FEMMEFANS UNITE!

*...feminist knowledge is rooted in imaginative connection and
hard-won, practical coalition—which is not the same thing as
identity but does demand self-critical situatedness and historical seriousness.*

↦ Donna Haraway (1997: 199)

The convoluted stories of women's arrival in sf traced by the last
chapter suggest the extent to which their entry was actively contested or questioned, rather than passively awaited or accepted. Women
confronted obstacles constituted by gendered discourses specific both
to the sf field and society more broadly. The ways in which women
negotiated such obstacles in sf provides an important context for the
activities of later feminist authors, readers, and fans. I am interested
in retrieving the stories of absent women not merely as a gynocritical
recovery, or as an historical corrective, but also in order to present a
more nuanced account of the kinds of countercultural activity possible in the genre at various times and places. That is, I wish to view
the development of woman-centered and feminist positions amongst
female sf readers and writers not just as an external import of wom-
en's lib into the sanctified space of sf (much as the "new wave" has in
many accounts been viewed as infecting the genre with literary values) but also as a specific response to, and evolution of, factors internal
to the field and community itself.

As Haraway's quote suggests, imagination is a powerful element
in collective political identity. In relation to sf there are resonances
here with L. Timmel Duchamp's insight that entry into sf feminisms
involves an imagining into community, even if only as an isolated
reader in conversation with texts alone (2004b: 4-5). The step from
a community of the mind to actualized engagement with existing,
self-identified feminist communities has of course become much sim-
pler since the widespread availability of online communities starting
in the 1990s. In the earlier decades of the twentieth century such a
step was more uncertain and potentially confronting. Female readers

and potential fans had first to become visible to one another, then to discover or develop the language and opportunity to frame their understandings as part of shared experiences. Thus I am particularly interested in locating expressions of a desire or need to identify as female fans or members of the sf community. Whilst such affiliations were likely to be based on an undifferentiated notion of collective identity as women, rather than shared political experiences or goals, it is here we find key influences on later feminist developments.

My focus on uncovering these herstories also complicates accepted explanations for women's increased presence from the 1960s on. Alongside the *Star Trek* rationale (noted in Chapter Two), many versions see women's presence due to a snowball effect—the presence of more female writers "naturally" attracted more readers, thus encouraging more writers. Yet many female writers (including Ursula K. Le Guin, Marion Zimmer Bradley, Katherine MacLean, James Tiptree Jr., and Joanna Russ) first encountered sf through the pulps, reading male authors.[1] If the increase in the number of women writers in the '60s and '70s was initiated in part by their exposure to sf as girls or young women, we should be looking for changes in the sf community from the 1940s on.

As I noted in Chapter Two, until recently few commentators looked to the '50s as a period of significance in sf history. A growing body of work interested in this era has identified developments that at least lessened the obstacles for female readers of sf. Larbalestier points to Samuel R. Delany's belief that a radicalization of sf began in the 1950s, a time when sf "began to deal directly with problems in the country. It began to touch on the racial situation, population growth, religious freedom, sexual roles, social alienation, 'conformity,' and ecology" (Delany 1984: 237; see also R. Latham 2006; Luckhurst 2005; Yaszek 2008). Another factor impacting on women's ability—and desire—to engage with sf was changes in the education system. In a letter to the feminist fanzine *Janus* in 1979, Linda Bushyager commented on the increase in women writers:

---

1   See Katherine MacLean, "The Expanding Mind" (MacLean 1981); Ursula Le Guin, "A Citizen of Mondath" (Le Guin 1992a); Margaret St. Clair, "Wight in Space" (St. Clair 1981); Marion Zimmer Bradley, "My Trip Through Science Fiction" (Bradley 1977/1978); Alice Sheldon, "A Woman Writing Science Fiction and Fantasy" (A. Sheldon 1988); and Joanna Russ, "Reflections on SF" (Russ 1975d).

I think there is probably a correlation between the push in science and math education in the late '50s and early '60s (after Sputnik) and the increased interest in science and SF among men and women now. The push caused a lot of women to begin taking an interest in science, and now we are seeing the women who were in grade and high school at the time becoming readers and writers. (1979: 7)

Such initiatives included the 1958 National Defense Education Act, which provided fellowships for any student in the areas of math and sciences, and the 1959 NASA program "Women in Space Early" (WISE) (Yaszek 2008: 13). On a broader societal level, Yaszek suggests that developments in the intersection of technology, domestic spaces, and women's work in the postwar period also impacted women's involvement in the field: "postwar women turned to SF as an important source of narratives for critically assessing the nature of feminine work and identity in a technology-intensive world" (8). While Yaszek focuses on writers rather than on readers as such, the notion that many women would be looking for narrative explorations of their increasingly technologized domestic and working lives in places other than ladies magazines is suggestive.

The invisible female fan/reader

It is difficult to develop a clear picture of women's activities in the earlier days of the sf community. For one thing, fan histories glossed over the presence of active female fans, and for another, there would have been many fans, and even more readers, whose activities never went beyond writing letters to fanzines or the pulps. As Harry Warner Jr. has commented on fandom in general, estimating numbers is complicated by the fact that "there must have been large numbers of fans not visible"(1969: 24).[2] Female fans were more likely than male fans to remain "not visible." As rich brown has observed, social pressure against reading sf would have been even greater for women than for men, which means that young women would thus have found it difficult to obtain or read sf unless it was brought into the house by a male relative (brown 1994: 90). Numerous female sf writers report having to hide their copies of the pulps, or getting them from male relatives,

---

2   For example, fans who were primarily collectors (Warner Jr. 1969: 24).

often without parental knowledge. Author Katherine MacLean provides a wonderful description of her furtive and fascinated discovery of the pulps and the less than approving reaction from her parents: "When I got home my mother burned the science fiction magazine, and pledged my brothers to take my bike away if they caught me with another" (MacLean 1981: 87; see also A. Sheldon 1988: 43-58). Apart from such tacit obstacles to women's involvement, there may well have been, as the last chapter suggested, much to actively alienate women from the magazines, particularly the attitude of male fans.

The possibility that many female readers and potential fans are "hidden from history" is also suggested by the fact that most subscribers to the magazines would have been male, even though female members of the family may also have been avid readers. Indeed, a number of letters noted by Larbalestier make reference to whole families reading sf (discussed below). Such considerations complicate the figures drawn from surveys conducted since the 1940s by the magazines in their attempt to build up profiles of the average sf reader/fan. One would assume that the number of female readers would necessarily be higher than that of female fans, as readers provided the base for fandom. Yet surveys of readers may be even more misleading than fan surveys (where chances were everyone knew each other), because magazine questionnaires presumed only a single respondent, so in the case of a household of multiple readers, the survey would most likely be filled out by the male subscriber. As sf reader and fan Mildred D. Broxon pointed out in the 1970s, estimates of readership have relied on, for example, magazine subscription lists which, "if sent to a couple, [are often] in the man's name... Since it was my husband's subscription he filled it out. Does this mean I don't read *Locus*?" (Broxon 1974: 22). The number of readers "hidden" by the subscriber who usually filled out such surveys is indicated by a 1971 *Locus* readers' poll, which asked the question: "How many other people read your copy of *Locus*?" Fifty-five percent replied that one other person read their copy, 23 percent that two others did, and 16 percent more than two.[3]

One of the earliest fan surveys that considered the proportion of women, conducted in 1944 by Bob Tucker, showed that out of 74

---

3   *Locus*, #79, Apr. 4, 1971, p. 7 (survey, 3-8); the sample for this survey was 201. The poll did not always include this question, and such "invisible readers" were unlikely to be included in demographic statistics of readership.

respondents, 11 percent were female fans (cited in Warner Jr. 1969: 25-6). Figures for readers of magazines, rather than fans, were actually lower in this period, with Campbell's 1949 survey of *Astounding* readers finding that only 6 percent were women.[4] Similar surveys in the following decades showed a gradual, though inconsistent, increase in the numbers of women, with *New Worlds* (UK) in the 1950s showing figures ranging from 5-10 percent to the comparative highs of *F&SF* in the 1960s with 29 percent and *Analog* with 25 percent in 1974 (Berger 1977: 234).

More concerted efforts to provide demographical and sociological information are apparent in a small number of studies by fan/academics carried out in the '70s and '80s. One of the earliest sociological analyses of fandom was Linda Fleming's "The American SF Subculture," which mentioned changes in fandom's social structure, such as the increased average age of members and the proportion of females, but did not engage specifically with the gendered divisions of fandom (Fleming 1977: 266).[5] In the same issue of *Science Fiction Studies* (*SFS*), Alfred Berger provided a thorough demographic outline of the socioeconomics of fandom based on questionnaires filled out at the 1973 World Convention in Toronto (Torcon II). Out of a base of 282, 35 percent were women, which was the highest figure shown in his comparative table of the sex ratio of various surveys from the 1940s. This finding did not, however, lead Berger to reconsider the traditional view that "science fiction has been a literature written by males for males" as, he argued, this figure was still far from the proportion of women in the general population (Berger 1977: 234). Another example by Phyllis and Nora Day, "Freaking the Mundane," provided demographics from a number of Midwestern (US) conventions, with 45 percent of their 700 responders being women. The Days marked this as a highly unusual result, since "fandom has the reputation of being mostly composed of white middle-class men," even though, apart from the Berger and Waugh studies, there have been almost no other surveys of the proportion of women convention goers (Day and Day 1983: 95).

---

4   As Warner cautions, one should be wary of extrapolating findings of this survey to fans (25).

5   Other interesting examples of sociological analyses of fandom include Colin Greenland (1982/83: 39-45) and Stephanie A. Hall (1989: 19-31).

Femmefans among the slans

Considering the unreliability and scanty nature of demographic figures for female fans and readers, a sense of women's early presence in the field can be gleaned from magazine editorials and letters, which often provided fans with their first point of communication and a forum for debate. In the remainder of this chapter, I look more closely at examples of female fans and readers from the 1920s to the 1950s. Reading "between the lines" of the fan histories available and drawing on sources such as magazine letters and fanzines, it is possible to at least outline a broader spectrum of female participation in fandom. Such readings also reveal evidence of numerous barriers to women reading and becoming active fans of sf, ranging from their isolation from other women fans to the patronizing and sometimes hostile reactions of male fans and editors. As I noted in the last chapter, individual opposition to female fans was often expressed in terms of the sociocultural discourses that positioned women as other to science and thus sf.

Writing of her first encounters with sf as a teenage "potential fan" in the 1940s, Juanita Coulson eloquently evokes the difficulties encountered on the road from reader to fan.

> I can testify from personal experience that a potential fan needed a thick skin in those days, to endure teasing and occasional downright contempt... It was rough for boys. It could be exquisitely painful for girls. Girls didn't even have the consolation of hoping to be pilots, astronomers, or scientists—those versions of SF's heroes—when they grew up; so far as any girl then knew, those professions were strictly male territory. That might explain why so few girls became fans in that era. America's standard of the "right" enthusiasms for women ran counter to SF. One had to swim long and hard upstream before finding the refuge of fandom. (Coulson 1994: 6)

A similar sentiment is expressed by Leigh Couch, also a fan in the 1940s, who wrote in 1977: "I don't think a young fan of today can realize how suspect we were for reading the pulps, and for a girl to read it, that was almost proof of perversion!" (1977: 10). For many, if not most, women interested in sf, their engagement may have gone no further than reading, or at best writing letters to the magazines, with little or no opportunity for participation in sf clubs full of single (and strange!) boys.

Many of the women's letters to the pulps identified by Larbalestier express this sense of being different or of concern about their reception. Indeed, such letters were often singled out by the editors, "signaled as anomalies with titles such as... 'A Kind Letter from a Lady Friend and Reader,'" while patronizing editorial responses emphasized their difference as members of the "fair sex" (Larbalestier 2002: 24).[6] A 1928 letter from a Mrs. H. O. De Hart (who described herself as a wife and mother of two babies) remarked "I do not really expect you to clutter up your comments with it" (De Hart 1928: 277). Other letters followed from women who had believed they were the only female readers of the magazine: "I was glad to know that there are other women readers of my favorite magazine, than myself" (Johnson 1929: 1140).

Another insight into women readers who may have wanted to write to *Amazing Stories* is provided by a letter written in 1953 by Lula B. Stewart, concerning her late entry into fandom.

> Way back thar, circa 1928, I read a science-fiction mag, and was infected. This chronic derangement might have culminated in the virulent stage known as actifandom at a very early date had not fate intervened to save me. While I was madly cerebrating over my first epistle...another damsel sent in a missive to ye ed.
>
> That dawdling undoubtedly saved my hide, but, Oooo! what happened to the other poor maiden! It shouldn't be done to a diploid! I can still hear the primitive screams of the man-pack echoing down the corridors of time. The rage of that mob was something awful to behold. Not only was I witness to that early kill, but cowered in my cave as other foolish females tried to run the gauntlet...
>
> Now, at last, in the dawn of a new era, I dare creep forth, and claim my heritage of egoboo... So, at last, backed by

6   See Gernsback's comments in *Amazing Stories*, vol. 3, no. 2, June 1928, p. 277; vol. 3, no. 7, Oct. 1928, p. 667; vol. 3, no. 12, Mar. 1929, p. 1140.

a formidable phalange of femfans, I dare speak up, brave lassie that I am. (1953: 133)[7]

Such letters reveal the loaded discursive space into which these women had to write themselves, in claiming a right to be interested in science yet simultaneously affirming their continued performance of "proper" femininity as wives, mothers, or sisters. Their interventions brought into sharp focus the conflicted discourses around gender, work, the future, and technoscience central to the field's subconscious. As Eric Drown notes, these letters reveal that "the letter columns of the pulp science fiction magazines became for a time, a place where the gender politics of science fiction and SF fandom were explicitly debated" (Drown 2006: 25).[8]

Throughout the 1930s female readers continued to assert their presence, and they increasingly referred to the presence of other women readers as a way of countering resistance to their presence. In 1931 a letter from Virginia E. McCay claimed: "A great many men and boys seem to think that girls do not care for science magazines but they are wrong. Almost all of my high school girl friends do read *Astounding Stories*, or other science fiction magazines" (cited in Drown 2006: 25). Larbalestier cites a similar letter from a 1939 issue of *Science Fiction*, written by five sisters who all read the magazine (and apparently shared it with male relatives):

> If you did not know that women read scientific fiction, give a listen:
>
> There are two housewives, an office worker, a high school girl, and a trained nurse among we five sisters and we all read SCIENCE FICTION (when we could snag it away from brother and two husbands)...
>
> We Read SCIENCE FICTION to help us picture what the world will be in years to come, or to get someone's idea of life in a different world. (Slimmer 1939: 118-19)

Such letters aim to justify women's interest in sf as readers and only rarely intimate more active engagement with the emerging fan

---

7 Reproduced in Larbalestier (2002: 26); In the same letter, Stewart also notes that she is a contributor to "that great, all-female *Femzine*."

8 See also references to other letters from women (24-27).

groups. However, one of the most famous accounts of early fandom, Sam Moskowitz's *The Immortal Storm*, provides evidence for women's involvement in active fandom in the 1930s. Moskowitz's account presents a strangely ambivalent picture of the few women who are briefly mentioned in this densely detailed text. Most are not singled out as women—to the extent that the gender of, for example, Morojo (Myrtle Douglas) and Leslie Perri (Doris Baumgardt) is at times unclear—although the women's connections to male fans is usually noted and they are marked as either girlfriend, wife, or sister.[9]

Describing one of the main events of the book, the exclusion of members of the infamous fan group, the Futurians, from the first "worldcon," Nycon, Moskowitz emphasizes the mediating role played by some female fans.

> Women Attendees such as Frances N. Swisher, wife of R.D. Swisher, PhD, and Myrtle R. Douglas, better known as Morojo, were particularly active in the Futurians' behalf, urging almost unceasingly that the barriers be dropped and that the Futurians be permitted to enter the hall without pledging good behavior. (1954: 243)[10]

Moskowitz mentions at least nine female fans by name, all of whom were members of clubs or involved with fanzines. Morojo was co-editor with Forrest Ackerman of *Imagination* ("*Madge*") and *Voice of the Imagination* ("*VOI*"); Leslie Perri was affianced to Fred Pohl and was one of the members of the Futurians allowed entry to Nycon. Others, such as Gertrude Kuslan, edited fanzines; Mary Rogers was a fan artist; and Kathryn Kelley was one of the board of directors of SFAA (Science Fiction Advancement Association of San Francisco).[11] Although this number seems small, these women could all be classified as active fans, which, considering Moskowitz's claim that only

---

9 Morojo's presence at the worldcon is also noted by Robert Madle (1994: 51) (the only mention of a woman in his article): "During the entire convention, Forrest J. Ackerman and Myrtle Douglas could be seen in their futuristic costumes, based on the movie *Things to Come*."

10 Moskowitz also mentions that many of the authors, editors, and artists attending the worldcon brought wives and children with them (213). This is the first time in the book that Moskowitz connects "Myrtle" with her pseudonym "Morojo," over one hundred pages after the first reference to Douglas.

11 Moskowitz, 1954; see pages: 63, 70, 137, 139, 184, 218, and 245.

around 50 fans (of either gender) existed at this time, is a fairly substantial proportion (114).

Reading issues of the zines *Madge* and *VOI* from the late '30s and early '40s reveals the presence of at least another twenty female fans (most members of the Los Angeles Sf League—LASFL). A regular column on members in *Madge* introduced the "First Feminine Member of the LASFL," Frances Fairchild, in 1938 with the comment: "Politics? None in particular. Believes in Women's Rights—& plenty of 'em" ("Among our Members," 1938a: 4).[12] Many of the women writing for these zines also contributed to what appears to be the first all-female zine (or femmefan zine), a one-off entitled *Pogo's STF-ETTE*, with material from Morojo, Pogo (her cousin), Gertrude Kuslan, Leslie Perri, and Leigh Brackett.[13]

Nineteen forties fandom is covered in the history monograph *All Our Yesterdays*, by another well-known fan historian, Harry Warner Jr. Warner restricts women's involvement in fandom to a two-paragraph discussion of "Feminine fans." The discussion mentions only three women and assigns Barbara Bovard "the pioneering role as an independent female fan," who, although not disqualified through familial connections to a man, was nevertheless aided by Forrest Ackerman, who "dragged her into Los Angeles fandom by brute strength" (Warner Jr. 1969: 26).[14] Warner also refers to Virginia Kidd as a "lone girl fan," but does not explain whether it is age or male affiliation that disqualifies her from Bovard's title. Also mentioned is the nine-year-old Mary Helen Washington, who was "more active than some more celebrated feminine fans, through her contribution of 'The Monster of the Cave' to her brother Raym's fanzine in 1942" (Warner Jr. 1969: 26).

---

12 Similarly, another female member was cited as saying: "I think we should hav a social systm...that woudnt b so wasteful, woud giv workingirls like me...th full fruits of their labor, & leav us all more chance to njoy life" (these are not typos: the LASFL under the direction of Forrest Ackerman had adopted for many of its zines a system of "simplified spelling" that removed many vowels and was based on phonetic spelling, also influenced by the interest in Esperanto among many members) (Among Our Members 1938b: 4).

13 *Pogo's STF-ETTE*, convention publication, nd, c. 1940 for Chicon (Chicago convention).

14 Bovard is first mentioned as an "upcoming fan" in a 1942 issue of *VOI* (#24, Aug. 1942, 3). Previously a number of female fans such as Morojo and Pogo were active and "independent" fans.

One female fan not mentioned by Warner is Marion Zimmer Bradley, who became a prolific letterhack towards the end of the '40s and is notable for being one of the first women to rise through the ranks of fandom to become a well-known pro.[15] Larbalestier notes that "[i]n the late 1940s and early 1950s there is a letter from Marion Zimmer (who became Marion Zimmer Bradley) in almost every issue of *Startling Stories*," and by the 1952 issue "she refers to herself as a BNF" (2002: 29). Another long-time fan, Leigh Couch, has commented of Bradley: "I remember her well from the old days when she battled one and all in the letter columns of the pulps... I admired her outspokenness in her letters" (1977: 10). It seems that Bradley's confidence was unusual; Karen Anderson has argued that many more female fans existed in the late 1940s than are remembered today, but that they were much less likely than men to become BNFs because they tended not to engage in this form of self-promotion.[16]

The 1950s saw a number of female fans becoming more visible. Camille Bacon-Smith's *Science Fiction Culture* for example includes reminiscences from a number of active female fans from this period, who comment that many more have disappeared from the collective fannish memory.[17] This decade also marks the appearance of Lee Hoffman, probably the best-known and most active femmefan of the

---

15 Others from around this time would include Virginia Kidd and Judith Merril. Bradley herself has noted this connection: "I have a great deal in common with such science fiction 'greats' as Harlan Ellison, Isaac Asimov, Ray Bradbury, Robert Silverberg and Donald Wolheim... I came up through the ranks of fandom to become a pro writer. My first works, like theirs, were published in the letter columns of the old pulp magazines"; (Marion Zimmer Bradley, "Fandom: Its Value to the Professional" cited in Jarvis 1985). In a later article, Warner does mention Bradley as one author (the only female name in the list) who had been involved in fanzines before turning pro (Warner Jr. 1994a: 178).

16 Cited in Andrew Hooper, "A Report From ConFrancisco, the 51st World Science Fiction Convention" (Hooper 1993: 43). Hooper's report includes a description of a panel on "The First Femmefans," which presented the recollections of early female fans Karen Anderson, Martha Beck, Catherine Crook De Camp, and JoAnn Wood.

17 See for example, Karen Anderson's recollections of women and fandom in the 1950s in Bacon-Smith (2000: 97-100). Bacon-Smith's ethnographic approach means she only begins her account of women in fandom in the '50s (279n2), and focuses on interviews and activity at conventions. Not as much attention is paid to fanzines, particularly early ones. Yet fanzines would have been key for women fans, since they were a much more accessible site for communication, especially for those situated outside urban centers of fan activity in terms of clubs or cons.

1950s and one of the first women to win the accolade of BNF. Because she used her nickname "Lee" (her given name was Shirley), according to rich brown, "most fans just 'naturally' assumed that Lee Hoffman was male":

> This assumption went unchallenged despite attempts by Lee H to tell her best fan friends the truth in a subtle way: She sent [Walt] Willis a Valentine's Day card (Walt just thought "he" was a little eccentric) and asked both Max Keasler and Shelby Vick not to betray her secret when she engaged in a round-robin wire correspondence with them (she assumed her voice would give her away; they assumed "he" was a young fan whose voice hadn't changed yet and thus were left scratching their heads, wondering what "secret" they were not supposed to reveal). (brown 1994: 91)

This "hoax" was ended when Hoffman attended the 1951 World Con, Nolacon, but by then her popularity was already established.

In the same year, a 21-year-old Bradley wrote in the anniversary issue of Lee Hoffman's *Quandry*: "My fan career has been notable mainly for the fact that I got along for years without claiming any feminine privileges" (Bradley 1951: 89).[18] Bradley did not elaborate on this statement, and it is intriguing in light of later comments that she felt there were no specific impediments for women entering the sf field. Already, Bradley emphasized the staunchly independent nature of her success and her ability to compete in the field as "one of the boys" without special consideration for the "mere" difference of her sex. Bradley's statement takes on added significance in light of the fact that the editor of *Quandry* had just been revealed to be female. Hoffman's identity remained hidden long enough for this fanzine to make her a BNF (leaving unanswered the tantalizing question of whether *Quandry* would have made her reputation had she used her given name Shirley instead of her nickname Lee). At this point, Bradley was already married, with a small child, and living in Texas—circumstances that made her rapid rise in fandom no mean feat,

---

18 Bradley continues: "I've published five issues of *Astra's Tower*, two of *Altitudes*, one of *Saporific*, one of *Ambuso* with another fan, and co-edited five issues of *Mezrab*. I've had dozens of poems and stories printed in fanzines, under my own name and that of Mario Stanza." At this point (age 21) her professional publications consisted of three poems.

considering the enormous constraints on her time, budget, and access to magazines (see for example, Bradley 1977/1978: 11-13).

Bradley obviously approved of and was happy to support other female fans such as Lee Hoffman, and she was a regular contributor and letter-writer to the fanzine *HodgePodge*, edited by sisters Nancy and Marie-Louise Share. One of Bradley's letters to this fanzine praised Theodore Sturgeon's exploration of "passionate human attachments" and went on to discuss "love":

> Many men believe that women hate all other women but at the risk of being re-crucified by Laney and other seekers out of base innuendo, I love women. I love men, too... What woman doesn't? But I love women, too. I'm proud that I am one! Granted that some women are asses half-wits and obese cheats—still women are a wonderful institution, as HODGEPODGE can proudly proclaim to the world. (Bradley 1954: 27)

Yet Bradley did not appear to have been involved in the all-female *Femzine* (discussed below). The *Fancyclopedia II* cites a letter from Bradley published in the January 1953 issue of *Femzine*, which is taken as evidence for lack of support for the fanzine:

> Frankly I think it's impossible for women, with no help from the "sterner sex," to do anything in the literary fanzine field. Man alone can manage something of strength and talent without feminine influence. It may be graceless, even ugly, but it will be strong. Women alone, sans masculine influence, impetus, or admiration, produce nothing of any worth. (Eney and Speer 1959: 62-3)

It is hard to know whether or not to take this at face value; these sentiments certainly run counter to Bradley's own history of producing solo zines, her support of Hoffman, and her staunchly independent progress ("sans masculine influence") as both fan and "pro" writer (not to mention her sales of early lesbian novels under a pseudonym). There were also by this time an increasing number of women publishing their own zines: one fanzine index list includes nine women who between them produced almost twenty fanzines and APAs between 1950 and 1952.[19]

---

19 *Fanzine Checklist*, Autumn 1950-Spring 1952, a National Fantasy Fan Federation Publication, compiled by Eva Firestone. An APA (Amateur publishing Association)

By the mid 1950s, according to Warner, "females without brothers or husbands in fandom became more numerous"; and he notes:
"England was particularly blessed with active female fans" (1994b:
70). This statement is supported by London fan Rob Hansen's aston-
ishingly detailed history of British fandom, *Then*, which provides a
wealth of detail about female fans. Hansen's work and fanzine lists
suggest evidence for over a dozen women publishing fanzines and amateur publishing associations (APAs), many of which appeared in the
first British APA, OMPA (Offtrail Magazine Publishers Association),
formed in 1954. Among them were Ella Parker, who went on to become the 1961 TAFF winner and chaired the second world convention
held in the UK, Loncon II, in 1965;[20] Ethel Lindsay, who produced
Scottishe from 1954 through to 1981 and was active right up until her
death in 1996; Joy Clarke, who with Vin¢ Clarke and Sandy Sanderson formed Inchmery fandom, the group that would become the focal
point of British fandom;[21] Irene Gore (later Potter), Pam Bulmer, and
Daphne Buckmaster. Women seem to have been much more prominent in British fandom than were their US counterparts at this time.
Warner accords greater status to British female fans than to American female fans, including Ella Parker and Ethel Lindsay in a list of
"large fannish names" and describing Parker as a "major stalwart in
British fandom" (Warner Jr. 1977: 169). The higher visibility of these
women may have reflected a more accepting and cooperative attitude
from male fans, perhaps resulting from the comparatively small and
close-knit nature of the British fan community (mostly centered in
London, but with important centers in Manchester, Liverpool, and
Northern Ireland).

Still, many women did not have access to this community and
were unaware of other female fans, as shown by a number of letters

---

is a compilation of mini-fanzines each compiled by individuals, then collated and
sent to all the members—it resembles a "paper version" of online communities such
as blogs or Live Journal.

20 TAFF stands for Trans-Atlantic Fan Fund, a means of raising funds to send fans
from North America to the UK (and Europe) and vice versa as an exchange visit
in alternating years. The fund is run as a ballot with at least two candidates, and
fans from both continents vote on the winner, who usually has to be well-known
to both fandoms in order to win.

21 'Vin¢' stands for Vincent. This is typical of fannish play with terminology, nick-
names and nomenclature.

to the British magazine *Authentic Science Fiction* (*ASF*). A letter from Irene Boothroyd in 1955 comments that, while she corresponded with a couple of other fans and had written material for *Femizine*, she was isolated by her geographical position in Huddersfield (Boothroyd 1955: 138). A few issues later, Patricia Baddock asked, "Am I the only female science fiction fan in this country?" and received an editorial response inviting her to the sf meetings held in a London pub, where she would meet other "girl fans." Baddock also expressed the hope that her letter would be published to "show the other would-be science fiction fans (female) that they are not alone in their madness!" (Baddock 1955: 125). A few issues later, Catherine Smith wrote in reply:

> In issue no. 57, a girl wrote to "Projectiles" [the *ASF* letters column] thinking that she was the only female SF fan. Obviously she was wrong, but I, personally, know of no other reader who is of my own sex. There must be some in Birmingham, somewhere. But where? If there are any girl readers of science fiction, or any science fiction clubs here, would they contact me? (C. Smith 1956: 159)

Despite the increasing numbers of women involved in well-known core fandom groups, many readers of sf magazines were limited by their geographical location, and, without attending meetings or conventions, they would have had little chance of joining the network of fanzines and APAs through which they could have corresponded with other female fans. These letters also indicate that while fan publishing was an important part of community building, face-to-face meetings were also crucial. Women, particularly, may well have desired the opportunity to talk to others who shared the madness of this "perverse" interest.

An important development in the 1950s was the appearance of a number of femme-fan zines: fanzines that marked themselves as written for and by women. Arising seemingly independently within a few years of each other, such femme-fan zines were produced in the US, Britain, and even Australia. These fanzines mark an important phase in the history of women's involvement in sf fandom. Although previously other women had edited their own fanzines, these were among the first to create a women-only space, with women providing all of the contributions. Like the American female fans of the 1940s, these women used the label femme-fan as a positive sign under which they could consolidate some kind of collective identity and presence. One of the first regular fanzines to be written entirely by women, the Australian *Vertical Horizons,* appeared in 1952 (and was defunct by 1955). This was followed by the American *Femzine,* which was produced by members of a female-only fan club, the Fanettes.[22] The last to appear—and longest-lived of this group—was the British *Femizine,* which ran from 1954 to 1956 (with a later revival in 1958-60).[23]

"Viewing Horizontally": women in Australian fandom[24]

Few though they may have been, women were involved in US fandom from the late 1930s, and at least a couple of women appeared on the British scene in the 1940s. Australian fandom, always small and isolated, maintained its adolescent male composition well into the 1950s. Vol Molesworth's history of Australian fandom before the 1950s mentions only one woman, his wife, Laura Molesworth, who was the first female member of the Futurian Society of Sydney (FSS).[25] By 1953, there were still only three "lady members," although many more were attending the less formal Thursday night meetings. So it is surprising to find appearing, almost immediately following the first few women to appear on the Sydney fan scene in the early 1950s, a fanzine produced for and by women. At the time of its first issue in 1952, only two women were members of the "official" fan group the FSS. With an initial membership of six, *Vertical Horizons* was not just a means of consolidating a small female presence in a male culture, but became for some their initiation point into fandom. The original members were editor Rosemary Simmons, Norma K. Hemming (also a pro-writer who published in the magazines *Thrills* and *New*

---

22 I have also seen the fanzine referred to as *Femizine.* I continue to use *Femzine* for the USA zine to avoid confusion with the UK zine of the same name.

23 I focus on the British and Australian zines, largely because I have been unable to locate copies of the US *Femzine.* Vincent Clarke (a London fan since the 1940s) kindly provided me with access to his extensive private collection of British fan sources and a great deal of background information during an interview; I am also indebted to fan Rob Hansen's history of British fandom, *Then,* which covers this period in detail. A member of the first Australian fan group, collector and bibliographer Graham Stone also kindly provided me with copies of *Vertical Horizons* and additional information during an interview.

24 "Viewing Horizontally" was the title of the news column in *Vertical Horizons.*

25 She is mentioned as attending an FSS meeting in 1947 (V. Molesworth 1994/ 1995: 26).

Worlds), Diana Wilkes, Pauline Roth, Norma Williams, and Laura Molesworth.[26]

Graham Stone, a member of FSS at the time, had suggested that the few female members should form a "women's auxiliary," an idea not well received by Rosemary Simmons and others but which may have contributed to the formation of the *Vertical Horizons* group.[27] Another catalyst was the 1952 convention SydCon, which brought the six members together for the first time (they were the only women present) (L. Molesworth 1953: 1-2). Initially providing only general news (albeit written by women), *Vertical Horizons* was specifically intended to help locate and contact other female fans and sf readers. Rosemary Simmons stated their aim in the second issue:

> The girls I really want to contact are those, who, like Chris Davison [a new member], for example, have been readers for years but have never entered fandom (by joining A.S.F.S. [Australian Science Fiction Society] or going to Thursday nights). (Simmons 1952: 2)[28]

The potential avenues for contact with fandom were limited for female readers. Although the largest fannish center in Australia, Sydney fandom was a small group with limited means (and at times desire) for advertising their presence.[29] Additionally, until the 1950s, the various permutations of the FSS were exclusively a male preserve,

26 Fans mentioned in later issues included Christine Davison, Loralie Giles, Mrs. L.M. Chalmers, Betty Bramble, Ronnie Beach, and Judy McGuinness. For more on Norma Hemming, one of the few recognized Australian female authors before the 1970s, see Russell Blackford and Sean McMullen, "Prophet and Pioneer: The Science Fiction of Norma Hemming" (1998).

27 Interview with Graham Stone, July 1997; hereafter, Stone interview.

28 The ASFS was started by Graham Stone in 1950 in an effort to establish communication with fans outside Sydney; it was the catalyst for the formation of local groups in Melbourne, Adelaide, and Brisbane. (My thanks to Graham Stone for providing me with this information.) (See also V. Molesworth 1994/1995: 29.) The Thursday night meetings were regular get-togethers of fans, not necessarily members of the FSS. Originally starting out as the venue for regular FSS meetings in the 1940s, by 1949 the society had lapsed into infrequent formal activity, but people continued to meet on Thursday nights into the 1950s, as a separate, though often overlapping group.

29 On conflicts over whether to actively recruit more members, for example, by advertising the existence of the FSS in magazines such as *Thrills* (see V. Molesworth 1994/1995: 30-1).

often divided by factional conflicts and internal organizational struggles.[30] Later issues of *Vertical Horizons* suggest that the members wanted to encourage women's participation in club meetings and formal sf organizations to alleviate some of the pressure (and perhaps tension) on the small number of women usually present. As Laura Molesworth stated in an editorial headed "Wanted: More Women Workers in Fandom": "We want to see greater numbers of girls at meetings, at Thursday Nights, and putting all their efforts into keeping the mere males in their place!" (L. Molesworth 1953: 1). The activities of Mrs. Joy Joyce were often singled out as an example of what women fans could accomplish in this very male preserve.[31] Offering congratulations on Joyce's role in organizing a fan group in Adelaide, Molesworth wrote "This is an achievement which all femme fans can proudly proclaim" (1). Joyce's example was all the more "edifying" because she was a wife and mother (*not* married to a fan) who was still capable of actively pursuing and promoting her interest in sf as much as any "mere male."[32]

The zine also provides evidence of a broader awareness of the gendered nature of science fiction texts and themes. In a review article in the second issue, Norma Williams offered a scathing picture of 1950s sf:

30 The FSS came into being in Nov. 1939 (following efforts at establishing a Science Fiction League and other junior clubs from 1935 on), and some form of the society existed, with regular lapses and changes in membership, organization, and goals, into the 1960s (see V. Molesworth 1994/1995).

31 Joy Joyce was one of two Adelaide fans to attend the 1953 convention in Sydney; her photo appears in the *Women's Weekly* coverage of the event; "Australian spacemen look into space: Science fiction fans are 'thinkers of tomorrow'" (1953: 16).

32 The difficulties faced, particularly by married women, in becoming involved in fandom are illustrated by articles and letters in another Australian fanzine from the early 1970s. Many female partners of fans became involved—if they weren't already—in fannish interests, not only to help out financially and physically, but also to understand an interest that could dominate a fan's life. Conversely this kind of dedication would have been much more difficult for women, especially once they were married or had children. Such problems were discussed in an issue of *Girls' Own Fanzine* on fan marriages: "The married housewife with fannish interests often has to fight tooth and nail in order to pursue them—for just one thing she's often financially dependent on her husband. This is part of the mundane double standard, of course": UK fans, Archie and Beryl Mercer (1973: 26). See also Jean Jordan (1973: 7). On the difficulties of being an sf fan in the 1950s, see Mrs. L.M. Chalmers, "I Refugee: An Addict Confesses All" (1953: 2-4) and Norma Hemming, "On the Trials and Tribulations of Being a Science Fiction Fan" (1953: 5-6).

[W]hat about women in science fiction? Most of 'em, according to present authors, exist solely as robots "to serve man," to provide an excuse for lurid cover paintings, admire the hero's muscles, be snatched by BEMs, and provide a pretext for shooting up someone with a ray-gun. Then, at times, we have the opposite extreme—matriarchal societies, or emerald-eyed goddesses with destructive tendencies (but still to provide the hero with an excuse for showing his muscles). [But] woman as a real character, as a human being is still a rarity in science fiction. (1952: 6)

This resonates strongly with later feminist critiques such as that of Russ: "There are plenty of images of women in science fiction. There are hardly any women" (1974b: 57).

Vertical Horizons had a fairly short life and seems to have had little impact on Australian fandom in general, beyond the initial impetus of attracting and encouraging female members, some of whom, like Williams, were active into the 1980s. Nevertheless, the group and fanzine represented a significant intervention into the all-male adolescent microcosm of Australian fandom. Along with its counterparts in the US and the UK, *Vertical Horizons* indicated the changes in the sf community (and broader society) in the 1950s that saw more women able or prepared to move from the relative obscurity of sf reader to a more active identity as sf fan.

British matriarchy or "Hoax" community?

The climate into which the British *Femizine* arrived in the mid-'50s was one in which women fans were establishing a presence in the small but influential London fandom (the hub of British fandom at that time). In 1955, the fanzine *Science Fantasy News* marked the change in fandom since the previous decade: "Any more for the Matriarchy? London fandom now has more active female fans than males in its ranks" (Clarke and Clarke 1955).[33] According to Vin¢ Clarke, previously Daphne Bradley had been the only woman active in London fandom in the 1940s.[34] She was now joined by others in the London

---

33 Vin¢ and Joy Clarke, *Science Fantasy News*, Christmas 1955.

34 Interview with Clarke, London, 23 July 1996 (hereafter Clarke interview). A couple of other women are mentioned in Warner's history of 1940s fandom: Joyce Fairburn and Joyce Teagle, who helped produce a 1940s fanzine *Operation Fantast*

Circle, including Joy Goodwin (later Clarke), Pam Buckmaster (sister of Ron who later married Ken Bulmer), and Dorothy Rattigan. There were also women involved in other groups, such as Ethel Lindsay in Glasgow, Roberta (Bobby) Wild in Slough, Frances Evans in Manchester, Shirley Marriot in Bournemouth (all of whom moved to London in the mid-'50s), Madeleine Willis in Belfast, and Ina Shorrock in Liverpool. Rob Hansen's history of British fandom, *Then*, notes that "[a]s male fans of the time have since observed, somewhat ruefully, most of their female counterparts were assertive and self-confident, many of them feminists" (Hansen 1993).[35] Although the number of active women was relatively small, they made an impression on male fandom, as Vin¢ Clarke recalled: "they were strong feminist types of course, because you had to be!" Clarke remembered Bobby Wild as "a fiercely independent female—feminist I should say—who did some very outspoken writing in our apa [OMPA]." Another notable fan was Ethel Lindsay, who according to Clarke, fascinated all the other fans because she was a "professional" (a nurse, later matron) who never married. She produced the fanzine *Scottishe* (originally as part of OMPA), which went on to become one of the longest lived in Britain, appearing from 1954 until the 1980s with over 80 issues.[36] (Lindsay's interest in women in fandom is suggested by the fact she later read some of the American feminist fanzines, as documented by a letter published in *Janus* in the 1980s.)

One of the most visible markers of women's presence and activity in British fandom was the creation of the "all female" zine, *Femizine*. The editorial of the first *Femizine*, in Summer 1954 declared:

when its editor, Ken Slater, was posted to Germany: "with the help of the girl he left behind him, Joyce Teagle, he produced from the continent a third *Operation Fantast*" (Warner Jr. 1969: 290-1).

35 "The Mid 1950s: Man and Supermancon." This is certainly the impression I got from Vin¢ Clarke, who told me "In the '50s there wasn't an awful lot of female fans around unfortunately, because they certainly brought up a different viewpoint," Clarke interview.

36 Clarke interview. Towards the end of the 1950s Ella Parker also emerged as a very active female fan, described by Harry Warner Jr. as "a major stalwart in British fandom during the latter part of the decade [1950s], both as a publisher and in socializing" (1977: 169).

In various groups and clubs in the UK, the femme fan is in the minority. "FEMIZINE" is designed to unite these minorities in order that they can get a better hearing in the fan world.

With one exception, all the material used will be written by femme-fans—but we hope men will still subscribe. The exception will be our letter section—"MAIL AND FE-MALE"... We are looking forward to receiving, and printing, comments from the males. (Carr 1954: 2)

The editorial was signed by the main editor, Joan W. Carr "on behalf of all femme fans" (and co-editors Frances Evans and Ethel Lindsay). Reading this zine for evidence of the interests and passions of female fans of the 1950s is, however, complicated by the fact that Joan W. Carr was not, in fact a woman, but a hoax, a fictional persona created by male fan Sandy Sanderson. While Frances Evans was aware of Carr's real identity, co-editor Lindsay initially was not, and the hoax was not revealed to UK fandom and the readers of *Femizine* until May 1956. Sanderson originally conceived of Joan Carr as way of stirring up the Manchester fan group to which he belonged, which had only one female member, Frances Evans. With the creation of *Femizine* and an increasingly widespread correspondence, Carr grew beyond Sanderson's early conception to become a well-known figure in British fandom generally. The success of this hoax is evident in Harry Warner Jr.'s claim that Carr (along with another "hoax" fan Carl Brandon) "remain[s] more vivid in the memories of fans who remember the 1950s than many real, less colorful fans of the same period" (Warner Jr. 1977: 88).[37]

The experience of reading *Femizine* is reminiscent of the peculiarly "doubled" reading position we now have when reading some of "James Tiptree Jr.'s" writings—only in reverse. The calls to unite femme-fans and "show up" the men would seem to be compromised by the fact that much of the material was written by a man, with the

---

37 "Carl Brandon," like Carr, was a hoax with potentially disturbing effects, since he was meant to be a black fan, and indeed became the first black fan to achieve prominence in US fandom. He was the creation of Terry Carr, along with "Boob" Stewart, Ron Ellik, Dave Rike, and Peter Graham (91-2). Warner also gives a brief account of the Carr hoax (89-90). In recent years Carl Brandon has been reclaimed by the black sf community, through the Carl Brandon awards for speculative fiction addressing race (see Chapter Five).

original intention of playing a trick on a group of male fans. Nevertheless, much of the material in *Femizine*, and the reaction to this all-female venture, still provides evidence for a desire among fans to recognize some form of commonality between the women scattered through fandom, and to achieve greater recognition for their contributions to fandom. Indeed, in the first issue, Carr notes that Evans and Lindsay were "really the originators of the idea" of a fanzine for women (following the model of the all-female *Femzine* in the US) (Warner Jr. 1977: 89-90) and that the contributions from other women such as Ina Shorrock showed "that there is a genuine need for FEMIZINE" (Carr 1954: 18).

In May 1956, Carr's true identity was revealed in the ninth issue of *Femizine*—the "hoax issue"—which contained extended commentaries and reminiscences from those involved. Evans and Lindsay, the two co-conspirators, wrote of their role in the hoax and detailed their increasing misgivings about Joan's role in *Femizine*. Their discomfort was caused by the whole-hearted acceptance not just of this "fake female," but also of *Femizine* itself, which was so "wildly successful that it drew up to 100 locs [letters of comment] per issue" (Warner Jr. 1977: 90). When, for example, the second issue drew an unfavorable review, Lindsay recalled that,

> the other femme fans rallied to our side, and defended us stoutly. They did all they could to help, and began to take a real pride in FEZ. That was when my troubles really started. I had been thinking of Joan as a separate personality... However, I began to wake up to the fact that I could not expect the rest of fandom to feel the same way. I began to worry what they would say when the news came out. At the same time so did Frances, who asked me if I ever woke up in a cold sweat thinking about it. I did. (Lindsay 1956: 10)

By 1955, as Hansen notes, "Evans and Lindsay were becoming increasingly uneasy about the lie at the heart of *Femizine*, that a fanzine that had become a rallying point for Britain's female fans was secretly edited by a man." They decided to try and alleviate the situation by suggesting that *Femizine* be opened to male contributors, and discussed this with other female fans at the 1955 national convention ("Cytricon" held in Kettering, from then on held over Easter) But, as Lindsay recalled:

It was no good. They turned the idea down cold, wanted us to stick to women alone. After they had gone Frances and I sat and looked at each other in dismay. "I feel sick," she said. "I think we'd better emigrate," I replied. We got hold of Sandy as soon as we could and told him firmly that, in one way or another, this monster Joan was going to have to be killed off. (Lindsay 1956: 10-11)

By this stage, the trepidation felt by Evans and Lindsay, "caused by the whole-hearted acceptance of FEZ by the femmes, by their pride in this 'all female' venture," had overcome their amusement (Evans 1956: 11). So, as Sanderson reflected, "it was decided to make FEZ a really all-female fanzine by having Joan withdraw from it completely and ask Pamela Bulmer to take over the reins" (Sanderson 1956: 8).[38] Sanderson could not carry through his original plan to avoid confrontation by slowly "retiring" Carr from the fan scene, because too many people were aware of Carr's real identity, so issue 9 was rushed together to prevent someone else from revealing the hoax.

Ultimately, fannish reaction to the revelation of the hoax was not the catastrophe Evans and Lindsay feared. According to Hansen, "[p]eople had been so completely taken in that they were stunned by the revelation and immediate reactions to it were muted" (Hansen 1993).[39] Vin¢ Clarke recalled that for many fans, it was as if a friend had died, producing "a sense of loss rather than laughter, or anger or anything like that."[40] Many of the fans' responses printed in *Femizine* and elsewhere expressed genuine regret at the passing of this fan—suggesting the welcoming and open climate of the British fandom, which could come to respect, admire, and feel so much friendship for a female fan whom they had come to know through correspondence

---

38 In the end, issue seven was put together by Vin¢ Clarke and Joy Goodwin, with only the 8th (March 1956) edited by Pamela Bulmer, who also let husband Ken into the secret.

39 "The Late 1950s: Gotterdammerung"; Thus Ron Bennett mourned "what I prefer to think of as Joan's passing from the fannish scene, an enforced gafia as it were." Ron Bennett, *Ploy*, no 6, Jun. 1956, cited in Hansen (1993).

40 Clarke interview. Another fan, Dean Grennell, responded: "I think it's the most gloriously hilarious hoax I've ever heard of and I think anyone who takes offence is a blooming sorehead," cited in Warner Jr. (1977: 90).

alone.[41] That the response of women fans was not as bad as the editors feared may have been due to the fact that many had secretly not found "Joan" as enticing as the men. As fan Pam Bulmer commented:

> The success of Sandy's hoax lay in the reality of Joan's personality. Not everyone liked Joan wholeheartedly. My own reaction was that she was another of those masculine sergeant-type women—horribly competent and out to prove they are as good as any man by acting like a man! (cited in Warner Jr. 1977: 90-91)

Inevitably, a hoax of this kind was detrimental to the growing strength and independence of the female fan community promised by *Femizine*'s beginnings. In Hansen's view,

> [h]aving such a prominent "female" fan and the editor of the fanzine they had taken as their rallying point turn out to be a man was to take the wind out of the sails of the emerging female fandom of the fifties. That issue of FEMIZINE was the last for two years, and revealing the hoax was to have just the effect that had been feared. (Hansen 1993)

The verdict of the American *Fancyclopedia II* in 1959 was even more dire: "When the hoax was revealed it dealt British female fandom a jolt from which it has yet to recover" (Eney and Speer 1959: 26). This was a rather harsh judgment; while the potential for a more solidified community of female fans may well have been undermined, women continued to publish their own zines and were active in various organizations (especially the London circle and OMPA). *Femizine* itself made a comeback, appearing as *Distaff* in September 1958 under editor Ethel Lindsay. Hansen reports that "[t]he fanzine was welcomed by Britain's female fans but the name-change wasn't," so the title reverted to *Femizine* and it "continued to be a showcase for the talents of female fans, until its fifteenth and final issue in September 1960" (Hansen 1993).[42]

---

41 Though apparently the photo of Joan (actually Sanderson's young cousin) that circulated amongst fans (on request) reinforced many male fans' positive views of her. See Hansen, "The Mid 1950s: Man and Supermancon" (1993).

42 This was quite a respectably long run for a fanzine. The numbering followed on from the original *Femizine*; thus *Distaff* was no. 10, the new *Femizine* began with no. 11 and so on.

Certainly it appears that the hoax and its fallout overshadowed the achievements of the real women involved in *Femizine*, with attention directed instead toward the male fan. In retrospect, however, Sanderson's role in *Femizine* does not diminish its success or the fact that female fans were so enthusiastic about a collective women's endeavor. For, despite the hoax and its ramifications, *Femizine* was significant in providing a forum for women's writing and a focus for female fan activity. *Femizine* helped build a strong sense of collective femmefan identity, with articles often raising issues of gender equality in fandom and the "mundane" world.

The first issue of *Femizine* contained a "call to arms" from Ina Shorrock, declaring that "we — the feminine side of Fandom — must start to push much harder than we have been doing in order to equal the men in science fictional affairs" (1954: 17). This rather mild call for action from the women in fandom received a reply from Harry Turner: "Ina sounds like a belated follower of Mrs. Pankhurst...I've not noticed any of those poor down-trodden femmes, but then that may be just because I'm one of these arrogant fans that treads on 'em."[43] While obviously intended as a jocular comment, Turner admitted he shared Henry Ernst's disparaging view (in the tellingly-titled "Romping through Fandom with the Little Woman") that there were three types of femm-fans, and even the best could only be secondary or "fake fans" (Ernst 1953: 14). Much of the response to the first issue consisted of such letters from men "ribbing" the girls, in a manner that was obviously expected. Three letters, for example, asked who had modeled for the first cover: this cover was a joking dig at male fans and their proclivities, featuring a girl in a bikini with a bubble on her head. Carr's editorial stated: "Our cover is mainly for the men. Take a long last lingering look. Wave a fond farewell to the cover girl. From now on, we join Frances Evans in her campaign for 'more beef-cake'" (Carr 1954: 2). Others responded with weak cries that women fans did not need to unite as they already had a powerful presence. Stuart McKenzie, for example, responded to the call to "unite the minorities to get a better hearing in the fan world" with amazement, saying that "the feminine element in this part of the world, at any rate (and indeed at all costs) gets a better hearing than the male. We HAVE to listen? <u>They</u> just ignore our 'idle chatter'" (McKenzie 1954).

---

43 Harry Turner, letter, *Femizine*, no. 2, December 1954.

His list of women who attended meetings at the Globe was indeed impressive: (his "ever-loving") Constance, Dorothy, Iris, both Pams, Daphne, Joy, Cathie, Hetta, and Margaret.

A much more strident "call to arms" appeared in the second issue from Pam Bulmer, signing herself as "Gloria Famhurst" (a pun on Pankhurst using fam as shorthand for female fan). While obviously tongue in cheek, with its opening "Women of fandom unite!," it targeted the pervasive stereotype of the woman as a secondary, nonproductive fan whose role was to support the fanac of the active male.

> Now we cry out against their unjustness, we will fight to the bitter end. Break down the doors of their dens, snatch the duplicators, seize the ink, the stencils and all the paraphernalia of fanac that we have guarded so faithfully and so thanklessly.

> We will chain ourselves to the lamp-posts outside the Globe and every fannish club or meeting place and we will not go until we are acclaimed with due respect. We will go on hunger strike, and if any of us die in such a brave cause our deaths will lie like an inky black smudge on every fanzine...

> There will be no lack of volunteers to be the first martyr crushed beneath the wheels of the bearded motor-bike and the stain of her militant blood will turn in the wheels of the rider's mind... She will go down in history as the first martyr of famdom and we shall see that her sacrifice is not in vain.

> To arms you shackled slaves of marriage! You who economise with the housekeeping, going short yourselves, nay all but starving so that they might buy their duplicators, their ink and paper, their stencils and their infamous magazines. An end to all this. United we are strong. Let them brew the tea whilst we besmear ourselves with ink and swearwords, producing the gems of wisdom for which we are justly famed. Women for fams! Fams for women! (Bulmer 1954: 7)

Amongst the parody and references recalling the suffragists, Bulmer paints a picture that suggests a realistic characterization of many fan couples. Such women were often involved in the dirty work without receiving any of the glory, offering a range of emotional *and* economic supports to their active fan partner, whilst receiving little or no credit themselves.[44]

This second issue received a cutting review in the fanzines section of *Authentic Science Fiction*:

> We thought that the girls of fandom would be able to turn out something that would at least rank equal with some of their male counterparts. Instead, maybe because mistakenly chivalrous comments on the first issue and the venture as a whole have gone to their heads, the editoresses have turned out a thing which is so obviously trying hard to be intelligently witty and just hasn't got what it takes. Also there is an emphasis on the smutty side of things that may well be unhealthy. No doubt these women will one day stop trying to act a part and will be themselves. (Fanzines 1954: 137)

These comments have a certain irony considering that at least one of the "editoresses" was indeed playing a part, which may also have accounted for the level of "smut" obviously considered by the reviewer to be inappropriate for women writers.[45] The reaction of female fans, as noted by Lindsay above, was to rally round *Femizine*, and an "advert" was inserted in the well-known zine **i** (Eye) by "LC [London Circle] femme-fans on behalf of FEMIZINE":

> BERT CAMPBELL LIES IN HIS BEARD! He alleges in *Authentic* that FEZ 2 is a Filthy Fanzine. Get one and judge for yourself! Then tell Bert what you think of him! (Classified Page 1954: back cover)

---

44 The femmefan entry in the *Fancyclopedia* (cited in the last chapter) confirms this picture. A similar scenario is suggested in a later article in an Australian fanzine, *Girl's Own Fanzine*. In response to the theme "Would you marry a fan?" Christine McGowan responds in the negative:

> The frequently itinerant nature of fannish employment and interests is another cause for concern... I wouldn't like being married to a man who only took a desultory interest in a series of more or less uninspiring jobs. Still less would I like a husband who spent every spare dollar on cruddy science fiction paperbacks and inky, clanking machinery. (McGowan 1973: 4)

45 The "smutty" side of Joan Carr was mentioned by others. In a conversation with Frances Evans, a fan known as "Machiavarley" (Brian Varley) commented that "from certain recent correspondence I've had with her [Joan] I feel sure that even tho' she is a sergeant she'll be a very 'amenable' type of girl. 'S'matter of fact, some of the sex and sadism she dishes out sounds quite shockin' coming from a woman." Evans replied "that's probably 'cos she's in the Army" (Evans 1956: 11).

Always a vocal and active group, for a brief time the women in London fandom had a unified presence in *Femizine*, which, along with their writing in other fanzines and apazines, challenged the male dominance of fandom. Although it may be problematic to describe these women as "feminist," the steps toward community they took obviously had some significance for the later development of consciously feminist fandom. In this period, mapping women's equality in terms of "feminism" was complicated by the lack of organized feminist groups or even singular role models—thus the references back to suffragettes and the Pankhursts. These women fans stand out for their interest in science and sf, in their outspokenness, their unwillingness to be given a supplementary role by male fans, and their belief in "equal rights" in matters such as pay. Yet, unsurprisingly in the post-war era of re-affirmation of feminine roles and the construction of the ideal female as the professional housewife and mother, such proto-feminist values were couched in (almost Victorian) terms of "equal but different" (see also Yaszek, 2008). Many of these women were opposed to an idea of gender equality that elided "essential" differences between the sexes, and often conflated "ardent feminists" with a "masculine" type. For example, in an apazine for OMPA around this time, Roberta Wild wrote "Let us have equality with men by all means, but equality does not mean similarity." Wild contrasted her view to those of women she met while in the forces who were "mannish types" (her description having resonances with the "mannish lesbian" stereotype of the '20s and '30s) and asked, "why are the most ardent feminists among my sex so damned masculine?"[46] The British female fans of the 1950s did not want to participate in the masculine world of sf as "one of the boys," but insisted on retaining their "femininity" whilst demanding equality under the inclusive yet distinguishing label femmefan.[47] Importantly, they obviously saw benefits from claiming this identity as a collective rather than on an individual basis, which would leave them more open to charges of aberrant performances of femininity.

---

46 She describes these women as wearing pin-striped slacks, man-tailored jackets, collars, and tie with no make-up and cropped hair! (Wild [1950s]: 13).

47 See for example references to beauty in Pamela Bulmer's "A Call to Arms" (Bulmer 1954: 6) and Ina Shorrock's, "A Call to Arms" (Shorrock 1954: 17). See also a letter from the 1930s, which makes similar claims both to intellect and beauty: Irene Frechette Bats, letter, *Amazing Stories*, July 1930, p. 379; cited in Drown (2006: 24-5).

While certainly fewer in number than the women involved in fandom in the USA, British female fans arguably maintained a stronger presence in British fandom as a whole than their US counterparts did. Judging by the limited lifespan of the US *Femzine*, community efforts were not as successful as those that sustained *Femizine*. None of the British fans attained the status of a Lee Hoffman, however, and none made the transition to professional writer, as did both Hoffman and Marion Zimmer Bradley.

However ephemeral or forgotten, these collective actions from the 1950s are important both for their attempts at community building and in their use of overt references to equal rights and opposition to sexism in fandom (even if often conducted in a jocular fashion). Like the US letter writers from the 1930s, these fans protested the reduction of women's role in sf to either sex/romance interest or as mere appendages to male readers or fans. A final example indicates the extent to which such sentiments might coalesce in direct critiques of the gendered nature of sf and its cultures, providing precedents for later feminist critique.

Proto-feminist criticism: The 1950s look forward

A fascinating instance of proto-feminist critique is found in a letter by sf author Miriam Allen deFord responding to an article by Dr. Robert S. Richardson in a 1955 issue of *Magazine of Fantasy and Science Fiction* (*F&SF*) (Richardson 1955: 44-52).[48] Richardson's "The Day after We Land on Mars" examined the practicalities of future expeditions to Mars and proposed that the all-male crews should take along a few "nice girls" to relieve their sexual frustration. Richardson did not consider the possibility that women could be present as members of the crew in their own right and dismissed the inclusion of married partners—"Family Life would be impossible under the conditions that prevail. Imagine the result of allowing a few wives to set up housekeeping in the colony! After a few weeks the place would be a shambles" (50). According to the *F&SF* editors, this article elicited more letters than any other non-fiction article had, and yet "not a single correspondent expressed moral shock and outrage." This is an interesting comment intimating the (sexual) open-mindedness of *F&SF*

48 See also the responses in vol. 10, no. 5, May 1956: Poul Anderson "Nice Girls on Mars" (1956) and Miriam Allen deFord, "News for Dr. Richardson" (1956).

readers. It stems from Richardson's belief that his proposition would (only) cause problems because of moral objections to what was essentially a proposal for publicly condoned prostitution (Editor 1956: 47).

Two responses to Richardson's article were published, those by sf authors deFord and Poul Anderson. Anderson's letter took seriously the "practical" problems raised by Richardson's scenario and argued that girls would take up room and cost money, so the best solution would be a drug to inhibit sex drive. In contrast to Richardson, Anderson raises the possibility of husband and wife teams and the inclusion of trained women in the crew. But he believed this would still cause problems because some girls would be more attractive than others, producing frustrated lovers with no chance of escape. In any case, he stated "few women are good explorers; you might say they are too practical. Feminists pardon me" (P. Anderson 1956: 50). The editors commented that, in contrast to Anderson's strictly "male viewpoint," the attitude of most correspondents (male and female) was "an immediate rejection of the basic male-centered assumptions." They introduced deFord as the perfect writer "to express this—no, not feminist, but merely human point of view" (deFord 1956: 53). The use of the term "feminism" here and in Anderson's article is worth noting, since most histories assume that feminism was little discussed in the 1950s. The use of "feminism" in this exchange (and indeed in other fannish publications from the 1950s and up to the 1990s) functions negatively—signaling an extreme position and bringing automatic condemnation from men such as Anderson, in contrast to the more justifiable (and "fannish") position of "humanism."

Despite the editors' attempt to situate deFord as a more moderate "humanist," however, deFord's article is a thorough attack on the sexism inherent in much of the sf and scientific community. Not surprisingly, given her Suffragist background, her article is overtly proto-feminist, foreshadowing later feminist criticism and invoking Simone De Beauvoir to support her argument. Her article begins "I am going to tell Dr. Richardson a secret. Women are not walking sex organs. They are human beings" (deFord 1956: 53). DeFord challenges the arguments about women's physical capacity or potential ability to become colonists to Mars. Instead, she attributes the low numbers of women in the sciences to "the discouragements and obstacles set in their path by people with Dr. Richardson's viewpoint." She also points to the real world examples of women who have trained as physicists, chemists, astronomers, and engineers (54).[49] DeFord's rebuttal of Dr. Richardson could be extended to much of the sf culture at this time:

> It is pretty disheartening, after all these years, to discover how many otherwise enlightened and progressive-minded men still retain in their subconscious this throwback attitude toward half of humanity which relegates women to the position of possessions, of ancillary adjuncts to men—what Simone de Beauvoir calls the "second sex." (56)

In her defense of women's scientific abilities, and her condemnation of the "covert" sexism that informed "merely intellectual" scientific hypotheticals, deFord here raised one of the first critical feminist voices in sf.[50] Such challenges to the masculine world of sf were the basis

---

49 Along with the other attributes of women personnel, deFord stated that "there is much less bickering and backhand knifing in conventions of feminine organizations than in those of masculine" (1956: 54).

50 DeFord published her first sf story in 1946 (at the age of 58) and went on to publish over seventy stories (including a number in F&SF), but no novels, which may account for her obscurity today. Born in 1888, she was also a noted Suffragist (see Fran Stallings 1984).

One of the first analyses of sf to recognize the exclusion of women as a significant characteristic of the genre appeared in Ednita P. Bernabeu's "SF: A New Mythos" in a 1957 issue of Psychoanalytic Quarterly (1957: 527-35). I have not included it in my analysis because it appeared outside the sf community; however, it provides a remarkable discussion of feminine symbolism in sf. Although somewhat dated in its positivist application of Freudian psychoanalytic readings, Bernabeu's use of this theory to read popular fiction led her to insights that foreshadowed later feminist readings. Outlining the various psycho-dynamic elements of sf, Bernabeu remarked that sexuality and women were "conspicuously absent," and argued that this constituted a "denial of femininity and feminine strivings." Her analysis situated the exclusion of women as deliberate (although perhaps unconscious) and integral to the sf mythos, rather than symptomatic of a general conservatism, or a narrow focus on "science." The presence of "Woman"—whether actual, threatened, or symbolically represented (i.e., as an alien)—signified concerns and fears immanent in even the most scientifically pure, technically focused sf. Bernabeu argued that:

> Women are feared as mothers and as sexual objects; yet there is a persistent preoccupation with "seeding" the outer galaxies with the human race... The insoluble question of childhood—where do babies come from?—is reopened on a cosmic level, denying the female as mother and conferring on the male the exclusive processes of direct reproduction. (1957: 532)

of woman-centered or gynocentric critiques that would intersect, and continue conterminously, with the development of feminist criticism into the 1970s and beyond.

"Will the Real James Tiptree, Jr. Please Stand Up," poster by Jeanne Gomoll, 1978. advertising a monthly meeting of The Society for the Furtherance and Study of Fantasy and Science Fiction (SF3). The program presented at this particular meeting was a rehearsal for a program of the same name showcased at WisCon 2.

4

Birth of a Sub-Genre: Feminist SF and Its Criticism

The current version of women in science fiction before the 1960s (which I've heard several times lately) goes like this: There weren't any. Only men wrote science fiction because the field was completely closed to women. Then, in the late '60s and early '70s, a group of feminist writers led by Joanna Russ and Ursula Le Guin [sic] stormed the barricades, and women began writing (and sometimes even editing) science fiction. Before that, nada.

If there were any women in the field before that (which there weren't), they had to slink around using male pseudonyms and hoping they wouldn't get caught. And if they did write under their own names (which they didn't), it doesn't count anyway because they only wrote sweet little domestic stories. Babies. They wrote mostly stories about babies.

There's only one problem with this version of women in SF — it's not true.

      ↝ Connie Willis (1992: 4)

Following the example of Katie King's attention to "the local aspects of discourse, very much historically—at times almost 'momentarily'—located" (1994: xi), I chart some of the trends in the production of feminist criticism(s) of sf that developed coterminous with, although somewhat detached from, feminist literary criticism. Feminist sf criticism marks itself—through naming, subject matter, and oppositional situation from both malestream sf criticism and mainstream literary feminist criticism—as the critical/theoretical project that most clearly speaks for and about feminist sf. A central facet of the production of feminist sf criticism is the construction of feminist sf. One of the primary sites of disjuncture between feminist (and other) critiques of sf has been the contesting definitions and mappings of this object. As in feminist theorizing more generally, the borderlands between the spaces of feminist fiction and women's writing have been traversed in multiple and conflicting ways: constituting for some a site of continuity, or easy slippage; for others a gradated spectrum, or even clear-cut division between opposing objects labeled woman and feminist.

Following its scattered beginnings in sf magazines, fanzines, and feminist journals in the early 1970s, feminist sf criticism became more established and accepted in the 1980s, signaled by the special issues on women and sf in the early 1980s, edited collections, and the first monographs on women and/or feminism in sf. Toward the late 1980s, feminist criticism really arrived in the sf field, as the first in a chain of monographs on feminist sf were published. This neat linear, teleological narrative does not tell the whole story, however; for me, this history is complicated by counter-feminist narratives such as that voiced by Connie Willis, by my dissatisfaction with the limitations of the feminist sf canon, by my curiosity about older female sf authors, and by my prejudices against atopic literary analyses. Reading Katie King's travels through the conversations that produced the object of knowledge that is feminist theory helped sensitize me to the complex, highly politicized, and situated nature of the threads that collectively I (and others) had referred to as feminist sf criticism.

As a discipline or field of study, feminist sf criticism has figured itself, to paraphrase Hollinger, as a unified body, motivated by the construction of a singular object "feminist sf" (Hollinger 1989: 235). One way of expanding the contours of this monolithic object is to pay attention to the multiplicity of historical and political positionings subsumed under the label "feminisms," usually represented through what Chela Sandoval has described as the hegemonic taxonomies of liberal, Marxist, radical/cultural, and socialist trends in feminism (Sandoval 1991; K. King 1994). Another way of exploding unitary conceptions of feminist criticism is to acknowledge the critical commentary and productions outside the institutions of academic, official publishing. Much influential work on women, sf, and feminism is not found in journal articles, but in those meta-textual spaces that have traditionally served in sf as forums for critical commentary and review: forewords, editorial columns, introductions to collections, and letters to fanzines. This chapter surveys constructions of feminist sf criticisms in a range of sources, written by critics, authors, anthologists, and fans, pursuing a variety of feminist trends, from patriarchal deconstructions, to gynocentric herstories, feminist constructions, resistances, and counter-narratives. My account of these trends aims to disrupt the hegemonic narrative of academic feminist sf criticism, with its focus on a restricted canon of texts.

The first steps in conversations about sf informed by a feminist perspective can be traced in a year-by-year account of the 1970s, which produced a handful of articles and essays situated in various locales, from women's studies and sf journals, to sf fanzines and introductions to collections. A survey of these articles locates many of the themes that were to be engaged, re-engaged, and contested through ensuing publications, and demonstrates the non-linear, circular nature of the "development" of feminist critiques. Incorporating and developing earlier ideas, while also foreshadowing later approaches, these articles can begin to be marked as feminist by the authors' enunciation of critiques of sf in light of the theories and praxis of the 1970s women's movement. Like the broader development of feminist literary criticism, the founding texts of feminist sf critique located their "permission to speak" in the deconstruction of patriarchal norms, a move which in the case of sf manifested as a challenge to the perceived or actual masculinism of the values and demographics of sf.

(Re)constructing the absence of "Women" in sf

If Cornillon's *Images of Women in Fiction* constitutes an originary moment in the dominant narrative of feminist literary criticism,[1] then Joanna Russ's essay in that collection forms an appropriate starting point for the consolidation of a feminist critique of sf. Originally published in 1970, "The Image of Women in SF" was the first critique of sf's representation of women consciously informed by the women's movement; appropriately enough, it appeared in a feminist journal, *The Red Clay Reader*. Although Russ's essay did not seem to be circulating in the sf community until its publication in the magazine *Vertex* in 1974, the substance of Russ's critique was almost certainly known

---

1 Where this dominant narrative is one constructed by white Anglo-American critics—cf King's discussion of the erasure of black feminist critics from early conversations about the history of feminist theory (K. King 1994: 12).

to a portion of the sf community, and critics interested in women's fiction would probably have seen Cornillon's collection.[2]

Indeed it is somewhat ironic that the "founding text" of feminist sf criticism initially issued from the domain of feminist literary studies—indicating a relatively free exchange across the boundaries of "literature" and "popular fiction," feminist theory and "genre" criticism, that decreased as sf scholarship lagged behind feminist criticism in terms of institutionalization in the academy. "The Image of Women" is a useful marker for Russ, indicating her multiple positioning inside the academy as well as in the women's movement and the sf field, drawing on her experiences as academic, sf reader, author, and critic. Contemporary readings of this article are also informed by the knowledge that around this time, Russ was writing the text that would be considered by many as *the* quintessential "feminist sf text"—*The Female Man*.[3] Certainly the responses to her article when it was reprinted in *Vertex*, discussed in the previous chapter, suggest influences from outside the text, particularly in their references to her anger, militancy, and charges of sexism.[4]

Russ's essay also signals a change in the *reception* of such critiques. Previously situated as part of ongoing internal "quality control," following Russ's article, critiques of women in sf were seen in the context of a feminist intervention, a politically-motivated challenge (or attack) informed by the women's liberation movement. For, at first reading, the substance of Russ's arguments do not differ radically from earlier critiques (such as those by Amis and Lundwall), which focused on the stereotypical nature of female characters and the fact that this stereotyping signaled a failure of sf's extrapolative imagina-

---

2   Thus I begin my consideration with "The Image of Women" rather than the 1972 article by Beverly Friend "Virgin Territory: Women and Sex in Science Fiction," even though Russ originally published outside the sf field.

3   For example, Ellen Morgan called it "the truest, most complete account available of what it feels like to be alienated as a woman and a feminist" (cited in Rosinsky 1982: 67). Rosinsky also notes that *The Female Man* is acknowledged as "a classic of feminist polemical literature."

4   Anderson's and Dick's replies invest the article with passions and accusations presumably extrapolated from extra-textual sources, perhaps personal interactions with Russ, or awareness of her fictional texts, such as "When it Changed." Although not published until 1975, *The Female Man* had been in circulation in the sf community for a number of years previously, according to Samuel Delany (as told to Tom Moylan, *Demand the Impossible* [Moylan 1986: 57]).

tion. Russ's position was distinguished by her particular investments in making such a critique: she was not only a woman, but a feminist, and she demanded a better standard of sf texts and authors. The image of women, in Russ's hands, is not a just a "failing" (mostly located in sf's past) to be rued and mentioned in passing, but is a central faultline in sf that, if addressed, would disrupt sf's "business as usual." Putting "real women" in sf would not just produce "decent sex" in Russ's schemata, but would also, in a true feminist revisioning, potentially disrupt some central shibboleths of sf (Russ 1974b: 56). Russ's framing of the problem strikes with more emotive force than previous incarnations; her article concludes: "There are plenty of images of women in science fiction. There are hardly any women" (57). This is the body of a "real" woman, with all its complications, demanding entry to science fiction.

The influence of Russ's feminism was most evident in her analysis of the causal factors that produced and continued to reproduce this lack of real women in sf. The lack of "social speculation," argued Russ, was due not to a "failure of the imagination outside the exact sciences," but rather to an acceptance of cultural conditioning and stereotypes that sf authors, in particular, should strive to oppose. While Russ located sexism (not actually mentioned in her article, Anderson notwithstanding) in sociocultural relations, she also attributed responsibility for reproducing these relations to the author as an individual. Suddenly it was not "history" that was responsible for women's image in sf, but the sf authors and readers themselves. That she had a bit of a chuckle in asserting this, accounts for some of the vehement reactions from individual male authors:

> [E]ven if readers are adolescents, the writers are not. I know quite a few grown-up men who should know better, but who nonetheless fall into what I would like to call the he-man ethic. (1974b: 55)

Most damning of all, Russ dared to be patronizing: "the [male] authors want to be progressive, God bless them, but they don't know how" (56). As Russ only listed three male exceptions, Mack Reynolds, Samuel Delany, and Robert Heinlein, all other male authors—like Dick—could take this comment as a personal attack. A respected sf critic and author (at least until her more overtly feminist work of the early 1970s), Russ charged sf with a failure to fulfill its potential of responsible and educated speculation. This failing was most obvious, Russ argued, in writers' employment of stereotypical characterizations of masculinity and femininity: "science fiction writers have no business employing stereotypes, let alone swallowing them goggle-eyed" (55).

The issue of the representation of women characters in sf was not, for Russ, directly linked to the presence of women writers of sf. While she acknowledged that, generally, "stories by women tend to contain more active and lively female characters than do stories by men, and more often than men writers, women writers try to invent worlds in which men and women will be equals," (1974b: 57) women writers were not automatically immune from cultural stereotypes. Russ's stance had a number of important consequences both for male and feminist critics. First, male authors and critics could not shift responsibility for non-sexist portrayals onto the growing number of female writers. Second, at a point when feminist literary criticism was defining itself in opposition to an androcentric tradition (through what was later called "images of women" criticism), Russ refused the basis of this conception. Merely being a woman writer was not enough to produce texts that escaped conventional ideas and prejudices concerning women's status and cultural role.

Russ also set up a distinction between certain kinds of women's writing and "feminist" writing, observing "the usual faults" in women's sf. Interestingly, Russ's categorization of "women's fiction" contains four categories, none of which seems to contain the seeds of feminist sf. The first category, in particular, distanced what was commonly called "women's sf" from an emergent tradition of feminist sf: "Ladies' Magazine fiction—in which the sweet, gentle, intuitive little heroine solves an interstellar crisis by mending her slip or doing something equally domestic after her big, heroic husband has failed" (56). The story Russ is probably referring to here is Zenna Henderson's "Subcommittee," in which an intergalactic war is prevented by the wife of a high official, who has secretly communicated with one of the alien forces whose son has befriended her own. In the climax of the story, the narrator proves that she has indeed made contact with the alien mother by displaying her pink slip to the human and alien members of a high-powered military meeting. The other two categories, "galactic suburbia" and space opera also firmly removed authors like Leigh Brackett from a possible tradition leading to feminist sf.[5] No examples of "galactic suburbia" are given, but considering earlier references by male critics to "domestic" sf that focused on housewives, this category likely refers to writers like Judith Merril and Anne McCaffrey.[6]

Despite the incensed responses from some quarters, Russ actually invested more power in sf's potential as a serious literature of ideas, change, and "cognitive estrangement" than did many male critics. Her whole critique was motivated by a great respect for sf, a form that she thought provided her a way out of the "old stories." "The Image of Women in SF," although directed at sf, described the androcentric state of fiction (and criticism) in general, as outlined in her article "What Can a Heroine Do" in Cornillon's collection (Russ 1972). It is also worth noting that at this "founding point" in feminist literary criticism, Russ gestured towards a problem in literary and feminist criticism that would not be tackled by the dominant body of white critics until well into the 1980s: the problem of reading counter-cultural fictions by black writers (and by implication other racial and ethnic bodies) in terms of the inherited mythos of white western culture. As an example, Russ asked what the American black writer would make of the "still-current myth…that Suffering Brings Wisdom": "When critics do not find what they expect, they cannot imagine that the fault may lie in their expectations" (15).

Beverly Friend's "Virgin Territory: Women and Sex in Science Fiction" (1972), was the first critique of the image of women to appear in sf critical commentary, in the only sf journal then existing, *Extrapolation*. Like Russ and earlier critics, Friend emphasized the negative portrayal of "women as appendage," singling out writers like Lester Del Rey (for his "Helen O'Loy") and Robert Heinlein.

---

5   This attack may seem somewhat at odds with her comments later in the same article that issues such as childcare and family structure should be considered in sf. (For example, on p. 57, Russ criticizes Le Guin's *Left Hand of Darkness* for not fully explaining family structure or child-rearing.) However it is likely that Russ's motivation was to demonstrate that such stories should not be claimed by (male) critics as an example of the "progress of sf" (i.e., the triumphant "trotting out" of female authors to prove a point) because, while they may have privileged women and "feminine" experience, the dominant mores of gendered behavior and patriarchal authority were not questioned or challenged.

6   In Yaszek's re-assessment of post-war women's sf set in "galactic suburbia," she indeed covers these authors as well as others such as Marion Zimmer Bradley, Carol Emshwiller, and Mildred Clingerman (Yaszek 2008).

Friend made explicit the link between her critique and "women's lib" that was subtextual in Russ's essays: "While speculative writing often reaches conclusions advocated by women's lib today (and did so as early as Wyndham's story ["Consider Her Ways"]), it may also point up the foibles of what we view as unchangeable" (Friend 1972: 57). Friend provided a much more positive judgment than Russ did of the trend against stereotypes, arguing that Farmer, Sturgeon, and Le Guin went beyond role reversal (super-man into super-girl) into "true extrapolations."

Just as Russ projected a standard against which contemporary sf was to be judged, Friend too delineated the possibility of a non-sexist sf, which would go beyond asking 'What if women were treated realistically in sf?'; to questions such as:

> "What if only females existed?" "What if different, even repulsive sexual characteristics were discovered?" "What if the sexes were combined to create a new, uni-sexed individual?" (51)

In Friend's analysis also, the standard by which sf is judged wanting is, in contrast to previous critiques, not the "already existing" social relations of the late '60s and '70s, but that of the much more radical possibilities implied by the theories and praxis of the Women's Liberation Movement.

The next "images of women" critique to appear in an sf journal was Le Guin's short essay "American SF and the Other," in a 1975 issue of *Science Fiction Studies*. Le Guin also drew on the example of the women's movement to substantiate her argument (along with Frederick Engel's use of the status of women as an index of societal civilization). The critiques discussed so far were subsumed by Le Guin into a feminist moment:

> The women's movement has made most of us conscious of the fact that SF has either totally ignored women, or presented them as squeaking dolls subject to instant rape by monsters—or old-maid scientists desexed by hypertrophy of the intellectual organs—or, at best, loyal little wives or mistresses of accomplished heroes. (Le Guin 1975: 208)

In a much more direct attack on male authors than that of Russ, Le Guin names "male elitism" as a cause, but goes on to locate the problem as lying much deeper, in the very mythos of sf: "Isn't the 'subjection of women' in SF merely a symptom of a whole which is authoritarian, power-worshipping, and intensely parochial?" (208). SF's treatment of women, in Le Guin's analysis, was symptomatic of a broader, multi-layered oppressive system metaphorically represented by the "alien": "there is the sexual Alien, and the social Alien, and the cultural Alien, and finally the racial Alien" (209). American sf had, Le Guin argued, "assumed a permanent hierarchy of superiors and inferiors, with rich, ambitious, aggressive males at the top, then a great gap, and then at the bottom the poor, the uneducated, the face-less masses, and all the women" (209). Le Guin's preferred object was sf tempered by human idealism: "and some serious consideration of such deeply radical, futuristic concepts as Liberty, Equality, and Fra-ternity. And remember that about 53% of the Brotherhood of Man is the Sisterhood of Woman" (210).

In the introductions to her collections of sf by women, *Women of Wonder*, Pamela Sargent offered some of the most comprehensive in-vestigations into the images and roles of women in sf (Sargent 1978b, 1978c, 1979).[7] A central facet of Sargent's critique of sf was the influ-ence of the masculine culture of science and technology on the field: "The effort and longterm commitment that our society demands of those studying the sciences are seen as inimical to the roles women are supposed to play" (1978a: 12). Sargent linked this discouragement of women to the lack of female readers of early sf: "Already discouraged from having an interest in technology, many girls found little for them-selves in books where men had most of the adventures and fun" (12). Sargent's innovative focus on the centrality of scientific discourses and cultures as a facet of sf's continuing masculinism was seldom repeat-ed in later feminist criticism. Her assumption that the convention-ally proscribed female reading position would have kept most girls away from sf, however, is challenged by later commentators. Susan Wood and others such as Marion Zimmer Bradley and Kathe Davis have argued, on the contrary, that the absence of "feminine" roles, plots, and settings were exactly what *did* attract certain girls to sf. It was, as Bradley remembered, a desire to escape the stifling gendered categories that assigned women to domesticated "ladies fiction" (sans

7 Another similar article, but targeted at a different audience, appeared in the jour-nal *Futures* (Sargent 1975: 433: 41).

adventure) that made sf so appealing (Bradley 1977: 34; see also Davis 1995: 178). Wood, writing in 1978, succinctly described the strategy later formalized in feminist reading theories such as Judith Fetterly's "resisting reader":

> My own "click" of consciousness came in 1972, after I had been reading what the library clerk coldly informed me were "boys books" for some 15 years, happily substituting my female self for their male protagonists. (Wood 1978/1979: 10)[8]

References to the adolescent male readership of sf became, in the 1978 analysis by Mary Kenny Badami, a three-pronged challenge to sf as a community and field, rather than just a collection of texts. The first article to proclaim itself "A Feminist Critique of Science Fiction," it is at once a consolidation of the trend to "images of women" critiques as well as a moment of transition (Badami 1978: 6-19). Although the article's overtly feminist positioning later became familiar, Badami's multi-layered analysis of the field in terms of subject, authorship, and readership became much rarer as feminist critical engagements with sf coalesced into feminist literary critiques of women's or feminist sf texts.

Badami's focus substituted the more expansive "role" of women for "images of women" in sf and stated more explicitly than did Russ or Friend the effects of sexism in every level of the sf field. Her thesis presented a more subtle take on the "absence" of women, directing attention crucially to the processes of validation and reception:

> Women have *not* been important as characters in sf;
> women have *not* been important as fans of sf;
> women have *not* been important as writers of sf. (6)

Badami forced readers to examine their preconceptions of women's role in the field (as opposed to "good intentions" regarding views about sexism or equality) by means of a quiz entitled "The Invisible Woman," which, for instance, asked for examples of ten women sf authors, novels told from a female viewpoint, and Andre Norton's real name (6). Despite the publication of articles such as those by Russ and Friend, anthologies such as Sargent's, and the testimony of authors like Aldiss and Harlan Ellison, Badami contended that

---

8   What prompted Wood's feminist change of consciousness was in part a story that, unusually, featured a female protagonist, but one so stereotyped that it caused Wood to throw the magazine across the room.

feminist appraisals needed to be reiterated. Her reasons included the "backlash" against feminist analyses already (or always) in evidence; the continuing reproduction of older values in both new books and the continuing popularity of "golden age" sf; nostalgia for "good old-fashioned sf"; and the fact that despite recent changes, women were not "secure as characters, readers, and writers of sf" (15). Badami was adamant that feminist critiques not be diverted by the tokenistic trotting out of exceptions to the rule:

> Disproving allegations of unequal representation by mentioning the very rare exception is akin to older arguments which sought to prove that Sidney Poitier in film and Ralph Bunche in the U.N. were evidence of racial integration in U.S. society. Even as we take pride in the presence of achieving women in traditionally male enclaves, we know the difference between tokenism and equal representation. (11)

What to Badami was tokenism could, of course, be seen by others as nascent efforts at reconstructing women's history within sf: the potential tension here was one that would resurface again and again in the development of feminism within sf.

In many ways, Badami consolidated the emerging identity of "feminist sf critic" (13). In an effort to avoid the kind of negative knee-jerk response to feminism as an "extremist" intrusion of "mundane" politics, Badami personalized her feminist standpoint ("'a' feminist critique, not 'the' feminist critique") and emphasized the multiplicity of positions inferred by the signifier "feminism": "I do not agree completely with everyone else who claims to be a feminist." A commonality amongst feminist positions is offered by Badami: "feminists are committed both to breaking the stereotypes in our own lives and to working for social change. That includes scrutinizing the books we read" (13). Badami's position thus intensifies the assumptions less explicit in Russ, Friend, Sargent, and Le Guin: that issues of sexism and representation in sf are important—not only because of sf's personal value to readers and authors like Russ, but also because such fiction is a reflection of, as well as a site of, struggles over cultural representation.

The publication of an article by Susan Wood (in the same year as Badami's) clearly signaled that the development of a visibly "feminist" critical stance was not a linear progression of gradual accretion and natural development from ("mother-critic") Russ. Rather than being an extension of Badami's *feminist* critical stance, Wood's "Women and Science Fiction" focused on an "images of women" critique (1978/79). Much of the difference may have stemmed from the publication sites of these two articles: Badami was writing for the established critical journal *Extrapolation*, addressing critics and students of sf, whereas Wood's article appeared in a fanzine, addressing readers, fans, and authors. (Interestingly, as I noted in Chapter Two, both Wood's and Russ's articles—neither of which signaled "feminism" as their context—received heated responses.)

These critiques of sf patriarchy already made moves to construct woman as subject, reflecting changes in the broader women's movement and critical trends such as gynocriticism. Although, as Sylvia Kelso observes, phases of feminist critique can be characterized in terms of a movement from "critiques of androcentrism," through "remedial research," to a phase that "reconceptualises subject fields," this movement is not simply a diachronic progression (Kelso 1996: 58). The doubled movement of de/reconstruction continues to be a facet of feminist sf criticism right up to the present and is the source of apparent inconsistencies between deconstructive narratives emphasizing the absence or invisibility of women and those constructing herstories that emphasize women's presence.

Dialogues: herstories and women's sf

The eddies of critique and construction that eventually initiated the production of "feminist sf" were already present in the negative formulations of patriarchal, androcentric sf and manifested as a much more conscious attempt to formulate a feminist subject in the mid-to-late 1970s. A sample of publications from 1974-1976 provides a sense of the dialogue between different impulses in such productive moves. My reading of these critiques highlights the differences brought about by an emphasis either on a feminist object (feminist sf) or on women in sf, which can intimate a gynocritics (criticism of women's as opposed to men's sf) or a recovery project of "herstory" (women writers of sf—not necessarily the same as a unified women's or feminist *tradition* of sf).

Many of these conversations took place outside "professional" journals and books, in fan publications and exchanges between fans and authors, often sparked by the publication of collections of sf by

women. The years 1974 and '75 saw the appearance of the first feminist fanzines, *The Witch and the Chameleon* (*WatCh*) and *Janus* (later
Aurora), and also Pamela Sargent's first *Women of Wonder* collection.
Both fanzines situated themselves as feminist in allegiance, providing
feminist perspectives on a range of authors and topics.[9] In the pages
of these zines, numerous articles, reviews, and letters consciously patrolled the emerging borders of "feminist sf," while others contributed to the historical project of reclaiming female authors.

The kind of exchanges circulating amongst women and feminists
at the time are evident in the "round-robin" letter correspondence
between sf authors edited by Jeffrey Smith for his fanzine *Khatru*
(Smith 1975).[10] This symposium on "Women in Science Fiction" is
not only a wonderfully representative "slice" of sf discussions about
women as subjects and authors of sf, but also a unique document of
social history, as nine women, two men, and one woman masquerading
as a man debated, raged, and agonized over sex roles, gender roles, literature, violence, and rape—all those topics so much at the forefront
of the feminist "consciousness-raising" atmosphere of the 1970s.[11] As
Gwyneth Jones commented in 1993, "It rather takes you aback, to realize how much of what's passed into the SF record—on feminism, on
women—comes from this single source" (Jones 1993: 131).

Much of the symposium centered not on sf but on broader feminist issues and critiques of sexism. The editor, Jeffrey Smith, assumed
a stance that figured women's entry into sf as a recent change and
attempted to direct the discussion through questions such as "what
attracted women writers to SF?" Kate Wilhelm responded: "Asking
what attracts women to science fiction is perpetuating the myth that it
is a man's field, and that reinforces the myth that any intellectual area
is a man's area" (Smith 1975: 9). As Jones later observed, ultimately, "the debate on women in SF cannot be sustained... What you're

9   The first editorial of *WatCh* situated its goals in feminist terms, and a later letter
    referred to it as a "feminist fanzine," *WatCh*, no. 2, Nov. 1974, p. 4; the second is-
    sue of *Janus* also promoted a feminist perspective, vol. 1, no. 2, 1975, p. 39. These
    fanzines are discussed in more detail in Chapter Five.

10 Second edition (with additional introduction and material edited by Jeanne Gomoll
    (Gomoll 1993). All subsequent page references refer to this second edition.

11 The contributors were Joanna Russ, Ursula Le Guin, Suzy McKee Charnas, Kate
    Wilhelm, Vonda N. McIntyre, Chelsea Quinn Yarbro, Virginia Kidd, Raylyn Moore,
    Luise White, Samuel R. Delany, and James Tiptree Jr.

talking about, immediately, is the position of women, the effects of gender-role, in the real world" (1993: 132). This, in fact, was the substance of one of Tiptree's first long contributions, which earned him a "trashing" from most of the "female participants": "First, to hell with talking about "women in sf"" (18). One of the most intriguing and valuable aspects of this document of feminist social history is the chronicling of the tensions and struggles over the meaning of feminism between women of different generations, different backgrounds and positionings (for example, middle-class liberal, socialist feminist, radical lesbian), and the contemporary reflections by women like Le Guin, Russ, and Charnas on their "previous selves" and also their treatment of others.[12]

Slowly, women writers in sf (and their fans) were establishing a collective identity or community, seen in the *Khatru* symposium, dialogues in fanzines and at conventions, and also reflected through the collections of women writing sf that appeared in the mid- to late-1970s. Published in the same year that Russ's article was printed in *Vertex*, Pamela Sargent's first anthology of women sf writers was helping to establish a complementary (often competing) "counter-canon" to masculinist sf. The earliest story in the collection was Judith Merril's "That only a Mother" (1948) and the latest Vonda McIntyre's "Of Mist, and Grass, and Sand."[13] In addition to the stories, Sargent's introduction, "Women in Science Fiction," constructed a lineage of women writing sf, beginning with nineteenth-century precursors, Mary Shelley and Rhoda Broughton, and also listing women who had begun writing in the 1960s and '70s (Sargent 1978a).[14] The authors

12 A number of the contemporary responses concern their re-assessment of different positions, such as Tiptree's proclamations on Motherhood, or, in Russ's words "how very radical Kate Wilhelm was then and how little I...perceived this" Russ, Dec 1, 1992 in "Symposium" (Gomoll 1993: 115).

13 The other authors in the collection were Sonya Dorman, Katherine MacLean, Marion Zimmer Bradley, Anne McCaffrey, Kit Reed, Kate Wilhelm, Carol Emshwiller, Ursula Le Guin, Chelsea Quinn Yarbro, and Joanna Russ.

14 In this introductory survey, Sargent provided more critical commentary on early women writers than any other critic would until Jane Donawerth's examination of women writing for the pulps in the '20s and '30s. Of this period, Sargent mentions only Francis Stevens, whom she situates as the first woman to write sf since Broughton's 1873 story "Behold It Was a Dream," not mentioning the many utopian stories authored by women that later feminist critics have included as part of a feminist sf or speculative tradition. In the 1995 expanded edition, *Women of*

cited included Francis Stevens (*The Heads of Cerebus*, 1919), C.L. Moore, Leigh Brackett, Wilmar Shiras, Judith Merril, Mildred Clingerman, Katherine MacLean, Margaret St. Clair, Zenna Henderson, and Andre Norton (Sargent 1978a: 15-22). Sargent's attention to authors such as Norton should be seen as part of an important recurring trend to "salvage" authors who "slipped through" this consolidation period, not becoming part of the emerging feminist sf canon and consequently suffering critical neglect.[15]

Contributions to canon formation in the form of anthologies continued in 1976, when two more collections appeared. Edited by sf writer Vonda N. McIntyre and academic Susan Janice Anderson, *Aurora: Beyond Equality* could be considered the first collection of "feminist sf" (although not named as such), even though half of the authors represented in it have been almost forgotten—or at any rate not incorporated into the feminist sf canon (McIntyre and Anderson 1976).[16] What is surprising, however, is the number of authors and stories that *would* become canonized: Racoona Sheldon's "Your Faces, O My Sisters! Your Faces Filled of Light" and James Tiptree Jr.'s "Houston, Houston, Do You Read?";[17] an excerpt from Piercy's *Woman on the Edge of Time*; a lesser-known story by Joanna Russ; and an essay by Le Guin. Although not specifically targeted as "feminist sf," the editors look to "non-sexist" sf futures as the best expression of feminism and sf.

In contrast, in her second collection *More Women of Wonder*, Sargent aimed to present a "picture of how the role of women in science

---

Wonder: The Classic Years, Sargent modifies her position, reflecting the impact of studies of feminist utopian fiction and the overlap critics have created between early utopias and feminist sf. In 1995, Sargent states, "other women, now largely forgotten, contributed to fantastic literature in the nineteenth century. Marie Corelli, Rhoda Broughton, Sara Coleridge, and Jane Louden, among others produced works bordering on science fiction." Sargent also cites Mary Bradley Lane's *Mizora* and Charlotte Perkins Gilman's *Herland* (1995: 3).

15   Thus, Sargent argues for Norton's talents, especially in the characterization of alien peoples: "In several novels she uses American Indians as protagonists (this in a field not noted, even today, for its use of minority characters)" (1978a: 21).

16   The lesser known authors are Dave Skal, Mildred Downey Broxon, P.J. Plauger (male), and Craig Strete.

17   Both pseudonyms of Alice Sheldon, whose identity was still unknown at the time of publication.

fiction developed."[18] Feminism is much more to the forefront in this introduction than in her 1974 collection, along with a certain amount of defensiveness. In both collections, Sargent took an historical approach, including "examples of both the 'old-fashioned' story and the more 'innovative' one. Because of this approach, some readers might conclude that the stories are not really feminist" (1974: 37). Thus Sargent was concerned more with the preservation of "herstory" than with the construction (or reflection) of feminist sf, and situated her collections as complements to feminist collections such as *Aurora* (37-8).

While the first *Women of Wonder* collection was seen by fanzine editor Amanda Bankier as fulfilling "a long-felt want," by 1976 that "want" was more likely to be expressed in feminist terms. Thus Jeanne Gomoll's review of *More Women of Wonder* expresses her disappointment with the first collection: "I was expecting Sargent to choose stories that were praiseworthy on a number of levels, and did not take seriously her proclaimed purpose to simply present what-has-been-done, good or bad, by women" (1976: 35). Most of Gomoll's dissatisfaction with the second collection stemmed from its failure to live up to its back cover blurb, which promised "to explore feminist themes in science fiction." The sticking point here was a struggle over what could be defined as "feminist fiction" or even feminist themes in sf. Already, in the emerging contours of "feminist sf," writers like Leigh Brackett and C.L. Moore were excluded (today Brackett is still excluded, whereas much of C. L. Moore's work has been "reclaimed" for its proto-feminist sensibilities).[19] The emerging process of canonization proceeded through dialogue between many participants in the nascent feminist sf community, with particular tensions between those who desired texts reflecting their engagement with contemporary feminist issues and others focused on women's long but unrecognized work in the field before the advent of women's lib.

---

18 Sargent, *More Women of Wonder* (14). Included in her introduction was discussion of a broader range of earlier sf, such as Francis Stevens's "Friend Island" (1918). This story (reprinted in *New Eves*) is a fascinating example of early women's sf, set in a role-reversal world, where women are admitted to be the superior sex. It does not, however, concern a battle of the sexes, but tells the tale of a fantastical island that is "alive," a female ship's captain and a man she is attracted to, until his ridiculous "mannish" behavior disillusions her.

19 See, for example, Susan Gubar (1980: 16-27) and Thomas A. Bredehoft (1997) who argues for C.L. Moore to be repositioned as the "mother" of feminist sf, rather than Shelley.

Synergy: "feminist sf" is born?

Although the desire to connect their interests in feminism and sf was a common underpinning of the interests of both authors and fans, the sub-genre/object of knowledge "feminist sf" was not "named" until 1978, formalized in the title of an article by Pamela J. Annas in the critical journal *Science Fiction Studies*: "New Worlds, New Words, Androgyny in Feminist Science Fiction" (1978: 143-56). Annas proffered a genealogy or history of feminist sf that grounded the emergence of feminist sf firmly in the rise of the women's movement: "feminist SF is as much a result of recent feminist literature as it is of SF" (144). This narrative was reinforced by her argument that sf was an "overwhelmingly male-dominated genre" where "male SF writers have avoided any discussion of sex and sex roles"; in contrast, Annas argued, "[a]lternatives to sex role stereotyping are central to the utopian visions of feminist writers" (146-7). Annas not only consolidated the work of various writers into a feminist "tradition" or community, but read them through the common concept of "androgyny" (145). Reflecting an earlier emphasis on androgyny in feminist theorizing, Annas incorporated a wide range of strategies under this umbrella concept:

> from visions of worlds which have entirely eliminated men and therefore sexual polarization, through visions of worlds which are biologically androgynous, to visions of worlds in which male and female functions and roles simply are not sharply differentiated. They can nevertheless be grouped together loosely under the concept of androgyny. For the feminist writer, androgyny is a metaphor...which allows the writer to structure utopian visions that eliminate or transcend contradictions which she sees as crucial. (146)

The newly-constituted breed of "feminist sf writers" had, according to Annas, a surprising number of revolutionary assumptions in common: "a politics of anarchism, a metaphysics of the organism, a psychological and social vision of unity, wholeness, balance, and cooperation" (155). The texts Annas employed for this construction were Russ's *The Female Man*, Le Guin's *The Left Hand of Darkness*, *The Lathe of Heaven*, *The Word for World is Forest*, and *The Dispossessed*, and Marge Piercy's *Woman on the Edge of Time*. Not surprisingly, the feminist status of some of these texts would be contested in later analyses as each critic incrementally advanced their own ideas of tradition and contributed to the canonizing of some texts as "feminist sf."

Another construction of "feminist sf" also published in 1978 (the first feminist critique to appear in an sf critical anthology) examined quite different texts, within a very different feminist context. Catherine Podojil's emphasis was not "feminist sf" but "the specific themes that women explore when they write science fiction from a feminist point of view" (1978: 71). Podojil's article may be seen as an attempt to bridge the creation of feminist sf with ideas about a women's tradition in sf by looking at women writers, feminist themes, and variations in these themes according to historical period. Podojil examined the work of Russ, Tiptree, and Sondra [Sonya] Dorman, "all of whom have written the bulk of their work within the framework of the recent feminist movement," in comparison with the earlier writer, Judith Merril, whose work is situated as "important for the period in which it was written, a period in which support for feminist ideals was very limited" (72).[20] She identified four "major feminist themes" in the works examined: the importance of daughters, the success of worlds run completely or equally by women, the human male as an alien form, and the importance of the individual woman creator. Other important but secondary themes traced by Podojil included lesbianism, "women as competent technicians, scientists, or artists," and "ethnic diversity" (observed in the work of Merril and Tiptree).

The critical awareness of "feminist sf" was matched by the publication of three new anthologies, also in 1978: *New Women of Wonder*, *Cassandra Rising*, and *Millennial Women*. These three collections illustrate a range of possible "canons," with Sargent's *New Women of Wonder* the one that most coincided with the group of texts identified as "feminist sf" by critics, authors, and fans. Reflecting the amount of debate within the community, "feminism" was also much more prominent in her Introduction, and Sargent was by this time able to draw on a body of feminist critique, such as the essays by Russ, Badami, and McIntyre, and from other sources such as the *Khatru* symposium and *Janus*. Many of the texts and authors in Sargent's collection

---

20 The works considered are Merril's *Daughters of Earth*; Russ's "When it Changed"; Tiptree's "The Women Men Don't See" and "Houston, Houston, Do You Read?"; and Dorman's "Building Block." Russ's and Tiptree's texts soon became canonized as "feminist SF," whereas Dorman's and Merril's received little critical attention until recently, see Yaszek (2008).

would become central to the feminist sf canon: James Tiptree Jr.'s "The Women Men Don't See," Eleanor Arnason's "The Warlord of Saturn's Moons," Chelsea Quinn Yarbro's "Dead in Irons," Josephine Saxton's "The Triumphant Head," Joan D. Vinge's "Eyes of Amber," Vonda McIntyre's "Screwtop," Joanna Russ's "When It Changed," Pamela Zoline's "Heat Death of the Universe," Kit Reed's "Songs of War," and Sonya Dorman's "Building Block." (Indeed, it may well have been such collections that made this work readily available to feminist academics and critics, who increasingly did not necessarily have a background in fandom and thus knowledge of, or subscriptions to, the magazines in which they originally appeared.) Gomoll situated *New Women of Wonder* along with *Millennial Women* and the earlier *Aurora* as the three best feminist-orientated sf anthologies yet published (1978/1979b: 36). The third collection, *Cassandra Rising*, was, as Gomoll observed, more an anthology of sf written by women than one of "women's sf" (37).

So at this point in the late 1970s, there were clearly observed gradations and polymorphous expressions of women's engagement with sf; the same was true for feminism and sf. Whereas Gomoll grouped *Millennial Women* with both *New Women of Wonder* and *Aurora*, its editor, Virginia Kidd, emphasized an "equisexist" approach: "one of the most impressive aspects of the collection is that all of these science fiction writers avoid hard-core science fiction for sociology, soft-pedal radical feminism for humanism, and write about women simply as women" (1978: 3). A long-time sf fan, author, and agent, Kidd may be seen as part of a "counter-feminist" initiative that is a vital thread throughout women's engagement in sf: seen in the attitudes of many earlier writers such as Leigh Brackett and Marion Zimmer Bradley, but also through the 1970s, '80s, and '90s in collections like *Cassandra Rising* and in the work of writers like Connie Willis.[21]

Consolidation and solidification

The 1980s was a period when feminist sf criticism consolidated its concerns and subject of study and became a more consensually recognized "object of knowledge." The years 1980-82 saw the publication

---

21 This is also seen in fan debates, where many women who wanted to encourage the participation of women and believed in equality issues such as equal pay, rejected "feminism" as a context for their position. See discussion in Chapter Five.

of a number of "landmark" texts that helped formalize feminist sf criticism within the critical field: special issues on women and sf by the critical journals *Science Fiction Studies* (*SFS*) and *Extrapolation*, and the publication of two critical anthologies.

The 1980 *SFS* issue "Science Fiction on Women—Science Fiction by Women," signaled a somewhat belated recognition of the developing body of feminist sf criticism.[22] The rather defensive editorial introduction declared that the issue was "not a token gesture," claiming that *SFS* had "published studies of women writers long before it was fashionable," although as the editors indicated, "women" here could be substituted for Shelley and Le Guin.[23] While the editorial refused to recognize the specificity of either women's (let alone feminist) writing or criticism, the essays themselves confirmed and consolidated certain trends in feminist sf criticism—namely, the turn away from negative critiques of masculine sf (and indeed from male

22 The journal *Extrapolation* had performed better in terms of articles by and about women. The British journal *Foundation* fared even worse; up to 1988 when they too published a special issue (no. 43, Summer, 1988) on women, there had been only half a dozen articles authored by women. One was a piece by Le Guin (as part of their series The Profession of Science Fiction), one was a (non-feminist) piece on Le Guin; Roz Kaveny, "Science Fiction in the 1970s" mentions some feminist authors. (In the same issue is an interesting piece on Mitchison and J.B.S. Haldane, which mentions *Memoirs of a Spacewoman*.) The first article on "Feminism in Science Fiction" in 1984 was by a male critic, Stefan Lewicki. In 1982 (no. 26) there was an interview with Pamela Sargent, prefaced by the following acknowledgment: "*Foundation* has never featured an interview with a woman writer: surely a disgraceful display of rampant testosterone, which we are glad to amend with the following piece" (56).

23 "Editorial Note," *Science Fiction Studies*, vol. 7, pt. 1, #20, Mar. 1980, p. 1. The editors also claimed "the analyses herein of gender stereotypes reaffirm and extend our long-standing concern with these and related socio-formalist questions." The evidence given for this concern consists of the Le Guin special issue (in which only one article mentions gender concerns), the Annas article discussed above, and a couple of other articles by male critics (one of which is a rather unsophisticated "demonstration" of Tiptree's pessimistic "belief" that the two sexes constitute different species or races—Lowry Pei, [Pei 1979].) This meager list concludes "and so forth," which is misleading since there remains very little else to add! In the nineteen issues to this date, there were only another couple of articles that included some mention of gender or women, four more on Le Guin; as contributors, Le Guin authored 10 pieces (mainly reviews), Russ had two articles, and only four other articles were written by female critics (including Annas). The editor did admit that the number of women contributors had not yet "alas" reached the level of proportional representation, judging by the number of female SFRA members.

writers altogether) and the constitution of feminist writings within sf in terms of "utopia."[24] Russ's "*Amor Vincit Foeminam*: The Battle of the Sexes in SF" signifies both the apogee of feminist critiques of the sexist tradition in sf as well as the formalization of a group of feminist texts that in a later article she would codify as "feminist utopias" (Russ 1980: 2-15). Although what Russ termed "flasher" stories situated conflict between the sexes in the private sphere, Russ claimed that these "feminist utopias see such conflict as a public, class conflict, so the solutions advocated are economic, social, and political" (14).[25]

Extrapolation's special issue in 1982 also described itself in terms of "women and sf," although nearly all of the actual contributions dealt with feminism and feminist sf. The authors discussed were Tiptree, Russ, Brackett, McCaffrey, and—more unusually—Anna Kavan, Octavia Butler, Phyllis Eisenstein, and Marlys Millhiser. Contributors ranged from critics well-known in the sf field, such as Beverly Friend and Marleen Barr, to more mainstream literary critics Natalie Rosinsky and Daphne Patai. An indication of the consolidation of feminist sf criticism is the inclusion of a bibliography of secondary material and a checklist of female sf writers.[26] In contrast to the *SFS* issue, a guest editor was employed who was a fan and teacher of women's sf. Mary Brizzi's editorial begins with the paradigmatic questions "Why is there no sex in science fiction? Why are there no women in science fiction?" in order to argue, in contrast, that women had always been writers and readers of sf and that women wrote hard sf (not just

---

24 The articles are Joanna Russ's "*Amor Vincit Foeminam*: The Battle of the Sexes in SF"; Susan Gubar's "C.L. Moore And the Conventions of Women's Science Fiction"; Linda Leith's "Marion Zimmer Bradley and Darkover"; Robert Galbreath's "Holism, Openness, and the Other: Le Guin's Use of the Occult"; Nadia Khouri's "The Dialectics of Power: Utopia in the SF of Le Guin, Jeury and Piercy"; and Jean Pfaelzer's "Parody and Satire in American Dystopian Fiction of the 19th Century."

25 The focus on the utopian element of contemporary feminist sf was reflected also in Nadia Khouri's article in this issue; while the use of utopia as a means of constructing a feminist heritage for this writing was reflected in Jean Pfaelzer's examination of dystopia.

26 Anne Hudson Jones's "Women in Science Fiction: An Annotated Secondary Bibliography," (1982), is an extensive survey of secondary articles with useful annotations; Roger C. Schlobin's "Farsighted Females: A Selective Checklist of Modern Women Writers of Science Fiction Through 1980" (1982) lists 217 female sf writers.

fantasy). [27] The editorial indicates Brizzi's desire to treat a large range of female authors and regrets the absence of articles on Tanith Lee, C.J. Cherryh, Chelsea Quinn Yarbro, Jean Lorrah, Jacqueline Lichtenberg, Doris Piserchia, and Joan Vinge (most of whom have still received very little critical attention). [28]

One of the most notable features of this journal issue is the use of feminist theorists and literary critics to situate and inform readings of feminist sf. Natalie Rosinsky drew on Hélène Cixous to read Russ's *The Female Man*, with reference to the critics Mary Ellman and Rachel Blau DuPlessis (1982: 31-6). Similarly, Marleen Barr discussed the work of Anne McCaffrey in conjunction with Cixous and Tillie Olsen (1982: 70-6). Both these articles situated feminist sf as deserving of attention from feminist literary criticism. Barr in particular was keen to make connections between a popular, female (rather than necessarily feminist) writer like McCaffrey and feminist literature and criticism. Such a move connected with efforts to recover earlier female authors as part of mainstream gynocritical literary criticism, suggesting that sf had a "herstory" worth recovering in contrast to the prevailing opinion of both the sf field and feminist literary criticism. This kind of approach often appears to be an attempt at "legitimation" of sf in feminist terms. The *Extrapolation* issue also saw the first "professional" publication of articles on African American writer Octavia Butler, by Frances Smith Foster and Beverly Friend (F. Foster 1982; Friend 1982). [29]

---

27 Brizzi also makes a characteristically feminist personal connection. She begins with an anecdote about a male bookshop owner, who told her women don't (can't) write science fiction, juxtaposed with the statement "the science fiction writer whom academics are soonest willing to accept as a mainstream writer of significance is a woman: Ursula K. Le Guin" (Brizzi 1982: 3).

28 Such attempts to dispel narrow trends to canonization were also indicated by the decision to exclude articles on Le Guin (as an earlier issue was devoted to her work) (Brizzi 1982: 4, 107). Unlike the *Science Fiction Studies* special issue on Le Guin, *Extrapolation*'s (vol. 21, no. 3, Fall 1980) included a number of feminist perspectives on her work: Rosemarie Arbur, "Le Guin's 'Song' of Inmost Feminism," (223-6); and Barbara Brown, "The Left Hand of Darkness: Androgyny, Future, Present, and Past" (227-35).

29 Although interviews and appreciations had appeared in fanzines: Janice Bogstad, "Octavia E. Butler and Power Relationships" (1978/79); and Claudia Peck, "Interview: Octavia Butler" (1980). Butler had also received critical attention outside the sf field, in magazines and journals devoted to African American literature—for example, Veronica Mixon, "Futurist Woman: Octavia Butler" (Mixon

In 1981, Russ offered a classification of feminist sf utopias that in many ways set the parameters for succeeding criticism: naming a group of texts and establishing connections and continuities between them—in short, establishing one of the first canons of feminist sf, one that continued to be influential as a touchstone for defining "feminist sf" well into the 1990s. This classification was in "Recent Feminist Utopias" in *Future Females: A Critical Anthology*, the first collection of critical articles about women in sf, edited by Marleen . The collection comprised a diverse assortment of essays, ranging from standard studies of authors like Le Guin and Piercy to examinations of themes such as sexism in sf and feminist utopias. It also included essays on Star Trek and a "juvenile" novel by Alexei Panshin as well as a reflective piece by the sf author Suzy McKee Charnas (Barr 1981).[30] The subject of Russ's article is clearly fictions influenced by the women's movement, fictions that present societies "conceived by the author as better in explicitly feminist terms and for explicitly feminist reasons" (1981: 71). Although Russ qualifies her use of "utopia" to describe all these works,[31] she nevertheless constructs them as "a remarkably coherent group in their presentation of feminist concerns and the feminist analyses which are central to these concerns" (71). The texts in this group are *Les Guérillères* (Monique Wittig), *The Female Man* (Russ), *The Dispossessed* (Le Guin), *Motherlines* (Charnas), *The Shattered Chain* (Marion Zimmer Bradley), *Woman on the Edge of Time* (Marge Piercy), *The Wanderground* (Sally Gearhart), *Triton* (Samuel Delany), "Houston, Houston, Do You Read?" (Tiptree), "Your Faces, O My Sisters! Your Faces Filled of Light!" (Racoona Sheldon), and "Commodore Bork and the Compost" (Catherine Anne Madsen). Only the last piece, by Madsen (published in the fanzine *WatCh*), has *not* remained within the critical canon of feminist sf. In an oft-quoted phrase, Russ defined the commonalities that marked these texts as a coherent group:

1979); Rosalie G. Harrison, "Sci Fi Visions: An Interview with Octavia Butler" (1980); and Carolyn S. Davidson, "The Science Fiction of Octavia Butler" (1981).

30 Also included was a comprehensive listing of sf by women (Schlobin 1981: 179-89).

31 For example, *Triton* and *The Dispossessed* "present not perfect societies but only ones better than our own," and the "utopia" in *The Shattered Chain* is a group, rather than the larger society of which it is a part.

Classless, without government, ecologically minded, with a strong feeling for the natural world, quasi-tribal in feeling and quasi-family in structure, the societies of these stories are *sexually permissive*...the point of the permissiveness is not to break taboos but to separate sexuality from questions of ownership, reproduction and social structure. (76)

Russ's essay marks the configuration of a specific use of the term "utopia" in criticism of feminist sf and, in retrospect, encapsulates a particular manifestation of "contemporary feminist utopianism" and, in many ways, of "feminist sf." The emphasis on "feminist utopia" satisfied Barr's editorial aim for the collection: "scholars who are interested in women and literature should devote more attention to science fiction's future visions... Science fiction should form a major current in the contemporary stream of feminist thought" (1981: 7). This theme, which recurs in all of Barr's later work, reflects the tenor of much feminist sf criticism for at least the following decade.

Carol Pearson's analysis of four feminist utopias (1981) offered another construction of feminist sf as "utopian" (and part of a more distinguished feminist literary heritage). A revised version of an earlier article on feminist utopias published in 1977 (which influenced Russ's 1981 essay),[32] Pearson's analysis extended the notion of a commonality of utopian vision to include historical precedents, arguing for similarities between Mary Bradley Lane's *Mizora* (1890), Charlotte Perkins Gilman's *Herland* (1915), and such contemporary works as Dorothy Bryant's *The Kin of Ata are Waiting for You* (1971) and Mary Staton's *From the Legend of Biel* (1975). Pearson argues that although these works stemmed from the diverse backgrounds of the nineteenth-century and twentieth-century women's movements, their "surprisingly numerous areas of consensus" derive from "the similar conditioning and experiences women share": that they are thus manifestations of a tradition of *women's* writing, conditioned by "feminist" political analyses (1981: 63).

---

32 This was a revised version of her earlier article "Women's Fantasies and Feminist Utopias" (C. Pearson 1977), which discussed Mary Bradley Lane's *Mizora*, Gilman's *Herland*, Piercy's *Woman on the Edge of Time*, Russ's *The Female Man*, Le Guin's *The Dispossessed*, Dorothy Bryant's *The Kin of Ata are Waiting for You*, Mary Staton's *From the Legend of Biel*, and Tiptree's "Houston, Houston, Do You Read?" Russ acknowledges her debt to this article in her own essay. This material also appeared in the final chapter of *The Female Hero in British and American Literature* (Pearson and Pope 1979).

Resistance: Counter-hegemonic narratives

The critical emphasis on utopia may have dominated feminist sf criticism at this time, but it was not the only approach evident in critical consideration of feminist sf. A number of texts may be considered part of a "counter" trend that continued to focus on pre-feminist women writers. The *SFS* special issue, for example, included both an article by Linda Leith on Marion Zimmer Bradley (1980: 28-35), a writer whose inclusion within feminist canons was always problematic (and would be resolved by Russ through referring to only one Bradley text), and Susan Gubar's article on C.L. Moore. Moore continued to receive some critical treatments in various collections, and Gubar, well-known as a feminist literary critic, limited her engagement with sf mostly to Moore, writing a number of essays on this subject. In her article for *SFS*, Gubar used Moore as a means of connecting a contemporary "tradition" of female sf to Mary Shelley (1980: 20).[33] Gubar differs from many earlier critics in casting Moore as a proto-feminist of sorts: not just (as is usual) for her role-reversal heroine Jirel of Joiry, but—through a revised reading of "Shambleau"—for having developed a potent reworking of a powerful feminine myth.[34]

Another example of a focus on women in sf was the 1982 collection *The Feminine Eye: Science Fiction and the Women Who Write It* (Staicar 1982). Aimed at "the non-specialist," editor Tom Staicar identified its topic as "women who have chosen SF as a vehicle for their views" (vii). The particular emphasis of this book, with each chapter treating the work of a separate author, resulted in the evaluation of a number of popular writers rarely discussed in feminist criticism, such as Andre Norton, C.J. Cherryh, and Joan Vinge.[35] The importance of this collection for the history of feminist sf criticism lies in its early demonstration of a chasm between the works considered appropriate

---

33 Gubar also commented that Moore's stories were important as a reminder that there were successful and pioneering female writers from the 1930s and '40s, including Sophie Wenzel Ellis, Amelia Reynolds Long, Lilith Lorraine, Leslie Francis Stone, and Minna Irving. She also mentions Leigh Brackett, Katherine MacLean, Francis Stevens, and Kate Wilhelm.

34 Gubar's lack of familiarity with the sf field is suggested by a couple of errors in the piece: for example, Kate Wilhelm's novel *Juniper Time* is attributed to Judith Merril.

35 Other writers discussed are Brackett, Moore, Tiptree, Bradley, Charnas, and Elgin.

for feminist critical evaluation and those by female writers who may treat similar themes but are more popular in terms of readership than are many feminist authors.

Nineteen eighty-four provides a convenient (and ironic) point for considering the "establishment" of feminist sf criticism and of its proper "subject"—feminist sf—since it brings the first monograph on feminist sf, *Feminist Futures* by Natalie Rosinsky (1984). In the same year, Betty King published a study of female main characters in sf, in some ways harking back to the "images of women criticism," but certainly influenced by feminist critique, in her construction of a teleology leading to progressively more liberated female characters (1984). Thus "Women in sf" at this stage could be seen as a separate, often complementary critical stream: although differently focused, it often provided evidence or texts for the construction of a "feminist sf" tradition.

This year also saw a special issue of a feminist journal on feminist sf, edited by Marleen Barr, "Oh Well, Orwell—Big Sister is Watching Herself: Feminist Science Fiction in 1984" (Barr 1984). Barr's introduction notably reads as a manifesto for feminist sf and its criticism: "'women in science fiction' is no longer a sufficient synonym for 'feminist science fiction'" (84).

> To date, every scholarly critical essay collection devoted to the work of female science fiction writers (*Future Females, The Feminine Eye* and the special issues of *Science Fiction Studies* and *Extrapolation*) has been safely labeled and packaged as "women in science fiction." In 1984, it is time to recognize that "women in science fiction" is not an adequately inclusive term for all the science fiction produced by female writers. There is a difference between Leigh Brackett's space operas, Ursula Le Guin's humanism, and Jessica Amanda Salmonson's swordswomen. (83)

In one of the first taxonomies of feminism in sf, Barr clearly demarcated "feminist sf" from "humanist sf," women's sf from women writing sf, and indicated the kind of writers *she* would "name" as feminist authors: Russ, Salmonson, Charnas, Tiptree, and Elizabeth A. Lynn. Barr concluded that "feminist scholars and writers are busily engaged in the creation and understanding of a new feminist subgenre," but Barr's only gesture toward definition of this new object was: "It is women who are the heroes of feminist science fiction; relationships between women receive its chief attention" (1984: 84).

Writing for a general feminist audience, Barr reiterated her critique of the gulf between feminist critics working on sf and feminists in the broader literary critical community:

> With only a few exceptions, our most renowned feminist theorists have devoted little attention to texts written by feminist science fiction writers. Most of the articles on these texts have been produced by a coterie of nonfeminist men and women who comprise the surprisingly conservative science fiction critical community. Hence, feminist critics of feminist science fiction can find comfortable niches neither among feminist/women's studies scholars nor among science fiction critics. (1984: 84)

The decline in communication between general feminist critics and feminists in sf since the 1970s seems to reinforce Cora Kaplan's belief that theorists were increasingly cut off from the grass-roots of popular writing; certainly as feminist journals became more "academic" and professionalized, there seems to have been fewer openings for articles on sf (Kaplan 1989: 18).

The increasing disjuncture between a newly consolidated feminist sf criticism and its "sister" in the mainstream is reflected in the increasing substitution of the term "speculative fiction" for science fiction, beginning with the first single-author study of feminist sf, *Feminist Futures* by Natalie Rosinsky. Although obviously familiar with material produced within the sf community (and herself a participant in fan activities), Rosinsky to some extent rejected the newly-constituted object "feminist sf" in favor of the term feminist speculative fiction. Rosinsky also considered more "mainstream" texts, thus sidestepping the emergent canon that had been the focus of criticism within the sf community. Consequently, her study was later situated by feminist sf critic Robin Roberts as part of a trend within mainstream feminist criticism that distorted feminist sf's genre legacy by forging links with the mainstream (R. Roberts 1995: 186-7).

A few years later, in 1987, the first single-author study to be firmly situated within the sf field was published: Barr's *Alien To Femininity: Speculative Fiction and Feminist Theory* (1987). To remedy her concern about the lack of connection between feminist theory and sf, Barr linked prominent feminist theorists with a number of feminist sf texts, bringing to bear, often for the first time in feminist sf criticism, the insights of critics such as Nina Auerbach (linked with Charnas, Tiptree, and Russ), Annis Pratt (Butler, Piercy, and Phyllis Eisenstein), Jane Gallop (Tanith Lee, Joan Vinge, and Lisa Tuttle), and Nancy Chodorow (Zoe Fairburns, Kate Wilhelm, and Jody Scott).

The late 1980s and 1990s saw the appearance of many more book-length studies of feminist sf, which worked to consolidate the position of feminist sf criticism (and initiate a "canon" of critical work). The larger scope and length of single-author studies allowed discussion of a broader range of texts as well as the elaboration of personal theories and taxonomies of feminism(s) in sf. Rather than viewing such studies as evidence of the consolidation of a long tradition of feminist criticism, however, many commentators heralded these works as entrants in "the still-new field of feminist SF criticism" (Davis 1994: 84).[36] In the remainder of this chapter, I consider how these texts synthesize the twenty-year history of feminist critiques in sf, while also tracing the re-assertion of "counter-hegemonic" or resistant narratives.

Counter-narratives: Re-asserting herstories

Throughout the 1980s, alongside the trend to consolidate feminist sf and its criticism, counter narratives persisted, seen in continuing searches for earlier women writers and analyses of more popular female writers, as well as claims that women's influence in the field predated the women's movement. This counterposition notably resurfaced in 1992, in the midst of the most active period for the publication of book-length studies of feminist sf, voiced by a writer outside the critical community and part of a newer cohort of female sf authors more likely to be considered "post-feminist." In "The Women SF Doesn't See," Connie Willis challenged the history of the field reiterated in many feminist critiques; namely the notion of sf as a masculine field that only recently saw changes which, if not initiated by the women's movement, were at least contemporaneous with it. The quote from Willis prefacing this chapter is her parody of feminist critical narratives about sf, which she challenges by recalling women writers who

36 Although at least one critic was less enthusiastic, asking, "Do we really need yet another book on science fiction and feminism?" (L. Williams, cited in R. Roberts 1995: 184).

had been neglected by feminist critics. Her list corresponds almost exactly with those writers of the 1950s Sargent discussed in 1974 and 1976: Kit Reed, Mildred Clingerman, Zenna Henderson, Shirley Jackson, Margaret St. Clair, Judith Merril, and C.L. Moore. Willis's stated rationale for this "recovery" was: "Not because of their historical importance, but because they wrote great stories, stories I'd remembered all these years." But as Willis herself suggests, these texts *do* have historic importance—even if only in terms of her personal reading history, as stories that she had "loved as a teenager" and was later surprised to find "how many of them had been written by women" (1992: 4-5).

In this emphasis on the personal, Willis's essay does not have to be read as a "counter-feminist" move, for, in Angela McRobbie's words, "politics occurs in the act of breaking away from the claim to be represented" (1994: 73). Willis here was rejecting the dominant feminist narrative that claimed to talk of the experience of liberated women in sf, with a focus on a small group of contemporary writers according to a taxonomized "feminism" with its roots still firmly in the (white) utopianism of the 1970s. Reading Willis's article marked a significant change in my own constructions of feminist sf and criticism, as it did for other critics such as Justine Larbalestier (who first brought this article to my attention) and Lisa Yaszek. As Larbalestier recalled, it was Willis's article that made her go back and read these authors. She, like myself, had accepted the covert (and often overt) dismissal of these authors by feminist (as well as sf) critics and had removed them from her conceptual space of "feminist sf."

However, not all earlier feminist sf criticism had devalued earlier women's writing as insufficiently feminist. In the mid-'80s, Diane Cook not only presaged many of Willis's objections to the lacunae in feminist narratives, but was also one of the few critics at the time to make a convincing argument for linking women's sf, herstory, and feminist sf. "Yes Virginia, There's Always Been Women's Science Fiction...Feminist Even" was originally a paper given at the World Science Fiction Convention in Melbourne, Australia (Cook 1985). Cook began with the popular perception that women and sf were incompatible: "When I tell people that I am researching women's science fiction, the response...is almost inevitably: *is* there any?" (133) Instead of the usual reference to the male-dominated character of sf, Cook emphasized women's *presence*, however marginalized or lacking in "visibility and creditability":

> But women writers have contributed to sf since its inception, and although feminist sf has only recently become a genre or sub-genre in its own right, there have always been feminist elements in women's sf. (133)[37]

In a discussion of the history of women's sf from Shelley through the nineteenth century utopias and Gilman's *Herland*, Cook, like many other critics, situates C. L. Moore as a focal writer who "reintroduced strong, complex women to speculative fiction." Cook provides a more critical view of Moore's work than, for example, Gubar (particularly Gubar's suggestion that "Shambleau" can be taken as an ambiguous metaphor for female sexuality) (Cook 1985: 137).[38] Cook argued that while Moore's work was not explicitly feminist, it helped establish a precedent for strong female protagonists, especially characters such as Deirdre of "No Woman Born," who "constitute[d] a significant challenge to patriarchal authority." In discussing the writers to follow Moore, Cook was concerned to challenge the trend to categorize women's sf from the 1940s-1950s as "wet-diaper" sf: "Derogation of domestic sf, for example, has obscured the significance of the bulk of more than a decade of women's sf" (143-4).

Emphasizing the constraints on women writers in this period of cold war conservatism, Cook argues that the emphasis on domesticity in women's writing, while not surprising, was not necessarily reactionary: "the 'wet-diaper' label is a ridiculously superficial and sexist dismissal which...denies the artistic integrity of a large body of women's work, and ignores a considerable amount of covert feminism" (138). The label "domestic sf" had been perpetuated not only by male critics such as Amis, but also by feminists such as Russ. In contrast, Cook emphasized that writing about such "trivial" subjects as domestic work and childcare could itself be a progressive measure—"[j]ust

---

37 Cook defined "feminist elements in women's sf" as "implicit or subtextual references to women's status, as concerns for women's welfare which lie beneath a work's more ostensible concerns" (134).

38 Cook also points out the troubling aspects of the Jirel of Joiry story, "Black God's Kiss," where, although Jirel successfully fights off the conqueror Guillaume, Jirel's remorse after her revenge (and subsequent discovery of her love for him) can be seen "as a woman's ultimate recoil from retaliation against a rapist, and her right to fight back is consequently undermined" (138).

putting women's domestic lives onto the sf agenda was a remarkable feat." Further, she argued that "domestic sf" considered the social consequences of science in the arena where they often were felt hardest—"Women may have had little knowledge of or power over science, but they have always been well-versed in its effects"—and cites Merril's "That Only a Mother" and Zenna Henderson's "Subcommittee" as examples (139).[39] Whilst an emphasis on the domestic sphere alone may not constitute in and of itself a "progressive" measure (unless its purpose was as a means of reassessment and critique of women's domestic role), Cook indicates the problems of a feminist criticism that (even inadvertently) colludes with the binary discourse trivializing the actions of women within their "appropriate" sphere. In a new formulation of "women in sf" and "feminist sf," Cook situated the work of earlier women writers as the basis for progression towards the overt questioning of gender roles in Russ, Tiptree, and Wilhelm. Cook emphasized that such writers did not "spring spontaneously from the so-called 'second wave' of feminism" but from numerous influences, including the "development of humanist and feminist ideas in women's sf since Frankenstein. There is a heritage of ideas, if not a tradition" (140).

Consolidating the object: Deconstructing the subject

Sarah Lefanu's *In the Chinks of the World Machine* (1988) may be seen as the first in a group of texts appearing in the 1990s, accompanied by work by Marleen Barr, Robin Roberts, and Jenny Wolmark, all of whom drew on postmodern theories to define and canonize various feminist sf texts in a dialogue with both overlapping and diverging positions. Sarah Lefanu was one of the first critics to provide a clear taxonomy of women's sf and feminist sf and to offer a more detailed analysis of how various interventions—such as women protagonists, role reversals, or the privileging of biological and life sciences over physical sciences—interrupted sf conventions, tropes, and narratives. For example, Lefanu argued that although an emphasis on "traditionally feminine values" (using a female hero or emphasizing "soft sciences" or "nature" over the hard science of traditional sf) did challenge science fictional norms, "there is a danger that this SF might

---

39 These connections between science and domesticity are taken up in greater detail in Yaszek's *Galactic Suburbia* (2008).

slip too much into sentiment, and become ghettoized precisely as 'women's sf'" (92).

Thus for Lefanu, writers like Le Guin, McIntyre, and Joan Slonczewski, who she sees as representing a "progressive" strain within the sf mainstream, "function within the paradigm of woman writer and patriarchal tradition: their concerns come from a sense of the exclusion and peripheralization of women" (92). The problem with such a position for Lefanu, informed by poststructuralist theories, was that this "women's positioning" skirted an essentialist position:

> [I]t accepts, somehow, the naturalness...of sexual difference. While it runs counter to prevailing ideology by prioritising women over men, and feminine over masculine, and thus challenges the end result of that ideology, it does not interrogate its construction. (92-3)

Such work is termed by Lefanu as a "feminised body of work" rather than "feminist" sf (93). It is here that the crux of the difference between "feminist" and other positions lies in Lefanu's analysis—between challenges to and inversions of sexual difference on the one hand and the *deconstruction* of sexual difference and gender roles on the other. Lefanu claimed she was "not trying to construct here a hierarchy of feminism, to measure one writer against another and find one lacking. I want to show the ways in which science fiction is feminism-friendly" (95). However, Lefanu does establish a specific manifestation of feminism—that influenced by poststructuralism—as the benchmark for her examination of sf's "feminist-friendly" potential.

In one sense Lefanu provides a super-consolidation of the object "feminist sf," a label referring to a small group of writers that partially overlaps, but also departs from, previous nascent canons. Writers speaking from "a position of (transformed) authority" (including Mary Gentle, C.J. Cherryh, Octavia Butler, and Cecilia Holland) (88-9)[40] and those speaking from "a position of (newly validated) sen-

---

40 Lefanu situates texts by these authors as ones that retain much of the structures and institutions of traditional sf, while placing authority in a central female character. Lefanu compares her analysis with that of Jenny Wolmark, who suggests that such undermining of stereotypes within a traditional framework produces more of a sense of dislocation than is found in texts that rewrite sf's "narrative conventions" from a feminist perspective. However Lefanu argues that the "undermining of sexual and racial stereotypes exists in an uneasy tension with...unquestioned assumptions," defined by Wolmark as the "social and economic structures of

timent" (Le Guin, McIntyre, and Joan Slonczewski) (90-94) fall outside her category of "feminist sf." For Lefanu, "feminist sf" applied
to writers who "deconstruct notions of essentialism from a relativis-
tic position: Pamela Zoline, Rhoda Lerman, Monique Wittig, Angela
Carter, Joanna Russ, and James Tiptree Jr." (94).

Russ is the one author on Lefanu's list who is included in every
feminist sf canon and whose presence is never contested. James Tiptree Jr. holds a similar position (since "her" identity was revealed at
any rate), although some critics have provided more complex readings
of "his" feminism (Boulter 1995). Pamela Zoline is one of the few
writers simultaneously claimed for the new wave tradition by male
critics as well as by feminists—all on the basis of one short story, "The
Heat Death of the Universe." Monique Wittig is similarly claimed almost universally as one of "the" canonical feminist sf writers, and her
novel *Les Guérillères* used to exemplify a mode of theorizing. Most
definitely written outside the Anglo-American sf community, this
radical French novel holds perhaps a stronger position in the feminist
sf canon than in the feminist literary canon. Angela Carter, whose
eclectic style resists classification simply as fantasy, sf, or magic realism, similarly rides both the mainstream and sf canons; a number of
her works are claimed by critics for the feminist sf canon.[41]

A reading of Zoline's story helps situate what for Lefanu is the
central problematic in her taxonomy of feminism:

> ["Heat Death"] at once centralises and deconstructs "wom-
> an." This, I think, exemplifies a problem that structuralist
> and post-structuralist criticism poses for feminists: the radi-
> cal, or transgressive aspects of the structuralist subversion of
> the subject do not allow for an analysis that shows "woman"
> never to have been the subject in the first place. (98)

While Lefanu's taxonomy of "feminist sf" per se is rather restricted,
her approach leaves open possibilities for a more fluid categorization

---

patriarchal, capitalist society which are incorporated wholesale into the stories"
(Wolmark 1986: 51).

41 Unlike a number of other mainstream authors however, Carter was open to her
texts being read as sf and indeed commented favorably on the reading strategies of sf readers: "I'm not worried about alienating readers by all my allusions,
as science fiction addicts are quite prepared to look up things they don't know,"
Kenyon, Private conversation with Carter, 3 Aug. 1985, (cited in Kenyon 1991:
16). See also Luckhurst's reading of Carter and feminist sf (2005).

of feminist engagements with sf (or feminist friendly work), not all of which would necessarily produce "feminist sf'" texts. The second half of her book covers writers who engage with feminism and sf in different ways, devoting a chapter each to the work of Tiptree, Le Guin, Charnas, and Russ. In Lefanu's words, the work of these authors "expresses, in different ways, the conjuncture of politics and the imagination" (101).

A different tactic is used by Robin Roberts in *A New Species: Gender and Science in Science Fiction*, which she describes as "the first overview of science fiction from a feminist perspective" (1993: 1). Roberts also draws on postmodernist theories, primarily to authorize readings of a number of texts outside the usual canon, including, for example, nineteenth-century sf, pulp magazine art, and the novels of Doris Lessing. A central thesis of her book is that "the genre has always acknowledged the power of the feminine through its depictions of the female as alien" (1). Roberts expands this theme through her readings of pulp sf art, whose depictions of female aliens are described as a legacy to feminists (40).[42] She argues that pulp sf had a more proto-feminist configuration than any critic has acknowledged: "[p]ulp science fiction is one of the 'stones available in the house' of patriarchy; and, wisely, feminist science fiction writers have not hesitated to use these stones against the house or even as the material for new texts" (47).[43]

Roberts' book is an important attempt to provide a historical overview of feminism in sf. She constructs an unusual taxonomy, which separates feminist sf from feminist utopian texts, a model that may have resulted from her focus on discrete historical periods. This distinction seems contradictory at times, delineated neither by historical period (e.g., '70s utopias) nor by a postmodernist-feminist positioning such as Lefanu's. Roberts' chapter on postmodernist feminist sf, for example, predictably focuses on Le Guin's *Always Coming Home* and Atwood's *The Handmaid's Tale*, but also rather strangely on Joan

---

42 Although Roberts calls on poststructuralist theory to "license" her readings of these visual images, the problematic relationship (in production and content) between the image and the text is not satisfactorily resolved.

43 In a footnote to this statement, Roberts defines protofeminist as "containing characteristics that resemble modern feminist ideas, but in a primitive or undeveloped form. Unconsciously, pulp science fiction writers and artists created female characters who are potentially feminist heroines" (65).

Slonczewski's *A Door into Ocean* and Sheila Finch's *Triad*. Roberts distinguishes postmodernist feminist sf from feminist utopias, which she characterizes as limited by their "separatist demarcation" with less room for "ambiguity and difference" (90). Following this categorization, she assigns *The Female Man, Motherlines,* and *Woman on the Edge of Time* to the "limited" feminist utopia, whereas much less overtly feminist texts are "privileged" (according to Roberts' own classification) as "feminist sf," including Andre Norton's *Witchworld,* Joan Vinge's *Snow Queen,* and C.J. Cherryh's "Cassandra." Thus whilst Roberts integrates a variety of texts in order to disrupt hierarchical canon-building practices, and invoke a broader "sense of history," she nevertheless re-creates definitional categories codifying narrative practice and thematic concerns that ultimately disengage texts from their historically specific conditions of production.

It is instructive to compare Roberts with Lefanu, especially on the issue and meaning of "essentialism." At first sight, Roberts' definition of feminist sf does not seem to deviate significantly from Lefanu's:

> Feminist science fiction looks at the dualities of masculine and feminine, traditional science and feminist science, and shifts the terms of the pairing to privilege the marginal over what is usually central. And in the process it deconstructs the binarisms of patriarchy. (1993: 90)

Roberts claims that feminist utopias frequently espouse a form of essentialism (because they resolutely idealize all-female societies), whereas feminist sf does not. She classifies as "feminist sf" texts such as Sheri S. Tepper's *Gate To Woman's Country,* which, in Lefanu's terms, is "essentialist" as it does not challenge the construction of binary notions of gender (Lefanu 1988: 91). But where Roberts portrays the deconstructive act as somehow inevitably produced by the act of reversal or privileging, in Lefanu's analysis, it is precisely the *difference* between these two acts (i.e., that of mere "reversal" as opposed to "deconstruction") that constitute the division between feminized and feminist sf. Lefanu's distinction is much more subtle and far-reaching. It is not enough, in Lefanu's taxonomy, to write of strong women, role reversals, or even very unconventional women; to be feminist sf, the writer must "deconstruct notions of essentialism" and interrogate the very construction of gendered identity (Lefanu 1988: 94). Lefanu's analysis suggests a spectrum with women's sf at one end, moving through "feminized sf," which, while challenging traditional sf narratives and conventions, still retains "the naturalness of sexual difference" and is thus distinguished from the other end of the spectrum, feminist sf. But, as Gwyneth Jones comments, in Lefanu's argument "an illusion remains of progression away from the fatal error of essentialism." Jones further notes the importance of this essentialism in the often "inadequate" feminized role-reversal stories to the very existence of the phenomenon of feminist sf: "It is extremely difficult to accuse, or even to question gender roles without first awarding them a powerful presence in the narrative" (Jones 1988: 60). Veronica Hollinger offers a more positive view of Lefanu's enterprise, which she argues invites reflections on the construction of the "subject" of feminist sf: "Her theoretical position invites the reader to conclude that a simultaneous deconstruction of exactly that subject may also be in order" (Hollinger 1989: 226).[44]

In *Aliens and Others*, Jenny Wolmark uses themes or patterns of feminist sf to structure her analysis in a similar fashion to that of Lefanu, but engages with a broader range of theorists (1993). Postmodernism is followed through the work of critics such as Andreas Huyssen, Brian McHale, Frederick Jameson, and Jean Baudrillard, and its relation to feminism explored through reference to Linda Hutcheon, Linda Nicholson, and Toril Moi, and the cautionary views of Meaghan Morris and Christine Di Stefano.[45] Thus the context for Wolmark's study is provided by the intersections between feminism, postmodernism, and sf, which can draw our attention to "the need constantly to redefine positions and meanings" (3).[46] Wolmark defines her contextual basis further:

---

44 cf. Hollinger, "Feminist Science Fiction: Breaking up the Subject" (1989: 229-39).

45 This provokes the comment from reviewer Frances Bonner that *Aliens and Others* has "'higher' theoretical underpinnings than Lefanu's... I cannot imagine it having the same number of readers, for its address is not at all to the general reader, nor even to the feminist who has failed to keep up with postmodernism" (1994/1995: 89). Considering the implication that the audience is thus more likely to be academics, it is even more significant that Wolmark discusses popular texts that many sf readers would be familiar with, but literary academics may not be.

46 Hollinger characterizes Wolmark's work as a significant entry into "the ongoing dialogue among cultural theorists about the complex interactions between feminism and postmodernism" (1994: 235).

The use of the term "intersections" is intended to suggest those cross-over points where discourses become openly contradictory, and boundaries become flexible and subject to renegotiation. Feminist science fiction exists at just such a point of intersection, or intertextuality. (3)

Wolmark recognizes the differences inherent in the sf texts she discusses, produced by the varied responses to the "unstable terrain of cultural and gender politics," but sees a certain shared agenda that is "concerned in some way with redefining the female subject outside the binary oppositions that seek to fix gender identities in the interests of existing relations of domination" (4).

While echoing elements of Lefanu's definition, Wolmark extends her analysis to a wide range of sf texts, including a *Star Trek* novel by Vonda N. McIntyre and work by Cherryh, Tepper, and Mary Gentle, for example. Particularly interesting is the final chapter on "Cyberpunk, Cyborgs and Feminist Science Fiction." Here Wolmark covers not only the work of Pat Cadigan (often dubbed the "only" female cyberpunk writer), but also that of Marge Piercy and the lesser-known writers Rebecca Ore and Elisabeth Vonarburg, whose work confronts "questions concerning the impact of information technology on social relations...from outside the framework of cyberpunk" (1993: 127).

Wolmark's discussion of the intersection of postmodernism and feminism concurs with those feminist theorists who warn against conflating the two. Her positioning in this debate appears in sharp contrast to the other major treatment of postmodernism and feminist sf in works by Marleen Barr. Barr's argument in *Feminist Fabulation* (1992) and *Lost in Space* (1993) is that feminist sf should be reconfigured as "feminist fabulation" in order to assume its "natural" and rightful place in "the postmodern canon." Her position here, as in all her work, stems from the frustration shared by so many feminist sf critics at the marginalization of feminist sf within mainstream feminist criticism. While numerous critics have concurred with her sentiment, many disagree with her tactics. Wolmark herself emphasizes the differences in their approach:

> In an extraordinary about-face, Barr has turned from being a vociferous advocate of the significance of the writing practices of feminist SF, to becoming an ardent supporter of a postmodern literary canon which has expanded to

accommodate what she calls "feminist fabulation." Since
this term includes what used to be known as feminist SF, it
is clear that generic specificity has been abandoned in favour
of "an umbrella term for describing overlapping genres..."
The claim that "Reinventing the canon coincides with reinventing womanhood" emphasises the essentially conservative nature of the position Barr has adopted: the reinvention
of the canon unquestioningly puts in place the same binary
opposition of high and popular culture against which Barr
insists she is arguing; in the same way, the reinvention of
"womanhood" places gender back into the context of the
binarisms of fixed subject positions, against which feminist
SF has been arguing. (25)

Barr's position is problematic for some critics for two reasons: first
because of the way such an approach removes feminist sf from its
generic context and second in its conflation of a feminist position
with postmodernism. As Hollinger notes, "[i]t may be the case, in
fact, that most feminist cultural production—including feminist
sf—is definitely *not* postmodern" (1993: 274).[47]

Next generations

Single-author studies of feminist sf reached their apogee in the
early 1990s, and in many ways the object "feminist sf criticism" began to disperse seemingly at the very point of its coherence. The flur-
ry of single-author studies of feminist sf came to a temporary halt
with Wolmark's text, but feminist criticism in sf continued to grow
and develop through numerous journal articles, special issues, collections, and even the appearance of *Femspec*, an academic journal
explicitly devoted to feminist sf. The subject of feminist sf criticism
became less unitary, with a broadening of interest in gender, race,
and queer theory. While canonical authors such as Le Guin, Russ, and
Tiptree continued to attract significant attention, at the same time
the breadth of criticism appearing, covering popular authors, newer
writers, and also different media, began the task of "breaking up the
subject" of feminist sf. Both the major sf journals again published

---

47 Indeed, this relation came under scrutiny in the mid- to late-1990s in relation to
    cyberpunk, discussed in Chapter Six.

special issues on feminist sf (*SFS* in 1990 and *Extrapolation* in 1995). From the early 1990s a number of studies focused on feminist sf as part of a utopian tradition (Andermahr 1992; Bammer 1991; Burwell 1997; Crowder 1993; Donawerth and Kolmerton 1994; Kessler 1995), while the gathering of herstories continued with the republication of the 1970s *Khatru* symposium (Gomoll 1993); and the fiction collections *New Eves* (Frank, Stine, and Ackerman 1994) and Sargent's new *Women of Wonder* collections (Sargent 1995a, 1995b).

The turn of the century saw a shift in the kinds of feminist criticism of sf being produced, marked appropriately by Barr's collection, *Future Females, the next Generation* (Barr 2000). Articles in collections such as this, along with others on cyberpunk or queer theory provided theoretically sophisticated and wide-ranging analyses of a gradually expanding set of texts (Merrick and Williams 1999; W. Pearson 1999; Wolmark 1999). The sorts of canon-building solidified in the first flush of single author studies was thus diluted through the sheer volume of articles and a shift away from the earlier attempts to develop taxonomies of feminist sf.

In contrast to their predecessors, the most recent spate of monographs approaches feminism and sf predominantly from the perspective of cultural history, rather than that of literary criticism, producing very different kinds of critical subjects (and objects). Presaged by Donawerth's 1997 *Frankenstein's Daughters*, this group of studies is not so much concerned with feminist sf, as with the differing texts and strategies produced by the intersection of feminisms and sf. Both appearing in 2002, Attebery's *Decoding Gender in Science Fiction* and Larbalestier's *The Battle of the Sexes in Science Fiction* (along with the later *Galactic Suburbia* by Yaszek) reconcile the continuing schism between women's and feminist sf by attending to and emphasizing the operation of gendered discourse over the course of sf history. *Daughters of Earth: Feminist Science Fiction in the Twentieth Century* (2006), a collection of largely noncanonical stories matched with critical essays, both implicitly and explicitly challenges the notion of a fixed feminist sf canon. These histories make clear the fact that the gendered dichotomies surrounding sex, sexuality, bodies, nature, and science are overtly and uniquely rendered in sf, producing the overriding anxieties about gendered binaries that make the genre ripe for feminist critique and appropriation. Thus, even when operating

outside feminist frameworks, the work and presence of women challenging and disrupting such discourses are framed as central to a feminist reading and appreciation of sf.

The consolidation of critical readings into a "sub-genre" like
feminist sf criticism has proceeded through dialogues around "shared
texts" and a basis of common reading experience. Whether intended
by each critic or not, each of these readings contributes to the classification of certain texts as the appropriate objects of study. While
for Robin Roberts, critical attention to more popular sf writers demonstrates "a resistance to canonization within the genre" (R. Roberts
1995: 191), in another sense such attention merely enacts a different
strand of canonization that may serve different constructions of the
object feminist sf. Also crucial to the formation of feminist sf criticism
are the theoretical, political, and critical positionings in relation to
feminism or feminist theory that differ according to institutional and
national location and generation. Readings informed by postmodernist or French feminist theorists produce very different demarcations
between feminist and women's sf than do those drawing on Shulamith Firestone or Adrienne Rich, for example. Given such a relatively
small field, gathered under a singular label, each reading and canonical taxonomy tends to be seen in a contestual debate, rather than a
complementary dialogue. But if we think instead, in terms of multiple and co-existing sf feminisms, much more complex and nuanced
conversations become possible. Doing so also reaffirms the readings
and activities of non-academic feminists in sf. For many readers and
fans of women's and feminist sf, talking and writing about these texts
is indeed a mark of feminist praxis, that, being driven by much more
personal and affective relations to sf texts collectively, produces quite
different taxonomies, genealogies, and herstories than those of literary criticism.

"FIAWOL," poster by Jeanne Gomoll, 1977, advertising a monthly meeting of The Society for the Furtherance and Study of Fantasy and Science Fiction (SF3). The Madison Wisconsin group met weekly, but produced formal programs once a month and marketed the events with flyers posted on the UW-Madison campus kiosks. The group recruited many members at these events.

5

FIAWOL: The Making of Fannish Feminisms[1]

As we work in the present...we must have the hope of a better
future to sustain us. Women's studies conferences, SF conven-
tions, smaller group interactions, women's and SF small press
publishing, these are our praxis as well as the place where we
can develop our theory, and from our theory, our future.

⇒ Janice Bogstad (1981: 2)

Coterminous with the development and establishment of academic sf criticism, similar struggles over the meaning of feminism
and women's fiction in sf occurred in the informal spaces of sf magazines, fanzines, and conventions. In the formative years of the early
'70s, these dialogues often featured many of the same voices, since au-
thor/critics, like Russ in particular, participated in fan debates. As the
epigraph from Bogstad suggests, in these conversations the "feminist
question in sf" was perhaps even more loaded, because these interactions were figured directly as feminist praxis and intervention. Clashes around the meanings of feminism, the sexual politics of fandom,
or even the key texts for consciousness-raising were, as the slogan ran,
intensely personal as well as political. Unlike the more formalized
spaces of academic debate, the feminists involved in fandom were frequently called on to explain or justify "feminism 101" to men and
women they were in direct contact with—often face to face. Despite
the creation of feminist-friendly spaces in fanzines and conventions,
to retain one's cultural connections to fandom, it was presumably necessary (no matter how difficult) to sometimes just walk away from or
ignore anti-feminist sentiment.

Encounters and tensions with earlier generations of female fans
could also be difficult, especially if these women perceived feminism
as an attack on their accomplishments as writers or fans in the days
when women's presence was less obtrusive. Thus in thinking about
the constitution of sf feminisms in fandom, recognizing the persis-
tence of counter-narratives is crucial, even more so than in academic

---

1 FIAWOL is a famous fannish acronym for "Fandom is a way of life."

feminist criticism, since such narratives reveal the very personal politicized debates conducted around feminist issues and the way sf acted as a frame for feminist praxis and cultural activity. This is particularly evident in engagements with non-feminist women or those who preferred to think of themselves as humanist or equi-sexist. Such tensions and conflicts reveal very clearly the terms of these debates and what was at stake in claiming a feminist space in sf and fandom. In drawing together evidence of such points of tension, an interesting figure emerged as a focal point—one who might seem out of place in a narrative about feminist fandom—author Marion Zimmer Bradley.

Bradley holds an ambiguous place in feminist sf criticism; recognized as an influential early female writer, her resistance to "mainstream" feminism and her very popularity has meant that she remains a fairly marginal figure in critical studies. However, from a lesbian and queer perspective, her fiction offers some early examples of challenges to heterosexuality. Bradley was at the center of a number of often heated debates about feminism, women's writing, and the history of women in sf. Thus in addition to framing the emergence of feminist fandom and tracing some of its key directions, publications, and political effects, this chapter also examines some of the exchanges involving Bradley as a case study of the complex stories and counternarratives circulating around feminism in 1970s fandom.

Becoming human

The 1960s is most commonly identified as a transitional period for women's involvement in fandom. Although greater numbers of women were entering fandom and becoming more visible, they still remained in the minority. Consequently, the stereotype (and atmosphere) of fandom continued to be masculinist, despite social rights movements and the increase in women's participation. The existence of femme-fan groups in the '50s did not appear to have any direct effects on women's entry into fandom in the '60s, beyond the influence of certain key individuals. The earlier cooperative efforts to construct a women's space in fandom seem to have left little impression a decade later. In a number of retrospectives on her experiences in fandom in the late '60s, for example, Susan Wood does not refer to any of the pioneering women editing fanzines in previous decades. The only reference to earlier femme-fans is a negative one: "Women's organizations in the '50s in fandom withered" (Wood

1978: 5). Wood's recollections of the fannish environment in the late-1960s are worth quoting at length.

> The stereotyped fan, in my generation, was still the bespectacled young, white, middleclass male, highly intellectual and socially inept. Some notable women, "femme" fans (as distinct from real fans?) (boyfen anyone?), published, wrote, ran conventions: Lee Hoffman had gafiated, but Bjo Trimble was involved with artshows and the *ST Concordance*, Juanita Coulson and Elinor Busby were coediting notable fanzines, as was Joyce Katz, then Fisher, whose woman-produced *What About Us Grils?* directly inspired my own first fanzine, several years later. Still, women were accepted mostly as appendages to notable fans, or as Token Men, at least until the WPSFA Phenomenon, which was, as Joe Siclari notes, "the largest invasion of single females ever to hit fandom til [sic] the Star Trek Eruption." (Wood 1977: 44; see also Wood 1978)[2]

Anecdotes from other sources reinforce Wood's view that in the '60s female fans were often considered little more than "appendages." A 1968 article by Robin White asks "Are Femme-Fans Human?" In the view of most male fans, she concludes, this depends largely on whether or not they are married. Before Robin White became involved with BNF Ted White, she reported being "chased" by "the guys," and regarded as a "sexy object"; after she "went out" with Ted, however, "[i]t was as if I had suddenly been born a real human being before their very eyes... I was no longer up for grabs. Once I was no longer a possible potential girlfriend, I was treated more like a common garden variety human-type person" (White 1968: 52).[3]

---

2   The WPSFA (Western Pennsylvania SF association) was a group formed by a number of female fans: "founding mothers" Linda Bushyager, "Ginjer" Buchanan, and "Suzle" (Suzanne) Tompkins in 1967. The term "gafiated" is a form of the fannish acronym GAFIA, "getting away from it all" which signals a temporary or more lasting stepping back from active fandom.

3   A similar anecdote was related by Jerry Kaufman to the timebinders electronic list: "At some con in the very late '60s, I met a young woman while wandering the hotel halls, and we decided to visit some room parties together. We walked into the first one, and a mass of men looked our way. With one voice, they roared, 'A GIRL!' and surged toward my companion. She turned and fled, and I never saw her again." Kaufman, timebinders list, 21/10/97, http://lists.sflovers.org/mailman/listinfo/timebinders.

Wood also wrote revealingly of the ambivalent status of the '60s female fan in her 1978 article "The People's Programming" (Wood 1978). In her early impressions, fandom was a welcoming space where fans would talk seriously to her, where people did not "play silly sex-role games, those games in which I was a misfit 'girl' in the 'real' mundane world. They accepted me as one of themselves" (4). In retrospect, Wood qualified the terms of her reception: "They accepted me as an Honorary Man" (4). Like Robin White, Wood perceived a significant change in her status after marrying a fan; but (writing from a '70s perspective) her analysis is expressed in explicitly feminist terms. Wood's experience of fandom was colored by the fact that she soon "became Partnered and then Married: as a woman (= 'sexual being') I was neutralized, safe. I could talk to men, without them, or their partners, feeling I was a Threat" (4).

In Wood's narrative, her gradual transition from "Honorary Man to Woman Fan" is accompanied by a change in fannish attitude from acceptance to incomprehension (and a measure of hostility).

> Saying that fandom was one big happy family earned me a couple of Hugos. Saying that fandom, like the rest of North American society, was sexist and did not necessarily treat women as individuals unless they denied the existence of sexism and denied their womanhood, earned me abuse. (5)

Wood earned those Hugos for her fanzines. Among the issues she started to complain about in fandom that earned abuse were the appearance of strippers or near-naked women as part of worldcon masquerades: "Complaining about dirty-jokes panels and strip-tease acts at...conventions was 'crazy libbers' behavior, 'making a fuss about nothing' (again), and terribly 'uptight'" (5).

Many of the women joining fandom in the late '60s and early '70s were also in the process of having their consciousness raised by feminist ideas—a development that jarred with many of the attitudes in their "second home" of fandom. As Wood noted, feminist fans were stimulated and encouraged in their efforts to change fandom by the writings and debates (in fanzines, magazines and cons) of authors such as Joanna Russ and Vonda N. McIntyre.[4] Not all fans were so re-

---

4   Wood mentions that McIntyre got "into a shouting match with Lester Del Rey about women" on a "women in sf" panel at PgHlange in 1970—perhaps the first such panel (1978: 5).

ceptive, however, as in some venues, "Joanna, Vonda, and a very few supporters were rousingly trashed for being bitter, vicious feminist bitches" (5).

In 1974, Wood was asked to moderate the first worldcon panel to address women's issues, "Women in SF: Image and Reality," at Discon II. Feminist fans such as Jennifer Bankier felt the panel was constrained by the presence of Leigh Brackett and Betty Ballantine—older women "who had made peace with the male-dominated field [and] said that women had suffered no discrimination" (Wood 1978: 6; see also J. Bankier 1974). The real debate happened in the hall and other rooms afterwards—an event many feminist fans pinpoint as their first realization of the potential and strength of feminist feeling amongst fans (see, for example, Gomoll 1986-87: 9). From this event flowed many other panels on women in sf and feminist issues: a Women's APA (AWA) started by Janet Small and Victoria Vayne, a women-only space at cons (A Room of Our Own), and feminist fanzines such as *Janus* (Wood 1978: 7). WisCon, held in 1976 (and continuing to this day), was the first sf convention to concentrate on feminist programming.

Feminist community building: The 1970s

The feminist fanzines produced in the 1970s are some of the few sources available for tracing the formation and development of feminist fan communities. The first, edited by Canadian Amanda Bankier, was *The Witch and the Chameleon* (*WatCh*), which only ran for six issues, from August 1974-1976. *Janus* was the longest running feminist zine, beginning in 1975 and continuing as *Aurora* from 1981 through to 1987, with a delayed final issue in 1990.[5] There were, however, other fanzines concerned with issues of gender and sexuality during this period. Jessica Amanda Salmonson edited *Windhaven*, and Seth McEvoy's *Pig Runners' Digest* (c. 1975) was described as "a discussion forum for writers on the topic of sexism and sexual preference in science fiction" (A. Bankier 1975: 42). *Women and Men* edited by Denys Howard (c. 1977) was considered in a review by Susan Wood as "the

---

5 *Janus* was initially edited by Janice Bogstad and Jeanne Gomoll, with help from the Madison sf group, SF³, then by a collective from 1981, with Bogstad leaving to form another zine, *New Moon: A Quarterly Journal of Feminist Issues in SF*. (Unfortunately, apart from a couple of specific articles, I was not able to obtain copies of this zine.)

most open and challenging of the new fanzines...an anti-sexist fanzine and letter-forum. Editor Denys Howard is a self-styled 'faggot'—an 'effeminist'" (Wood 1977: 44). Another feminist personalzine was *Orca* by Jennifer Bankier (sister of Amanda, editor of *WatCh*), which aimed to publish "items with a feminist, socialist-anarchist...humanist, or aesthetic persuasion" (cited in Wood 1977: 44). Avedon Carol's genzine (sometimes personalzine) *The Invisible Fan* (first published in 1976) also reflected, as its title suggests, Carol's feminist commitments.[6]

My construction here of feminist fan communities is necessarily constrained by my access to sources, with *Janus/Aurora* and *WatCh* being the only fanzines available to me.[7] However, since *Janus/Aurora* was so long-running and the Madison group has, with the yearly WisCon, remained at the forefront of feminist fan activity well into the twenty-first century, this community is an important one in the interaction of feminism and sf. Other forums vital to this construction process are now largely inaccessible, such as the debates and planning of club meetings, APAs, formal programming and informal chats at conventions. Some of the fervor and excitement of this period is, nevertheless, suggested through the letters and con reports available in these fanzines.

Jointly, *Janus* and *WatCh* signaled the growing number of fans (particularly women) who wanted to bring together their commitment to women's liberation with their fan interests.[8] As Rhoda Katerinsky, an editor at *Ms.* Magazine, commented in a 1976 letter to *WatCh*:

> There is a growing feminist movement within SF fandom, and results can be seen already. At the cons and meetings, sooner or later a little knot of women gathers in a corner and has a small c-r session, that covers not only SF but the whole feminist field, and we get support from each other and swap stories, feelings, and sisterly raps. Sometimes we also have sisterly fights, but almost everyone comes away from one of those mini-raps with another friend, and a feeling of belonging. And that is what fandom is all about. (1976: 25)

6 Background information provided by personal interview with Carol, 22 July 1996.

7 And these only as I managed to buy or get copies of them at WisCon 20. My thanks to editors Jeanne Gomoll and Amanda Bankier for their assistance in obtaining these copies.

8 For example, a letter from fan Kris Fawcett commented on the "steadily growing feminist element" in sf fandom in the early 1970s (1974: 4).

Rather than an all-male preserve celebrating the (masculinist) concerns of sf, fandom was seen by many women as a potential haven for the kinds of community and networking inspired by Women's Lib—a place to build "a room of one's own." Indeed, at the 1978 WesterCon, the first women-only space at a con was organized by Susan Wood, called "rooms of our own," which became features of other conventions (Gomoll 1986-87: 9).

The response to *Janus* (and *WatCh*) was an enthusiastic welcome from many female fans. Linda E. Bushyager's review of *Janus* commented: "It's basically a genzine, but fairly oriented towards SF—in particular, they've been running some of the best feminism-in-sf discussions around (it's popping up all over, gang! Whoopee!)" (L. Bushyager 1977: 11). The appearance of forums for feminist debate was similarly welcomed by Wood in a review of *WatCh*.

> For many of us, it's become indispensable: a rap group with friends, a support system, a source of laughter, insight and ideas. And...I am recommending it equally for...its approach, its politics, its community of interest: women, and the few men joining with us, concerned with sexism in the supposedly visionary SF world. (1977: 44)[9]

For Wood, such fanzines signaled a "real, positive change...in fandom and fanzines: a broadening of the community and its approaches, not primarily to SF, but to living" (1977: 44). *Janus* in particular served a number of functions within the fan community. It provided a site for critical analysis, gathered information on contemporary and earlier female writers, and was a forum for debate through letters and editorials. *Janus* created a space where the editors' and readers' dual interests in feminism and sf could interact, and in the process, function as a kind of praxis.

The editors' vision for *Janus* was outlined by Janice Bogstad in 1977.

> As my co-editor, Jeanne Gomoll, so aptly put it when we were criticized for militant feminism and political stances in some editorials, at this point we are not so much trying to change other people's minds with our writing as we are trying to develop our own consciousness. The kind of amateur

---

9   Unfortunately, this was the last issue of *WatCh* to appear.

writing and publishing that exists in fandom offers us a vital opportunity to explore such issues as feminist consciousness and language...even the possible effects of scientific developments on women... Increasingly as time goes by, feminist issues have become easier to explore in the context of fandom, partially because SF novels themselves explore such issues. (1977: 7)[10]

Readers and fans were thus developing feminist ideas in tandem with (and sometimes ahead of) the writers and texts they engaged with in the sf community; just as the writers were also "communicating with fan organizations and publications about their ideas in the process of developing them" (Bogstad 1977: 7). The tide of letters debating feminist issues indicates that many other readers—women and men—participated in this "development of consciousness." Indeed, the letters of comment (locs) in these zines often displayed evidence of struggles over the meaning and impact of feminism between male and female fans. Readers Adrienne Fein and Karen Pearlschtein, for example, expressed impatience with "male travelers" who "expect to give us equality in return for rewards" or who merely "tolerated" feminism (Fein 1977: 50; Pearlschtein 1977: 28; see also B.E. Brown 1978: 62).

"An evolution of consciousness": Bradley, fandom, and feminism

Of course it was not only men who might display antagonistic or ambivalent attitudes to feminism in fandom. A fascinating exchange occurred between Bradley and feminist writers and fans in the pages of *WatCh*, a debate that illuminated her uneasy relationship with the women's liberation movement generally and with the feminist fan community (and latterly, feminist sf critics). One of the best-selling contemporary sf authors, Bradley's beginnings were in the fan community, a link she maintained and encouraged through the specialized Darkover fandom, with which she was intimately connected for

---

10 This article was taken from an academic paper Bogstad delivered at the Symposium on "Post Industrial Culture" at the University of Wisconsin-Milwaukee; organized by the then-head of the Center for Twentieth Century Studies, Teresa de Lauretis, who along with Bogstad, Samuel Delany, and Darko Suvin participated in a workshop on sf.

a number of years, editing collections and publishing a magazine (*Marion Zimmer Bradley's Fantasy Magazine*).

The exchange was sparked by McIntyre's stringent feminist critique of Bradley's *Darkover Landfall* and included letters from writers such as Russ and Tiptree (using the name Racoona Sheldon), as well as two from Bradley herself (McIntyre 1974; Bradley 1978). *Darkover Landfall* begins with a spaceship crash-landing on an unknown planet and follows the survivors' attempt to re-create civilization. Their efforts are complicated by a conceit of the plot postulating a heavier gravity than that of Earth, which apparently dramatically increases the risks of pregnancy and necessitates the inactivity of pregnant women. One of the central female characters, Camilla Del Rey, becomes pregnant and is forced by the needs of the community to accept her condition against her will and relinquish her scientific duties for a life of largely inactive breeding.[11]

The plight of this character, the motivation for rendering women in such a compromised situation, and various passages about women's role in society and the women's liberation movement are the focus of McIntyre's critique. "In *Darkover Landfall*, MZB shows that she deeply distrusts and dislikes the feminist movement... She has, it seems, taken her views from anti-feminists who believe feminism to be the result of raging hormones, over-crowding, and a pathological hatred of children" (McIntyre 1974: 20). McIntyre's overall judgment is that the book is nothing less than a "strike against the feminist movement" (1974: 24).

The notion that *Darkover Landfall* was Bradley's deliberate attack on feminism was highlighted by McIntyre's citation of a particularly damning speech by one of the male characters, addressed to Del Rey:

> Man is a rationalizing animal, so sociologists called it "women's Liberation" and things like that, but what it amounted to was a pathological reaction to over-population and over-crowding. Women who couldn't be allowed to have children,

---

11 The name of this character appears to be a deliberate reference to Lester Del Rey. Bradley claimed that this book was a direct response to a statement made by Del Rey: "Once Lester Del Rey stood up at a conference and said that it didn't matter a particle to him if 95% of the human race died out. 'As long as enough survive to keep our technology alive,' he said, 'That's all it needs to take us to the stars. And that's all that matters.' That outraged me." And the result was *Darkover Landfall* (see Bradley 1977/1978: 16).

had to be given some other work, for the sake of their men-
tal health. But it wears off... By the time the baby comes,
you'll probably have normal hormones too, and make a good
mother. (Bradley 1978; cited in McIntyre 1974: 23)

McIntyre's attribution of this opinion to Bradley was perhaps misleading—as Bradley herself later pointed out, a character's statements
do not, of course, always reflect the beliefs of the author.[12] However,
the undertow of anti-feminist feeling in the book was further suggested by a statement made elsewhere by Bradley (which was pointedly
placed after Bradley's rebuttal of McIntyre's review in the third issue
of *WatCh*): "My latest book, *Darkover Landfall*, is supposed to be my
attack on a world which equates civilization with energy consumption
(with a few scathing snarls at Women's Lib)" (Bradley 1975a: 30).[13]
Bradley's initial reaction to McIntyre's review was to argue that the
feminist and anti-feminist statements in the book were only a secondary theme (1975a: 29). In one of the few letters supporting Bradley,
Jacqueline Lichtenberg wrote that she,

> flatly disagree[d] with Vonda's review... I know something
> of what went into that book, and polemics was *not* one of the
> ingredients. For every anti-feminist statement there is a pro-
> feminist statement elsewhere to balance it and the emphasis
> is on the TEARING IRONY of *technological Woman* thrown
> back to the status of breed cow. (Lichtenberg 1975: 28)[14]

In a second letter in issue four, Bradley gave a more detailed response,
along with some fascinating background information on her personal
convictions. Allowing the reproduced quote about "Women's Lib" to
stand, Bradley clarified her position as an attack on a certain sub-strata
of feminism—what she termed the "man-hating" castrating "variety"/stereotype, which was her only understanding of the movement
at the time of writing *Darkover Landfall* (1975b: 19).

---

12 Bradley accused McIntyre of falling into the trap of viewing this character as a
    "voicepiece of the author stating...her private convictions" (Bradley 1975a: 29).

13 Quoted from *The Alien Critic*, vol. 2, no. 4, #7, 1973, p. 22.

14 Lichtenberg began as a writer of Trek fiction for zines, then wrote professional
    Star Trek novels and her own series of Sime/Gen novels. She was a friend of
    Bradley's, and they used to exchange drafts of their work daily when writing
    novels (see Bradley 1977/1978: 19).

In a review of her life experiences, Bradley argued that sf was the first "genuinely non-sexist world" she encountered outside her own family, and that women who railed against sf's sexism were merely looking for a scapegoat to cover their own failure (1975b: 20).[15] Recalling her own experiences, Bradley argued that "freedom" should be seen in perspective:

> I grew up on a farm, and one takes it for granted there that women can work as hard as men. I did a man's work until I was in my late teens, and it seemed a positive pleasure to be able to spend my days at housework... The woman who spends her adolescence stacking hay, driving cows, milking and mucking out barns is not going to scream with agony at being allowed to spend her twenties and thirties making a few beds, cooking a few meals, washing a few dishes, and having the rest of her time, as I did, to do as much writing as I wanted. (1975b: 19)

She continued "Thank God I can [make my living]...at a dishpan and over a crib, where my hands are busy and my mind free, instead of working at some brain-grating office job which leaves my mind too jangled to <u>think</u>" (21). This argument would seem to be what "Racoona Sheldon" (her true identity still secret) termed the "I've made it why can't you" syndrome in an earlier issue of *WatCh*. Responding to a similar argument presented by Katherine Kurtz at a con panel, Sheldon called for a united front, as "the woman who makes it personally and alone is impoverished by the plight of her sisters, and has in effect accepted an insane reality" (1975: 26; The Katherine Kurtz comment was outlined in J. Bankier 1974).

Bradley's views here contrast sharply with a moving article written by a woman of a similar generation and circumstance (married with children), Kate Wilhelm (1975). Wilhelm was also seen as a problematic figure by feminist critics; indeed, Wilhlem's *The Clewiston Test* was the subject of a number of critical letters to *Janus* concerning the negative representation of lesbianism in the book (see, for example, Lynn 1977: 26; Salmonson 1977: 19, and Gomoll 1977,

---

15 "[W]hen I hear a woman say that her work has been rejected because she was a women, I can only assume that she would rather think it was rejected because she was a woman, than accept the hard fact that it was probably rejected because it just wasn't a good story" (Bradley 1975b: 20).

ed. comment). Wilhelm emphasized the immense difficulties faced by women attempting to make a career of writing. "There is prejudice from the first, originating in the beginning with the family. They'll think it's cute, or precocious, or at least, not dangerous, when a woman starts to write stories" (1975: 21).[16] Wilhelm's article addressed the generational conflict that seems to inform Bradley's difficulty with many feminist critiques, between women who had "made it alone" and those decrying an "unequal playing ground." Wilhelm recognized the impatience shown by some women who had succeeded in writing sf (including herself), "when we have had it with too many young writers who want someone else to come along and chop down the maze for them... What the older, established writers can give is not a secret of how to do it, but rather encouragement, testimony, support, and occasionally a good swift kick"(23). In the following issue "Racoona Sheldon" pointed to "the genuine generation gap" between Bradley and the younger feminists: "I've known some of those strong, inner-directed women who grew up on farms or in small towns and simply decided the world—not themselves—was crazy when they hit the social barriers." Such women, argued Sheldon, were not necessarily competitive with other women—including Bradley—but had the luck to "grow up unsquashed" (1976: 30).

One of the most interesting facets of the *WatCh* debate is the changing response to Bradley as she reveals more of herself in subsequent letters. The letters from Russ, in particular, gradually retreat from strident critique of Bradley's work toward a "gentler" negotiation of issues and acceptance of the political validity of differing personal experiences. Russ's first letter is an analytical critique of the assumptions about feminism displayed in Bradley's response, which notes that the question "of whether a woman's uterus belongs to her or to the community she happens to find herself in" was from the mid-'60s a "very hot political issue" that would necessarily provoke "vehement

---

16 She described a number of hurdles, such as convincing yourself to be a writer when others won't accept you as such, knowing the limits of outside responsibilities and learning to say "no." "I realized the world, everyone in it practically, will give more and more responsibility to any woman who will continue to accept it. And when the other responsibilities are too great, her responsibility to herself must go... It is generally expected that the children, the house, school functions, husband's needs, yard, etc. all come first, and the time left over is hers to use as she chooses. A woman who is determined to write has to reverse that order, and it is hard" (Wilhelm 1975: 21).

reactions" (Russ 1975a: 15). Russ argued that books such as *Darkover Landfall* (and all sf) could not be separated from the political and social assumptions underpinning them, and concluded that by relying on such assumptions, the book could be considered anti-feminist. Russ summed up the anger felt by feminist readers such as McIntyre:

> [T]o falsify biology (which Bradley does grossly in assuming that high gravity will have no effect on men, and no other effects on anyone) and to drag Anatomy-is-Destiny out of three-thousand-year-old mothballs in order to do so, is not an answer. Or an advance. It's the old you-can't-win slap in the face again. (1975a: 18)

The debate takes on quite a different tone following Bradley's second letter (in issue 4), where Bradley talked of her experience with local women's groups and about her sexuality:

> I have not really *intended* to become the spokesperson for the gay community in science fiction, but I have always known... that I was just as strongly homosexual as I was heterosexual...I have always felt free to write for lesbian publications, etc., under my own name, and have never made any secret of the fact that I consider myself at least bisexual, and probably, more honestly, an offbeat lesbian who simply manages to form occasional strong attachments to men.
> (Bradley 1975b: 22)[17]

Bradley also claims to have been among the forefront of writers who were open about sexual and homosexual relationships in sf. She describes herself as "the first writer...to deal with a woman character as a fully sexual being" in her book *The Bloody Sun* (1964); in *World Wreckers* (1971) she depicted "explicit homosexuality," and again in *The Heritage of Hastur* (1975); in *Centaurus Changeling* (1954) she "dealt with an intense, strongly emotionalized friendship between two women." In *The Shattered Chain* she creates the Guild of Free Amazons (which in later books features lesbian relationships) although she claims she "chickened out on lesbianism" in this book (Bradley 1975b: 22-23).

---

17 Bradley goes on, rather strangely, to claim that "mainstream [fiction] has been wide open to lesbianism for forty years or so; in 1962, with two lesbian friends, I catalogued over a thousand titles" (Bradley 1975b: 22)–a view in sharp contrast with Russ's discussion of lesbianism in her letter to the third issue of *WatCh* (Russ 1975c) and taken up by her second letter (Russ 1976: 11).

In Russ's second contribution, "A Letter to Marion Zimmer Bradley," she apologizes for her previous letter, describing it as "too flip" and "heartless," and admits admiration for Bradley's "hard work, her grit, her honesty, and her bravery"—whilst still disagreeing with Bradley on many points (1976: 9). In this letter, Russ provides an incisive review of the feminist movement, including the problems of "class snobbery and what...one might call... 'motherhood-snobbery'"—a result, argued Russ, of the initial, vehement reaction to sexism (9).[18] This letter—the final contribution to the debate—is a wonderfully informed and persuasive delineation of many of the tenets of feminist arguments, which would have been at home in any academic journal. It demonstrates the sophisticated and committed level of engagement that could occur in a small, amateur publication in the "ghetto" of the sf field.[19] The conflicts of generational, class, and personal difference evident in this "conversation" are neatly summed up by Russ, whose argument signals the importance and influence of personal "travels" through or against feminism(s):[20]

> I wish I could castigate Bradley as a sexist—which would make everything so easy!—but clearly she's not. I do have a horrible feeling, though, that much of what she says in her letter is exactly what I would've said in or about the winter and spring of 1968, which is when I first met feminism... I do feel that, having made sacrifices (including part of one's own personality) to get what one wanted, there's a strong human tendency to insist that the sacrifices were necessary. (1976: 12)

This was the last issue of *WatCh*, and thus the end of the "conversation." However another debate featuring Bradley occurred in *Janus/Aurora*, provoked by comments about her book *The Shattered Chain*, which continued for five issues.[21] In response to criticism from

18 This phrase is cited from Philip Slater (no reference given).

19 A good overview of the sheer volume, scope, and brilliance of Russ's writings, reviews, and letters can be sampled in her collection *The Country You Have Never Seen* (2007).

20 I use "travels" here to connect with Katie King's observations on personal reading histories (K. King 1994).

21 Lunch and Talk with Suzy McKee Charnas, Amanda Bankier, Janice Bogstad, and Jeanne Gomoll 1976; Round 2: Reactions to "Lunch and Talk" 1977.

Suzy McKee Charnas and Amanda Bankier, Bradley wrote: "I am not ashamed of *Shattered Chain*; it may have been a disappointment to women on the cutting edge of the front line of feminism, who wanted their ultimate wishes fulfilled in fiction." She continued:

> But from the reactions I have received, it reached the audi-
> ence I wanted: women still weighted with their "invisible
> chains" who, maybe, have begun to realize that maybe they
> are not as free as they thought they were, and may start won-
> dering, thinking, maybe doing something, however small. I
> am not an innovator. I realized that long ago. I take radical
> ideas and make them popular, I sneak them in under the de-
> fenses of conservatives. (Round 2: Reactions to "Lunch and
> Talk" 1977: 32) [22]

Establishing a demarcation between the "front-line feminists" associated with the *Janus* readership and newer writers (such as Charnas) and her own, more "populist" approach, Bradley called for recognition and compassion from "movement" women. A particularly interesting part of the exchange was Bradley's exploration of her bisexuality, sparked by comments that her status as a married woman protected her from the disapprobation accompanying the label "lesbian." She countered: "I am also sick and tired of having people think that being bisexual is somehow having the best of both worlds, that my marriage is some kind of 'protection.' Christ, no!" (Bradley 1977: 31; see also 39). An interesting plea for understanding appeared in a letter from lesbian author, Elizabeth Lynn.

> [Writers] balance our own changing, growing consciousness,
> the needs (as we perceive them) of our audience, our editors'
> prejudices, and the demands of our characters... We all do it
> differently, as the controversy in *Janus* [8], centring around
> *The Shattered Chain*, points out. Writers change, writers
> grow (often through the medium of their own book). We
> are not consistent all the time. (Nor are the demands of the
> reading public.) It would be just, I think, if that public when
> it wears its critical hat remembers these facts and attempts
> to be kind. (1977: 26)

---

22 Russ's response takes up Bradley's charges of feminist sf as "wish-fulfilment," and her argument for the worth of a populist (if less radical) approach (Round 2: Reactions to "Lunch and Talk" 1977: 34-35).

Not a feminist, but...

As Lynn's words remind us, people change, as does feminism it-self, and its relation to or resonance for individuals. A few years after these exchanges, Bradley offered some quite different reflections on women, sf, and feminism. In the article "My Trip Through Science Fiction," she gave an alternative perspective on the "ease" of her achievements in sf, referring to the debate over *Darkover Landfall*. In contrast to her earlier picture of the housewife happily "fitting in" her writing, she painted a more oppressive image of her life in a small town, where her "strange obsession" with sf was not well understood by her husband. This is made clear in a description of her "escape" from her first marriage and Texas to go to Berkeley,

> where I found a world sympathetic to writing as a career, and a husband who took it for granted that when there was an editor's deadline coming up, the laundry could lie un-washed on the floor, and registered mail for a manuscript wasn't something you had to sneak out of the housekeeping money. He's a writer, too. I sometimes think a woman writer should only marry another writer. (Bradley 1977/1978: 14)

A mark of Bradley's changing consciousness is her admission, which she had previously refused to divulge, that the source of her first sf novel sprang from personal experience. From the perspective of the late-1970s, Bradley recognized in *The Door Through Space* (1961) (a "rough sketch" for her later Darkover novels), "a portrait of [her] own younger self, trapped and savage in a hopeless marriage; a woman chained" (Bradley 1977/1978: 17). Bradley traced her evolv-ing personal consciousness through to her recent work, which pro-duced a better resolution—and a more feminist one—than her first, "hidden" image of herself as Dallisa, the chained wife.

> Not for twenty years did I see that in Dallisa I had created a portrait of myself, dying inside in the bleached and bar-ren lands of the Texas desert; and not for twenty years did I manage to create for myself, in *The Shattered Chain*, a band of Amazons who ride to the Dry Towns to set a chained woman free. (17)

Bradley's "Trip Through SF" also contains a reconsideration of the debate around *Darkover Landfall* (1977/1978: 16). Here Bradley accepts, to some extent, the "outrage" felt by feminist readers and situates the book as part of a dialogue, initially between herself and Del Rey, and carried on by Russ:

> I am told...that Joanna Russ has written a novel where, in similar straights, the women of the colony refuse to bear children at all, on the grounds that a colony based on ex-ploitation of women has no *right* to survive. Science Fiction writers are constantly amending, correcting, embellishing the ideas of their colleagues. (16)

The book referred to is Russ's *We Who Are About To...*, in which ac-tually only one woman refuses to have children and becomes embroiled in what Duchamp reads as a "life-and-death struggle over the politics of the body and a total breakdown in discourse" (2006a: 6). Russ totally overturns the precepts of Bradley's book, where "the common good was held more important than the personal convenience of any one wom-an" (Bradley 1977/78: 16). Russ's character declares: "*I* think that some kinds of survival are damned idiotic. So you want your children to live in the Old Stone Age? Do you want them to forget how to read? Do you want to lose your teeth? Do you want your great-grandchildren to die at thirty? That's obscene" (Russ 1987: 24-25).[23] Placed alongside *Darkover Landfall* and the *WatCh* debate, these texts provide a perfect example of some of the tensions, arguments, and possibilities evident in the cross-pollinating feminisms and sf stories of the mid-1970s.

At this stage, in the late 1970s, Bradley was more open about the constraints faced by women writers prior to the advent of feminist influences. Bradley admitted that, like other women writing for the pulps, her novels were constructed to appeal to a "masculine view-point" (which, well into the 1950s, meant few if any female charac-ters, especially in active roles)—a necessary decision to ensure sales (see Bradley 1977/1978: 16; 1977: 34-35). After the failure of her first couple of novels (which centered on female characters), Bradley admitted that her desire for publication brought the realization that she "would have to write about men... This was simply the rules of the game, the economic facts of life in the market" (1977: 35). This would presumably have been in the early 1950s, before her first major

---

23 And in response to the standard argument that "Civilization must be preserved," she answers: "Civilization's doing fine...We just don't happen to be where it is" (Russ 1987: 31).

sale, *Centaurus Changeling*, in 1953. *The Web of Darkness* (eventually published in 1983) is a fantasy about two sisters; *Window on the
Night* (unpublished) was about the first moon flight, "according to a
theory then current about the superior physical stamina of women, it
dealt with a crew entirely composed of women" (35).[24] In "An Evolution of Consciousness" (1977; a title inferring at least some connection to the women's movement), Bradley traces an impulse to present
strong, independent women from her earliest writings: an impulse
that (although curtailed by the pressures of the market) had, since
the 1960s, developed into a focus of her work. Whilst "An Evolution"
is colored by a rather defensive call to recognize her contributions to
the development of women characters in sf, the earlier essay "My
Trip" openly acknowledges the constraints imposed on her writing
by the market and herself. Here, she admitted that "[n]ot till 1976
did I dare write openly about women, in *The Shattered Chain*." By
this time other women were entering the field, welcomed by Bradley
as "sisters" and as an "exciting new development" in the sf world
(Bradley 1977/1978: 19).[25] However, in "An Evolution," she also re-
vises her rather optimistic viewpoint concerning homosexuality. In a
discussion of the lesbian possibilities of the Free Amazon "freemates"
(Darilyn and Menalla) in her novel *Winds of Darkover*, she admits: "I
didn't stress their 'marriage'; the book was written in 1970, and the
lesbianism was (and is) a stronger taboo in science fiction than male
homosexuality" (Bradley 1977: 39).

The narrative Bradley weaves around herself in such articles is of
a writer whose desire to present equal female characters has gradually
been allowed to (re)surface as the climate of sf "changed":

> I can now write of [women] as I always knew them to be:
> strong, independent, courageous, no longer yielding even lip
> service to the custom that they must sit and wait for the men
> to rescue them. I don't have to cover up their strength with a
> mask of conventional femininity. (Bradley 1977: 45)

24 Around this time there was an article in the British magazine *Authentic* on this issue,
arguing that women would make better astronauts than men (Downe 1955).

25 This article also refers to a time when Bradley wanted to quit sf, until Anne
McCaffrey gave her a copy of Le Guin's *The Left Hand of Darkness* (Bradley
1977/1978: 15); as a result, she wrote: "my discouragement with the whole
world of science fiction suddenly left me" (1977/1978: 19).

Yet this is not to say that Bradley suddenly became comfortable with "feminism" or would have seen herself as part of a developing movement of feminist writers and readers of sf. Bradley's reflective articles certainly display some revision of her opinion regarding feminist critiques of sf—partially redolent of Le Guin's "Redux" with its reconsideration of her own earlier work. Unlike Le Guin, however, Bradley's various commentaries remain contradictory, never comfortably resolving her position with regard to "feminism" and the "movement" (see Le Guin 1992b). In a later article published in the 1980s, much of Bradley's antagonism to "mainstream" feminism (or its stereotype) is again prevalent. In this case, Bradley may have been reacting against one of the side effects of the growing feminist critical attention to sf, which reiterated the absence of women. Like Connie Willis, Bradley was at pains to contradict this myth: "I have often heard the conventional wisdom about women in science fiction; namely, that there aren't any, or weren't before 1961. There's just one thing wrong with the conventional wisdom; it isn't true" (Bradley 1988: 84).[26] As in Willis's 1992 article, Bradley provided a list of female predecessors, from Tiptree, Norton, C.L. Moore, Leigh Brackett, and herself to Shelley and Inez Haynes Irwin, along with editors Dorothy McIlwraith and Mary Gnaedinger (Bradley 1988: 84-87).[27]

Bradley also attacked what she saw as the accepted feminist view of earlier writers such as Leigh Brackett: that in their use of "male" pseudonyms, male characters and points-of-view, they were writing "like a man" and "selling out to the male establishment" (1988: 87).[28] In Bradley's narrative, a legitimate feminist critique of the restrictive circumstances of the early sf field—from audience expectations to editors and publishing concerns—is perceived as a personal attack

---

26 Unfortunately, the original publication details for the articles in this collection are not given.

27 Inez Haynes Irwin (who also published under the name Inez Haynes Gilmore) wrote the fantasy *Angel Island* in the 1920s, which, according to Bradley, "proved, without alienating the male audience for whom it was written, to be a most powerful metaphor of feminism" (Bradley 1988: 85). (Note Gilmore was her first husband's surname and Irwin was her second husband's.) Dorothy McIlwraith was editor of *Weird Tales* after the death of Fritz Leiber, and Mary Gnaedinger edited *Famous Fantastic Mysteries* (see also C. Willis 1992).

28 Bradley cites Pamela Sargent's view of Brackett presented in the introduction to *Women of Wonder*: "She writes like a male, and a male steeped in machismo at that" (Bradley 1988: 87).

on the credibility of the individual women who, despite these constraints, succeeded in the field. Indeed Bradley herself implicitly recognized such constraints, arguing that Brackett "filled the perceived needs of the marketplace."

> True, her stories told of the dealings of men; so did mine...
> *All* science-fiction stories in the forties and fifties were about
> men; Leigh could not have sold them otherwise. Had she
> chosen to write solely about women, she could only have
> published them at a vanity press. (1988: 88)

Bradley exaggerated here; Judith Merril, Carol Emshwiller, and Zenna Henderson among others wrote stories from a woman's perspective in the 1940s and 1950s—and they, too, have been subject to similar feminist critiques of the limitations of their work (whether or not dictated by the social and cultural context).[29] Bradley, along with a number of other female writers whose careers started before the 1960s, has until recently been largely absent from feminist taxonomies within sf (see for example, Yaszek 2008). Throughout the numerous articles in which Bradley erratically engages with "women's issues," a common thread is her determination to be able to define her own "brand of feminism." Indeed, in a 1985 article, Bradley shows awareness of and concern for many issues central to feminism. Commenting on the rise of Darkover fandom around her books, she felt that she had made available a site for fans to discuss,

> especially sensitive subjects on which I can only touch in my
> books. It is easier, and safer, for these young people to talk
> about women's rights, homosexuality, unusual approaches to
> religion, gender roles in society, and extrasensory perception
> on Darkover rather than in the worlds of suburbia or middle
> America where they themselves live. (Bradley 1985: 80)[30]

This "trip" through some of Bradley's interactions and altercations with certain sections of the women's movement suggests the

---

29 Indeed, Bradley goes on to mention one of Merril's novels, *Shadow on the Hearth*, as a "successful attempt to write typical women's fiction within the context of science fiction"; however, she classes it (as some feminist critics have done) as a story more suitable to the *Ladies' Home Journal* (1988: 91-92). See Yaszek (2008) for a more nuanced consideration of these writers.

30 See also Bacon-Smith for reports from fans and writers who found a "haven" in darkover fandom and its conventions, such as Melissa Scott (2000: 116-20).

boundaries of the feminist community/ies being built in sf in the early to mid-1970s. Like a number of other authors (from Russ and Le Guin to Norton), Bradley engaged in dialogues with excited, younger sf readers with feminist commitments in the pages of *WatCh* and *Janus* (and with different communities of fans and writers in other fanzines). An important focus for this communication between young feminist fans (and authors) and older female writers was the fans' attempt to reconcile their current (1970s) desires with the material that guided their entry into sf. Work by authors such as Bradley, Norton, and McCaffrey, which had portrayed strong women, had often served as "rite of passage" books for the '60s and '70s generations of female readers. Yet by the mid-1970s, such material no longer produced the "click" of consciousness some readers required for a *feminist* "sense of wonder" (Wood 1978/1979: 10; see also Kelso 2000).

Writing feminist fandom into being

In the late 1970s, *Janus* provided the only dedicated space for serious, feminist analysis of sf, producing criticism that was as sophisticated as the articles that had begun to appear in sf journals a few years earlier. This is not really surprising, since most of the earlier articles appearing in the more "academic" forum of the journals were written by women who were also fans, or writers involved in the fan community, such as Russ, Badami, and Friend. Examples included critical reviews of collections of women's sf such as *New Women of Wonder* and *Cassandra Rising* (Gomoll 1978/1979b: 32-36; Kidd 1978; Laurence 1978; Sargent 1978b), articles such as Gomoll's "Post-Holocaust Themes in Feminist Science Fiction" (1980), and reviews of feminist anthropology and science texts (Lucas 1981/1982, 1982). Another important critical function of the zine was the effort to recover "herstory" by building a bibliography of female and feminist writers. Sparked by an interest in the rapidly increasingly proportion of female sf writers since 1970, Bogstad began a project to document this "manifestation." The project included interviews with newer female sf writers and the compilation of an audio and visual archive of readings and interviews with a broad range of female authors (Bogstad 1978/1979). Bogstad's editorial announcing the project included a preliminary list of 49 female writers, which Bogstad invited readers to expand on (1978/1979: 7). A couple of issues later the results of readers' suggestions were published as a "compendium" that added another 131 names, making a list of 180 female sf and fantasy writers (Compendium 1979).[31] Letters followed praising the project from readers desiring more information on "excellent and grossly underrated 'older' writers" (Logan 1980: 34). A campaign began to collect nominations for under-appreciated female writers for an issue on "Invisible Women." Readers such as Anne Laurie Logan complied, observing that,

> a lot of the new feminist SF writers of both sexes owe a real debt to Andre Norton, whose "juvenile" novels said that it was okay to be different...okay to cherish the thought of independence, community, and communication over the goals of domination and power and money. (1980: 34; see also Logan 1982/1983)[32]

Jessica Amanda Salmonson mentioned Miriam Allen deFord and also Margaret St. Clair, who "was writing SF with themes of sexuality in the '50s; no one else was. She always included strong female characters one way or another; it was quite rare when she started" (1982/1983: 6). Long-time British fan Ethel Lindsay commented on the "practically unknown book" *Restoree* by Anne McCaffrey, which had provided one of her first encounters with a strong woman character in sf: "I can remember at the time the great feeling of satisfaction to find the woman rescuing the male for a change" (1984: 6).[33]

The resultant "Invisible Women" issue contained articles on authors such as deFord and Katherine MacLean, who have to this day received little feminist critical attention, and also provided valuable discussions of the work of Norton, Lee Killough, and Sonya Dorman (Chavey 1984; D'Ammassa 1984; Frazier 1984; R. Roberts 1984; Stallings 1984). These articles provide clues as to why some prolific

---

31 This list is a classic illustration of the invaluable bibliographic work produced by fandom because of the extensive resources and knowledge of its members, and their willingness to contribute to a collective effort.

32 In this letter she also mentions Doris Piserchia as a writer who deserves a wider audience. Another writer mentioned was Naomi Mitchison, whose *Memoirs of a Spacewoman* later attracted feminist interest through the Women's Press reissue in 1985 (Chatelain 1984: 7).

33 Here is evidence of the fact that Lindsay—part of the 1950s group of female fans in Britain—was still active and indeed showed interest in the new generation of female fandom.

and respected female writers had come to be almost totally forgotten. A pertinent example is deFord, whose reputation diminished rapidly, because she wrote only short stories, collections of which quickly went out of print. Yet, as this article points out, her work was quite radical: "A veteran of the first women's movement, she had already re-visioned perspectives the second movement had to discover again" (Stallings 1984: 18).[34] A couple of the "Invisible Women" articles are predecessors to the feminist academic interest in the nineteenth-century origins of women's sf writing, with an excellent examination of Gilman's *Herland*, which, although "rescued" in the 1970s was not often discussed in terms of the speculative/sf tradition (Cline 1984; Enrys 1984).

"Feminism isn't fannish"

Although the feminist readers of *Janus* recognized and valued the contributions made by "pre-movement" women writers, other "femme-fans" were not as ready to consider female contributions to sf and fandom in terms of feminism. The very precept on which this feminist community was based—as a space for the interaction of sf fan interests and feminist commitments—was still an issue of some controversy, with at least one (female) fan declaring that "feminism isn't fannish" (attributed to Victoria Vayne in Gomoll 1978: 3). The notion that fandom should be a haven for "apoliticism" is evident in some of the debate surrounding *Janus*'s Hugo nomination for best fanzine. In a 1978 editorial, Gomoll reported that fans had complained that *Janus* was nominated for its politics rather than its quality (Gomoll 1978: 3). In a letter, Victoria Vayne expressed her unease that the nomination resulted from the backing of "politically motivated voters," and added that she would be happier if *Janus* was on that ballot solely because of its quality (1978: 65). Objections followed: Adrienne Fein argued that *Janus*'s feminism was *part* of its quality, adding "I would not feel comfortable nominating a zine which went in for tired old sexist jokes even if the quality was otherwise good" (1978/79: 49-50). Others agreed that they would not vote for offensive zines, and pointed out the over-reaction implied by charges of bloc voting. "A few female fans vote for *Janus*, and we hear loud cries of bloc voting;

---

34 DeFord was born in 1888, published her first sf story in 1946 (age 58), and published more than 70 more before her death in 1975 (Stallings 1984: 17).

if a majority of male fans vote for, say, *Locus*, do we postulate that *this* is bloc voting?" (Logan 1978/1979: 51). Terry Garey also good-humoredly criticized the notion of a bloc vote:

> Come now, Victoria, surely from your personal experience with *A Woman's APA* you must realize that we never presented a united front about *anything*. At the time of the nominations, several members were not speaking to one another... What you have managed to do, Victoria, is perpetuate the rumor that feminist fans are out to take over fandom. Come to think of it, what a great idea! Thanks! Today, Madison, then the Hugos, and then...then...why, then the *world*! Heh, heh, heh! (1978/1979: 50)[35]

The question of whether or not "politics" had any place in fandom arose even more forcefully with reference to activities at conventions: two interesting examples surrounded the second WisCon and the 1978 WorldCon. *Janus* contained numerous reports on the state of feminist programming at various conventions, including the worldcons, with details of events such as a "gay party" (distributing buttons "Happy Gays Are Here Again") and programming on items like "sexism in fandom" and "Feminism and Fandom."[36] Although such feminist programming was becoming more frequent in the late 1970s, it was not without opposition, also becoming "the target of more and more frequent jokes and sometimes, too, of open anger and resentment by those people who think fandom is no place for feminism...or that sexism simply doesn't happen in fandom and doesn't need to be dealt with" (Gomoll 1977: 22). Gomoll gives an example of such opposition, an article by Ted White in *Scintillation* #13, which "speaks for the people who are angered by what they see as a separatist movement within SF fandom that is detrimental to its structure" (1977: 22). Even within the sf group that organized WisCon and *Janus*, there was controversy over the place and function of feminist activities, with debate after the second WisCon over whether or not

---

35 It is interesting to note that Vayne was not necessarily anti-feminist, being a member of the Women's APA.

36 These examples are from Suncon, 35th World Sf Convention, 1977 (reported in Gomoll 1977). (Also at the gay party was Avedon Carol in what would become an infamous masquerade costume—holding whips and accompanied by two "Slave Boys of Gor"!)

to continue with its "feminist slant." This was, apparently, a difficult convention, and complaints were heard afterwards about the feminist bias; although, as many readers commented, only about a quarter of the programming was feminist, and as Jane Hawkins remarked, "[a]nyone who went there and didn't expect a lot of feminist stuff was a fool." Hawkins continued:

> Hey, two feminist GoHs, a fanzine known as feminist, and a con billed that way—where is the surprise? Sure, someone who was hostile to or bored by feminism wouldn't have liked WisCon. BFD. They can go to over a hundred different cons for their belly dancers and sexist jokes. WisCon drew people from all over the country *because* it was a feminist con, and where else do you find that? (1978: 66; see also Morse 1978)[37]

The divisive opinions concerning the presence of feminism in fandom were illustrated even more clearly in a conflict arising over IguanaCon in 1978, concerning the Equal Rights Amendment Bill (ERA). The National Organization of Women (NOW) led a campaign for economic boycotts against the states that had not ratified the ERA, and in a perfect example of feminist praxis in fandom, this became a pressing issue for a number of fans because IguanaCon was to be held in an unratified state, Arizona.

Debate about the issue surfaced in *Janus* with the publication of "A Statement of Ethical Position by the WorldCon Guest of Honor," Harlan Ellison (Ellison 1977: 32-33). Ellison apparently was torn between his position as GoH (accepted before the NOW campaigns began) and support for the ERA, which he felt meant he should boycott the con. After consultation with writers and fans such as Le Guin, Russ, McIntyre, Bradley, and Susan Wood, Ellison decided to attend the con, but "in the spirit of making the convention a platform for heightening the awareness of fans," and he promised to coordinate with NOW and other pro-ERA elements to publicize the situation (Ellison 1977: 32). He urged fans to follow his lead in withholding as much money from the state as possible, by camping out rather than staying in the

---

37 Another expression of support came from Sara Thompson: "I came away from WisCon with a very positive belief that I *can* integrate the feminist and fantastic fiction...aspects of my life, 'cuz other women fans are doing it, and helping each other, and growing stronger" (Thompson 1978: 67).

convention hotel and even bringing in their own food (33). Arguing that, despite the rhetoric of sf as a socially conscious literature, the sf community generally shied away from pressing contemporary issues, Ellison asked, "let's *just for once*, in the world of SF, walk the walk and not just talk the talk" (33).

A selection of the replies Ellison received was published in a later issue, arguing both for and against his position, or various facets of it. A number of feminist fans voiced their support, including a staff member of NOW, and another who described the "excitement we feel that an Important Person is doing something difficult for him to help the cause of the ERA" (Crimmins 1978: 70; see also Fein 1978; Lucero 1978; Quindlen 1978). Others supported the ERA but not Ellison's method of protest, which they felt would hurt both the convention and local small businesses without any effect on the county or state.[38] A number of fans were apparently diametrically opposed to Ellison's stance; he received six letters in one day "from SF fans—all male, five in states that haven't ratified—assuring me I'm an asshole, subversive beyond belief in my efforts to 'undermine fandom' and piss on their convention" (Ellison 1978: 70).[39]

The fairly common fannish distaste for the intrusion of "mundane" politics into fandom did not alone account for the animosity towards the ERA boycott displayed in some quarters. Ellison pointed out to potential opponents that there was a "recent precedent for utilizing a worldcon for moral ends" in Robert Heinlein's publicizing a drive for blood donors (1977: 33). Many fans, however, obviously saw feminism as somehow more "political" than other "liberal" or moral issues. As Anne Laurie Logan's letter noted, "no charges of 'politicking' were raised when Heinlein used his position as GoH to ask for blood, or when numerous fans made themselves loud and even obnoxious in defense of L-5 or NASA" (1978/1979: 51). Upholding the status quo (including sexism) was, apparently, not seen as a "political" act.[40]

---

38 See also letters from Michael A. Armstrong, Mark Wakely, Barbara Delhotel, and R. Laurraine Tutihasi (Armstrong 1978; Wakely 1978; Delhotel 1978; Tutihasi 1978).

39 Another negative response came from F. Paul Wilson, who wrote "I'm shocked to hear you support a measure that will further increase the near-totalitarian power the federal government now holds over our lives" and later "I've noticed an inherent fascism in the women's movement" (1978: 70).

40 The ERA issue caused controversy again in 1980, *Janus #17* 6 (1): 4-6.

The outcome of Ellison's position at IguanaCon was not discussed in the following issues of *Janus*, although a con report by Gomoll praised the "fantastic" feminist programming ("there was *not* just the one or two obligatory 'women's panels' at which all women participating in programming were to be found") (1978/1979a: 3).[41] Feminist issues and the ERA were obviously a visible presence, generating much excitement and enthusiasm amongst feminist fans.

> People *changed their minds*, they *were moved* as a result of [the] panels. Ask Susan Wood, who during her participation on a number of panels, encountered women who were reconsidering their opposition to the ERA as a result of some of the talking that went on... It was exciting!... It occurred to me then, and I still feel so now, that we've passed some sort of great divide.... We don't have to argue for *basic* programming and discussion on these vital subjects any longer. We won't often be "given" a token women's panel to appease us and keep us quiet any more. (It's a *tradition!*)
> (Gomoll 1978/1979a: 3-4)

A number of fascinating letters and articles from male fans testify to the impact that feminist programming had on some fans previously underexposed to literate feminists. Jon Singer wrote of WisCon 3 that he was "still boiling with ideas... I came away also, perhaps a notch more radical than I arrived" and went on to outline his changed understanding of "patriarchy" and women's oppression (Singer 1979: 16).

How (not) to suppress feminist fandom

The feeling that feminism was in fandom to stay, that feminist, gay, and lesbian issues could no longer be excluded from fan debate, did not last for long. By the 1980s, many conventions had not embraced Wood's ideal of "people's programming," but had remained at the level of the ubiquitous "women in SF panels," which slowly settled into a "generic" panel subject to mild ridicule (Gomoll 1986-87: 9). In her "Open Letter to Joanna Russ," published in 1987, Jeanne Gomoll expressed her fear that the history and achievements of feminist fandom were being forgotten, suppressed, or rewritten:

---

41 The programming was organized by Hilde Hildebrand.

Today I sit in the audience at all-male "fandom of the '70s panels"...and don't hear *anything* of the politics, the changes, the roles that women played that decade (except sometimes, a little chortling aside about how it is easier now to get a date with a female fan). (1986-87: 9)

In this account, feminist influence appears as a brief hiatus, with fandom reverting to the scenario portrayed by Wood of the "All Our Yesterdays" fanhistory display in 1973 (Wood 1978: 5).[42] The only response to this suppression was, as Gomoll suggested, a concerted effort by feminist fans to re-tell their histories and ensure that their memories were available to new generations of fans: "If we ourselves forget, why should we expect new generations of readers and fans to dig up the truth about what really happened?" (1986-87: 10). Unfortunately, one of the best avenues for ensuring continued visibility and "balanced retrospectives" was itself in the process of disappearing. Four years after Gomoll's essay appeared in *Aurora* 26, the last issue was published, fulfilling Gomoll's fears that the fanzine was floundering because of a "failure of energy" (10).

In a later retrospective, Gomoll noted that WisCon, as well as their fanzine, was under threat because of this lack of energy, as well as the general anti-feminist feeling resulting from the 1980s "backlash" years (2000). Despite almost "walk[ing] away from the convention towards the end of the 1980s," Gomoll continued her involvement, as WisCon was revitalized in the 1990s and indeed grew far beyond expectations, celebrating its 30th anniversary in 2006 (co-chaired by Gomoll). The source of this revitalization was, for many, the announcement of the James Tiptree Jr. Award. At WisCon 15, in 1991, Diane Martin reported "participating in panel discussions that in feminist content and enthusiasm, rivaled the WisCons of the late '70s" (1992: 3). Part of this excitement stemmed from Pat Murphy's announcement during her GoH speech of a new sf award. Murphy talked of the need to challenge assumptions that feminism was passé—in both sf and society more generally. She related a conversation with Richard Kadrey, in which he suggested, "You know what would really piss people off? You ought to give out a women's science fiction award" (Murphy 1991: 9). Murphy continued:

---

42 Wood wrote of her realization that "'All Our Yesterdays' was a display of all *men's* yesterdays, plus a photo of Joni Stopa in a fountain in a bikini" (1978: 5).

Okay, it was just a joke, nothing more. But a few weeks later, I had dinner with Karen Fowler and I mentioned this joke. Karen is also a trouble-maker, but a very thoughtful one. She looked thoughtful and said, "You know, there is no science fiction award named after a woman."...

And then Karen, who tends toward brilliance, said, "What about James Tiptree Jr.?" And it seemed like such a perfect idea. James Tiptree Jr. winner of multiple Nebulas, revealed in mid-career as Alice Sheldon, and forever after, in every introduction, revealed as Alice Sheldon. James Tiptree Jr., who helped break down the imaginary barrier between "women's writing" and "men's writing." James Tiptree Jr., author of "The Women Men Don't See."...

And so I would like to announce the creation of the James Tiptree Jr. Memorial Award, to be presented annually to a fictional work that explores and expands the roles of women and men. We're still in the planning stages, but we plan to appoint a panel of five judges and we plan to finance the award—and this is another stroke of genius on Karen's part—through bake sales. (If you want to volunteer to run a bake sale, talk to me after the speech.) (9)

The response was immediate, and the resulting "juggernaut" more than the founders could have dreamed. As Gomoll commented,

Pat was standing in front of a critical mass of people, all of whom cared deeply about the kind of science fiction that speaks to feminist values...who were feeling frustrated by politics of the day... Frankly, we were all in a mood to Do Something. So it shouldn't have been a complete surprise that after Pat made her historic announcement, the crowd rose and cheered and clapped and laughed for a long, long time. And that we started to Do Things.... (2000: 3)

Within a few months, the first Tiptree Award cookbook was published, bake sales had been held, and the award was on its way to becoming a fixture, which as of 2009, is still going strong. Notwithstanding its success, the humor underlying the award has remained central: Murphy talks of the award as a subversive joke "that takes you by surprise and makes you blink and turns the world into a different place, much stranger and more wonderful than you ever thought possible" (Murphy and Fowler 2005: vii). The first joke is of course the name: the male pseudonym of a female sf writer whose work and life challenged so many assumptions about gender and sf, writing, and authorship. The bake-sales funding model (a deliberate ironic political statement) has become a feature of the award, as well as other non-traditional activities, including the publication of two cookery books.[43] Apart from a monetary and travel award, the winners also receive an original piece of artwork specially commissioned each year by a female artist (as well as something made of chocolate, such as a plaque or typewriter).

The constitution and function of the panel of judges also attempts to disrupt traditional hierarchies and biases in sf (and other) awards. Central to Murphy and Fowler's motivations in starting the award was the problem of ensuring realistic representation of women writers in the field, anthologies, and on award panels, rather than "tokenism." Fowler reports that at the time, the Philip K. Dick Award had a "token female spot" on the jury:

> And Pat and I started saying to each other, "Wouldn't it be irritating to people if it were the other way around? What if we had a jury of five, and there was always one man, and never more than one man? Wouldn't people find that outrageous in a way that they don't find the situation on the Philip K. Dick jury outrageous?" (Lawrence 2004)

Beyond the "token man," the jury also subverts the "usual hierarchy that is maintained by many literary awards, where only professionals are invited to be on the jury panel. The jury has included fans, writers, editors, booksellers, academics, even postgraduate students" (Larbalestier 2002: 215). The judging process itself is also a distinctive and important characteristic of the award, which works to acknowledge as many texts as possible, rather than just isolating one or two "of the best." The traditional format of winners and losers is subverted through the simultaneous publication of the names of the winner/s, the titles short-listed for the award (now termed an Honor list), and

---

43 *The Bakery Men Don't See* and *Her Smoke Rose Up from Supper*, Both titles are puns on Tiptree stories, "The Women Men Don't See" and "Her Smoke Rose Up Forever."

the "long list" of all fiction considered, usually with fairly extensive annotations identifying why a text has won or been short-listed.

As Larbalestier has noted, many people "explicitly link the Tiptree to a renewal of a tradition of feminist science fiction" (2002: 208). For writer Susanna Sturgis, "the Tiptree Award has made feminism visible once again in the f/sf community and many believe that it has significantly affected what is being written and published" (1995: 52). The effects of the award on the broader sf community can be gauged not only from the enthusiasm and energy of the many fans who have contributed to the cook books, bake sales, and auctions, but also by the hostility shown in some quarters toward the award. To quote Sturgis again, "Even the grumbling—e.g., 'I bet no man ever wins this award'—indicated the growing seriousness with which the Tiptree is taken" (52).[44] Ironically, one of the most infamous complaints about the award became transformed into one of the best "in-jokes" and rallying calls for both the award and the feminist sf community. David Brin complained about the award's failure to recognize his 1993 novel *Glory Season* (originally claiming in an interview that it was not considered, despite being listed on the short list, and later asking about the judging process during a WorldCon 1996 panel on the Tiptree Award) (Larbalestier 2002: 216). The notion that there was some sort of "feminist cabal" behind the Tiptree was consequently taken on board as yet another gleeful, humorous point of identification. The first anthology arising from the award, *Flying Cups and Saucers*, was edited by Debbie Notkin and "the Secret Feminist Cabal" (1998), while the 1998 WisCon t-shirt featured the iconic Tiptree Award "Space Babe," with the motto "WisCon: home of the Feminist Cabal."[45] By 2000, the cabal had even spawned its own placeholder website (not much more than the statement "The cabal is a secret

---

44 For negative commentary, see for example Charles Platt (responding to the reprinting of Murphy's "Illusion and Expectation" speech in the previous issue): "Awards are always a bad idea, and the Tiptree Award is even worse than usual, because it separates books by men from books by women as if the difference matters" (1992). The Tiptree Award, however, was never limited to work by women. Only a few years later, the Tiptree Award for 1995, presented at WisCon 20 was jointly awarded to Elizabeth Hand and Theodore Roszak, and indeed a number of men have won the award since.

45 The Space Babe image and tattoo is the mascot of the Tiptree Award; see <http://www.tiptree.org/?see=spacebabe>, which states: "Who roams the galaxy, single-handedly fighting injustice, oppression, and outdated portrayals of gender roles in

organization dedicated to gender-bending science fiction, temporary tattoos and bake sales" with a link describing WisCon as the "feminist cabal's family reunion."[46]

Growing alongside and in support of the reinvigorated feminist sf community represented by WisCon and the Tiptree Award was the online face of feminist fandom. From early electronic lists such as Fem-SF and Feminist-SF, to the current explosion of websites, livejournal communities, blogs, and wikis, feminist fandom has a strong presence on the web. In addition to providing an invaluable forum for discussion and promotion of venues such as WisCon, use of the internet has seen feminist fandom extend its reach to a much broader community of readers who in the past may never have made the step to active involvement such as convention-going or fanzine-reading. Electronic communication has brought new people into the extended sf community, allowing them more insight into and greater potential for participation in fandom than ever before. Indeed, for many, lists such as Fem-SF have been their first and only experience of fandom. Feminist-SF, a list begun in 1997 as an alternative and supplement to the "closed" Fem-SF list, is an interesting example. It quickly attracted a diverse range of members, many of whom are feminist academics, students, and science/technical workers who have been long-time sf readers in isolation, outside the confines of fandom. Amongst general debate on feminist issues, works of sf are discussed, bibliographical information shared, reading lists built, and advice on teaching courses given, in an expanded community that overlaps the writer/fan sf community. Thus, amongst feminist fans and well-known authors, such as Griffith, Charnas, and McIntyre, are "neos": sf readers who have in some cases not even heard of fannish traditions like the Worldcon.

More recently, initiatives such as Feminist SF—the Blog (http://blogs.feministsf.net/) and the feminist sf wiki (http://wiki.feministsf.net/) have appeared, alongside homepages and blogs for feminist sf groups such as Aqueduct Press, the Broad Universe organization (for promoting genre fiction by women), and the Feminist SF carnival (a

speculative fiction? Space Babe! Join her in her quest, and be recognized by her allies everywhere when you wear the sign of The Secret Feminist Cabal."

46 This site used to be available at http://www.feministcabal.org/; the text can still be found at Broad Universe: http://www.broaduniverse.org/links.html.

regular round-up of blog postings relating to feminist sf).[47] Apart from providing key forums for discussion outside physical spaces such as WisCon, a greater diversity of fans and feminisms are visible, in particular on sites by women of color such as "The Angry Black Woman" Blog and author Nalo Hopkinson's site.[48] Efforts to call attention to race in the sf community have also been galvanized by the establishment of the Carl Brandon Society, sparked at the 1999 WisCon (which programmed more items on race in response to calls from people of color). Taking its name from the "fake" black fan of the 1950s, the society gives out two awards, The Parallax Award, for speculative fiction by a person of color, and the Kindred Award, for speculative fiction dealing with race and ethnicity.[49] In 2007, the society also presented the first Octavia E. Butler Memorial Scholarships, to enable writers of color to attend Clarion workshops.

These activities have, as Duchamp observes, culminated in the "creation of a feminist sf public sphere," one that is more accessible and geographically and demographically diverse than WisCon alone or the sphere formed around early fanzines (2004a: 35). Having a greater presence in the "public sphere" of the Net also means, of course, greater opportunities for contact and conflict with non-feminist parts of the sf community. Just as the Net has facilitated unique actions such as the "slushbombing" of sf magazines (coordinating the submission of stories by women to certain magazines), it also means such actions are subject to greater critique and even hostility. For some, these reactions signal the rather depressing feeling that "we're back at the beginning" and having to argue yet again that sexism does exist (Swirsky 2007: 19-21).[50] For others, the Net lives up to its promise of free and open communication or, in Liz Henry's words, "the internets work how they're supposed to." Reviewing the multitude of responses to the "open source boob project," Henry delighted in the fact that so

---

47 See http://www.broaduniverse.org/ and http://carnival.feministsf.net/. Other key blog carnivals include the People Of Color In Scifi & Fantasy Blog Carnival, see http://willow-dot-com.livejournal.com/21136.html.

48 See http://theangryblackwoman.com/ and http://nalohopkinson.com/.

49 See http://www.carlbrandon.org/awards.html.

50 Other online incidents of note that have galvanized both sexist debate and feminist response are the 2006 Hugo Award incident where Harlan Ellison groped Connie Willis (the very same Ellison who so vocally fought for the ERA amendments back in the '70s), and the related "open source boob project."

many women (and men) made the internet "EXPLODE with mockery, outrage, anger, orneriness, analysis, questioning, and criticism. THAT'S how it's supposed to work! The feminist blogosphere is swift and fierce! It lays out the issues, it gets its hands dirty, it disagrees and shouts and does it right. Go team!"[51]

For most of the women (and men) involved in feminist fan activity since the 1970s, sf has provided a space in which to debate ideas about their life, society, and the future in a relatively open atmosphere where most voices are granted a hearing. Every hue of feminism(s) is apparent, ranging from "women's interests" to radical lesbian-feminism and all points in between. Although disagreements and differences are evident within and between various groups and sub-communities, a common feeling running through these "sites" is that under the broad umbrella of sf fandom, these women and men have found a "home" — a place of belonging, creativity, and political praxis, where beliefs and identities can be affirmed. For some fans, sf groups or zines have been only one strand in a broader engagement with other feminist groups and publishing forums. For others, it has been the only sphere in which they would (or could) practice their personal form of feminist praxis. The sense of "homecoming" and "belonging" is a constant theme in accounts of the discovery of fandom: many fans describe their sense of being "outside" the dominant culture, of being "alien" — a feeling with obvious resonances for women.

Considering the amount of debate and often antagonistic conflict over the problems of sexism, chauvinism, and conservatism of much sf writing, the question arises — how then, has sf seemingly been such a fertile site for feminist activity, engagement, and thinking? An answer suggested by various discussions with fans is that while fandom

---

51 The "open source boob project" reported a (male) fannish experiment at a convention, in which male fans approached women and asked permission to touch their breasts. Henry's post sums up both the original post and its fallout in the blogosphere. "The Internets work how they're supposed to," April 22nd 2008, http://blogs.feministsf.net/?p=340. Another fabulous response came from an Australian fan and cyberfeminist, Sarah Xu, "the Real Open Source Boob project" (online instructions for making a crochet "boob") http://fiftytwoacts.wordpress.com/2008/04/29/act-16/; http://fiftytwoacts.wordpress.com/2008/05/20/act-17/.

(and sf) *was* (and is) sexist, it was not always as sexist as the "real world" and presented an opportunity for feminist women (and men) to actively change their environment. As Avedon Carol remarked, "We got a reaction in fandom that we didn't get in the rest of the world—I mean, it worked!"[52] And despite various setbacks and continuing conflicts, the feminist communities forged in fandom in the 1970s seem to have survived the coming of new generations—bringing in their wake the hope that, perhaps this once, our recent feminist histories will not be forgotten.

---

52 Interview with Avedon Carol, London, 22 July 1996.

6

CYBORG THEORISTS: FEMINIST SF CRITICISM MEETS CYBERCULTURAL STUDIES

I want to conclude with a myth about identity and boundaries which might inform late twentieth-century political imaginations. I am indebted in this story to writers like Joanna Russ, Samuel Delany, John Varley, James Tiptree Jr., Octavia Butler, and Vonda McIntyre. These are our storytellers exploring what it means to be embodied in high-tech worlds. They are theorists for cyborgs.

⤙ Donna Haraway ([1985] 2004a: 31)

Previous chapters have traced the ways in which for many critics, writers, and readers in the field, sf was a central site for the working through of feminist debates and ideas. The next two chapters examine how recognition of the cultural work of sf feminisms filters out into other critical communities, specifically cultural and philosophical studies of science and technology. Central to these broader feminist explorations are the ways sf encourages consideration of the interpenetration of bodies, subjectivity, and identity in relation to contemporary technoculture. A significant moment of such interchanges can be seen in the feminist engagements with technology and science fiction in the 1980s and 1990s. Ironically, just as feminist sf had been formalized as an object of study, critical attention was arrested by a male-dominated movement that seemed to eclipse the impact and import of feminist sf: cyberpunk. Beyond the bounds of sf, a more wide-reaching event horizon was signaled by the publication of Haraway's socialist-feminist "Manifesto for Cyborgs." Whilst very different figures, both Haraway's cyborg and cyberpunk's cowboys are crucial players in the conversations examined in this chapter: together staging the limits, as well as the contradictions, implicit in this cross-cultural and boundary-confronting encounter.

Both cyberpunk and the Harawayan cyborg seemed to demand a feminist sf criticism more attentive to technology, provoked by cyberpunk's foregrounding of technology in techno-human relations (Hollinger 1990a), as well as by Haraway's demand for socialist feminists to refuse "a demonology of technology" (2004: 39). In fiction too, critics like Wolmark observed a shift in '80s feminist sf to confront "the question of gendered subjectivity more explicitly within the context of the masculinist hegemony of technology" (1999: 231-2). These considerations of technology and subjectivity characterized a broader trend, such that from the mid-1980s, "sf has almost obsessively (re) imagined the post-human subject at a variety of 'conjunctures' with the technological" (Hollinger 2008: 140). Thus consideration of the cybercultural turn in feminist sf and cultural criticism also confronts the emergence of and contests over the "posthuman." Critical debates around the posthuman, cyborg, and cyberpunk not only reflect key developments in feminist technocultural studies, but also serve to emphasize a crucial site of productive tension in contemporary feminist theory—how we factor the material body into theorizing about subjectivity, identity, and ontology.

The critical studies I examine here fall roughly into two camps: literary studies of sf where "cyberpunk" (often intersecting with "postmodern literature") is the primary focus, and cultural studies of science and technology that emphasize the metaphor of the cyborg in their analyses of popular representations, including cyberpunk sf. Dealing first with the sf field, I survey the various meanings attributed to the "movement" within the genre and examine a range of feminist responses and critiques.[1] Coterminous with these critiques, feminist cultural studies of science and technology were also confronting cyberculture and cyberpunk, following Haraway in calling on sf to explore human-technology relations. I conclude by examining some more recent texts that revisit cyberpunk and the cyborg and the different elements at play in the construction of a feminist genealogy of "cyberfiction" or "cyborg writing."

---

1   The first feminist academic articles on this '80s phenomena did not surface until the 1990s. Articles from Joan Gordon and Veronica Hollinger appeared in 1990 (Gordon 1990; Hollinger 1990a) followed by Nixon's "Cyberpunk" (Nixon 1992a). Feminist reader/fan commentary on cyberpunk appeared from about 1986, for example in the fanzine *Aurora*.

Sf reviews cyberpunk

"Cyberpunk," the title of a story by Bruce Bethke, was employed by Gardener Dozois in a 1984 *Washington Post* article to refer to the "bizarre hard-edged, high-tech" sf of the 1980s (Bethke 1983; see also Shiner 1992: 17; Dery 1996: 75). Associated with a small group of writers (almost all male, from Texas, and fond of "mirrorshade" sunglasses) critics were soon referring to a "movement" whose contours were virtually defined by William Gibson's 1984 novel *Neuromancer*, and the anthology edited by Bruce Sterling, *Mirrorshades* (1994b; see also L. McCaffery 1991b; Latham 1993; Shiner 1992; Sterling 1991). *Neuromancer* has often been taken as defining the style, content, and mythos of cyberpunk, while *Mirrorshades* delineated membership of the movement: who was "in" the cyberpunk club. Outside interest was signaled by an article in *Rolling Stone* in December 1986 and a special issue of the academic journal *The Mississippi Review* in 1988.[2] By this stage, however, cyberpunk was already seen by many in the sf field as passé; and in 1991, Lewis Shiner reported the "death" of cyberpunk in the *New York Times* (1991).[3] Nevertheless, as Mark Bould observes, the "academic response to Cyberpunk was unprecedented"; the 1990s saw the intensification of critical interest in cyberpunk both inside and outside the field, with articles appearing fairly regularly in critical journals like *Science Fiction Studies* from 1990 onwards and another dedicated collection, *Fiction 2000*, published in 1992 (Bould 2005: 228; Fitting 1990; Slusser and Shippey 1992).

For critics both inside and outside the field, cyberpunk captured a particular zeitgeist, resulting in an unprecedented valorizing of sf as a cultural text necessary to, and revealing of, our techno-cultural moment. Critical attempts at definition ranged from "a group of writers striving to bring sf into the information age" (Latham 1993: 267), to a "new subgenre of hard sf which expressly considers the changing

2 Interestingly, this issue of a "mainstream" literary journal predated analysis in sf critical journals, though the articles were mostly written by sf critics. Special issue: "The Cyberpunk Controversy," *The Mississippi Review*, vol. 16, no. 1/2, #47/48, 1988. Most of this material was later reprinted in *Storming The Reality Studio* (L. McCaffery 1991b). See also Darko Suvin, "On Gibson and Cyberpunk" (Suvin 1989).

3 Not all cyberpunk writers concurred with his view—see the responses from Sterling (1991) and Pat Cadigan (1993: 4-9).

status of human subjects under late capitalist conditions of production" (Whalen 1992: 75), to "near-future science fiction that appeared to be capable of cognitively mapping the conditions of the emerging global order" (Moylan 1995: 183). For Claire Sponsler, cyberpunk had become "a widely accepted term for describing a specific kind of cultural production found in music, film and fiction in 1980s America," a "reinterpretation of human (and especially male) experience in a media-dominated, information-saturated post-industrial age" (Sponsler 1993: 251). Cyberpunk's transcendence of its original literary moorings implied to some that it "provided a popular framework for conceptualizing new relationships to technology" (Foster 1993b: 13), a view reinforced by Sterling's comment that the cyberpunks were "perhaps the first SF generation to grow up not only within the literary tradition of science fiction but in a truly science-fictional world" (Sterling 1994a: ix).[4] Such grandiose claims aside, cyberpunk certainly exerted a "particular kind of cultural and masculinist hegemony over questions concerning the impact of information technology on social relations" (Wolmark 1993: 127).

Although the classic texts of the cyberpunk movement constitute a mere handful of works from the mid-1980s, they represent a defining moment in contemporary sf history. Initially a number of critics seemed to accept Sterling's claims that cyberpunk represented a new revolutionary movement, revitalizing sf by giving voice to a subversive avant-garde, the Bohemians or "new punks" of the 1980s. Critics such as Larry McCaffery enthusiastically extended this view to incorporate a critical avant-gardism, claiming cyberpunk as "postmodern sf," constituting a radical post-humanist critique of the modernism and humanism that continued to (de)limit the bulk of genre sf (see for example, L. McCaffery 1991a). The prevailing critical view has, however, been more skeptical and often downright disdainful of the inflated "revolutionary" claims made for cyberpunk (Moylan 1995; Nixon 1992a; Ross 1991). The casting of cyberpunk as sf's salvation not only offended many of the sf "old guard," but was also seen to eclipse other kinds of sf that had gradually been effecting change

---

4 This "sf world" really refers only to white western culture, its "science fictionality" dependent on cultural, economic, gendered, racial, and generation factors; see for example Darko Suvin, "On Gibson and Cyberpunk SF" (Suvin 1989). My thanks to Sylvia Kelso for bringing this point to my attention.

in the genre—particularly the writings of feminist, gay, and lesbian authors. Thus, it is hardly surprising that feminist sf critics should be amongst the most severe critics of cyberpunk. Less enthusiastic critiques of cyberpunk focused on what was perceived to be a gap between "cyberpunk's self-promotion and textual performance" (Easterbrook 1992: 378). Nevertheless, the longevity of critical attention renders this ossified moment of sf history significant. Casting cyberpunk as the product of a "multiplicity of influences within and without sf," Hollinger noted that, at the least, "cyberpunk helped to generate a great deal of very useful controversy about the role of sf in the 1980s" (1990a: 41).[5]

Most importantly, cyberpunk foregrounded technology in a way that spoke to the concerns of late 1980s and '90s technoculture. Focused on the near future and extrapolating from current (and what seemed to be immanent) information and computer technology, cyberpunk also emphasized the political and economic forces shaping contemporary and future technological development (Ben-Tov 1995: 176). Cyberpunk seemed to literalize Teresa De Lauretis's notion that "technology is our historical context, political and personal" and suggested how intimate this context could be(come) (de Lauretis 1990: 167; see also Hollinger 1990a). Cyberpunk took for granted the inevitability of a total "interface," thus departing from a number of standard sf traditions, such as "the positive or negative valorization [of technology] so central to earlier sf" (Fitting 1990: 302). Similarly cyberpunk skirted the political values of dystopia or utopia and distanced itself from the traditional sf tropes of apocalypse and holocaust, indeed displaying what Claire Sponsler termed a "boredom with Apocalypse" (1993: 253; see also Hollinger 1990a: 38; Fitting 1990: 300; Pask 1995: 182).

---

5 Samuel Delany similarly argued that cyberpunk was an exciting phenomenon amongst fans and critics:

> [I]t produced a lot of exciting speculation and argument that woke many of us up to various nuances of writerly tone; it made us look at new, possible relations between science fiction and the world; and it foregrounded a real and important attitude toward technology that was constituted as much by numbness as it was by ease and accessibility...There was a lot of criticism. There was a lot of argument, back and forth... All of it made a bright and informative dialogue that shed its flashes and glimmers all about the SF field. (Delany 1988: 29)

Various academic accounts have situated cyberpunk as a fiction uniquely reflective of postmodern culture, with Bukatman going so far as to claim Deleuze and Guatari as cyberpunks (1991: 354).[6] Fredric Jameson called cyberpunk "the supreme literary expression if not of postmodernism, then of late capitalism itself" (1991: 419n1). Critics such as Istvan Csicsery-Ronay saw in cyberpunk "the apotheosis of bad faith, the apotheosis of the postmodern," reflecting a culture of despair or malaise (1991: 193). In contrast, Hollinger argued that cyberpunk was one of a number of sf projects (including some feminist sf) that could be seen as "anti-humanist" because of its deconstruction of the subject and nature/culture, human/machine oppositions (1990a: 30).[7] Interestingly, Sterling himself claimed that the anti-humanist conviction in cyberpunk was not a "literary stunt," but "an objective fact about culture in the late twentieth century. Cyberpunk didn't invent this situation; it just reflects it" (1991: 40). However, the critique of humanism implicit in the themes of cyberpunk were, as Hollinger noted, at best incomplete (1990a: 41).

Another focus for critical commentary was the reactionary nature of gender politics in cyberpunk scenarios. In the conclusion of his article "Futuristic Flu," Csicsery-Ronay briefly notes that "one difference" left untouched in cyberpunk "is that between male and female" (1992a: 43).[8] Andrew Ross was amongst the most trenchant critics of "Cyberpunk in Boystown," which he described as the "urban fantasies of white male folklore" (Ross 1991: 145). "Cyberpunk's idea of a counterpolitics...seems to have little to do with the burgeoning power of the great social movements of our day: feminism, ecology, peace, sexual liberation, civil rights" (152). Others such as Terence Whalen, Peter Fitting, and Tom Moylan similarly noted cyberpunk's

---

6   See also Richard Kadrey and Larry McCaffery, "Cyberpunk 101" (1991), which gives such a list of critical and fictional influences.

7   See also L. McCaffery (1991a), who cautions against the ease of claiming cyberpunk as postmodern, since other sf movements also produced postmodernist fiction. And see Roger Luckhurst on the fashionable traffic between postmodern critics and sf (Luckhurst 1991).

8   He suggests, however, that such explorations should take place in a "different" arena—that of feminist futurism. In an ironic fashion, he suggests that women (and feminists) would automatically be uninterested in cyberpunk, noting that the cyberpunks are "canny men—almost all of them men (why would a woman care about a technological society she had no role in creating?)" (Csicsery-Ronay Jr. 1991: 183).

disparagement of a progressive political agenda and questioned the implications of "alienated subcultures adopting the hi-tech tools of the establishment" (Whalen 1992: 75).[9] Not surprisingly, feminist critics also refused to bypass considerations of cyberpunk futures as merely signaling a postmodern failure of, or resistance to, utopian imaginings.

"Not our revolution": Feminist critiques of cyberpunk

The initial target of feminist critique was not cyberpunk's futures, however, but its history, in particular the absence and even denial of feminist forbears in the self-constructed cyberpunk genealogy.[10] In "An Open Letter to Joanna Russ," Jeanne Gomoll (the editor of feminist fanzine *Aurora*) aired her misgivings about Sterling's introduction to *Burning Chrome*. Comparing Sterling's dismissal of 1970s sf as "confused, self-involved and stale" with the examples of suppression in Russ's "How to Suppress Women's writing," Gomoll observed a new "strategy" in operation— "They wrote it, but they were a fad" (1986-87: 7). The enthusiasm for cyberpunk was, for Gomoll, part of a "backlash" against feminist writing and activity in sf:

> With a touch of the keys on his word processor, Sterling
> dumps a decade of SF writing out of critical memory: the

9   Though as Ross points out, there are examples of more successful appropriations of similar hi-tech, such as the black hip-hop music counterculture; in contrast, he argues cyberpunk displays an "urban fantasy" of a subculture that remains a "dominant white middle class conception of inner-city life" (Ross 1991: 144-5; see also Moylan 1995; and Fitting 1990). While Fitting adopts a more positive view of Gibson than Ross does, this is qualified, noting that Gibson's "is a violent, masculinist future, one in which feelings and emotions seem to have disappeared along with...the "human" (307). See also Easterbrook (1992) on the loss of humanity and commodification of the body: "In cyberpunk, tears become spit, love becomes decadence, body collapses into an amalgam of hormones, blood vanishes altogether, or becomes barbecue sauce or beer suds" (391-2).

10   The first feminist critique came from fan writer and editor Jeanne Gomoll (see below), predating academic feminist articles by almost four years. The next feminist articles appeared in 1990 (see above); Ross's chapter, "Cyberpunk in Boystown," appeared in *Strange Weather* in 1991; Nixon's "Cyberpunk" in 1992. A special issue of *Genders* (no. 18, 1993) edited by Thomas Foster explored cyberpunk and feminism, whereas Jenny Wolmark's book *Aliens and Others*, including a chapter on cyberpunk, was published in 1993. In 1995 *Science Fiction Studies* published Karen Cadora's "Feminist Cyberpunk" and Mary Catherine Harper's "Incurably Alien Other."

whole decade was boring, symptomatic of a sick culture, not worth talking about. Now, at last, he says, we're on to the right stuff again. (7)[11]

Gomoll's article sparked a widespread debate—a "furore" according to Samuel Delany (Tatsumi 1988: 8). It was widely circulated amongst fans and writers, being reprinted in a one-off fanzine *Six Shooter* and in the journal *Hot Wire* as "The Me Decade and Feminist SF," and read at the 1988 Corflu convention.[12] In a well-known interview, Delany also criticized the elision of feminist sf ("the explosion that lights the whole cyberpunk movement") produced by the "endless anxious search for fathers" amongst cyberpunk critics (Tatsumi 1988: 9).[13] Interestingly, many subsequent feminist analyses omit reference to the "mother" of this debate—Gomoll—and instead engage with Delany's argument, focusing particularly on his claims that Gibson's Molly was a direct descendant of Russ's Jael.[14] A number of critics emphasized the "apolitical" nature of cyberpunk razor girls, developing a feminist counter-argument against the often celebratory academic accounts cojoining cyberpunk with postmodern and posthumanist narratives.[15]

For feminist critics, gendered roles and identities in cyberpunk were constrained by the phallocentric structures and desires of its

11 Similarly, Nixon also argued that Sterling does suggest "the gender of those producers of stale futures when he posits a connection between drugs, personal computers, and cyberpunk as 'definitive high-tech products'" (Nixon 1992a: 220) when he states: "No counterculture Earth Mother gave us lysergic acid—it came from a Sandoz lab" (Sterling 1994a: xiii).

12 "Dear Editorial Horde," *The Last Aurora*, vol. 10, no. 2, Autumn 1990, 6-11. In this issue of *Aurora*, Gomoll printed some of the many letters she had received, including a highly defensive and antagonistic response from Sterling.

13 Similarly, Wolmark argued that feminist sf had "an undeniable impact on cyberpunk" (1993: 110).

14 Although critics such as Nixon, Wolmark, Harper, and Cadora all cite Delany's argument, they do not refer to Gomoll. In contrast, Sarah Lefanu situates Gomoll's article as an important part of the history of feminist sf, though she does not specifically discuss it in terms of cyberpunk (Lefanu 1988: 6-7).

15 For example, Nixon describes the women in cyberpunk as "effectively depoliticized and sapped of any revolutionary energy" (1992a: 223). Similarly, Ross argued that cyberpunk "razorgirls" like Molly exist in a survivalist environment, a "zero-sum game" where their only possible roles are as "predator or prey" (1991: 158-9; see also Gordon 1990: 198).

technocultural context. Thus, feminist critique focused on the representation of the body and human subjectivity in cyberpunk texts, with Gibson (and *Neuromancer*) in particular criticized for the apparent retention of the old humanist dream of transcendence—here refigured as that of "meat vs. mind," where "advanced technology erases human morality…beyond the need of ethical justifications" (Easterbrook 1992: 383; see also Hollinger 1990a: 32). The familiar hard-boiled masculinism of the console cowboys of cyberpunk and the legitimation of their drive to escape the feminized "meat" of the body was the focus of most feminist criticism of the movement. Paralleling similar work on computer culture by Sandy Stone and Zoë Soufoulis (aka Sofia), for example, feminist sf critics emphasized the gendered and inherently sexualized language coloring the human-computer interface in cyberpunk.[16] For Nixon, not only was the matrix feminized, but also the means of entering it—while hackers generally "jack in" some female characters have a mystical power to enter cyberspace without jacking in, acting as "horses" that the cowboys can "mount" and "ride" into the matrix (Nixon 1992a: 227).[17] Nixon's analysis is based on her observation that "[t]he computer matrix, a construct culturally associated with the masculine world of logic and scientific wizardry, could easily constitute the space of the homoerotic. But it doesn't…the matrix itself is figured as feminine space" (227). For Karen Cadora the absence of gay, lesbian, and female characters necessitates the construction of "a feminine space in which male heroes can establish and assert their masculinity. The feminization of cyberspace is necessary to insure that these male characters remain heterosexual" (Cadora 1995: 361).[18]

---

16 Feminist critics of computer culture also examine the sexualized and gendered language surrounding the hacker culture, though they are not brought into the feminist sf narratives of cyberpunk. See, for example, Allucquére Rosanne Stone (1991), Zoë Sofia (1993), and Nicola Nixon (1992a: 227).

17 "The cowboys have to 'interface' with the matrix through 'slotting into' feminized cyberspace decks; certain females, however, require no such mediation: they are already, by implication, a part of it" (227). She is here referring to Gibson's work, especially *Count Zero*. The reference in *Neuromancer* to the time "When it Changed" (which, as Nixon also notes is surely invoking Russ's story of the same name) is cast by Nixon as the change to a dangerously feminized matrix.

18 See also Moylan, who argues that a similar repression of sites of opposition operates in terms of race, as well as gender and sexuality:

When examining feminist fictional responses to cyberspatial scenarios, critics often tried to distance this work from cyberpunk through the constitution of separate sub-genres variously labeled feminist cyberpunk or cyborg writing. Pat Cadigan, the only woman associated with the Movement, was situated as a problematic figure in feminist criticism. Whilst some saw in her work an attempt to "avoid the kind of technological essentialism" of writers such as Gibson, others claimed it was limited by its very association with cyberpunk (Wolmark 1993: 121). Wolmark, for example, notes that while Cadigan's novels include "a significant number of strong female characters... the depiction of women as other in cyberpunk goes unquestioned" (125). Similarly Cadora accused Cadigan of conflating technology and masculinity (1995: 358).[19] These views contrast with those of cultural critics such as Anne Balsamo and Claudia Springer (discussed below), who drew on Cadigan's work to complicate dominant notions about gender and technology. In *Synners*, for example, Visual Mark's realization of the transcendental urge to escape the "meat-prison" is constructed as undesirable, in contrast to Gina's decision to return to the trials of embodied existence. Gina and Sam, the female hackers and "synners," have a much more partial, fluid, and practical engagement with their technological world and in fact are the ones who are left with the responsibility of "cleaning up" after the catastrophic effects of Mark's abandonment are released onto the net. As Harper argues, although *Synners* is similar to texts such as *Neuromancer* and *Schismatrix*, in that for the male hacker "a choice is made between the material body and a transcendent state," *Synners* enacts an anti-humanist move by suggesting that "the consequence of such an

---

In an appropriation of non-white cultures that resembles little more than a form of a "yuppie postmodernism"...engaging in a trendy consumption of the life and art of racial Others, Gibson has created three textual populations that serve as happy helpers: the Rastafarians and the voodoo priests—and especially the women of the Brotherhood who are doubly subordinated as helpers to the helpers—never become actors in their own right, never claim a different voice or space within the narrative. (1995: 190-1)

19 Yet Cadora also provides a more positive reading of Cadigan's *Synners*, observing that the masculinity of characters like Visual Mark is destabilized and feminized by the means in which they connect to cyberspace, through the use of "sockets" implanted deep in their brains—"[t]hey are the penetrated, not the penetrating" (362).

operation would be a disastrous one" (Harper 1995: 412). Sherryl Vint agrees, noting that "[l]ike Haraway, Cadigan asks us to attend to the material consequences of scientific endeavour" and suggests that no technologies should be allowed to "replace our connection with the material world" (2007: 117). As Vint argues, "*Synners* shows us that it is possible to imagine a cyberpunk world grounded in the material, in ethical uses of technology, and in respect for other human subjects both on and off the Net" (122).

Invoking the feminist cyborg

Although feminists criticized the conservative "body politics" of cyberpunk, the intimacy of its human/machine interface certainly posed challenges to modernist concepts of subjectivity, a project central to both feminist and postmodernist critiques.[20] Cyberpunk's paradigmatic hold over the representation of future technoculture, however, demanded a feminist counter-narrative that incorporated more than the work of the one "movement" woman writer. Many feminist analyses of cyberpunk turned to readings of feminist sf as a corrective to masculinist cyberpunk narratives. Cadora employs the label "feminist cyberpunk" to represent a "revolutionary blend" of "the conventions of cyberpunk with the political savvy of feminist sf" (1995: 357). In contrast, Harper offers a congruent subgenre, the "parallel and developing literature of feminist cyborg writing," which is distinguished from cyberpunk by a "set of cultural and technological transgressors whose politics may not be reduced to simple mind/body oppositions" (1995: 400).[21]

The critical contextualization of a feminist sf engaged with such technocultural concerns depended crucially on the critic's construction

---

20 As Jenny Wolmark notes, technology "provides the context in which both cyberpunk and feminist science fiction deal with the central questions of difference and identity in a post-industrial, postmodern society" (1993: 109). Similarly, Scott Bukatman has argued that cyberpunk is the "literary form most centrally concerned with the rhetorical production of a complex imbrication between the human subject and the electronically defined realities of the Dataist Era" (1991: 347).

21 In a similar formulation, Moylan has argued (in the face of the "death" of 1980s cyberpunk) for a "late" or post-cyberpunk movement "that appears to be dominated by women writers" (1995: 185, 195n9). A few years later, Lisa Yaszek employs a broader notion of "cyborg writing" as a "genre" that explores the impact of technological mediation on "understandings of human identity and agency" (2002: 3).

of "cyberpunk." For Wolmark, "Cadigan's attempt to suggest an oppositional stance to existing relations of power is largely defeated by the reification of gender roles that is implicit in cyberpunk" (1993: 125). Thus, she concludes that "cyberpunk is fairly intractable as far as the representation of gender relations is concerned" (126). The construction of cyberpunk as a fixed, intractable mode, within a context where it dominated investigations of contemporary technoculture, was not conducive to opening a discursive space for feminist contestation of these representations.[22] A solution provided by many feminist critics was to (re)establish the feminist techno-cultural metaphor of the cyborg as formulated by Haraway as the context for reading feminist cyberpunk. As Harper argues, "[f]ar more so than cyberpunk's inversions, feminist cyborgs radically reconfigure humanness and expand the potential within humanist subjectivity" (1995: 415). The invocation of Haraway's cyborg seemed to offer more libratory and expansive possibilities for feminist "cyberfictions" than the central cyberpunk figure of the Gibsonian cyber-cowboy.[23] Thus for Harper, "Haraway's cyborg is a self-declared deconstructor of humanism while Gibson's cyborgs deviate from, then reinstate, the humanist position" (1995: 404). Yet there are similarities, since both offered an "imaginative bio-technological form which by its nature undermines the split between humanity and its technology," and are also "still undeniably the dream-children of a positivist, rationalist American technology built by middle-class men of the previous two generations" (404-5).

Critics such as Harper, Cadora, and Wolmark thus employed Haraway's cyborg as license to extend the scope of cyberpunk beyond the "neuromancers" and reassert a feminist presence in contemporary sf. In "Incurably Alien Other," Harper discusses the work of Pat Cadigan, Misha (a Native American writer), Laura J. Mixon, and Lisa Mason as

---

22 Cf Cadora (1995: 358), who describes Wolmark's dismissal of cyberpunk as "a little too hasty... Feminist sf cannot afford to dismiss the potential of cyberpunk."

23 While for feminist critics of cyberpunk, the appeal to a more politically "committed" figure such as Haraway's cyborg seems an obvious critical trajectory, one male critic complained, as early as 1992 (before most of the articles discussed here were published) that "the fashionable pitting of the cyborg against the cyberpunk, the emancipatory radical feminist theory-being versus the juvenile male neuromantic outlaw, is, as the saying goes, already tired" (Csicsery-Ronay Jr. 1992b: 409).

"feminist cyborg writing" (1995: 403).[24] The most important feature of such "feminist-centered writers of cyborg literature," according to Harper is the "knowledge that subjectivity is an interchangeable and mutable set of identities, powers, and strategies" (417). Tracing feminist (re)workings of techno-social relations through writers who "utilise the metaphor of the cyborg rather than that of cyberspace," Wolmark focuses on Rebecca Ore, Marge Piercy, and Elisabeth Vonarburg, arguing that these writers engage more fully with the revisions suggested by Haraway's cyborg (1993: 127).[25] Wolmark remains cautious in her assessment, noting that Piercy's deployment of the cyborg was limited by a focus on masculine identity through the male cyborg Yod,[26] whereas Vonarburg's character, Elisa, was restrained by the technological determinism and "negative politics" embedded in the Project and its male originator's "genetic ambitions" (1993: 134-7).

Cadora's examples of feminist cyberpunk exemplify Haraway's cyborg by attempting to blur boundaries not just between human and machine, but also between human and animal and the "real and

24 Later she describes this work: "Feminist cyborg literature is one kind of articulation of our culture's own sense of alienation from its 'incurably informed' rationalist humanist project" (418). Harper analyzes Cadigan's *Synners*, Misha's *Red Spider White Web*, Mixon's *Glass Houses*, and Mason's *Arachne*; and also looks at "Sue Thomas's didactic, yet imaginative and highly meta-fictive, cyborg novel *Correspondence*" (416).

25 The texts examined here are *The Illegal Rebirth of Billy the Kid,* Rebecca Ore; *Body of Glass,* Marge Piercy; and *The Silent City,* Elisabeth Vonarburg. As Fitting observes, Marge Piercy's *Body of Glass* has received little attention in the North American sf community (though it did win the British Arthur C. Clarke Award for best sf novel in 1992), despite its obvious "dialogue" with cyberpunk (Fitting 1994: 4). Piercy notes in her acknowledgments that a student told her that "the alternate universe that Connie blunders into [in *Woman on the Edge of Time*]... anticipated cyberpunk"; she also acknowledges the influence of both Gibson and Haraway (Piercy 1992: 583-4) (first published in the US as *He, She and It,* Alfred Knopf, 1991). In my Penguin edition, the back cover blurb reads: "Interweaving cyberpunk and ecology, Jewish history and mythology, Marge Piercy gives us a giant of a futurist novel." It is interesting that, as cyberpunk gained such wide parlance, a book could be promoted as "cyberpunk," without mentioning sf at all.

26 As Fitting points out, it is actually quite misleading for Piercy to term Yod a "cyborg" since he is more properly an android, and the "true cyborg is Nili," a member of a community who have created themselves to protect their enclave (1994: 5). See also (McCarron 1995: 268-71).

unreal."[27] Mary Rosenblum's *Chimera*, Maureen McHugh's *China Mountain Zhang*, and Laura Mixon's *Glass Houses* all move beyond the heterosexism of cyberpunk and include lesbian, gay, or bisexual characters (Cadora 1995: 362-4). These texts also center on the issue of embodiment, and, as Cadora observed, "almost all feminist cyberpunk depicts virtual reality as a space that must be navigated with a body of some sort" (365).[28] Often, animal forms are also incorporated, leading Cadora to argue that,

> feminist cyberpunk improves on some other feminist sf in that it acknowledges a love for the organic without making an essentialist connection between nature and the feminine. Because technology is the medium through which the transgressions occur, electronic animal personas in feminist cyberpunk do not signal innocent longings to return to Mother Nature. Rather, these personas hint at the ironic but potent links between embodied humans and endangered species. (367)[29]

One problem with these positionings of feminist cyborg alternatives or reworkings is, however, precisely the way they are situated fairly narrowly in terms of the "male" cyberpunk sf movement. Although this is perhaps inevitable given the level of debate provoked by cyberpunk, it seems strange that "cyberpunk," which came to signify a whole array of cultural practices and products relating to contemporary views of technology—from the internet, hackers, and electronic magazines to more "academic" concerns about cyborg and posthuman identities—has in much sf criticism been limited to a handful of texts mostly by white men from the mid-'80s.[30]

---

27 Male cyberpunk, as she observes, generally only deals with assaults on the first boundary (Cardora 1995: 359-60).

28 Another example she gives is Piercy's *Body of Glass*. Also relevant here would be Scott's *Trouble and Her Friends* and Mason's *Arachne*.

29 Cadora gives as examples *Glass Houses* and *Chimera*. Similar electronic animal personae are central to Mason's *Arachne*.

30 Especially when most of these authors have themselves moved away from "cyberpunk" in their works and seem to be more responsive to feminist and other political issues. For example, see Gibson's *Virtual Light* with a teenage female protagonist and more emphasis on exploring the "sprawl-like" community around the San Francisco bridge; or the Gibson and Sterling "steampunk" collaboration, *The Difference Engine*. In an interview about this book, Gibson and Sterling discuss

Feminist techno-cultural studies read sf

At the same time as these debates in the sf field, cyberpunk and science fictional cyborgs became a focal point for the expanding field of cultural studies of techno-science focused on "cyberculture" and "cyborgology." [31] Feminist cultural studies of science and technology such as the collection *Between Monsters, Goddesses and Cyborgs* pursue "cross- and transdisciplinary approaches in order to grasp the webs of text, myth, machine, organism, matter and society which postmodern science, medicine and technology seem to put on the agenda in a more pressing manner than ever before" (Lykke 1996: 6). Indicative of the leaky boundaries of cyber-discourse, insightful analyses of feminist sf issue from such studies, not necessarily centered around cyberpunk sf, but employing sf to inform and reflect cyborg feminisms, cybernetic theories, and feminist critiques of technology. Within the framework of these cultural studies, cyberpunk (and feminist sf) are situated as expressions of and ways of reading our technoculture(s).

Although in 1993 Thomas Foster noted the scarcity of feminist cultural critiques of cyberpunk sf, this lack was quickly remedied (1993a: 6-7). Within their broader examinations of cyberculture, critics such as Anne Balsamo and Claudia Springer drew on cyberpunk (and other sf) texts to demonstrate the presence of consistent gendered formulations. Balsamo's study reads cyberpunk as one of an array of popular representations of technocultural concerns, situating "cyberpunk mythologies in relation to the emergence of a new cultural forma-

---

issues such as the socio-cultural re-production of women's bodies and fashion ("the female body is reinvented every decade") and the ecological problems left for the next generation, such as the "mounds of disposable diapers" (Fischlin, Hollinger, and Taylor 1992: 3, 5).

31 For example, the eclectic collection *The Cyborg Handbook* acknowledged sf as the site of most theorizing about cyborgs, claiming that:

> The compleat [sic] cyborgologist must study science fiction as the anthropologist listens to myths and prophesies. Science fiction has often led the way in theorising and examining cyborgs, showing their proliferation and suggesting some of the dilemmas and social implications they represent. And several important critics—Kate Hayles, Scott Bukatman, Fredric Jameson, Anne Balsamo, and Donna Haraway...have used these fictional resources to explore the cyborg and the ways he/she/it affects our ideas of the "human." (Gray, Mentor, and Figueroa-Sarriera 1995: 8)

tion built in and around cyberspace."[32] Fiction has been an important part of feminist attempts to construct narratives that help make
sense of technocultural transformations as they emerge: "Fictional
narratives serve dual purposes in this effort. On the one hand, they
can thematize cultural preoccupations... However, they also serve as
expressive resources that offer cognitive maps of emergent cultural
arrangements" (Balsamo 1996: 161). Many critics also observed that
sf offers a highly appropriate mode for telling stories that traverse the
traditional boundaries of the sciences and the arts, technology and
culture. Much of N. Katherine Hayles's work has engaged in an inte-
grated analysis of the oft-divided spheres and discursive concerns that
hover around the signifier "sf"—mediating between the emphasis
on discourse characteristic of literary studies and the often reductive
material practices of the sciences.

Like the feminist critics of cyberpunk in sf, these cultural critics
emphasized cyberpunk's conservative gender relations and the ways in
which computer technologies and cyberspace are sexualized. In general, sf critics focused on the issues of identity, subjectivity, and embodiment in cyberpunk, seeing its questioning of traditional divisions
between self and technology as exemplary postmodern challenges to
humanism. Feminist critics of cyberpunk sf continue in this framework, but emphasize the extent to which cyberpunk also retains humanist conceptions such as the Cartesian dualism of mind over body,
which is deemed a failure to follow through on postmodern deconstructions. Feminist cultural critics, however, situate the "masculinist"
traits of cyberpunk as a reflection of the more obviously conservative
cultures of computer hackers and celebratory "new edge" magazines.
Indeed, many of the feminist critics I examine below locate contempt
for the "meat" and the gendered differentials of cyberpunk's exploration of subjectivity as a *reflection of*, rather than an incomplete gestur-
ing towards, postmodern theories. Different readings emerge when
diverse cultural and technological discourses are read alongside cyberpunk literature and postmodern literary theory. The question of

---

32 Although here discussing specifically cyberpunk sf, Balsamo points to the much
more extensive sites where cyberpunk mythologies may signify. A mapping of
cyberpunk sf, though difficult enough, is only a fraction of the practices of a "much
broader formation" labeled by *Mondo 2000* as "The New Edge," which could, as
Balsamo observes, include comic books, electronic newsgroups, bulletin boards,
MUDs, and on-line journals (Balsamo 1996: 134-5).

the body is foremost in these readings, which employ the metaphor of the cyborg to address new permutations of post- or anti-humanist embodiment in contemporary technoculture.

The immaterial body vs. the embodied cyborg

In a 1997 review of technocultural studies, Hollinger observes: "There is a determination on the part of many critical thinkers to reinsert the 'meat' into the picture, to resist those dreams of a disappearing body which have been influenced by technological fictions of its looming obsolescence" (Hollinger 1997: 126-7).[33] In different ways, Balsamo, Springer, Hayles, Rosanne (Sandy) Stone, and Vivian Sobchak all challenge what Sadie Plant describes as "a cerebral flight from the mysteries of matter" in postmodern theory, cyberculture, scientific research, and cyberpunk (Plant 1995: 60). Hayles provides a framework for pursuing this concern across a range of discursive borders, identifying a collaborative construction of the "dematerialization of embodiment" in the oft-separated areas of postmodern literary studies and techno-scientific narratives (Hayles 1992: 147). This idea has become a postmodern "orthodoxy" according to Hayles, reinforced by three cultural currents: discourse theory, information theory, and information technology. In order to "excavate" the connections between these sites Hayles suggests the need for a way of talking about the body "that is responsive to its postmodern construction as discourse/information and yet is not trapped within it" (148). Hayles draws on the heuristic distinctions between what she terms embodiment, inscription, and incorporating practices in order to understand the "connections between the immateriality of information and the material conditions of its production" (148).[34]

---

33 This article refers specifically to Dery's *Escape Velocity*, Balsamo's *Technologies of the Gendered Body*, and Springer's *Electronic Eros*.

34 Hayles's example of interactions between inscription, incorporation, and discourse within the "technologies of informatics" is the development of word processing, worth quoting at length:

> As the technology has advanced from manual to electric typewriters to computer keyboards, the touch needed to produce the inscriptions has grown progressively lighter. At the same time, the material resistance of the text to manipulation has dramatically decreased. To erase an error on a manually typed page, it was necessary to interact physically with the paper. Touch was heavy...and the resistance of materiality

In her "Materiality of Informatics" (and later *How We Became Posthuman*) Hayles shows how the "disappearance of the body into a fluid and changing display of signs" is enacted by various postmodernist, cultural, and information theorists, from Baudrillard to Arthur and Marilouise Kroker and Hans Moravec (Hayles 1992: 148; 1999: 192-3). Building on information theory, researchers such as Hans Moravec redefine human minds as cybernetic systems that could be replaced by a *representation*—that is, as a system of code that could be downloaded into a computer "brain" ("transmigration" in Moravec's words). There are obvious resonances here with postmodern arguments for the discursive and linguistic construction of the body.[35]

Also troubled by the apparent obsolescence of the body was Rosanne Stone, whose article "Will the Real Body Please Stand Up" is a key document in the history of virtual communities and cyberspace research. Stone castigates those who would "forget about the body," arguing that "virtual community originates in, and must return to, the physical. No refigured virtual body, no matter how beautiful, will slow the death of a cyberpunk with AIDS. Even in the age of the technosubject, life is lived through bodies" (Stone 1991: 113). And these bodies, despite the early liberalist claims for cyberspace and the internet, continue to be unavoidably marked by race, sex, and gender, no matter which "side" of the screen one is on. Yet, Hayles's tracing of the "superfluous body" in varied discourses leads her to ask: "Is it necessary to insist that the body, far from disappearing, remains essential to human life? No human has yet succeeded in living for even a few seconds without a body" (Hayles 1992: 149). Hayles views such

---

was immediately and physically present. Moreover, the strength of the touch was directly related to the inscription it created... Inscription and incorporation were joined in an arrangement that was visually apparent every time a key lever moved... With word processing, the touch grows lighter and the friction of textuality decreases almost to zero. The smallest keystroke can completely reformat the text, move it to a new location or erase it altogether. The text seems to have lost its materiality, existing not as pages dotted with erasures but as lights flickering on the screen. The relation between incorporation and inscription, no longer proportional and mechanical, is electronic and exponential. (165)

35 Springer comments: "Humans, according to Moravec's misanthropic plan, should consent to their own extinction and cede the future to their computerised progeny"—a scenario that has not been seriously entertained in sf for some time (Springer 1993: 164).

"ecstatic pronouncements and delirious dreams" of disembodiment as evidence "not that the body has disappeared, but that a certain kind of postmodern subjectivity has emerged"—a subjectivity constituted by "the crossing of the materiality of informatics with the immateriality of information" (149). These critiques also make apparent the limiting dualistic logic surrounding discussion and construction of the body when reduced to the either/or of a "flesh and blood entity" versus a "symbolic construct" (Balsamo 1996: 23). The dualist nature of such arguments, Balsamo reminds us, arose from the historical circumstances of feminist challenges to biologically determinist accounts. For Balsamo, the best way to circumvent "the effectivity of essentialist versus anti-essentialist perspectives" was to focus "attention on the ways in which nature and culture are mutually determining systems of understanding" (23).

Like Hayles, Balsamo links concern about the body directly with developments in postmodern thought, and asks: "Is it ironic that the body disappears in postmodern theory just as women and feminists have emerged as an intellectual force within the human disciplines?" (Balsamo 1996: 31).[36] The efforts to deconstruct the "organic foundation of feminist thought" such as corporeal feminism, Balsamo argues, were confronted with a postmodernist discourse "that gleefully joins it in deconstructing biological essentialism. In the process, feminists encounter unsolicited assistance in doing away with 'the body' which served—at one point, if not now—as the necessary foundation of women's empowerment" (31).[37] Vivian Sobchak was another critic who cautioned against the "dangerous libratory poetry of cultural formalists like Baudrillard who long to escape the lived-body and its limitations and write it off (quite literally) as just another sign of its times" (Sobchak 1995: 210). Sobchak links this disavowal of the lived-

36 A similar argument has of course been put for the female "subject." Carol Mason argues that there "is much slippage between the ideas of 'the Body' and 'the self' as historical, hence denaturalized and political 'constructs'"; she gives as an example arguments about abortion in the '60s, '70s, and '80s, when radical feminist interrogations "of the political *subject* gave way to liberal feminist's protection of the political *body*" (Mason 1995: 236).

37 Balsamo goes on to warn of the dangers of being once more "strategically eclipsed," arguing that "feminists have a political stake in constructing and critiquing theories of the body within postmodernism... The final fate of 'the body' should not be left entirely to the panic postmodernists" (31).

body to other cultural trends, such as the obsession with physical fitness and "hard bodies," and to theorists like Moravec (211-12).[38]

> This alienated and highly fetishized fascination with the
> body-object (the body that we *have*) and the devaluation of
> the lived-body (the body that we *are*) is a consequence of a
> dangerous confusion between the agency that is our bodies/
> our selves and the power of our incredible new technologies
> of perception and expression. (211)

The trope of the immaterial body—evident in postmodern theory, information theory, and computer culture—is of course also present (or reflected) in cyberpunk fiction. For critics such as Springer,
cyberpunk offered visions of "worlds where the computer metaphor
for human existence has triumphed" (1993: 164-5). The activities of
cyberpunk characters, argues Springer, erase the boundary between
human and computer and "the nature of the human psyche is rede-
fined in accordance with the computer paradigm" (165). Similarly,
Balsamo writes that while "cyberpunk appeals to the pleasure of the
interface seem to reassert a material body at the heart of new technological encounters, in actuality they are appeals that rest on repression
of the material body" (1996: 161).

These feminist critiques of (dis)embodied relations in cyberpunk
and cyberculture indicate the utility of the cyborg for feminist technocultural engagements in both theory and sf. Many cultural critics
situated the cyborg as a figure that could be re-constructed against the
grain of (immaterial) cyberpunk and postmodern formulations in order to re-situate and re-read cyberspatial relations.[39] In contrast to the
technophilic eclipse of the body (mirrored in much cyberpunk), the
descendants of Haraway's cyborg were seen to enable "a reconstructed
fiction of gender identity" based in a "discursively constructed material body" (Balsamo 1996: 32). Balsamo, for example, argues that "[b]y
reasserting a material body, the cyborg rebukes the disappearance of

---

38 For analysis of the 1990s trend towards lean, hard, "machinelike" bodies and ab-
horrence of yielding flesh among female dieters and fitness fanatics, see for example Susan Bordo, "Reading the Slender Body" (Bordo 1990).

39 See Chris Gray's analysis of the cyborg subject: "on the one hand, it participates
in a decentring of traditional subjectivity, of the metaphysics of presence, of the
organic or essential identity and body; on the other, it offers a physical and bodily
experience of what some feminists call strategic subjectivities" (Gray and Mentor
1995: 458-9).

the body within postmodernism… Ultimately, the cyborg challenges feminism to search for ways to study the body as it is at once both a cultural construction and a material fact of human life" (33).[40]

Feminist cyborgian readings of sf

Drawing on such feminist cyborgian reading practices, these cultural critics utilized cyberpunk much more directly as a way of critiquing and interrogating contemporary technocultures. Unlike in feminist sf criticism, critics such as Springer and Balsamo provided feminist critiques of popular texts such as cyberpunk and popular films, rather than searching for feminist sf alternatives. Springer, for example, displays a fascination with the ambivalence of cyberpunk's razor girls:

> She is simultaneously one of the most compelling and one of the most problematic figures in cyberpunk, for her appeal on a feminist level is frequently undermined by her conventional patriarchal presentation. Her ambiguous status has inspired contradictory interpretations and has sparked debates among commentators on cyberpunk. (1996: 135)[41]

Hardwired women such as Gibson's Molly Millions "clearly embody a fetishized male fantasy, but they also represent feminist rebellion against a brutal patriarchal system. It is difficult to either condemn or celebrate them, since a single interpretation cannot entirely explain their appeal" (138).[42] Springer's both/and approach does not

40 This possibility was already present in some cyberpunk texts, which, as Thomas Foster argued, called into question "distinctions between mind and body, human and machine, the straight white male self and its others, even while they remain dependent on those distinctions to some degree" (1993b: 12).

41 Springer refers to Nixon's critique of cyberpunk's depoliticized "strong" female characters and the exchange between Nixon and John Pierce in the pages of *Science Fiction Studies*—an exchange that Springer observes emphasizes "the ambiguity of cyberpunk's angry woman and her ability to evoke multiple, even contradictory responses" (135-6). (See Nixon 1992a, 1992b; Pierce 1992.)

42 A well known example of such an ambiguous character is Sarah Connor from the *Terminator* films. Springer argues that Connor "fits into a long tradition of phallic women in films whose fetishized bodies are designed to ease castration fears for the male spectator made uncomfortable by the sight of a fleshy woman on screen. However, she also provides an attractive figure in the realm of fantasy for angry women" (138). A different view is provided by Joan Gordon's claims that cyberpunk provided a means of "rescuing" what she termed "overt" feminist sf from its

attempt to resolve the ambiguous figure of this "angry woman," but acknowledges its potentially pleasurable appeal (for both feminists and hackers). "Because of the ambiguities and contradictions of her presentation, however, cyberpunk's figure of the angry woman can neither be hailed as a feminist paragon nor repudiated as a mere sex object; she incorporates aspects of both but fully embodies neither" (139). What most interested Springer about these cyberpunk women was that their metaphoric transformation into computer was not realized; "these cybernetic women do not achieve a radically non-human, computerized existence" (Springer 1993: 171). Thus, in contrast to the claims of "scientists" like Moravec, that human downloading into computer existence would make gender obsolete, "cyberpunk points instead to a future in which gender and sex not only exist but have become magnified" (171). Despite the ambiguity, Springer was clearly unconvinced of cyberpunk's radical potential in terms of refiguring subjectivity, especially as it related to women: "Most cybernetic women in cyberpunk, however, fail to give us a radically nonhuman vision of computerized existence" (1996: 140).

As in feminist sf criticism, Cadigan's *Synners* was often employed by feminist cultural critics to suggest a different model of cyborgian relations and cyber-embodiment than is the norm in cyberpunk and computer culture. For Balsamo, a pivotal message of *Synners* is encapsulated by the refrain "change for the machines?," which "morphs from a literal question at a vending machine to a philosophical comment about the nature of the technologized human" (1996: 134). Again reflecting Hayles's concern with the "materiality of informatics," Balsamo's focus is on the relation of the material body to cyberspace, the "constitution of the informed body," in a text where "information is never merely discursive" (140). In Balsamo's view, *Synners* offers a feminist alternative to cyberpunk narratives, "that begins with the assumption that bodies are always gendered and always marked by race" (144). Gendered differences are suggested by the way the characters relate to cyberspace. Thus, like Vint, Balsamo reads *Synners* as being closer to Haraway's cyborg politics than to cyberpunk culture, as "the gendered distinctions among the characters

---

"rut" of pastoral, organic utopias, seeing a direct link between "angry women" such as Russ's Jael and cyberpunk women such as Molly Millions. She does, however, also admit the political limitations of the latter (Gordon 1990: 196-7).

hold true to a cyborgian figuration of gender difference whereby the female body is coded as a body-in-connection and the male body as a body-in-isolation" (144). Indeed, *Synners* encompasses a spectrum of embodied relations, which for Balsamo represents "four different versions of cyberpunk embodiment": the marked body (Gina), the disappearing body (Visual Mark), the laboring body (Sam), and the repressed body (Gabe) (140).[43] In this embrace of myriad possibilities, *Synners* provides an "alternative vision of technological embodiment" (155).

> In offering gendered descriptions of multiple forms of postmodern embodiment, *Synners* sets the stage for the elaboration of a feminist theory of the relationship of material bodies to cyberspace and of the construction of agency in technological encounters... *Synners* suggests a beginning point in the elaboration of a map of contemporary cyberculture, where technology serves as a site for the reinscription of cultural narratives of gender and race identities. (146)

Thus, for critics like Balsamo and Springer, it is crucial for feminist technoscience studies to contest the discursive spaces and formulations of cyberpunk, and indeed the more utopian refigurings of the cyborg.

Cyborgian readings of feminist-inflected cybernetic narratives such as Cadigan's *Synners* demonstrate the possibilities for constructing embodied cyborgian relations, resisting determinist accounts that could locate problematic "immaterial" behavior in the new technologies themselves. Particularly in the overpopulated and over-determined world of cyberculture in all its literary, scientific, and media manifestations, the predominance of the computer, networks, and "cyberspace" obscured the importance of other technologies implicated in and contributing to cyborg and post-human formations. Biotechnology has been central to feminist technocultural concerns (and also a vital thread of sf and popular science narratives) from the late 1980s on.[44] Genetic manipulation and reproductive technologies

---

43 "Where Sam hacks the net through a terminal powered by her own body, Visual Mark actually inhabits the network as he mutated into a disembodied, sentient artificial intelligence (AI). Although both Gina and Gabe travel through cyberspace on their way to someplace else, Gabe is addicted to cyberspace simulations and Gina endures them" (142). Gina's body is also marked, of course, by its color.

44 A more detailed examination of feminist and sf responses to reproductive technologies is provided in Chapter Seven.

are also central to cyborgian and posthuman reconfigurations, and sf narratives provide ways for critics to map out some of the monstrous hybrids inhabiting the borderlands of feminist critique and scientific progress stories.[45] Susan Squier, for example examines the (re)production of the posthuman body through the cultural images of the ecto-genetic fetus, surrogate mother, and pregnant man. Despite being sites for "potentially oppressive scientific/technical interventions," these bodily figures should not, she argues, be seen as either "inherently oppressive nor inherently liberatory" (Squier 1995b: 113). Instead, such bodies can be read as examples of the "contemporary preoccupation with reproduction as the object of expert knowledge and power," as well as representations that have played "a crucial role in setting the social and cultural boundary conditions for their use" (113, 115).[46] Sf is an exemplary source of such representations, and Squier reads texts such as Octavia Butler's *Xenogenesis* trilogy and Angela Carter's *The Passion of New Eve* as narratives that both develop and challenge such posthuman bodies.[47]

Biotechnologies were also central to Haraway's construction of the cyborg, which was a figure for thinking through not just communications technologies, but also biologies. Indeed, the "Cyborg Manifesto" draws explicit links between the two: "communications sciences and modern biologies are constructed by a common move—*the translation of the world into a problem of coding*" (Haraway 2004a: 23). The

---

45 These other technologies do not seem to have the same resonance as that of computer technology in this "cybercultural" moment, perhaps because they lack the same "hands-on-appeal," operating in the specialized arenas of scientific communities remote from "society" but mediated through sensationalist reporting. Although people can read about and discuss, for example, the cloning of sheep or use of animal genes in food products, they may feel unable to participate in or influence these developments, unlike the potential avenues (albeit mediated by economic status and geographical position, class, race, and gender) for interaction with communication technology and computers.

46 Squier argues that most feminist critiques of these NRTs have failed to adequately assess the social and cultural conditions of their use, and the important gap between this range of medical practices and their representations (115).

47 Similarly, Balsamo's chapter on "public pregnancies and cultural narratives of surveillance" utilizes Margaret Atwood's *The Handmaid's Tale* as a text that "narrativises current anxieties about reproduction in a technological age" (1996: 81). Balsamo observes that in reading *The Handmaid's Tale* as something other than an sf dystopia she is reading "against the grain," instead locating it as a "speculative ethnographical account of our collective life in a technological era" (114).

cyborg figure helped reveal the extent to which these two "natural-technical objects of knowledge" had already blurred the difference between machine and organism, and thus enabled a countering of this "myth of a common language" and a way out of the "maze of dualisms" underwriting humanist subjectivity (39). Ironically, whilst in the past Haraway had criticized the tendency of feminists to concentrate on "uterine politics" and thus gravitate to issues like reproductive technology, her increasing influence on cultural studies of science and technology produced a situation where feminists might "naturally" be drawn to a focus on IT and computers, overlooking many other aspects of contemporary technology and technoscientific relations. As this chapter suggests, much of the feminist cultural and literary criticism of technoscience in feminist sf focuses on the cyborg and cyberpunk. Haraway's work on the cyborg, however, has functioned not only as a metaphor for human-technology relations, but also as a sign of more complex interpenetrations of human/animal/nature than the traditional distinctions perpetrated in scientific discourses.

In turning to sf to explore her construction of a "potentially helpful cyborg myth," (2004a: 32) it is significant that many of the texts Haraway cites include cyborgs produced through, or concerned with, biotechnologies, including the fiction of Octavia Butler. In her 1989 article, "The Biopolitics of Postmodern Bodies," Haraway explores the *Xenogenesis* trilogy as an exemplary cyborgian resistance to the "imperative to recreate the sacred image of the same" (Haraway 1991: 226). The bodies of Butler's alien Oankali are described as "immune and genetic technologies, driven to exchange, replication, dangerous intimacy across the boundaries of self and other" (227). Haraway points to an important difference between human and Oankali technology: rather than building "non-living technologies to mediate their self-formations and reformations," the Oankali "are complexly webbed into a universe of living machines, all of which are partners in their apparatus of bodily production, including the ship on which the action of *Dawn* takes place" (228).

Such readings highlight the ways in which, even for feminist critics, cyborg theorizing has been almost compulsively framed by, and responsive to, cyberpunk. The enthusiasm for cyberpunk as a representative fiction of techno-social engagements placed restraints on the kinds of texts that were privileged as cultural expressions of this technocultural moment. Hollinger's review of the work of critics like Balsamo and Springer makes this limitation explicit, observing that,

> [e]ven their clear-headed critiques of the various political failings of cyberpunk...function—in spite of themselves, as it were—to maintain its centrality ...As it is, the rather unswerving focus on cyberpunk that we see in these studies results in its construction as sf's most representative body of stories engaged with contemporary techno-culture; I do not think that this particular construction is as accurate as it once was. (Hollinger 1997: 131)[48]

While such an observation may well seem obsolete from the vantage point of 2009, a similar critique can still be leveled at the continued "unswerving focus" on the cyborg as a critical tool for reading contemporary techno-relations.[49]

What's in a name?

Around the same time that cyborgs and cyberpunk were at the forefront of feminist sf and cultural criticism, a quite different conversation about feminism and cyberpunk was taking place between writers and readers in the feminist sf community. These exchanges reveal yet another way in which cyberpunk held sway over such debates, but also points to the broader range of texts Hollinger wished to see as representative of sf's engagement with technoculture.

On an electronic discussion list devoted to feminist sf, Fem-SF, a question posed by Karen Joy Fowler in 1995 precipitated a wide-ranging debate about feminism, women, and cyberpunk. Fowler had recently written a review of Joanna Russ's *To Write Like a Woman* and

---

48 Other critics had made similar observations: Stephanie Smith argued that the enthusiasm for the hi-tech style of cyberpunk obscured the significance of work by authors such as Butler. However, in making her case, Smith reads the Oankali's "genetic" technology as a cybernetic system, thus relating Butler's texts to cyberpunk (S. Smith 1993: 76). As Vint would finally observe in 2007, readings of the Xenogenesis series had neglected their connections to contemporary debates over biotechnologies such as IVF and genetic engineering, an oversight corrected by Vint's own reading of the trilogy.

49 See, for example, Cornea (2005), Hayles (2006), Mitchell (2006), and Shabot (2006). In citing these examples, I do not mean to devalue their analyses—Hayles for example, is critical of the cyborg as metaphor. Nevertheless, the continued reference to the cyborg indicates the tenacity of its hold on techno-critics' imaginations.

was asked by the editors to include a discussion of "the many female writers who are now inhabiting cyberpunk and making it their own," with the suggestion that one such writer was Melissa Scott. Fowler wrote: "I hadn't thought of Melissa's work in that way. Maybe I thought the sexual politics of cyberpunk were so intrinsic that Melissa's work couldn't possibly be classed this way" (Fem-SF 29/11/95). There followed arguments both for and against Scott as a "cyberpunk" writer. Editor and fan Debbie Notkin described *Trouble and Her Friends* as "a brilliant example of taking the stuff of cyberpunk, including the sexual politics, and braiding it into a feminist weave. I would say that 'inhabiting' cyberpunk, or perhaps squatting on it, is exactly what that book does" (12/11/95). In contrast, sf critic Brian Attebery suggested that "women writers are recombining the elements [of cyberpunk] in such a way as to equal something that isn't cyberpunk" (12/11/95). A number of other writers were suggested as examples of a different perspective on cyberpunk, including Cadigan, Wilhelmina Baird, Candas Jane Dorsey, Emma Bull, and eluki bes shahar.[50]

References to writers outside the "mainstream" of cyberpunk provoked an effort to define cyberpunk in more explicit terms, producing constructions based variously on texts, authors, content, politics, or style, and oscillating between cyberpunk as a referent for an sf "movement" and as a broader cultural phenomena. Scott's own responses to this question are very interesting. In her view, Cyberpunk as expounded by Bruce Sterling "...is ultimately a pretty useless thing—a carnival sort of genre, in which straight middle-class white men imagine themselves as oppressed and end up reaffirming the status quo" (29/11/95). According to Scott, the contemporary technocultural concerns and techno-social relations considered the *sine qua non* of cyberpunk could be explored in much more radical ways that "could add up to more than just the status quo."[51] Scott's comments on whether her work could be considered cyberpunk are worth quoting at length.

---

50 Brian Attebery, 29/11/95; and Sylvia Kelso, 30/11/95. Wilhelmina Baird, *Crashcourse, Clipjoint,* and *Psykosis;* Candas Jane Dorsey, "(Learning About) Machine Sex" (described by Attebery as "the single best Woman and Computers story that I know of"); Emma Bull, *Bone Dance;* eluki bes shahar, *Hellflower* trilogy (which Kelso includes "if the parameters include using cyberspace [or anyway virtual reality] and gritty underclass women, not to mention a wisecracking style").

51 She adds that "Cyberpunk is also one of the few subgenres of SF that lets you talk about class because it's one of the few genres that takes economics seriously."

I share a lot of the same concerns as the well-known cyber-punk writers, though my conclusions are a lot different, and for that reason what I write shares many of the same images and technological ideas: they're the best way of articulating, literalizing, these same vague and theoretical concerns. My assumptions about the ways the world works are a lot differ-ent, and therefore my books are very different.

My point in all of this is whether or not Bruce Sterling's definition is *the* definition of cyberpunk. If it is, then, no, nothing I've done can be considered cyberpunk. If, however, the definition is something like "fiction about the effect of computer networks, the creation of a global economy, and popular culture on individuals"...then there's room for a whole lot more—and obviously my work fits in there...

So, yeah, I guess I write cyberpunk. Certainly *Trouble and Her Friends* is cyberpunk.

Besides, the coffee-table *Encyclopedia of SF* says I'm a cyber-punk, so I guess I must be. (29/11/95)[52]

For Nicola Griffith, cyberpunk was "more about attitude than tropes":

If there are computers and cyberspace and crime and miser-able, cynical protagonists always on the lookout for number one, then it's cyberpunk. If there are computers and cyber-space and crime and protagonists who are struggling to make their life and/or someone else's a bit better, then it's not. So I don't think of *Trouble and Her Friends* or *Slow River* as cy-berpunk; they both have *hope*, something definitely missing from big chunks of fiction by writers whom everyone agrees work in the genre such as, say, Jeter. (30/11/95)

Whereas Scott's definition of cyberpunk was determined by its subject, which could be expanded to include feminist writers (even though remaining associated with writers like Sterling and Gibson), Griffith defines cyberpunk in terms of its rather regressive class and

---

52 The *Illustrated Encyclopedia of SF* has a section on "The Cyberpunk Years," and apart from Gibson and Sterling, the list of cyberpunk writers includes ("whether or not they actually use the label") Greg Bear, Pat Cadigan, K.W. Jeter, Melissa Scott, Richard Kadrey, and John Shirley (Clute 1995: 88-9).

gender politics, and thus rejects it as a label for feminist work. Fowler also based her view of cyberpunk on "attitude," which she associated much more obviously with gender and sex, rather than individualism or nihilism (in the process suggesting an interesting distinction between Cadigan and other movement writers):

> [T]o me Gibson is all about sex. The secret motto is, yes, you're a loser, but you're really cool and that not-at-all-conventionally pretty, but yet terribly sexy woman with the retractable claws—she sees how cool you are. Your life is a dangerous adventure! And you won't die, although you may be attractively disillusioned and weary by the time it's over... After that you're not going to believe that I really like Gibson's work, but I do. It's a race, it's a rush, and he's really, really good at it... What it's not, I think, is nihilistic, unless James Bond is nihilistic. The appeal of cyberpunk, a la Gibson, is the sexiness. Pat Cadigan is a far grimmer writer, which is probably why her audience is smaller. (30/11/95)

The reluctance of authors like Scott and Griffith to be marked with the "cyberpunk" label stemmed from a highly critical view of the male "movement" and the continued monopoly of male writers over what was defined as cyberpunk. On the whole, the members of Fem-SF were very sensitive to the "masculinized" nature of cyberpunk, and were totally unconvinced of its "revolutionary" potential or liberating possibilities. Reflecting the feminist critiques of cyberpunk's Cartesian transcendental moves, Duchamp argued that,

> [f]or me, Cyberpunk...first and last promotes a hatred of the body. This carnephobia is an underlying attitude of the genre (again, in its narrowest definition by the boys) that I believe is the machine driving some of its most cherished conventions... The works by women with strong cyberpunk elements either ignore this attitude, or negotiate with it, or outright dispute it. The body's something that just does not get dismissed by women writers. (30/11/95)[53]

---

53 Cf Bukatman:

> Science Fiction by women simply does not indulge such fantasies of technological "oneness." The interface with the cyberspatial realities takes a toll on the female subject rarely acknowledged by the cowboy heroes of cyberpunk. In cyberpunk the desire to merge with the

Scott agreed that 'carnephobia' was a defining characteristic of cyberpunk, adding,

> [i]t's actually one of the things I was trying to articulate in *Trouble and Her Friends*—that's why the brainworm translates the nets as a full range of physical sensation, that's why women/queers/people of color use it, they being traditionally (and particularly in the western, which was the other model I was working with) associated with the body and its indulgence as opposed to the intellect and the denial of the body, and that's why so much is made of the fact that Trouble and the others meet in the real world, not just on-line. (1/12/95)

More so than for the feminist critics discussed above, contesting the meaning of cyberpunk had immediate consequences for these sf authors, constituted as it was as the "vanguard" of contemporary sf and thus, for publishers, eminently desirable (in marketing, economic, and critical terms). Many of the authors on Fem-SF were mindful of the effects of labels on their potential readership, critical attention, and remuneration of their work.[54] As Scott wrote,

> [t]he thing that bugs me about the whole question is that there's a huge status issue involved in the field—like "hard SF," "cyberpunk" so often gets redefined to exclude anything that isn't by a straight, white, middle-class man—and then those of us who aren't all of that end up agreeing that "people like us don't write [fill in the blank]," which not only prevents us from having our views heard on the issues that are being considered but also prevents us from being considered important (god forbid, canonical), and makes it easy to dismiss not only our work but the ideas behind that work. It also means that we don't get to debate the definitions, and that's the really bad part... Because I think my

---

machine is romanticized as a necessary but voluntary action, the next evolutionary step. In feminist science fiction, this desire to merge with the machine is viewed as aberrant, and is often presented as an act of surrender rather than empowerment. (Bukatman 1993: 316)

54 Interestingly, by 1997 this issue seemed to have lost some of its force, with Nicola Griffith's *Slow River*, regardless of its non/identity as cyberpunk, winning the Nebula Award.

definition of cyberpunk is a pretty good one, big enough to hold *Neuromancer* et al. but also big enough to include the works that question their assumptions. (29/11/95)[55]

Thus, whereas some writers objected to the use of the label "cyberpunk" to identify feminist work, others recognized the importance of retaining a feminist voice in the struggles over definition, naming, and ultimately, legitimacy (Griffith, Fem-SF, 13/11/95). For writers such as Scott, the crucial point was to recognize and validate the existence of alternative stories of technocultural relations found in feminist sf, stories in which the body was not disappeared.

Taking stock of all of these feminist conversations about technoculture, we see a very different process of critical engagement and canon formation than that of the earlier formative period of feminist criticism. By the late 1980s and early '90s, sf feminisms were partially incorporated into the mainstream of sf—to the extent that resisting or challenging cyberpunk was not as simple as the first forays into critiquing representations of women in the traditional sf canon. Having won a certain level of acceptance within the field, sf feminisms were undercut by cyberpunk's reclaiming of the radical forefront of sf. Attempts to delineate oppositional feminist narratives were also complicated by the ways in which cyberpunk seemed to promise a challenge to the liberal humanist subject—which at least in theory aligned with similar feminist projects. The dominance of postmodern theory in sf criticism through the 1990s and its seeming affinity with cyberpunk also complicated the situation, exposing an ongoing tension for feminist theory—how, then, to hold on to the body? Indeed, this dilemma is actually central to, rather than bypassed in all of Haraway's work—including the Cyborg Manifesto. This is made much clearer in later work (starting, in fact, from "Situated Knowledges") that explicitly

---

55 Another interesting comment about exclusion was made by the British author Gwyneth Jones: "But in dense, complex hard-sf post-modernist worldview fiction (yes, I mean you Ms. Scott) as in all other sf, if it is foolish to be a woman, to be a non-US woman is just about suicidal," Gwyneth Jones, Fem-SF, 3/12/95. I have never seen Jones referred to as writing "cyberpunk," although Clute and Nicholls in their *Encyclopedia* refers to Jones's work as an example of recent stories featuring humans "modified in such a way as to be able to plug directly into computers... particularly graphic images of this kind can be found in...*Escape Plans* (1986) by Gwyneth Jones; the notion is a staple background element of cyberpunk" (Clute and Nicholls 1993: 291) (under the heading "Cyborgs").

rejects a radical constructionism characteristic of some postmodern positions (Haraway 1988). The broader context of feminist politics is also clearly relevant: these critics were writing in the era following the 1980s backlash and the "postfeminism" of the 1990s. In this context it was no longer politically possible or viable to claim feminist sf as a unified, monolithic object, and the array of texts assembled under the label feminist sf often seemed far from what Joan Gordon had termed "overt" feminist sf (Gordon 1990).

Cybersexualities and cyberfiction

By the turn of the century, the situation had shifted; cyberpunk was no longer at the forefront of sf criticism, and radical visions of cyberculture had mellowed into a more pedestrian integration of the internet as part of everyday life. Writerly and critical concern with gender, technology, bodies, and cyborgs did not end in the 1990s of course. Cyberpunk has remained an indelible part of the sf canon, and the cyborg in various forms continues to hold sway in a range of cultural discourses. However, we have seen a shift in terms of the kinds of feminist theoretical and fictional texts called on to engage technocultural debate. A sense of this changing ground can be gauged from two key anthologies appearing at the tail end of critical excitement over cyberpunk: Jenny Wolmark's collection, *Cybersexualities: A Reader on Feminist Theory, Cyborgs and Cyberspace* (1999), and Mary Flanagan and Austin Booth's *reload: rethinking women + cyberculture* (2002). In contrast to Wolmark's emphasis on critical theory, *reload* includes fiction and theory; however, both acknowledge the traffic between criticism and fiction in bringing together sf with technocultural criticism, thus literalizing their common concerns as part of a broader conversation about gender and technology.

Flanagan and Booth wanted to remedy the lack of an anthology of women's cyberpunk or "cyberfiction" by providing examples of "women's fictional representations of cyberculture with feminist theoretical and critical investigations of gender and technoculture" (2002: 1). The critical works in *reload* encompass feminist critiques of cyberpunk and other sf (Hollinger, Foster, Flanagan) along with more pragmatic examinations of the realities of gender and women's lived experience in online culture (Adams, Nakamura, Stein). The essays in Wolmark's collection are all reprints, but she brings together the key feminist critiques of cyberpunk (such as Hollinger, Foster, Doane, and Nixon) with the writings of feminist technoculture critics such as Hayles, Balsamo, Springer, Stone, and Plant. Importantly, she also includes theoretical works by Zoe Sofia, Elizabeth Grosz, Chela Sandoval, and Jenifer González, as well as Haraway's "The Promises of Monsters" (rather than the "extensively anthologized" Manifesto) (Wolmark 1999: 3). What both anthologies also make very clear is the centrality of embodiment to feminist theorizing about gender and technoculture. Part 1 of *Cybersexualities* is titled "Technology, Embodiment and Cyberspace" and includes Stone's key argument for the inability to escape the body in virtual space, Sofia's feminist complication of "virtual corporeality," and the leading figure in Corporeal feminism, Elizabeth Grosz. In addition to "The Visual/Visible/Virtual Subject," one of *reload*'s three sections is called "Bodies" (see also their sequel collection *re:skin*, 2007).

These two volumes collect a different array of sf texts central to the re-imagining of gendered technocultures, reflecting a long-present and increasing concern with gendered bodies, technology, subjectivity, and cyborgian transgressions of natural/social/cultural boundaries. The editors of *reload* define these texts as women's cyberfiction, a genre that "predates the almost exclusively male cyberpunk movement." However, they figure contemporary writers such as Scott, Mixon, Mason, and Carter as "post-cyberpunks," whose texts appropriate "the style and setting of cyberpunk" and function as "both part of and resistant to the larger cyberpunk culture of which [they are] a part" (Booth 2002: 25). Nevertheless, both collections traverse texts rarely included in surveys of cyberpunk, including Laura Mixon's *Proxies*, Raphael Carter's *A Fortunate Fall*, Emma Bull's *Bone Dance*, Piercy's *He She and It* (alt *Body of Glass*), Sue Thomas's *Correspondence*, and Amy Thomson's *Virtual Girl* (Foster 2002; Hicks 2002; Wolmark 1999). All of these can be seen as contemporaries of texts by writers such as Cadigan, Scott, and Mason, suggesting they should not be viewed solely as offspring of cyberpunk fathers. Indeed, Cadigan, the only female associated with the movement, has claimed in an interview that while she was "drawn in" to the group of movement writers by exchanging stories and contributing to *Mirrorshades*, the concerns she was developing in her writing—later identified as generic "Cyberpunk"—were present before she had met any of "the boys" or read their fiction (Cadigan 1990).[56] Thus while at times still constrained by the cultural sway of cyberpunk, these collections begin to mark out a different genealogy of feminist sf concerned with technoculture.

As these readings suggest, a history of feminist precursors could traverse C.L. Moore's "Of No Woman Born," Tiptree's "The Girl Who Was Plugged In," and Anne McCaffrey's "The Ship Who Sang," all of which are reprinted in *reload*. Moore's oft-cited "No Woman Born" (1995; original ed. 1944) contains one of the earliest examples of a cyborg in sf. This story lends itself to feminist interpretations, with its theme of a woman saved from death by technological means (by a male scientist) who achieves pleasure and agency in her new non-human metal body—a nascent feminist cyborg. Moore's story presents interesting avenues for rethinking embodiment, female beauty, and power. The perception of the male narrator, mourning the loss of the beautiful female body, worried about the "fragility" of her "glowing and radiant mind poised in metal" (Moore 1995: 34) and about how audiences will respond to her "inhuman" appearance, is in tension with Deirdre's confidence and appreciation of the potentials and strengths of her new body. The doctor who created her metal body does not see her as human and worries about Deirdre's reaction when she fully realizes she is no longer human: "If only she weren't so...so frail. She doesn't realize how delicately poised her very sanity is. We gave her what we could... but she's so pitifully handicapped even with all we could do" (41). But, as Deirdre shows, she is far from powerless or sub-human, but is in fact a "superhuman" whose only fear is that of loneliness, and who desires "not to draw so far from the human race" (63).

Another early cyborg created by a feminist author is P. Burke of Tiptree's "The Girl Who Was Plugged In" (Tiptree Jr. 1990; original ed. 1973), which again deals with female bodies, "beauty," and identity, but with much darker overtones. The cyborg that P. Burke becomes is ultimately destructive, allowing the illusion that this friendless, physically "deformed" woman can be transformed into the stereotypical "beauty," as she increasingly lives a virtual life as the

---

56 She describes her experience of the WorldCon in Baltimore: "Rudy Rucker was there, [Bruce] Sterling was there, [Lewis] Shiner was there, Bill Gibson was there. John Shirley was there, and we were all talking about the *same* things. We'd all started—I don't know when they were are all writing about what their things were and everything, but I'd already started" (89-90).

mind of the "placental decanter" Delphi, remotely operated from an underground lab. Burke's body, grotesquely marked by "pituitary dystrophy," cannot ultimately be escaped, despite her temporary, illusory inhabitancy of the "godling" body of Delphi. Like the cyberpunk hackers who follow her, Burke desires transcendence of her "meat," not to a disembodied cyber-state, but to a re-embodied existence as Delphi, whose unreachable desirability of body and consumer accessories mark the unreal standards by which this society condemns Burke's body as "better off dead." Burke almost achieves her desire, leaving a ghost in the machine/Delphi that continues to propel her for a few hours after their "death." But Tiptree never lets us forget the "hulk" of P. Burke's body, "the monster down in the dungeon smelling of electrode paste" (1990: 67). And Burke, though she feels she is "in that sweet little body," is not allowed to forget it either and must let Delphi "sleep" while the "forgotten hulk in the sauna" is forced to eat, sleep, and exercise (51).

Tiptree's cyborg contrasts sharply with the unproblematic cyborg figure in Anne McCaffrey's *The Ship Who Sang* (1979). Although also inhabiting a "defective" body, Helva must become a cyborg in order to survive and attain mobility (of a limited sort). Given her lack of alternatives, Helva's life as the "brain" of a space ship is presented as positive and fulfilling. Hayles offers an interesting reading of *The Ship Who Sang* as a "cybernetic romance," with Helva moving "through a typical if vicarious female life-cycle despite her cyborg hyperconnectivity," which suggests there is "essentially no difference between a cyborg and a woman" (Hayles 1993: 164). Most readings of Helva emphasize the conservatism of Helva's "feminine" dreams, the inherent assumption being that a cyborg identity would preclude the assumption of feminine socialized roles. While Hayles agrees that the "Ship Who Sang" stories play "with a transformation they do not take seriously," she goes further:

> The pleasure they offer is the reassurance that human bonding will triumph over hyperconnectivity, life cycle over dis/ assembly zone, female nature over cyborg transformation. Nevertheless, the fact that it was necessary to envision such transformations indicates the pressure that was building on essentialist conceptions of gender, human nature, and traditional life cycle narratives [in the 1960s]. (166)

In tracing these precursors, it is worth remembering that both Tiptree and McCaffrey are called upon by Haraway as "theorists for cyborgs" in her "Manifesto" (2004: 36-7). Another story briefly alluded to by Haraway, but not named, is Tiptree's neglected novel, *Up the Walls of the World*, which like Butler's work is more concerned with biologically-modulated cyborgs (1980). In this novel, various cyborgian connections and interactions are enabled by the space-faring alien, Leviathan, who ends up hosting a multitude of humans and another alien species, the Tyrenni. An African-American woman, Margaret Omali, "merges" with the alien/ship (which could be seen as an "organic" computer), creating a sort of "cyberspace" in which the humans and Tyrenni interact. In this cyborgian/symbiotic relationship, Omali leaves behind a life of struggle and abuse to achieve power and agency, but also increased connection and empathy with other beings (including humans and animals); gendered roles are also broken down, as are the "othering" differences between species. In some ways, Omali seems to have "transcended" her human self, and unlike the other humans and aliens traveling as "negative entropy" within the Leviathan, she has "merged" with the "great entity around them" (281). Still able to take on a "human" form for communication, Omali tells one of the humans "We—I have learned the value of life. I have you all in my circuits" (291). (One can easily imagine Haraway penning such a line!) In an uncharacteristically optimistic tale, rather than emphasizing the alienation of human relations, Tiptree offers the embrace of the alien as a hopeful and redeeming possibility: "Oddly, it is the coming of the alien that is responsible for Dann's most human contact and the most touching one" (291). As with Butler's *Xenogenesis*, it takes an alien and a black woman to midwife a radically new understanding and experience of what it means to be human.

Posthuman—all too human?
Giving information back its body[57]

As we move further away from the cyberpunk's (and the cyborg's) originary moment in the 1980s, more texts are brought into play as evidence of feminist technocultural work in sf, while, increasingly,

---

57 This phrase is taken from the title of an article by Rosi Braiotti, "Posthuman, All Too Human: Towards a New Process Ontology" (2006).

cyberpunk becomes a bit player in, rather than the major attraction of, such investigations. (Similarly, in Haraway's work, the cyborg is demoted to a junior member of the litter in her new figurative tool of companion species.) Sherryl Vint's recent *Bodies of Tomorrow* positions itself simply as a study of "technology, subjectivity, science fiction," while bringing a feminist critique to bear on cyberpunk as well as various feminist sf and feminist "post-cyberpunk" works (Vint 2007). Continuing the conversation and concerns of the critics already discussed, Vint's study is more deliberately situated as an intervention in the "realm of the posthuman, the debate over the identities and values of what will come after the human" (2007: 7). As Hayles reiterates in *How We became Posthuman*, the fact that "information lost its body" is a key factor in the construction of the "posthuman," as is the "technological artifact and cultural icon" of the cyborg (K. Hayles 1999: 2). Thus a key subtext of earlier concerns about cyborg ontologies and embodiment is how we understand and construct a "post-humanist" subjectivity. Although the focus may now be the posthuman, rather than the cyborg, the feminist concern with embodiment is still paramount (and indeed Vint's readings of Haraway much more accurately than Hayles's reflect the complexities and nuances of her work). In contrast to Hayle's "cautious optimism" about the posthuman subject, Vint is concerned to construct an ethical posthumanism, one that is "attentive to embodiment" (2007: 218n13). Specifically, she argues for "an embodied posthumanism, one that remains focused on a subjectivity embedded in material reality and that seeks to be responsible for the social consequences of the worlds it creates" (182).

Vint's argument draws on sf texts that "exhibit current anxieties about embodiment and posthumanism" (2007: 22). In her reading, even cyberpunk texts such as Gibson's *Neuromancer* evidence such anxieties in exhibiting, rather than necessarily celebrating, the appeal of an "escape from the body," while Cadigan's *Synners* is appreciated as an ethical exploration of "embodied reality and subjectivity" (24). Carter's *The Fortunate Fall* (1996) is seen as "an ironic response" to cyberpunk, where those "who live only on the Net are shown to be less instead of more than human" (24). Moving into new territory, Vint also provides an exemplary reading of Gwyneth Jones's work, an author who (as noted in the Fem-SF exchange) has only rarely been discussed in terms of cybercultural concerns. Published at the height of cyberpunk in 1986, Jones's *Escape Plans* deals with computer technology and features characters "jacking in" but does not "feel" at all like cyberpunk (although it is cited in the *Encyclopedia of Science Fiction* under the "cyborg" listing as providing "particularly graphic images" of humans modified to plug directly into computers) (Clute and Nicholls 1993: 291).[58] As Wolmark notes, Jones provides at best an ambiguous take on the "pleasure of the interface," with those most fully interfaced with the computer (through "brain sockets") at the bottom of the social hierarchy: "Since the interface means one thing to the power elite and another to those who are subject to the needs of that elite, it is clear that the cyborg identities in this future are neither innocent nor free" (Wolmark 1999: 237; see also Booth 2002: 28). Vint, however, focuses on Jones's *Aleutian* trilogy, which she sees as most faithful to Haraway's cyborg figuration, in that the alien Aleutians "eschew the boundaries of man/animal or man/machine: both their technology and their domestic animals are made from their own biochemical secretions" (2007: 39). Such connections are not accidental—the Aleutians were Jones's attempt to imagine human identity and subjectivity as non-Cartesian (Jones 1999: 114). All the dichotomies that follow from this mind/body split are erased or complicated by the Aleutians, who cannot be understood through binary divisions of self/other, people/non-people, subjects/objects, or, crucially, male/female. And lest we dismiss the radical cyborgian transgressions of the Aleutians by categorizing their bodily techniques as "natural," Vint reminds us that they are, in effect, a sophisticated, corporeal biotechnology—not unlike the biotech of Butler's Oankali (2007: 193n9).

Extrapolating from Vint's position, I want to suggest some final examples that help us think through ethical, embodied post-human subjectivities that are more faithful to Haraway's non-innocent, boundary-blurring cyborg. A number of 1990s feminist sf texts can be read as dismantling the cyberpunk posthuman move, by giving information back its body. That is, rather than presenting us with humans or biologies translated into code, these texts imagine a *re/materialization* of information, through playing with the embodiment of

---

58 It is also possible to read Cho from Jones's *Divine Endurance* and *Flowerdust* through a cyborg framework. Jones notes that one Italian critic has undertaken such a reading, see Gwyneth Jones, "The Metempsychosis of the Machine" (1997: 10n16).

non-organic Artificial Intelligences (AIs)—a very different kind of cyborgian configuration.

Melissa Scott's *Dreamships* (1992) is a fascinating examination of the boundaries of what can be considered "human." In a world where AI constructs are commonplace, the "Dreampeace" movement fights for civil rights for AIs that have achieved "human" intelligence, opposed by the cartel who produce AIs but also by the lowest socioeconomic class of workers, the "coolies" whose own rights are virtually non-existent. Other examples exploring the "humanity" of AIs are found in novels by eluki bes shahr and Sarah Zettel (shahar 1991, 1992, 1993; Zettel 1997). Although these AIs are "all machine," their actions, desires, and relationships with humans implicate them in a less innocent cyborgian relation than the easy separation of machine/artifact from human/nature. In both examples, AIs exist in societies with limited though still advanced forms of computer and space technology, where hacking or interfacing with the system is outlawed or (even more interestingly, considering the claims made for technologies such as VR) not possible. These texts can be read as re-appropriations and critiques of cyberpunk. The lack of an advanced "cyberspace" setting is a reminder that robots and intelligent machines are old sf tropes that nevertheless take on new resonances when read against the "cyberpunk trend" in sf and technoculture.

In Sarah Zettel's *Fool's War*, "Dobbs" is a member of the Guild of Fools, who crew space ships to provide entertainment but also psychological assessment and covert counseling to relieve the stresses of long distance space travel. Dobbs can travel through the communication and computer systems, in a form similar to cyberspace but imaged only by packets of data. Eventually it is revealed that Dobbs and the whole Guild are actually independent AIs. This future system employs AIs to run most planetary and interstellar communication and organization but their intelligence is limited to the jobs they have to perform, and they are devoid of personality as such. Occasionally AIs become "rogue entities" and are triggered into consciousness, often causing catastrophic computer and even planetary breakdowns. The independent AIs who make up the Fool's Guild are "rogue" AIs who have become stable and are downloaded into organic bodies to pass for human. Dobbs explains that only AIs can travel in the computer networks:

"We can do it because we are born...we come into existence without human senses, and with patterns of consciousness that are measurable and repeatable in an inorganic net. Even then our bodies have to be carefully engineered"—she tapped the implant behind her ear—"to make the jump between environments."

"But, but," Yerusha stammered. "How can you be *Alive*? Are you saying any AI can just get dumped into a body and be human?"

"No." Dobbs shook her head. "Only the ones that become independent inside the net." (Zettel 1997: 316)

Yet even these AIs imported into human bodies have to live by the conditions imposed by their material existence. When Dobbs is propositioned by a renegade group of AIs working to take control of their existence (and thus human society), she is ultimately repelled by the arrangements made to maintain their net existence, which entails relinquishing control of their bodies to "life support" systems and IV lines (Zettel 1997: 352). This contempt for the "meat," which extends to "farming" humans for their bodies, is one of the factors that results in Dobbs's allegiance to humans. Finally, after a battle that necessitates Dobbs leaving her body to become a collective entity on the net to save Earth from destruction, she reflects: "I liked being Human. I liked it from the first day I had a body. I'm going to miss it, a lot" (454).

The overriding theme arising from all these sf feminist encounters with cyberculture is a (re)emphais on the body, materiality, and corporeality. Enthusiasm for feminist reworkings of cyborgs aside, this focus is central to, rather than at odds with, Haraway's original intent. As becomes clearer in her later work, the "body"—materiality—was never meant to be "disappeared" by her cyborg figure, which was intended to re-emphasize the tensions and contradictions of the Cartesian dualisms characterizing liberal humanism (and its consequent impress on western epistemology and ontology more generally). Nevertheless, the cyborg figure and thus Haraway have been called on to promote very different kinds of work—feminist and otherwise—and Haraway herself claimed as a poster academic for both overly utopian cyberfeminisms as well as cyberpunk/s. This connection between cyborg politics and a feminist concern for the body is, as Judith Squires argues, easily overlooked: "If we are to salvage the image of the cyborg we would do well to insist that cyberfeminism be seen as a metaphor for addressing the inter-relation between technology and the body, not as a means of using the former to transcend the latter" (cited in Adam 2002: 164). Despite the pull of cyberpunk, it seems clear that this inter-relation has not so easily been overlooked in sf feminisms.

Looking back on these encounters, the focus on the body that threads through these fictional and critical texts becomes vital as the intersections between cybernetics, cybercultures, and sf futures converge on the seeming inescapability of a "posthuman" future. As Vint notes, "Sf is particularly suited to exploring the question of the posthuman because it is a discourse that allows us to concretely imagine bodies and selves otherwise" (2007: 19). Unlike Vint and Hayles, however, I am not as comfortable with the term posthuman as a way of signifying the different kinds of bodies, selves, and relations we might imagine after humanism. Instead, I agree with Haraway, who warns that we should beware "getting beyond one troubled category for a worse one even more likely to go postal." Like Haraway, "I never wanted to be posthuman, or posthumanist, any more than I wanted to be postfeminist" (Haraway 2008: 17). That is, in sf terms at least, I'd still rather be a cyborg than a posthuman.

7

ANOTHER SCIENCE "FICTION"?
FEMINIST STORIES OF SCIENCE

*A number of friends remain surprised that I...discuss feminist
science fiction, as this seems to me to have a special relationship both to feminist culture and to technoscience. This relationship is both playful and serious; "we" read it—certainly
more of us than follow the feminist science criticism. My feeling is that, as a critical, wide-reaching engagement in feminist
debates around technoscience, feminist SF is quite simply far
too important to be left out.*

→ Hilary Rose (1994: 12)

What if the study and crafting of fiction and fact happened explicitly, *instead of covertly, in the same room, and in all rooms?*

→ Donna Haraway (1997: 110)

The mid-1980s through to the late '90s saw another example of sf
feminism engaged in a cross-disciplinary conversation—around feminism and science—that called on feminist sf as interlocutor. Occurring
over the same period, this interchange was intimately connected to
yet distinct from the dialogue focused on cyberpunk and cyberculture.
While both could count Haraway's "Cyborg Manifesto" as a primary
influence, these feminist challenges to the epistemology and ontology
of the sciences were overshadowed by the high-profile tussles over
cyberpunk. Nevertheless, the conversations traced in this chapter raise
questions and issues that have become pivotal for sf feminism/s, feminist theory, and sf criticism in general.

In recent years, the concerns and insights of science and technology studies have increasingly been considered central to critical accounts of sf. In 2006, Roger Luckhurst wrote of the need to "find new
connections between contemporary sf and a body of critical theory
that focuses on technoculture but that has largely been eclipsed by the
exhaustive finessing of the concept of postmodernism. There have
been some striking blindspots in this regard" (Luckhurst 2006: 1).

Both feminist and sf criticism have recently shown signs of more engaged conversations with feminist science theorists beyond Haraway's cyborg. Mark Bould, Sherryl Vint, and Luckhurst are among those critics turning to science studies as a key context for the study of sf (Luckhurst 2005; Bould and Vint 2006; Vint 2009), while Lisa Yaszek's cultural history of post-war women's sf argues for a "natural compatibility between feminist SF studies and…science studies, literary studies, and cultural history" (Yaszek, 2008: 6). Margret Grebowicz's collection *Sci-Fi in the mind's Eye: Reading science through science fiction* exemplifies this trend by juxtaposing sf and science and technology studies to "provoke encounters, conversations between people interested in precisely these aspects of the culture of science: the politics, the conflicts, the effects, the stakes" (Grebowicz 2007: xvi).

Such moves are significant not only for developing more comprehensive approaches to cultural histories of sf or revealing new contexts in which to explore the feminism of texts neglected in literary studies. They also signify an important exchange between what C.P. Snow termed the "two-culture" divide of the sciences and humanities (Snow 1965). Although the hybrid moniker of the genre would seem to situate sf as an obvious site of cross-cultural exchange, sf critics have been somewhat slow in pursuing this connection—due at least in part to the "exhaustive finessing" of postmodern theory noted by Luckhurst. For in constructionist accounts, the importance of science has often been underplayed, because culture is privileged over nature and the linguistic realm over the materialist (see Bould and Vint 2006). Additionally, just as feminist sf criticism has been marginalized within literary studies, mainstream feminist theory has, until very recently, "betrayed a certain chilliness to feminist science studies" (Squier and Littlefield, 2004: 123; see also E. Wilson 1992). In a postmodern critical climate in which responses from the humanities to the sciences have tended towards the hypercritical, both feminist sf criticism and feminist science studies occupy liminal locations, marked by their connections with science but also, more promisingly, by their potential to disrupt the two-culture divide.

Although science may have been an "exotic" place for feminisms to be generally, for critics of feminist sf, science would presumably be a familiar and necessary context. Such has not been the case, however, as the bulk of feminist sf criticism has approached the genre purely as literature, part of the humanities or "soft sciences" rather than the supposed "hard science" of masculinist sf. Amidst the confusion over exactly how science functions in sf, there seems to be an assumption that, if nothing else, the "science" in sf was what kept it a masculine field for so long and excluded women from its realm, whether it functioned as subject, object, or method (see for example, Donawerth 1997). Despite the tenacity of the two-culture divide (and its rather distorted mapping onto hard and soft sf), feminist studies of science and technology since the 1970s provide an important framework for reading feminist sf. The history of feminist sf demands consideration not only in terms of its status as feminist literature, but also in relation to struggles over the place of "nature," gender, and race in relation to scientific knowledge. Such struggles were at the forefront of feminist science studies through this period, and from the mid-1980s on feminist critics from both sf and science studies drew on feminist sf to work through these issues. Part of these explorations entailed a challenge to the ways in which science was seen to function in sf.

The meaning of science in sf

It is generally recognized that sf has long drawn on — and transformed — the tropes and epistemologies of technoscience. Certainly most attempts to define sf include some notion that it takes science seriously: whether as a privileged way of apprehending the world, a set of values or laws that must be adhered to, or the key driver in human and social development. Nevertheless, the place of science in sf remains a hazy area, with "little consensus on the ways in which 'science' is defined and used" (Mathur 2004: 120). Most obviously, science has been called upon in a naive way to enforce internal gate-keeping (between "hard" and "soft" sf for example) and is regularly employed as a way of delimiting sf from other genres (whether fantasy or mainstream). But what notion of the sf-science relation is employed in such definitional moves?

In studies of science in sf such as *Close Encounters? Science and science fiction*, "real" science (as opposed to science patter or pseudo-science) is associated almost entirely with hard sf: "science fiction in which the major impetus for the exploration which takes place is one of the so called hard, or physical, sciences, including chemistry, physics, biology, astronomy, geology and possibly mathematics" (L. David

Allen, cited in Lambourne, Shallis, and Shortland 1990: 37-8). In such accounts, the only place where the relation of science to sf figures in a serious way is in hard sf. Other forms of sf, such as that produced by the New Wave, are dismissed as being "more concerned *with the impact* of science than with the science itself" (my emphases: 37). In viewing science only as fact, critics can then "cast out all other facets of science employed by science fiction writers," including the social relations of science (M. Willis 2006: 17).

As many observers have noted, "hard SF often has less to do with its scientific content than with a particular stance that Kathryn Cramer calls 'technophilic'" (Attebery 2002: 48; see also Bartter 1992/1993). Just as in the similarly coded distinction between hard and soft sciences, the divide between hard sf and the rest of the genre is not so much about a proper or authentic use of "real" science, but actually proceeds from assumptions about the role of scientific authority and objectivity—a realist, empiricist, and positivist scientific attitude. Most hard sf adheres to notions of the authority of scientific discourse (over the eroding influence of the social and cultural) and a trust in the "scientific method" based on autonomous objectivity, arising from a reified separation between the active, human (usually male) subject and the subjugated, feminized object of knowledge, nature. (In other words, precisely that which is the focus of feminist critiques of science and technology and is often implicitly or explicitly challenged in feminist sf.) Although the hard/soft divide in sf is now generally seen—even by proponents of hard sf like Gary Westfahl—as fairly meaningless (Westfahl 2005), this division has nevertheless done damage to the potential for more nuanced explorations of the kinds of science constructed and explored in sf. In feminist sf studies, for example, the hard/soft sf rhetoric has to some extent constrained the ways in which representations of gender and science are discussed (see below). This reductionist approach characterizes only a certain portion of critical considerations of science in sf criticism. Many other definitions of sf encompass some element of the social context of the sciences and, it could be argued, have done so since Campbellian days.[1]

---

1   In tracing the Campbellian reworkings of Gernsback's scientifiction, Gary Westfahl himself notes Campbell's argument "that science fiction could go beyond creating new scientific ideas to consider thoughtfully the implications, and possible effects on society, of those ideas" (Westfahl 1998: 193). Bould and Vint have argued that we see in Campbellian sf "a foregrounding of the interconnection of science

In the 1960s, Judith Merril identified the social relations of science as one of the key concerns of New Wave writers, in contrast to those who framed such explorations as "anti-science": "The literature of the mid-20th century can be meaningful only in so far as it perceives, and relates itself to, the central reality of our culture: the revolution in scientific thought" (Merril 1971: 54). Merril's sentiments here are not so dissimilar from Haraway's argument, twenty years later, about science vis-à-vis feminist theory. Aside from some hard-sf aficionados, or science warrior types, most contemporary sf critics who deal with the sciences acknowledge their sociocultural contexts. Anne Cranny Francis, for example, argues that numerous sf texts show science and technology to be, "like any form of knowledge, context-dependent and socioculturally specific" (1998: 75). That is, like Haraway, Cranny-Francis argues that "science is culture"; unlike Haraway, however, Cranny-Francis distinguishes between fictive and "real world" science:

> Science fiction is fiction which uses science and/or technology
> to focus on issues of concern raised by the changing nature of
> a society's industrial base and by the ideological and discursive
> influences on and results of those changes; it is not (necessar-
> ily) fiction about actual science and technology. (77)

In being so careful to distinguish the science of sf from "real science" (since this may lead to the traps of accountability, prediction, or accuracy) in formulations such as Cranny-Francis's, the connections between (real world) science stories and (sf) science fictions are sharply delineated. But it is the potential of such fictions of science to speak to our construction and understanding of scientific knowledge and cultures that Haraway and others find most compelling in feminist sf.

Such distinctions allow an approach that reads the science of sf merely as a metaphoric vehicle for exploring gender, sex, or sexuality. For some texts this is indeed the case, but for many others a feminist revisioning or critique of scientific discourses and cultures is an integral function of the text. In other words, visions of scientific discoveries or thought experiments about new genetic technologies in feminist sf not only may function as a means of constructing a women-only world, or a world of five genders, but may also represent the primary

_____

and social world through its countering of the pernicious modern epistemological separation of fact-based science and value-based culture" (2006: 6).

focus of the text, enabling critique of the operation of the techno-scientific-social relations of contemporary society. As Karen Cadora has argued, "taking the science out of feminist sf strips the genre of its power to critique and re-imagine the intersections of technology and gender" (1995: 359).[2]

More importantly, such a separation fails to challenge the divide that drives the damaging modernist model of epistemology and ontology that separates nature from culture. This separation is highlighted and reinforced through the institutionalization of knowledge into different disciplines, as Nina Lykke explains:

> Marking one pole of this divide, the humanities and social sciences supposedly deal with those phenomena that differentiate the universal human being, traditionally identified as "man," from "his" others: things/artefacts and nature. Among these phenomena are the ability to think and the linguistic, aesthetic, ethical, imaginative and social capacities of the human being. At the other pole of the great divide we find the techno-, biomedical and exact sciences. They are expected to explore the non-human, which includes the biological dimensions of the human body, since universal man principally shares them with non-human creatures such as other mammals. (1996: 15)

It is this parceling out and separation of knowledges, and thus understandings of human relations to the world, that is most at stake in the critiques of science theorists such as Haraway and Bruno Latour. The work of both Haraway and Latour challenges the modernist divide between the scientific domain of the "real" and sociopolitical domain of the discursive. As the so-called science wars so vividly illustrated, it is futile to remain trapped in arguments over which realm (science or humanities) offers better access to our understanding of culture, nature, and the human. Such a position merely reinforces the divide and continues to allow the sciences to be the legitimate patroller and producer of (a non-discursive) "nature." It is for such reasons that Haraway has increasingly moved away from overly constructionist positions to what she calls a "relational realism" (Haraway in Schneider 2005: 141):

---

2   Like many other feminist critics who do discuss science and technology, Cadora here concentrates on technology and goes on to examine feminist cyberpunk.

I am neither a naturalist, nor a social constructionist. Nei-
ther-nor. This is not social constructionism, and it is not
technoscientific, or biological determinism. It is not nature.
It is not culture, It is truly about a serious historical effort to
get elsewhere. (Haraway 2004b: 330)

A number of recent articles from feminist science critics express
concerns about the lack of discursive exchange between their field
and related feminist theorizing in the humanities. Critics such as
Elizabeth Wilson, Vicki Kirby, and Karen Barad, for example, are concerned that much feminist philosophy fails to acknowledge or engage
with scientific understandings of "life" (from organisms, matter, and
nature to "bodies") in their accounts of human and gendered subjectivity and embodiment (E.. Wilson 1999; Kirby 1999; Barad 2003).
In contrast, feminist technoscience scholars have long called for the
pressing need to integrate "'nature,' including bodily matter, into the
extended framework of feminist cultural analysis" (Lykke and Braidotti 1996: 243). Within the "more unambiguously 'human'" realm of
the humanities, such a realization has been slow in coming. Haraway's
work has displayed an insistent recognition of the complicated entan-
glements involved in unpacking science stories and, crucially, science's
imbrication with "nature," or rather our stories of nature, signaled
by her preferred term, "naturecultures." From some of her earliest
work, Haraway argued the need for feminists to struggle "within the
belly of the monster," to engage and take seriously the stories of life,
nature, and the material that the sciences patrol and are implicated
with/in. As she wrote back in 1978,

> we have allowed our distance from science and technology to
> lead us to misunderstand the status and function of natural
> knowledge… We have challenged our traditional assignment
> to the status of natural objects by becoming anti-natural
> in our ideology in a way which leaves the life sciences un-
> touched by feminist needs. (Haraway 1991 [1978]: 8)[3]

---

3   Over the last three decades a similar warning has been reiterated by a number
    of feminist critics: "it remains inadequate (both theoretically and politically) for
    feminism simply to reject the biological" (R. Roberts 2000: 1; see also: E. Wilson
    1999; Severin and Wyer 2000; Kirby 1999). Increasingly, this rejection appears
    as both politically and epistemologically unproductive, given the turn in many life
    sciences to understandings that actually work against traditional dualistic binaries
    such as the mind/body split (Kirby 2008; Hird 2004).

The place of "nature" in scientific and feminist discourses is problematic and indeed is one of the most contested issues in sociological and philosophical studies of science. Tracing the construction of nature as an object of knowledge has been vital for contesting the appearance of the natural sciences as a "culture of no culture" (Traweek 1988: 162). Unpacking the signifier "nature" is a project of particular relevance to sf. Although women may often be absent and seemingly irrelevant to much masculinist sf, the figures of woman, the "feminine" and its traditional signifier and co-other, nature, are an overwhelming if negative presence in all sf, and of course in science also. Attebery argues that in pulp sf "sex is nowhere and everywhere," seen most obviously in the attempt to exclude women from the practice of science and interest of scientists such that "[w]hen women are excluded from the laboratory, everything the scientist studies threatens to become a substitute woman" (Attebery 2002: 46). Drawing on feminist science critics such as Evelyn Fox Keller and Sandra Harding, Attebery links this sf "megatext" to the sexualized master narrative of science, which codes nature as feminine (47-8).

The slippery polysemy of "Nature" in scientific, feminist, and postmodern discourses is a central focus of feminist science studies. As Lykke and Braidotti have argued,

> feminist science and technology studies can also be read as a kind of implicit or explicit argument for the integration of "nature" and "bodily matter." It is obvious that "nature" and "matter" are much more difficult to avoid when you move into the monstrous area of feminist studies of the natural, technical and biomedical sciences than when you remain within the "purer," more unambiguously "human," realms of the humanities or social sciences. (1996: 242-243)

As the conversations I examine in this chapter emphasize, taking the science of feminist sf seriously leads to a central problematic—how to account for nature and the material in feminist theory, or in Karen Barad's words, "how matter comes to matter" (2003). For feminist confrontations with science in sf ultimately disrupt the codes invested in the status of "nature" and thus the positivist model of scientific knowledge itself underpinning the sf megatext. In this way, feminist analysis of the science of sf engages exactly the questions and dilemmas central to much contemporary feminist theory.

Conversations about women, science, feminism, and fiction

Writing in 1997, Jane Donawerth noted that "no one has yet attempted to describe the paradigm of science in women's science fiction" (1997: 36n1).[4] Although she was correct that a systematic overview had yet to be attempted, from the mid-1980s through the 1990s a number of sf critics foregrounded feminist encounters with the sciences in sf. And beginning with Haraway's 1985 "Cyborg Manifesto," feminist critics such as Haraway and Hilary Rose also drew on feminist sf to pursue their critiques of the sciences. These cross-disciplinary encounters do not form quite the same inter-related conversation as those around feminism and cyberpunk recounted in the last chapter. It was not until the 1990s that feminist sf criticism began drawing on the resources of feminist science studies in a substantial fashion. Nevertheless, employing Haraway's use of "SF" to signal a field encompassing science fictions, science facts, and speculative fictions, I position these critical stories about feminism and science fiction/s as initiating an important conversation about feminism and science (Haraway 1989a: 5).

Also of relevance to this dialogue are the interests of sf authors themselves. A number of feminist sf authors have scientific training and bring this to bear on their work, including Joan Slonczewski (biology), Catherine Asaro (physics), Vonda N. McIntyre (genetics), and Julie Czerneda (biology). Other feminist sf writers follow up their interests in scientific developments through magazines such as *New Scientist* and conduct extensive amateur research. Gwyneth Jones's novel *Life*, for example, cites Short and Balaban's *Differences Between the Sexes* and Fox Keller's *A Feeling for the Organism* as its prime influences, and Jones spent time observing the work of a female geneticist and her lab team as research for the book (Jones 1999, 2004, 2009).[5] Author Nicola Griffith exemplifies the comment made by Hilary

---

4 The exceptions listed by Donawerth are Patrocinio Schweickart, Donna Haraway, Robin Roberts, and Hilary Rose; see discussion below. See also her "Utopian Science" (Donawerth 1990); there is also some discussion of science in her article "Science Fiction by Women in the Early Pulps, 1926-1930" (1994).

5 For example, Nancy Kress, talking at a panel on "women and hard sf" at WisCon 20, 1996; see also Janet Kagan, author's note (1991: 278), Kress (2007), and Duchamp (2007).

Rose that "'lay' people (and outside our narrow expertises we are all lay people) pick up particular areas of science, typically those which are important or have some special interest for them" (Rose 1996: 96). Griffith has explained how her book *Ammonite* resulted directly from research she carried out in order to find out more about her health problems (finally diagnosed as multiple sclerosis):

> When I was first ill in 1989, in the UK, I was misdiagnosed with myalgic encephalomyelitis, a chronic disease of the immune system. When I moved to this country, that mis-diagnosis was exchanged for another: chronic fatigue and immune dysfunction syndrome. All anyone knew about ei-ther of these two conditions was that a retrovirus *might* be involved, somewhere. I started researching viruses and the immune system. I found a book about lupus erythematosus, a terrible and often fatal systemic disease thought by some to be initially triggered by a retrovirus. Women, I learned, were nine times more likely to contract lupus than men. And, oh, I thought, oh: a sex-linked predisposition to deadly infection. Catastrophe on Jeep [the planet setting of *Ammo-nite*] would come not by fire or flood or alien invasion, but by virus: little packets of alien DNA. (Griffith 1996)

The incentive for this direct engagement with science parallels that of many feminist science theorists, whose critiques developed initially from concerns about the effects of medical science on women's bodies, seen in publications such as that by the Boston Women's Health Book Collective (Boston Women's Health Collective 1969).[6]

Constructing technoscience through feminist sf criticism

The history of feminist science studies provides a logical frame for the approaches to science seen in feminist sf criticism. Beginning with

---

6   In her *Love, Power, and Knowledge*, Rose provides a good overview of feminist the-ories of science, from their beginnings in the radical science and women's health movements, and early feminist concerns with sociobiology and medical sciences. See the chapters "Feminism and the Academy," pp. 51-70, and "Listening to Each Other: Feminist Voices in the Theory of Scientific Knowledge," pp. 71-96 (Rose 1994). Among the significant texts in the development of feminist science stud-ies are Haraway 1988, 1986; Tuana 1987; Longino 1987; Harding 1986; Bleier 1986; Rothschild 1983; Keller 1983; Merchant 1980. A useful reader is Keller and Longino's *Feminism and Science* (1996).

campaigns to train more women in scientific and technological fields and challenges to the "masculinist culture" of the sciences, feminist science studies increasingly focused on the gendered and raced nature of scientific language, knowledge, and practice. In recent years, key themes emerging from the various strands of this interdisciplinary field have included debates around objectivity (how we construct or position the knowing subject); the potential for a more democratic science; and how to maintain a feminist epistemology and praxis in the face of charges of relativism.[7] Paralleling these developments, both feminist sf and its criticism display a variety of deconstructive and reconstructive approaches to science. Whilst not a strictly diachronic progression, sf feminisms as well as feminist science studies begin with critiques of the masculinist bias of science, followed by an impulse to "improve" science by "adding" women, a focus on what different characteristics being a women scientist might entail, and various expressions of the desirability of a significantly altered—even feminist—science.

Within sf criticism, one of the earliest articles to focus on science in women's sf was Virginia Allen and Terri Paul's "Science and Fiction: Ways of Theorizing about Women" (1986). From what Sandra Harding termed a feminist empiricist position, Allen and Paul read women's sf as an example of scientific pedagogy, employing observation, hypothesis, and speculation (Allen and Paul 1986: 166). Beginning with an analysis of "The Women Men Don't See," they situate Tiptree's examination of gender as an example of "good science" in practice. In a move that makes science central to women's sf, they claim that an important part of a story's science fictiveness rests on the fact that it is "doing science": "It is this doing science—theorizing about curious phenomena and testing hypotheses—that makes the story science fiction in the best, the fullest sense" (1986: 166). Allen and Paul's position accords with a feminist empiricist stance, arguing that when science fails to take account of gender, it not being practiced "properly." They extend this belief to sf: "Good science fiction has a mandate to explore ideas with the methodology of science, particularly ideas that do not fit within the prevailing paradigm" (170).

---

7   For an excellent overview of some of these tensions, see Margret Grebowicz (2005). Other contemporary overviews include Harding (2004); Mayberry, Subramaniam, and Weasel (2001).

Allen and Paul conclude that theorizing about gender engages in that essential component of scientific inquiry, speculation, and will, the authors suggest, result in a better science.

> It is difficult if not impossible to carry out scientific research in good faith, responsibly, when the scientific community has a vested political interest in its interpretation—whether the bias is feminist or misogynist. (174)

Calling on a wide range of feminist sf texts from Tiptree to Russ, Charnas, Kit Reed, and Suzette Haden Elgin, Allen and Paul argue that sf, much more so than mainstream fiction, is suited to the exploration of non-masculinist social and scientific paradigms.

> Science fiction makes its unique contribution to greater understanding by providing something like a laboratory for investigating hypotheses about human nature... When feminist science fiction writers theorize about the nature of men and women...they engage in an essential component of scientific enquiry, speculation. (181-2)

In claiming this speculative function for sf, Allen and Paul foreshadow later claims by critics such as Rose, who describes feminist sf as a "dream laboratory."

A key element in empiricist critiques is the view that both scientific cultures and practices can be "improved" through better representation of women in the sciences. Donawerth's framing discussion of "women's participation in science" in *Frankenstein's Daughters* indicates the historical importance of such positions. The long-standing struggles to improve women's entry into scientific professions influenced women's sf not only from the 1960s and '70s, but in a number of texts from the 1920s and '30s. Stories such as Clare Winger Harris's "The Menace of Mars" (1928) and Louise Rice and Tonjoroff-Roberts's "The Astounding Enemy" (1930) feature women scientists, reflecting, according to Donawerth, the late nineteenth-century campaigns to gain science education for women (earlier expressed in utopias such as Mary Bradley Lane's *Mizora* and Charlotte Perkins Gilman's *Herland*) (1997: 4-5).[8]

---

8   Yaszek questions Donawerth's association of these pulp writers "with the feminist politics of preceding decades rather than, say, the woman-centered but ultimately nonfeminist politics of 'municipal housekeeping' espoused by socialist and New Deal women at this time" (Yaszek 2008: 108n. 3). Whilst Yaszek is right to cau-

The issue of more equal representation in the sciences was an important first step in feminist critiques and, as Donawerth argues, necessary in "imagining women as subjects of science, not as its objects" (5). Nevertheless, many feminist critics would later argue that constructing an "equal playing field" in science did not necessarily imply a radical change in the nature or practice of science itself. As Harding and other critics would point out, the empiricist arguments for women's inclusion emerged *not* from a desire to change the nature of science but from a belief that a "true" adherence to scientific methods and objectivity necessitated eliminating its androcentric bias.[9]

Apart from Allen and Paul (who in fact imply more radical effects than a limited empiricist position), most other critics exploring gender and science in sf presume that changes in the nature of science, and thus sf, are a necessary and natural result of feminist interventions. In "Feminist Epistemology in Piercy's *Woman on the Edge of Time*," Billie Maciunas explores Piercy's text in the context of Sandra Harding's *The Science Question in Feminism* (Maciunas 1992; Harding 1986). In this text, Harding categorized three different types of feminist epistemologies that challenged traditional, patriarchal ways of knowing—feminist empiricism, feminist standpoint, and feminist postmodernism. Harding also briefly referred to women's sf, suggesting that in challenging "science-as-usual," "we should turn to our novelists and poets for a better intuitive grasp of the theory we need" (20). Following Harding's suggestion, Maciunas reads Piercy's text as a way of tracing the emergence of all three of these feminist

---

tion against the search for feminist forebears despite the existence of more immediate historical contexts, I do not necessarily agree that Donawerth is incorrect in observing such a connection with the specific campaign around science education. In this regard, I am intrigued by a passing comment by Samuel Delany that female characters in sf were influenced by the women's movement of the "teens and '20s...which had been stabilized by the marginal position of pulp fiction outside that of the literary mainstream" (Delany and Freedman 2008: 213).

9   Indeed, many women within the sciences still reject what they see as an attack on the very basis of scientific knowledge and remain committed to the "practical" liberal project to encourage the increased participation of women in science. Wendy Faulkner, among others, has noted the difficulty of combining increased representation with a more radical project to transform the sciences (Faulkner 1995: 343). More recently, Grebowicz points out that even contemporary feminist analyses influenced by postmodern critiques leave certain tenets of scientific epistemology in place (Grebowicz 2005; see also Harding 1996; Wayne 2000; Roy 2004).

epistemologies. Dealing only superficially with science as such, Maciunas nevertheless indicates the relevance feminist sf has for critiques of science as it indicates "revolutionary changes in knowers, ways of knowing, and the world to be known" (257).

Perhaps the best example of a "feminist standpoint" critique is found in a 1983 article that in many ways presages Harding's later refinements on standpoint epistemology (Schweickart 1983, see also, Bartter 1992/1993; and Stocker 1989). In her "'What If...Science and Technology in Feminist Utopias,'" Patrocinio Schweickart questions the "othering" of women and nature seemingly inherent in the traditional model of the scientific method. Schweickart's examination was based on readings of texts such as Dorothy Bryant's *The Kin of Ata are Waiting for You*, Gearhart's *The Wanderground*, and Le Guin's *The Dispossessed* (Schweickart 1983: 204). Rather than the usual emphasis on the ways feminist utopias *rejected* science and technology, Schweickart figures this turn as a "radical critique of the masculinist logic of science and technology" and not simply an essentialist privileging of a feminine "Nature" (204; 201). Schweickart's analysis thus operates within the framework of "successor science projects" entailing a radical, feminist refiguring of the "scientific method" and epistemology (see for example, Kember 1996: 231, 236). Her approach produces a reading of Le Guin's novel different from many other feminist analyses, which have criticized the focus on a male scientist and retention of a male perspective. Instead, Schweickart identifies the utopian nature of the use and methodology of science, which, she argues, does not employ a "logic of domination" nor is "separated from moral and ethical concerns" (1983: 208-209). Schweickart's article demonstrates that a focus on science and technology can provide an alternative framework for assessing the "feminism" of texts, one that may be overlooked in analyses focused more narrowly on re-visions of the gendered social order.

The most sustained examinations of science in sf criticism appeared in the 1990s, in Donawerth's article "Utopian Science" (1990) and a chapter of the same name in her book *Frankenstein's Daughters* (1997).[10] Also declaring an interest in science, Robin Roberts' *A New*

---

10 Among the feminist and women's sf texts discussed by Donawerth (that have often received little if any critical attention to date) are James Tiptree Jr.'s *Up The Walls of the World* (1978), Sherri S. Tepper's *After Long Silence* (1987), Sheila

Species (1993) refers to feminist science theorists in contextualizing her approach to science, but does not bring these critics to bear in her reading of the sf texts themselves. Appearing after more than a decade of sustained feminist science studies, these more substantive engagements with science in feminist sf exhibit the major themes characterizing this body of critical work: namely, a focus on "women's issues" such as reproductive technology, the impact of women's standpoint on science, and the possibility of constructing a feminist science.

Women's issues? NRTs and sociobiology

The area of technoscience that had, at this point, attracted the most attention from feminists (including those outside the sciences) was that of the "new reproductive technologies" (NRTs). Such technologies can, problematically, be figured as a "natural" concern of women, or as Donawerth puts it, a "women's issue" in science—one that has immediate and visible effects primarily on women's bodies. In sf, interest in reproductive technology appeared as early as the 1930s. Donawerth considers a number of early examples by women writers, such as Lilith Lorraine's "Into the 28th Century," where women's fetuses are removed after conception to be grown in a laboratory (Donawerth 1990: 543; Lorraine 1930: 250-267). In Donawerth's reading, such writers offered "alternative technologies of childbirth and scientific child rearing" and often added "a reduction of childcare owing to scientific progress to the utopian abolishment of the dangers of childbirth" (Donawerth 1997: 12).[11]

Since the 1970s, a vast body of feminist writing has confronted the repercussions of contemporary medical technologies and NRTs, which, in contrast to work on the technological benefits of family planning and birth control, is much less celebratory of the "technological fix."[12]

Finch's *The Garden of the Shaped* (1987), Barbara Paul's *An Exercise for Madmen* (1978), Pamela Sargent's *Cloned Lives* (1976), Anne McCaffrey's *Dinosaur Planet Survivors* (1984), Judith Moffett's *The Ragged World* (1991), Janet Kagan's *Hellspark* (1988), C.J. Cherryh's *The Pride of Chanur* (1982), Phyllis Gotlieb's *Emperor, Swords, Pentacles* (1982), and Rebecca Ore's *Becoming Alien* (1988).

11 Among the examples discussed are Leslie F. Stone's "Letter of the Twenty-Fourth Century" (1929), "Out of the Void" (1929), and "Women with Wings" (1930); and Sophie Wenzel Ellis's "Creatures of the Light" (1930).

12 Some of the significant feminist texts on reproductive technology from this period included Scutt (1988); Arditti, Klein, and Minden (1984); Hartouni (1997);

Yet such work has rarely been brought into dialogue with feminist sf, with one of the few exceptions being the juxtaposition of Shulamith Firestone's arguments in *The Dialectic of Sex* with Marge Piercy's vision of utopian reproduction in *Woman on the Edge of Time*. Two texts that could be read very differently through the lens of feminist theories of NRT are Sheri S. Tepper's *Gate to Women's Country* and Pamela Sargent's *The Shore of Women*, in which artificial insemination is controlled by women, and rather than "farming" ova, men are "milked" for their sperm.[13] The re-emergence of sociobiology was one discourse about gender that fed into the idea of the '80s as a period of conservatism and backlash, and texts such as Suzette Haden Elgin's *Native Tongue* trilogy and Margaret Atwood's *The Handmaid's Tale* are conventionally read in terms of this conservative atmosphere (if not specifically in terms of the discourse of sociobiology).

As Donawerth suggests, other texts that could be read in the context of feminist reactions to sociobiology are 1980s "role-reversal" stories such as C.J. Cherryh's *The Pride of Chanur*, Jayge Carr's *Leviathan's Deep*, and Cynthia Felice's *Double Nocturne* (Donawerth 1997: 15-16).[14] Reading role-reversal texts as part of the feminist dialogue about sociobiology and reproductive technologies sets their relation with the 1970s feminist sf utopias in a more complex light. Piercy's text was the only one of the '70s utopias to directly address the issues of control and power entailed by artificial reproduction and to confront a potential feminist aversion to "babies in bottles."[15] In Piercy's

---

Strathern (1992); Squier (1994); Rowland (1992); Baruch, D'Adamo Jr., and Seager (1988); Franklin and McNeil (1988); McNeil, Varcoe, and Yearley (1990); Spallone and Steinberg (1987); and Corea (1985).

13 However, as Joan Haran pointed out to me, in Tepper's *Gate* these technologies are also still intrusive of women's bodies.

14 Donawerth reads a number of feminist sf texts and dystopias in terms of the feminist critiques of sociobiology, such as Anne Fausto-Sterling's *Myths of Gender* (1992).

15 Expressed through the voice of the "contemporary" Chicana narrator, Connie, who represents one of those groups who is most vulnerable to the sexist and racist implications of techno-scientific medical authority. Whilst Connie is appalled by the idea of both sexes mothering and breast-feeding, and reproduction by means of "Mother the machine," her despairing comments are revealing: "She hated them, the bland bottleborn monsters of the future, born without pain, multicolored like a litter of puppies without the stigmata of race and sex." Piercy (1991 [1978]: 104-6).

hands, this troubled offspring of twentieth century technoscience becomes the means by which gendered power differentials of parenting are eliminated. Racial and cultural differences are divorced from genetic inheritance in order to break down the (re)production of patrilineal purity of "bloodlines."

As Lefanu has observed, most other feminist sf writers rejected Firestone's view of pregnancy (as "barbaric") and her argument that technological control of reproduction is the means to liberation (Lefanu 1988: 59; Firestone 1979).[16] While some form of exogenetic reproduction is necessary for the all-female societies in novels such as *The Wanderground, The Female Man,* and *Motherlines,* the novels are somewhat ambiguous vis-à-vis contemporary feminist debate over the issues of control and choice in reproductive technologies; the absence of men meant that questions concerning this technology's troubling history and origins in a patriarchal system of techno-scientific domination could be bypassed. Such concerns, which have been at the center of feminist critiques of NRT, are confronted much more directly in other feminist sf texts. As Marleen Barr observes, Octavia Butler's *Dawn* can be read in the context of the late 1980s feminist critics of reprotech such as Gena Corea and Robin Rowland (Barr 1992: 87-8).[17] Here is Lilith, the central character and narrator of *Dawn:*

> In a very real sense, she was an experimental animal...Was that what she was headed for? Forced artificial insemination. Surrogate motherhood? Fertility drugs and forced "donations" of eggs? Implantation of unrelated fertilized eggs. Removal of children from mothers at birth... Humans had done these things to captive breeders—all for a higher good of course. (Butler 1988: 58)

Other examples occur in a collection of fiction specifically written as feminist meditations on NRT, *Angels of Power, and other reproductive creations,* which includes stories by Australian sf writers Lucy Sussex

---

16 This view became, of course even more widespread in the 1980s and '90s, as the rapid development of reproductive technologies and the question of control and "choice" became vital feminist issues.

17 See also Barr (1987: 125-32), which refers to the work of critics such as Gena Corea.

and Rosaleen Love (Hawthorne and Klein 1991).[18] One of the editors was Renate Klein, a well-known feminist critic of NRT and genetic engineering, who argued that such fictions have powerful potential.

> Imagination, vision and a good joke have the power to show up [reproductive] technologies for what they are and to carry us into a different future: one in which women are no longer "test sites" for science's fantasies of a grey future, and one in which diversity and human variation are not only valid, but also valued. (Hawthorne and Klein 1991: xi)

In contrast to earlier feminist utopias, one of the few post-'70s all-female worlds to address the process of "gynogenesis" does so in terms of female control over a technology of reproduction not fixed in the contested realm of "mother the machine." In Nicola Griffith's *Ammonite*, a virus has infected a planet's population and killed all the men. One of the effects of the virus on the original inhabitants of Jeep, who have assimilated the virus, is the ability to perceive and even influence their biochemistry, including conception. "The virus had altered everything. She saw how she could change the chromosomes, how she could rearrange the pairs of alleles on each one. If she reached in and touched *this*, enfolded *that*, the cell would begin to divide. And she could control it..." (Griffith 1993: 267)

Feminist critiques of reproductive and genetic technologies are animated by the re-assertion of women's right to control their bodies and thus to affirm experiences and affinities culturally encoded as "female" over the detached authority of "science." Moving beyond "deconstructions of patriarchy," feminist standpoint epistemologies maintain that the master narrative of the sciences can be re-made into a discourse that does not alienate women or people of color (a position that has sometimes appeared to invoke essentialist assumptions of an innate connection between "women" and "nature").

Women's science

Introducing traditionally feminine concerns such as empathy and emotion into the sciences is a hallmark of feminist standpoint approaches that posit a need for a "successor science" that acknowledges

---

18 Lucy Sussex, "Mother-of-All," pp. 95-127; Rosaleen Love, "Tanami Drift," pp. 228-51.

"women's issues." Many feminist sf texts design futures where science includes areas considered unscientific (or soft, social sciences) in western technoculture. Donawerth's study covers a number of examples that incorporate issues, work, and even spaces traditionally considered women's realm into their future sciences. For example, in the Sharer society of Joan Slonczewski's *A Door Into Ocean*, day-to-day living, childcare, and science are all part of a communal social space, and, in Donawerth's words, "laboratories look just like homes." "In this society, the person who cleans the labs is very likely the same person who does the science" (1997: 10). Similarly, Donawerth argues that communication—traditionally seen as a female attribute—operates as a "science" in texts such as Bradley's Darkover novels, Tepper's *After Long Silence*, Elgin's *Native Tongue*, Sheila Finch's *Triad*, and Janet Kagan's *Hellspark* (6). Another example cited by Donawerth as evidence for a "redefinition" of science to incorporate "women's values" is Naomi Mitchison's *Memoirs of a Spacewoman*. The spacewoman, Mary gives us a glimpse of her (future) history:

> I may be out of date, but I always feel that biology and, of course, communication are essentially women's work, and glory. Yes, I know there have been physicists like Yin Ih and molecular astronomers—I remember old Jane Rakadsalis myself, her wonderful black, ageless face opening into a great smile! But somehow the disciplines of life seem more congenial to most of us women. (Mitchison 1985, cited in Donawerth 1997: 1)

In this "history of science full of women," however, Mitchison goes beyond a simple role reversal privileging "women's work." In Mary's future, it is taken for granted that there *will* be women—not only white, but women of color—participating in all sciences, including the "hard" sciences (Donawerth 1997: 5).

Donawerth drew on such examples to argue that their re-valuing of "female" fields or "soft" sciences contributed to a *redefinition* of science. Yet the privileging of alternative areas of science does little to redefine what counts as the natural sciences and does not destabilize the hierarchical model that separates and devalues the soft sciences (in contemporary society *or* sf). Working from a more enigmatic feminist standpoint, theorists such as Harding, Keller, and Haraway were involved in a broader project of interrogating the practices and assumptions of the whole range of sciences.[19]

Within sf, areas and subjects considered more appropriate to women have historically been marked along the hard/soft divide— that is, as a binary with the hard sciences such as physics on one side and the softer social sciences (including, interestingly, biology) on the other. In *A New Species: Gender and Science in Science Fiction*, Robin Roberts reaffirms the notion that men write hard sf and women write soft sf, effectively leaving this gendered binarism intact (1993: 5). She instead reverses the traditional hierarchy to privilege the social sciences, imaginary sciences such as telekinesis and telepathy, and magic, arguing that writers who "depict magic as valorizing for women and as a legitimate science" may "overcome the dichotomy between valid hard science and invalid soft science" (8). However, exactly how this dichotomy could be overcome and the implications for science if successful remains unclear. In a discussion of Piercy's *Woman on the Edge of Time*, Roberts argues that in Mattapoisett, "soft science is explicitly contrasted to the negative hard science" of the contemporary western world (85). Piercy was not merely championing a "feminine" soft science over a masculinist "hard," however. What really differentiates the forms of science characteristic of contemporary society from Mattapoisett are the social and cultural contexts that inform the organization and implementation of this "utopian science." In contrast to the twentieth-century US, Piercy constructs a society and science in partnership, a relation of equilibrium, rather than one of exploitation and domination. In characterizing this relation as typical of a "soft," "feminine" science, Roberts' analysis omits the notion of a different way of constructing science and its subject(s) within the "social" field, leaving unquestioned the inevitability of the "mastery" rhetoric of the hard sciences. In this taxonomy, male/female and hard/soft are not challenged as social constructions, but appear as self-evident and fixed entities, where, for example, it is assumed that magic is a "female" and computers are a "male" paradigm of science (Roberts 1993: 98).[20]

---

19 For example, by investigating how molecular biological accounts of genes reproduce culturally specific human social narratives (see Keller 1992; Haraway 1989b).

20 This example is drawn from her discussion of Joan Vinge's *The Snow Queen*.

In contrast to Roberts' validation of a "feminine" paradigm, in *Frankenstein's Daughters*, Donawerth is more concerned with the possible transformations brought about by re-positioning science. Like Roberts, Donawerth also identifies a central problem for feminist science theorists and sf authors: the fact that the contemporary model of science constructs women as the objects, not the subjects, of science. Both Donawerth and Roberts look for examples of sf that fulfill the empirical goal of situating women as scientists and that broaden the definition of science to include areas that more easily situate women as "subject." Donawerth, however, focuses more on the kinds of re-visioning and reconstruction of science that occur in both feminist science theory and feminist sf.

Utopian science

Donawerth's central claim is that both feminist sf and feminist science theories have a shared goal—to create a "utopian paradigm" of feminist science, which would entail,

> [w]omen's participation in science as subjects not objects, revised definitions and discourses of science, inclusion in science of women's issues, treatment of science as a origin story that has been feminized, a conception of human's relation to nature as partnership not domination, and an ideal of science as subjective, relational, holistic, and complex. (1997: 2)

This listing indeed captures many of the goals pursued by feminist science theorists; however, it tends to suggest a unity of purpose (and methodology) that is not reflective of the complex reality; indeed the very feasibility (and even desirability) of a "feminist science" was the subject of much debate in feminist science studies (see for example, Fee 1983; Harding 1991; Longino 1987; Rosser 1987). Donawerth draws a detailed profile of what such a feminist science would look like.

> Besides changing the conception of nature, by including women in science, feminist historians and theorists of science have argued, a revised science would express the culturally different qualities assigned to women. A feminist science will acknowledge subjectivity in its methods; it will look at problems not just analytically but also holistically; it will aim for the complex answer as best and most honest; and it will be

decentralized and organized cooperatively. In all these ways, a feminist science is utopian, since these conditions, values, and goals do not describe contemporary science. (1997: 22)

Donawerth's assumption here that inserting "women" and women's values into science would automatically make for a different (and better) science is precisely the aspect of earlier feminist standpoint arguments that has come under challenge. Postmodernist theorists have critiqued feminist standpoint positions for naively evoking a unitary female experience that disregards race, class, and cultural differences.[21] And so from the early 1990s on, the notion of a feminist science has come to stand for a particularly intransigent problem in feminist science studies, which needs to argue from a position of political responsibility without falling back on a certainty secured through "the innocence of identity politics" (McCaughey 1993: 80; see also W. Brown 1991: 63-84; Haraway 1988).

Given this context, Donawerth rightly points to feminist sf as a space where alternative models of science can be tested.

Because almost no feminist science exists, many women science fiction writers and feminist science theorists have imagined an idealized system of science, creating it as a dialogue with and critique of contemporary scientific ideologies and practices. (1997: 2)

One of the texts Donawerth calls on to illustrate this utopian paradigm of a revised, feminist science is Judith Moffett's *The Ragged World*. Perhaps not immediately obvious as a feminist novel, its feminism inheres in the construction of an alternative practice of science, "its careful revision of the definition and discourse of science" (1997: 8).

Rather than presenting an abstract discourse about science, Moffett, through her biologist, stresses embodiment and connection to life: when the biologist finally does an experi-

---

21 Regardless of whether a standpoint position is essentialist or "constructed," some postmodernist critics take issue with the claim that the knowledge based on the lives of oppressed groups will necessarily produce a "better" science. Critics such as Jane Flax and Susan Hekman are opposed to the belief that feminist (or antiracist, anti-colonialist, anti-heterosexist) epistemologies as knowledge arising from (ontologically "privileged") oppressed groups can be "better," or "less false than those produced by the dominant western phallocentric sciences (see Hekman 1990; Flax 1992).

ment, she does so with melons and squash in her own back-
yard, not in her college laboratory. (8)

Donawerth sees Moffett's biologist as pursuing a science expressed
through what Hilary Rose calls the "language of love" that "current
science lacks and a utopian science would discover" (1997: 10).

> Moffett thus presents us with a utopian science that revises
> the definition of our science and offers a different vision, of
> science as full of choice (and accident), practised by loving
> caretakers who speak a language that includes connections to
> external environment as well as internal genetic mechanics.
> (Donawerth 1997: 11)

Donawerth here identifies many of the themes central to feminist science studies of the time—a more holistic approach to the life sciences,
a revaluing of what spaces and activities count as "scientific," and finally a deconstruction of scientific methodology that challenges what
Nelly Oudshoorn calls the "myth of scientific heroes discovering the
secrets of nature" (Oudshoorn 1996: 122-3). Although such a model
of scientific practice could indeed be construed as "utopian" in its
foregrounding of feminist concerns, it also provides a pragmatic and
achievable model of a different way of doing science (helped by the
fact that Moffett's biologist had given up any ambitions to be a career
scientist). And yet, in a sense, Donawerth's concern to valorize feminist
sf minimizes the potential of the very work she calls upon to enrich
and contextualize her readings, for situating these re-imaginings of
science-as-usual as "utopian" overshadows the similarly radical work
being accomplished in the discursive field of feminist science studies.[22] An essential element of feminist interventions in the sciences has
been the process of challenging the narratives, myths, and truth-claims
of science. As Haraway argued back in 1986, "feminist science is about
changing possibilities," and feminist interventions such as Haraway's
had in the early 1990s already begun to alter the possibilities of what
could and could not be claimed in the name of "science" (Haraway
1986: 81). Indeed, an exploration of what a "feminist science" might

---

22 In hindsight, however, it is important to recognize that the radical critiques and innovations of feminist science studies provided, in the post-backlash, "post-feminist"
   period of the 1990s, one of the few sources of such utopian visions. Thus, given
   the retreat from the utopian moment of 1970s feminist sf, it is easy to see the
   appeal of casting this particular strand of feminist sf as utopian.

constitute was the focus of one "real world" group of scientists in the later 1980s (Harding 1991).

Real life feminist science

The October 29th group at the University of Wisconsin-Madison was one such example of a real world attempt to intervene in science-as-usual. Inspired by Ruth Bleier, this discussion group asked "What would a feminist science be like?"—a question they, as working scientists and feminists found "not only philosophical, but intensely emotional, practical and urgent" (October 29th Group 1989: 253). Writing of their conclusions as well as "disagreements about a feminist critique of the natural sciences," the group described its collective process as "part of feminist science in action" and indeed claimed to be "in some ways a forerunner or prototype of feminist science" (253, 259).

> When the question of whether such a thing as "feminist science" could exist was first posed, our training in traditional science made it seem absurd: good science is good science whatever your politics, we thought. For some of us, this is still the case. Nevertheless, we all acknowledge the importance of a feminist critique of science, and we continue to struggle with the question "What is a feminist science?" (254)[23]

One of the more practical and immediate issues raised by the October 29th group was the importance of feminist sensitivity to matters such as the kinds of subjects chosen for scientific scrutiny, from the obvious concentration on sex differences in brain structure to the less obvious, such as "the fascination in molecular biology with 'master molecules' or in physiology with 'master glands'" (256-259).[24] The October 29th group was only one example of contemporary women grappling with ways to bring feminism and science together in their working lives. The difficulty of this task was indicated by Sue Rosser,

---

23 A vivid illustration of the difficulty of accepting such paradigm shifts is given by Evelyn Fox Keller in a series of personal anecdotes about her own transformation from "working scientist to feminist critic" (Keller 1992: 21-25).

24 Another example given is "selective publishing" or the preferential treatment given to the publication of work confirming scientific orthodoxy. See also Keller on the intrinsically competitive character of biological and evolutionary theories, "Language and Ideology in Evolutionary Theory: Reading Cultural Norms into Natural Law" (Keller and Longino 1996: 156-70).

who noted that most feminist scientists who became interested in pursuing a feminist sociology of science gradually dropped their "'hard science,' grant-supported research along the way" (Rosser 1989: 250).[25] Yet some women did, and do, manage to combine their science and feminism—the subject of Rosser's article, Ruth Bleier, being one example. Donna Haraway offered another example: Martha Crouch, a leading molecular plant biologist as well as an activist for environmental justice and "biodiversity conservation." Her activism led Crouch to question her "pleasure in the playful world of pure science," and she resigned her large grants and her consultations for agribusiness research companies (Haraway 1997: 110-111). In Haraway's words,

> Crouch felt that the psychological and practical separation of the political and the technoscientific, which was essential to the ordinary canons of objective scientific practice, and which functioned to keep her science and her activism apart, represented an immature technoscientific subject formation...In Sandra Harding's terms, she was developing a practice of stronger objectivity. (1997: 111)

As Haraway avers, "Crouch models a responsible life in science...one that offers hope," and one that could be considered an example of feminist practice in science (1997: 112). Both Crouch and Moffett's fictional biologist offer hopeful feminist models, a potential somewhat undermined in Donawerth's utopian paradigm. More recently a "new generation" of working scientists have written of how they integrate their feminism into their daily practice of science (see for example, Wayne 2000; Weasel 2001; Roy 2004).

Although in a note Donawerth acknowledges the "range and controversies in feminist science theory," (1997: 37n3),[26] the utopian

---

25 As Rosser and others point out, Bleier was an exception to this trend, continuing to research neuroanatomy whilst working on feminism and science as chair of the Women's Studies Program at the University of Wisconsin.

26 Donawerth refers to Hilary Rose (1983, 1986), Evelyn Fox Keller (1985), Carolyn Merchant (1980), and Joan Rothschild (1981). Other contemporary texts from this period that highlighted differences, particularly in terms of race and the theorizing of women of color, can be found in Harding's *Whose Science?* (1991), which provides a reading list of studies of science and race and studies authored by women of color (191-2n1&2). See also Haraway, *Primate Visions* (1989a); Sandra Gilman, *Difference and Pathology* (1985); Stephen Jay Gould, *The Mismeasure of Man* (1981); Darlene Clark Hine, *Black Women in White* (1989); Anne Fausto-Sterling

paradigm developed in her work remains closer to Rose's position in the 1983 article "Hand, Brain, and Heart," rather than Rose's later "fusion of standpoint theory with situated knowledges" (Rose 1994: 96). For critics such as Haraway and Harding, the re-construction of scientific knowledges also involves a commitment to intervene in contemporary scientific practices, with the aim of working towards "technoscientific democracy" (Haraway 1997: 95). The mediation between some form of feminist, anti-racist standpoint and constructivist epistemologies was at this point a pivotal dilemma for feminist science theorists, expounded here by Haraway:

> "[O]ur" problem is how to have simultaneously an account of radical historical contingency for all knowledge claims and knowing subjects, a critical practice for recognizing our own "semiotic technologies" for making meanings, and a no-nonsense commitment to faithful accounts of a "real" world, one that can be partially shared and friendly to earth-wide projects of finite freedom, adequate material abundance, modest meaning in suffering, and limited happiness. Harding calls this necessary multiple desire a need for a successor science project and a postmodern insistence on irreducible difference and radical multiplicity of local knowledges. (1988: 187)

It was Haraway and Harding's attention to race, combined with a postmodernist skepticism toward the notion of innocent, power-neutral knowledges, that led to much more nuanced concepts of objectivity such as Harding's "strong objectivity," and Haraway's "situated knowledges" and her concept of the "modest witness" (Haraway 1997, 1988; Harding 1996).[27] Sarah Kember figures this change as a move from a belief in "successor science projects" to an emphasis on "embodied knowledges" (1996: 231).

---

and Lydia English, "Women and Minorities in Science" (1986); Nancy Leys Stepan, "Race and Gender: The Role of Analogy in Science" (1986); and Zuleyma Tang Halpin, "Scientific Objectivity and the Concept of 'The Other'" (1989).

27 Such concepts have arisen from what Haraway calls the "objectivity debates," with some postmodernist critics rejecting any recourse to notions of "objective" knowledge. See, for example, Jane Flax: "Ultimately, Harding seems to think, as do Nancy Harstock and others, that the success of the feminist projects of creating effective analyses of gender and of ending gender-based domination depends on our ability to make truth claims about the 'objective' status or our knowledge and our rights" (1992: 456-7).

Donawerth does in fact allude to this dilemma in her reading of Mitchison's *Memoirs*:

> The British Mitchison develops the problems for a feminist science that might result from subjectivity by tying colonialism to the question of scientific objectivity: if one gives up as androcentric the concept of objectivity, does one have any place to stand?...so subjectivity provides the ground for as many problems as the older ideal of objectivity in science. (1997: 29-30)

Mitchison's text presages the problems with standpoint epistemology precisely because Mitchison was concerned as much with race and colonialism as with gender. A similar concern to represent women of color as scientists is also evident in novels by James Tiptree Jr. and Alice Lightner (a fact highlighted in Donawerth's article "Utopian Science") (see Mitchison 1985, 1995; Tiptree Jr. 1980; Lightner 1969; Donawerth 1990: 555-556). It is worth noting that Mitchison's and Tiptree's dual concern with race and gender, unusual in feminist sf (and in much white feminist theory) in the 1960s and 1970s may have been due to their positioning on the outskirts of the hegemonic Anglo-American women's movement.[28] Mitchison had an ambivalent relation to organized feminism throughout her life and was more vocal in support of various socialist movements and black civil rights, becoming the adopted mother of the chief of a Botswana tribe and consequently banned from travel in apartheid South Africa (see Benton 1992; Squier 1995a). In the 1920s Alice Sheldon traveled through colonial Africa and Asia with her parents and was obviously deeply influenced by the alienating experience of being a "little white girl" cast as the other (Haraway 1989a: 2, 377-379; Larbalestier 2002: 183-188).

---

28 I have been able to find little biographical information on Alice Lightner, who wrote mostly young adult sf in the '50s and '60s. In "Utopian Science," Donawerth reads Lightner's *Day of the Drones* alongside Butler and implies that Lightner was also African American. However Lightner is not mentioned in Donawerth's *Frankenstein's Daughters*. No biographical references describe Lightner as African American, and I was informed by an sf fan who had met her at a conference some years ago that she was not black. However, as Nalo Hopkinson has suggested to me, Lightner could well have been "passing" or presumed white because of the lightness of her skin. Regardless of her background, Lightner's picture of a black female heroine in a future post-holocaust Africa is one of the earliest sf texts to feature a non-white women as a main character, along with Samuel R. Delany's Rydra Wong in *Babel 17* (1966).

Although Donawerth emphasizes the race-blindness of much feminist sf and earlier feminist science theorizing, her utopian paradigm is at its most unstable when applied to Octavia Butler's short story "Bloodchild." In Donawerth's reading, "Bloodchild" presents "a future society reaching the utopian goals of the paradigm outlined in [Donawerth's] chapter, but remaining a dystopia" (1997: 35). Butler's texts may well be seen as critiques of the "vision of white feminists," but it is less convincing to situate the alien Tlic of her story as a direct critique of the "utopian vision of science" on offer in white feminist sf texts. The closest Butler comes, I feel, to engaging with "utopian" visions of a more responsible science is perhaps in the Xenogenesis series, in which the Oankali practice a science that is certainly relational, subjective, holistic, and intimately related to their bodies—while they are also capable of exploitation and manipulation to suit their own needs. As Donawerth herself notes in a brief concluding comment on *Xenogenesis*: "The Oankali, however, despite their achievement of an equal rights science for themselves, still exploit other species, calling what they take by force or coercion 'trade'" (1997: 36). Donawerth's reading of "Bloodchild" does not convince me of the story's "negative commentary" but instead of the limitations of engaging with feminist revisionings of sciences in theory and sf purely in terms of a utopian "paradigm," a move which smoothes over and silences some messy but productive areas of contestation and uncertainty.

In arguing for the importance of feminist sf in the context of feminist science theories, both Donawerth and Roberts made the important point that feminist sf provides women with a unique space in which they can control the narratives of science. However, in arguing for the distinctiveness of this space, they perhaps underestimate the extent to which feminist science theory of the time also constituted such an intervention. Like feminist sf, feminist science studies provides "narratives about science" that focus on "the gendered categories and myths that shape the world of science" (R. Roberts 1993: 6). Indeed, this is exactly what Haraway argues for in the "Cyborg Manifesto": "One important route for reconstructing socialist-feminist politics is through theory and practice addressed to the social relations of science and technology, including crucially the systems of myth and meanings structuring our imaginations" (2004a: 23). Moreover, it is the potential function of feminist sf as a "thought laboratory," not just for the construction of a utopian ideal of future science, but as a medium for experimenting with "non-innocent" knowledges and positionings such as "strong objectivity," "situated knowledge," and the "modest witness," that situates feminist sf as an important resource for feminist science theorists. Indeed, those science theorists who themselves discuss feminist sf employ the fictional texts as participants in the evolving dialogue between different groups over the meaning of "the science question in feminism."[29]

Dream laboratories: sf as feminist science studies

In 1986, Harding observed that feminists involved in critiquing the "sins" of contemporary science had "not yet given adequate attention to envisioning truly emancipatory knowledge-seeking" (1986: 19). As noted above, Harding wondered how feminist understandings of science would differ if they started not with current categories but with those of future worlds such as Piercy's Mattapoisett (although she did not follow this course herself). Prefiguring the sf criticism of Donawerth and Roberts, from the mid-1980s into the early 1990s a number of feminist science critics pursued such a course of imaginatively bringing together feminist sf with their science studies. Critics such as Rose and Haraway called upon feminist sf as cultural "texts" that comment upon, interact with, and critique scientific knowledge, methods, and cultures. Rose argued that feminist sf not only reflects contemporary feminist concerns, but is also a site for the development and configuration of feminist debates (H. Rose 1994: 209). Similarly, Lykke's account of the development of feminist science and technology studies situated Marge Piercy's *Woman on the Edge of Time* and Sally Miller Gearhart's *The Wanderground* alongside Shulamith Firestone's *The Dialectic of Sex* and the Boston Women's *Our Bodies Ourselves* as equally significant texts in the early feminist debate on the subject (Lykke 1996: 1-3).

Haraway, Rose, and Lykke all remain unusual for their willingness to cross and merge the boundaries of literature/science and fiction/

---

29 For example, Maureen McNeil and Sarah Franklin claim that attention to the cultural and textual production of the sciences could involve examining the meaning of science at popular levels by looking at sf, among other "popular" conduits of science (1991: 138).

theory.[30] As Rose notes in her introduction to *Love, Power, and Knowledge*, "[a] number of friends remain surprised that I here discuss feminist science fiction" (1994: 12). But for Rose, feminist sf is a "deeply political writing" whose myth-making plays a significant role in reconstructing techno-science (229). In 1986, Rose wrote of the "empowering visions offered us by feminist sf writing," from authors such as Russ, Le Guin, and Piercy, and commented that "it is not by chance that feminists writing or talking about science and technology constantly return...to these empowering alternative visions" (1986: 74, 59). Echoing many other critics of feminist sf, Rose viewed the genre as a "privileged space, a sort of dream laboratory—where feminisms may try out wonderful and/or terrifying social projects" (228).

Rose argued that sf can help feminists think through difficult processes of change, such as reproductive technology, "where new boundaries between the natural and the social are being negotiated" (1986: 229). In Rose's analysis, feminist visions of transformations in both "natural and social" worlds are important, signaling a difference from literary analysis that centers on changes in the social sphere. Rose linked her analysis of feminist sf directly with feminist critiques of science. She claimed, for example, that Piercy's *Woman on the Edge of Time* anticipated issues raised by feminist critics, especially in demonstrating "that not only is nature modified continuously by culture—and that includes our own nature—but that our conceptions of what is natural and what is cultural themselves undergo subtle changes" (1986: 223).

Another result of Rose's focus is the construction of a different genealogy than the usual literary history of feminist sf. Rose "respectfully" dislodges Mary Shelley as the "foremother of SF," arguing instead that this place is deserved by the natural scientist and philosopher Margaret Cavendish (1986: 210). In contrast to the literary arguments for Cavendish's place in the feminist utopian tradition, Rose foregrounds Cavendish's role in the "formation of mechanical philosophy" in mid-seventeenth century England, her writing on a number of scientific topics, and the fact that as a woman, despite her privileged rank and status, she was excluded from the Royal Society

---

30 In a note to "Manifesto," Haraway thanks Nancy Hartsock for discussion on feminist theory and feminist science fiction, although I have found no mention of feminist sf in Hartsock's work (Haraway 1991: 244n. 1). This section of her acknowledgments is omitted from the version of the Manifesto contained in the *Haraway Reader* (2004b).

(209-210). Like other feminist sf critics, Rose also notes that sf's low status made it a relatively accessible genre for women writers, but rather than drawing a literary comparison, she notes instead similarities with women's experiences in the fields of crystallography or biochemistry in the '40s (209).

Arguing that literary critics had only recently taken sf seriously, Rose observes that "both scientists and critics of science have long had a close and much less discussed relationship with SF'" (the exception being Haraway and Mary Midgley's *Science as Salvation*) (1986: 208, 282n2).[31] In contrast to the literary approach, which viewed feminist sf as "part of a general flowering of women's writing," Rose situates feminist sf as a "vehicle for exploring our pressing anxieties and experiences concerning science and technology," which in the 1970s and '80s had "both been reflective of and constitutive of the feminist critique of science" (209). Yet, she argued,

> the current recovery of SF by literary criticism and cultural studies, which is part of an important and welcome attempt to dissolve the divide between popular and high culture, has often underplayed the close relationship between science criticism and SF, not least within feminism. It is as if, while taking down that cultural divide, another between the arts and the sciences is allowed to reproduce itself uncriticised. It is this division, a sort of replay of Snow's two cultures, even though the categories themselves constantly shift, that I want to see removed. (74, 59)[32]

No such distinctions were allowed to stand unchallenged by the other central theorist to write of feminist sf—Haraway.

Haraway's ongoing project to expose and revision Western narratives of science has often proceeded by recounting alternative stories, from those of feminist primatologists to those of sf writers such as Octavia Butler. Haraway has written about feminist sf in a number of

---

31 Rose claims that few critics recognize that the 1930s and '40s were also a golden age for science criticism that "took writing futurist accounts of science...as a seriously pleasurable task" (1986: 208). Examples include Charlotte and J.B.S. Haldane who both wrote sf scenarios about genetic engineering.

32 Later, she also observes, "The significance of the SF feminist writing as an intervention in popular culture needs underlining, not least when we think about what was happening—and initially not happening—within left and feminist politics in terms of their capacity to ignore science and technology" (1986: 214).

her theoretical studies of science, notably in the "Manifesto for Cyborgs" and *Primate Visions*.[33] In "Manifesto," Haraway employs the figure of the cyborg as a "myth about identity and boundaries which might inform late twentieth century political imaginations"—a myth that Haraway claimed was indebted to feminist sf writers such as Russ, Tiptree, Delany, and Butler (2004a: 31).

Haraway mixes protocols of reading to illuminate the way meaning structures are solidified by the practice of reading scientific discourses as authoritative forms of knowledge about the "real" world. In *Primate Visions*, Haraway reads popular and technical discourses "out of context," deliberately "mixing genres and contexts to play with scientific and popular accounts...telling and retelling stories in the attempt to shift the webs of intertextuality and to facilitate...new possibilities for the meanings of difference, reproduction and survival" (1989a: 377).[34] As noted above, Haraway refigures the "narrative field" of "SF" to include "the narratives of speculative fiction and scientific fact" in order to encourage readers to "remap the borderlands between nature and culture" (1986: 81). In many ways, Haraway tries to construct her audience as sf readers. For example, Haraway's use of sf to include science fiction/fact undermines the boundaries between fact and fiction, scientific fact and representation, and foregrounds the narrativity of scientific discourses. This is a useful tool for feminist analysis, which has too often considered sf only as a literature of popular culture rather than as an intervention into discourses of science (although feminist fans and writers have been more aware of this possibility, as Sargent's introduction to *Women of Wonder* demonstrates).

Octavia Butler in particular figures prominently in Haraway's search for non-innocent, "monstrous" origin stories and narratives of nature and science. In "The Biopolitics of Posthuman Bodies,"

33 See also her "Biopolitics of Postmodern Bodies," "Primatology is Politics," "Situated Knowledges," and "The Promises of Monsters" (Haraway 1986, 1988, 1989b, 1992). Many of these essays are collected in her *Simians, Cyborgs and Women* (1991) and others in the more recent *Haraway Reader* (2004b).

34 In a review of *Primate Visions* for the journal *Science Fiction Studies*, Charles Elkins enthusiastically argues for the importance of Haraway's work for scholars of science, not just for her provocative "blurring" of distinctions such as science/literature and fact/fiction, but because "the narratives of science as *Primate Visions* constructs them can provide a richer more complete understanding" of sf—in this case the work of Octavia Butler (1990: 270-2).

Haraway remarks that *Clay's Ark* "read like" *The Extended Pheno-type*—with Butler's invaders "disturbingly like the 'ultimate' unit of selection that haunts the biopolitical imaginations of postmodern evolutionary theorists and economic planners" (1991: 226). The parallel drawn by Haraway suggests that because the implicit narratives of science—competition, invasion, colonization—are "writ large" in many sf narratives, their destructive implications may be rendered more obvious. Racist, sexist, and colonizing behaviors are more flagrantly rendered when their setting is virgin planets populated by sentient aliens, than in, for example, scientific "stories" about the operation of cells in the immune system of an organism. Correspondingly, feminist sf may both highlight the negative consequences of such narratives on all levels—from sf to science, microscopic to macroscopic—and investigate the possibility of different narratives or origin stories.

Haraway argues that Butler's sf is about "resistance to the imperative to recreate the sacred image of the same"—particularly *Xeno-genesis*, which offers "the monstrous fear and hope that the child will not, after all, be like the parent" (Haraway 1989a: 378). According to Haraway, Butler's fiction avoids the necessity of origin myths: "Butler's communities are assembled out of the genocides of history, not rooted in the fantasies of natural roots and recoverable origins. Hers is survival fiction" (1989a: 379).[35] The Oankali, in particular, fulfill Haraway's challenge to blur boundaries: "Their bodies themselves are immune and genetic technologies, driven to exchange, replication, dangerous intimacy across the boundaries of self and other, and the power of images" (Haraway 1991: 227). As a complex form of organic technology, the Oankali live in a "postmodern" network of living machines "all of which are partners."[36]

---

35 This statement could easily be applied to Butler's series *Parable of the Sower*, which interrogates that other grand narrative of western patriarchy—religion—converting it into a postmodern litany "God is Change"—and its originator/prophet is a young, African American woman.

36 An interesting example of a completely different reading is provided by Stacy Alaimo, who, strangely, draws on Haraway, and amidst a theoretical discussion briefly refers to Butler's work twice. Straight after discussing Haraway's "Manifesto," Alaimo declares "Octavia Butler reveals her unease with machines by replacing them with organic beings in her future world" (Alaimo 1994: 146, see also 143). Alaimo here positions Butler as technophobic, when in fact the Oankali are a radical example precisely of Haraway's cyborg metaphor in the sense that

Such readings of Butler, focused on science, nature, and the boundaries of the human situate the writing of Black sf writers as central to the field and also extricate Butler's texts from the white feminist utopian/dystopian narrative that has framed most other feminist sf critiques of her work. Both Haraway and Rose engage Butler's text in a wider debate about feminist epistemologies and the sciences, such that feminist sf becomes the terrain for intertextual debates in feminist science theory. Rose signals one of the changes in focus these critics bring to sf, placing Butler's writing not within the context of feminist literary history, but in the context of the cultural relations of scientific knowledge.

> Where Mary Shelley's Monster was a creation from a feminist reading of early nineteenth-century science in which electricity generated life, Butler's Lilith and her son Akin are located in a feminist and postcolonial reading of the embryology and genetics of the late twentieth century, set in a post-holocaust world. (H. Rose 1994: 227)

The risky reading strategies of feminist sf

Unlike Rose, Haraway's work from the mid-1990s continued to reference feminist sf. Although later texts do not always engage sf as directly as in *Primate Visions*, for example, sf has remained an important part of Haraway's theoretical and linguistic tool kit, forming one important strand of her multi-literate and transdisciplinary approach to the sciences. Apart from the cyborg, sf has offered her other imaginative figures to be of use. In her 1997 book *Modest Witness*, Haraway incorporates a canonical feminist sf image, employing the "Female-Man" (from Russ's novel) in conjunction with "OncoMouse" (a transgenic mouse carrying an oncogene—a "human, tumor-producing gene"—used in research on cancer, and the first patented animal in the world) as examples of boundary crossing figures in contemporary technoscience (1997: 79-82). Both of these "composite organs," writes Haraway, "force a revaluation of what may count as nature and artefact, of what histories are to be inhabited, by whom, and for whom" (119). The fact that such organisms are not only constructed but are

---

they are part of a cybernetic system and confuse the boundaries between human and machine, self and other, technoscience and nature.

also commodified is signaled by Haraway's discussion of patents and inscription of these creatures as "FemaleMan©" and "OncoMouse™."[37] FemaleMan© and OncoMouse™ are Haraway's tools, her writing technologies for intervening in the production and commodification of technoscience in what she terms the New World Order Inc. (3-8). Haraway finds inspiration not just from the texts themselves, but also from the very narrative modes and reading protocols demanded by sf, which she sees as invaluable aids to the kinds of altered, irresponsible, and in/appropriate(d) stories that she likes to tell.

> I wish to exercise the license that is built into the anti-elitist reading conventions of SF popular cultures. SF conventions invite — or at least permit more readily than do the academically propagated, respectful consumption protocols for literature — rewriting as one reads. The books are cheap; they don't stay in print long; why not rewrite them as one goes? Most of the SF I like motivates me to engage actively with images, plots, figures, devices, linguistic moves, in short, with worlds, not so much to make them come out "right," as to make them move "differently." These worlds motivate me to test their virtue, to see if their articulations work — and what they work for. Because SF makes identification with a principal character, comfort within the patently constructed world, or a relaxed attitude toward language, especially risky reading strategies, the reader is likely to be more generous and more suspicious — both generous and suspicious, exactly the receptive posture I seek in political semiosis generally. (Haraway 1992: 326)

Haraway's unusual and challenging reading of science stories such as those from the field of primatology emerges from exactly such a "generous and suspicious" stance, which is sensitive to the "plots and linguistic moves" of scientific writing and always questions why, and for whom, such "worlds" are made to work.

---

37 "Because patent status reconfigures an organism as a human invention, produced by mixing labor and nature as those categories are understood in Western law and philosophy, patenting an organism is a large semiotic and practical step toward blocking nonproprietary and nontechnical meaning from many social sites–such as labs, courts, and popular venues. Technoscience as cultural practice and practical culture, however, requires attention to all the meanings, identities, materialities, and accountabilities of the subjects and objects in play" (Haraway 1997: 82).

※

What this dispersed conversation suggests is, I argue, the depth and range of possible intersections between feminism, sf, and science studies. Since the late 1990s, when dialogue from the feminist sf critical side seemed to be in hiatus, feminist science studies has undergone a series of epistemological and ideological transformations, many of them led by Haraway. As more recent sf criticism, from Attebery, Yaszek, Vint, and others incorporates contemporary feminist science studies, we start to see more clearly the role that sf feminisms can play in the vital dialogue about science, nature, and culture that is of such importance to feminist politics and theory in the twenty-first century.

Adopting a Harawayan perspective on science and naturecultures, we might consider a much broader range of feminist sf texts as having something to say about science and a focus on science as central to their operation. All kinds of texts that engage with the practices, institutions, facts, and sociocultural impacts of science would be under consideration, texts often proffered in forms that do not gel with either hard sf or social critique notions of sf. For example, as Lisa Yaszek shows of postwar women's sf, texts by writers such as Marion Zimmer Bradley, Katherine MacLean, and Judith Merril all included "radical reassessments of science, technology, and women's work" (2008: 194)—stories that may in retrospect have been devalued by the more radical critiques of patriarchal technoscience that were to follow.

The recognition of popular cultural forms like feminist sf as participants in critical conversations around the sciences also works to highlight the fact that science itself is a cultural practice, a perspective that opens the door for "a motley crew of interlopers to take part in shaping and unshaping what will count as scientific knowledge, for whom, and at what cost" (Haraway 1997: 67). Further, the more accessible nature of creative forms such as fiction widens the field of potential "interlopers"; not an insignificant attribute, given the importance of continuing public debates about our techno-scientific futures and those "othered" by this culture. Such an intervention is vital in a climate where, as Hilary Rose has observed, there remains considerable apprehension "that a nontechnical expert should have an opinion and start talking as well as listening" (1996: 86).

Feminists should listen for and take seriously the stories about science told in feminist sf texts, which envisage social, cultural, and discursive formations that allow new narratives of gender, feminisms, and the sciences. The increasing attention to the social relations of science and technology, "including crucially the systems of myth and meanings structuring our imaginations" (Haraway 2004a: 23), suggests that feminist sf's re-workings of such myths can be seen as central to feminist reconstructions of the sciences. I believe that feminist sf could—and should—form a vital link in cross-cultural feminist stories and conversations about the cultures and discourses of the sciences, as they help make visible "the monstrous web of text, myth, politics, and materiality that constitutes the scientific enterprise" (Lykke and Braidotti 1996: 242).

Haraway has argued that feminist contests for scientific meaning do not work by replacing one paradigm with another; for example, "as a form of narrative practice or storytelling, feminist practice in primatology has worked more by altering a 'field' of stories or possible explanatory accounts... Every story in a 'field' alters the status of all the others" (Haraway 1986: 81). Having intervened in this "narrative field," feminists can take pleasure in experimenting with the different kinds of stories—about science, knowledge, nature, and the human—that become possible when the old narrative fields of science and enlightenment discourse are disrupted.

8

BEYOND GENDER?
TWENTY-FIRST CENTURY SF FEMINISMS

I find that we in the sf community sometimes like to think of ourselves as more progressive than other people. And while there's a lot of fodder for that argument, I'd say it's also true that we are reflective of the larger communities to which we also belong, and as those communities struggle with sexism, racism, queerphobia, classism, ableism, ageism, etc., so do we. And it shows. Sometimes the sf community can be quite oppressive and close-minded. But it's also a place that values openness and critical thought and exploration and the notion of diversity (even though we still have a long way to go to practise that last one more)... Science fiction as a literature probably helped to save my life. I suspect I would have self-destructed without it, and without the people I have met because of it. So even when I'm critical of it, I'm very happy that it's here.

-→≡ Nalo Hopkinson (in Johnston 2008: 214-5)

In the late 1990s sf feminism, like much of the feminist movement in general, was in a rather uncertain position, troubled by intimations of a "postfeminist" period. The feminist "third wave" signaled both an energetic, younger generation of riot grrls, as well as a widespread feeling that the work of the second wave was done. So too, in the sf field, alongside the entry of new generations of female fans and critics came expressions of indifference to feminism, not unlike the dismissals Gomoll worried about back in 1987 (Gomoll 1986-87). Duchamp, for example, pointed to the weariness with feminist issues displayed in Gary Wolfe's argument that the term feminist sf was "ready to be retired to the agenda farm" (Wolfe 1997: 18; Duchamp 2004a: 22).[1] Employing a different tactic, one recent study uncovered

---

1   Other attempts to delegitimate feminism argue that feminist critiques (e.g., of early sf) are misguided and a-historical. In 1993, for example, Gary Westfahl took to task male sf critics such as Eric Rabkin and Peter Nicholls for their alignment with feminist critiques of "the image of women" in sf. "These apologies for science

hundreds of female authors of sf in the pulps, in order to demonstrate that sf was not sexist, and thus feminist critiques were both misguided and unnecessary (Davin 2006). Throughout the 1990s, there were also fears about the increasingly restrictive economics of publishing and its impact on the publishability of feminist works, as the genre market was squeezed by the takeover of mega-corporate publishing (see for example, Sedgewick, 1991).

Writing from the perspective of 2003, however, Duchamp could observe that the "feminist public sphere, regardless of the main-stream's insistence that sf is "post-feminist," is stronger than it has ever been" (2004a: 36). WisCon and the Tiptree Award had continued to flourish, as had online forums, whilst in 1999 the inaugural issue of the feminist academic journal, *Femspec* was published. On the publishing front, too, fears about the future of feminist publishing were countered by the arrival of a number of independent specialist press-es such as Tachyon Publications (1995, whose motto is "saving the world…one good book at a time"), Aqueduct Press (2004, specializing in feminist sf), and initiatives such as Broad Universe, an organization promoting women writers of sf/f.

In bringing my journey through sf feminism/s to a close, I con-clude with an all-too brief overview of some of the more recent developments of the last decade or so. From a twenty-first century perspective, perhaps the two most important impacts on or challenges to the field have been (a) the increasing profile of women of color and the growth of critical attention to race; and (b) a revitalized at-tention to sexuality in sf, particularly as read through queer theory. Both these developments suggest a shift in priorities whereby gender is diminishing as a central focus for a more diverse understanding of sf feminisms. Similar questions about the continuing efficacy or util-ity of "gender" as an analytical tool are also evident in mainstream feminist theory, particularly in feminist science studies.

Taking the troubled relation between gender and feminism as my theme, I draw on the Tiptree Award as an exemplary case study for ex-amining this relation in contemporary sf feminisms. Whilst perceived

---

fiction," he argued, were "excessive." Westfahl's critique is representative of a move to recover sf history by situating the absorption of feminist revisions in mainstream sf criticism as unnecessary. Instead of berating the past, he argued, critics should accept that sf in the 1930s and '40s was "an unenlightened form of literature in an unenlightened age" (Westfahl 1993: 43).

by many as a feminist award and closely associated with WisCon and the feminist sf community more broadly, the award's mandate is specifically fiction that challenges *gender* roles. I am interested in what the Tiptree Award might signal about the shifting definitional terrain marking out sf feminisms and, in particular, about feminism's complex relation to gender as its central theoretical concept and tool.

The view from queer

From the late 1990s on, the field of queer theory, identified with the work of Teresa de Lauretis, Judith Butler, and Eve Kosofsky Sedgwick among others, began to impact feminist sf criticism. In particular, the pioneering work of Wendy Gay Pearson and Veronica Hollinger provided refreshingly different readings of some classic feminist sf and also suggested how a queer perspective might challenge the way sf feminisms have approached similar concerns with sexuality, gender, identity, and bodies (Hollinger 1999, 2008; Pearson 1999, 2002, 2003). Almost a decade after the special issue of *SFS* on queer theory (1999), the collection *Queer Universes*, edited by Pearson, Hollinger, and Joan Gordon appeared, offering a comprehensive review of queer theory's application to sf.[2] In the introduction to *Queer Universes*, the editors note that considerations of sexuality, especially alternative sexualities, have been surprisingly rare, particularly given the focus on gender in sf criticism (2008: 7).

Although queer theory and queer readings of sf are not always coterminous with feminist critical projects, they do of course significantly overlap. As the editors of *Queer Universes* point out, feminist theory is a key influence in queer genealogies (Pearson, Hollinger, and Gordon 2008: 4-6). Hollinger, for example, has performed illuminating re-readings of feminist sf writers such as Moore, Tiptree, and Russ based on the "strategic intersections" of feminist and queer theory, readings that "emphasize the fact that complex and sophisticated inquiries into gender issues are by no means new to science fiction" (Hollinger 1999: 23). Consequently, reading sf through queer

---

2 This gap suggests that perhaps sf criticism, or at least academic publishing, has not been as open as one might hope to the challenges posed by queer theory, or studies of sexuality, for despite their high standing in sf criticism and academe, the editors had great difficulties finding a publisher for this collection, which was consequently delayed for a number of years.

theory highlights the dynamic interaction between theory and fiction and, in particular, the view that "our theoretical representations of these issues have not always kept pace with the fiction" (Hollinger 1999: 23).

One of the most challenging insights offered by queer theory is, as Sedgwick argues, "that a damaging bias toward heterosocial or heterosexist assumptions inheres unavoidably in the very concept of gender" (cited in Hollinger 1999: 25). Expanding on this argument, Hollinger identifies a serious dilemma for feminist readings: "An emphasis on gender risks the continuous reinscription of sexual binarism, the heterosexual opposition which historically has proven so oppressive for so many women" (24). For Hollinger, Pearson, and Gordon, queer theory is about destabilizing and "rethinking Cartesian systems of knowledge" that underwrite all the self/other binarisms such as hetero/homosexual or masculine/feminine (2008: 4). In regards to sf, they argue that,

> Queer theoretical approaches, alongside feminist, postcolonial, postmodern, and critical race theories, allow critics to make visible the naturalized epistemologies of sexuality, gender, and race that underwrite the most conservative sf, as well as to explain some of science fiction's most striking attempts to defamiliarize and denaturalize taken-for-granted constructions of what it means to be, and to live, as a human. (6)

In challenging these naturalized ideologies, the operation of queer theory is thus seen to be inseparable from other theoretical projects concerned with challenging modernist notions of the white, humanist subject.

Building a color-full tradition

Postcolonialist critiques of the intersection of race and gender have also been slow in coming to sf, in spite of the centrality of the species and racial other to sf narratives and tropes.[3] Nevertheless, recent years have seen encouraging developments along these lines, with the increased visibility of writers and fans of color, and initiatives such as the Carl Brandon awards (for speculative fiction by writers of color, as

---

3   This problem was succinctly expressed by Gwyneth Jones (1997). (See also Rieder 2008.)

well as works that deal with race and ethnicity). Making race central to critical accounts of sf is slowly becoming more common. Previously, critical race studies in sf consisted in the main of analyses of Delany and Butler. In 1997 the first anthology dealing with race and sf/f appeared, *Into Darkness Peering: Race and Color in the Fantastic*, edited by Elisabeth Anne Leonard. Whilst representing an important first step, this collection still reflected the predominance of white perspectives in terms of both texts and critics.

Shortly thereafter, the beginnings of a new era of black sf was presaged by Walter Mosley in a 1998 *New York Times* article that predicted "an explosion of science fiction from the black community" within the next five years (reprinted in Thomas 2000: 407). Within two years, Sheree R. Thomas had produced the first of her groundbreaking collections, *Dark Matter: A Century of Speculative Fiction from the African Diaspora* (Thomas 2000).[4] Joined within a few years by *Dark Matter: Reading the Bones* (Thomas 2004) and Nalo Hopkinson and Uppinder Mehan's *So Long Been Dreaming: Postcolonial Science Fiction & Fantasy* (2004), a whole new group of women of color made their mark in the genre. Joining Tananarive Due, Jewelle Gomez, and Hopkinson were Thomas, Nisi Shawl, Nnedi Okorafor Mbachu, Andrea Hairston, and Hiromi Goto, among others.

The titles of these anthologies indicate one obstacle to the recognition of a larger, more diverse group of women of color as part of the sf field and community. Stories that foreground black characters and non-Anglo cultural traditions are often told through forms and language that differ markedly from the white Anglophone tradition of sf and thus do not sit comfortably within its normative (white) generic norms. As such, sf criticism may overlook or exclude certain texts or approach them with inadequate tools of analysis. Instructive in this regard are a number of recent critical articles by women of color who approach texts by authors such as Hopkinson from a very different frame than that of white feminist sf criticism. In the third of her "future female" series, Barr's collection *Afro-Future Females* collects important critical essays and reflections by black critics and sf/f writers. Alcena Madeline Davis Rogan, for example, contextualizes her analysis through a focus on the history of black women's experience of the

---

4   Both Dark Matter anthologies won the World Fantasy Award for best anthology in 2000 and 2005 respectively. A third volume is forthcoming.

struggles around motherhood and reproductive politics, while Madhu Dubey emphasizes the particularity of black encounters with scientific narratives of nature and the animal (Dubey 2008; Rogan 2008).

As we see more black women and women of color writing, participating, and reading within the field, our notions of what feminist sf encompasses in terms of genre should become more expansive. Certainly this seems to be happening if we look to the work being published by feminist sf press Aqueduct, for example, which has included the panoramic science fiction *Mindscape* by Andrea Hairston (2006), the breathtaking short stories covering all ranges of the fantastic by Nisi Shawl (*Filter House*, 2008), and the thought-provoking mediations on race, gender, and physics in Vandana Singh's *Of Love and Other Monsters* (2007) and *Distances* (2008). Similarly, since her debut *Brown Girl in the Ring*, Nalo Hopkinson has continued to challenge and stretch the limits of genre, as well as the intersections of race, culture, sex, and sexuality with works like *The Salt Roads* (2003) and *The New Moon's Arms* (2007).

Another important—and more direct site—of challenge to normative sf feminism in terms of race can be seen in the commentaries and debates emerging from the sf feminist community. The increased participation of women of color in sf fandom and publishing has resulted in demands to address the racialized power relations of the community—in other words, issuing a call to change the *praxis* of sf feminisms, not just the bounds or focus of its critical analysis. Given the unusual positioning of WisCon in the sf field, one would expect that this self-consciously politicized forum would be the first to show signs of a more progressive, race-conscious approach. On the contrary, recent WisCons have seen race emerge as a site of difficult and fraught conversations. This is not to criticize WisCon per se—as many organizers and critics comment, WisCon is not a utopian feminist space, but rather one that must accommodate a range of issues, politics, and people. It is, however, a site that overtly displays the real struggles and changes of consciousness necessary for feminism/s to seriously account for race in its theory and praxis. In this way, WisCon and the sf feminist community mirror, if not preempt, mainstream feminisms. "Doing" critical race theory and feminism in the academy only gets us so far—at a site like WisCon, participants are more likely to confront the manifest changes in discourse, representation, and engagement that are required to address the "reassignment of power" that situates race as central (on the difficulties of "reassigning power," see Duchamp and Delany 2007: 176). A good example is provided by K. Joyce Tsai's report on WisCon 31 (held in 2007), which expresses her outrage at sitting through a panel on revolution that reinforced colonialist, white, American-centric perspective and "unthinking racism" (Tsai 2008: 62). The panel was, she observed, "yet another example of how Western voices are central and active and how the voices of the colonized continue to be unheard or characterized as passive" (68).[5]

If sf feminisms are to seriously encounter the critiques and changes in perspective indicated by critical race theory (and queer theory), it is, I would argue, inevitable that the theoretical approach and analytical tools must also change. One obvious consequence of such critiques is the dislodging of gender as the principal category for (white) feminist analysis. Given the importance of the Tiptree Award to the feminist sf community and the centrality of gender to the process of this award, the Tiptree forms an important site for an assessment of the state of sf feminisms in this regard.

Reading sf feminisms from Tiptree texts

The dialogues and interactions of community participants in sites such as the Tiptree Award actively contribute to the discursive formation and mediation of "feminist sf" and indeed sf feminisms in general. As noted in Chapter Five, the award is continually in the process of being re-invented, in that every year each jury must decide for themselves what its parameters are. Each year, therefore the jurors engage in a unique process of self-reflection on the notion of "gender bending" and, by implication (or default), feminism and feminist sf. The award thus provides an interesting case study of the changing meanings and constitutions of "feminisms" and "gender" in the science fiction field. The parameters of this discussion can be inferred from the set of texts that win or are short-listed for the award, as well as from the jurors' comments on these texts. Also forming part of this dialogue are published reflections from past jurors (which I approach

---

5   See also Duchamp's perceptive and thoughtful commentary on the same panel from the perspective of being a panelist who also felt angered and constrained by these normative restrictions (2008).

with the experience of having been a member of the jury for the 2000 award).

In concert with sf criticism, book reviews, and events such as conventions and author readings, the Tiptree Award helps to delineate a shared set of texts that define and produce the object feminist sf. Since its inception, the Tiptree Award has become a significant site of—and just as importantly—a *focus* for such debates. Interestingly the Tiptree Award itself and the texts it recognizes do not necessarily equate with or map directly onto "feminist sf." As Larbalestier points out, people now refer to "tiptree texts," a term that has taken on rather complex meanings, invoking as it does texts nominated (or even potential nominees) for the award as well as the oeuvre of sf author James Tiptree Jr. (Larbalestier 2002: 202, 218). Either way, within the sf field the very name "Tiptree" signals a nuanced and complex history of engagement with gender, sexuality, postcolonialism, and feminism that does not always map neatly onto normative feminist genealogies.

In this context, it is useful to view the award as a continuation of the kind of dialogues and processes ongoing since the early 1970s in fanzines, letters, and forewords to collections like Sargent's *Women of Wonder*: the identification of potential "feminist friendly" authors, the ever popular fannish activity of constructing reading lists, and of course reviewing and commenting on recent publications. Although not all jurors would agree, and the award is not officially "branded" as feminist (other than its association with the secret feminist cabal), I would argue that the very existence of the award, its processes, and associated dialogues are all central to feminist production and practice in sf.

Expanding and exploring gender

Choosing nominees and winners is a complex, multilayered process, particularly because each panel decides for itself exactly what is meant by works that "explore and expand gender roles." As Larbalestier reports, each panel must engage with questions like:

> What does "gender bending" mean? What are we looking for?
> What are we rewarding and encouraging? And the arguments
> and discussion they are part of give voice to undercurrents

and debates within the broader science fiction community and beyond. Debates about popular feminism and "political correctness" are raised frequently… The award serves to show also that feminism is not a monolith any more than science fiction is—that there are many feminists and feminisms. (Larbalestier 2002: 220)

There is also no set format for deciding on the winner, which is again left up to the jury, although it has tended to be consensual. Reflecting on her experience (which very much matched my own), Larbalestier reports that her panel decided,

we didn't have to agree about the books on the shortlist… but that we did about the final winner. … So our short list was an eclectic mix reflecting the various passions of the various judges.

Agreeing to the final winner was hard. Some of us were passionate about books that other judges despised, muttering, "Over my dead body does that book win." We had a veto and we exercised it, which meant we were left with books and stories that we all loved, but about which, perhaps, some of us weren't as passionate as we were about other, vetoed, books. (http://www.justinelarbalestier.com/Musings/judgingawards.htm)

The openness of the award, the mix of judges, and the lively debates around texts and the award itself mean that, in Larbalestier's words, the award is "always in a state of becoming" (218), another facet appropriate to a feminist award. In this process of becoming, the award, its judges, and the texts it recognizes all provide indications of the fluctuating state of feminisms within the field and the shifting meanings and assumptions assigned to gender.

Some measure of the debates and conversations that characterize each jury's deliberations can be gleaned from the annotations to the winners and honor list (and sometimes long list) published on the award website, which is fairly extensive up until 2004. The subtext of these annotations are the "hidden" conversations the jury conducts in order to try to delineate what, exactly, it is the members wish the award to acknowledge (Notkin 2005). "Every jury has begun by inventing the wheel—by grappling with the phrase 'explores and expands gender' all over again" (Fowler, cited in Larbalestier, 2002: 217). As Fowler points out, the continual re-negotiation of the meaning or resonance of this phrase means that different values and criteria characterize each panel: "Some juries have valued expansion more than exploration of gender. Some have felt that feminism was a crucial component" (221). Fowler observes that judges often begin the process "with a long discussion over where the cutting edge is now and whether it's moved since last year and what they think of last year's selection" (219). Similarly, Jeanne Gomoll comments that the term "gender bending" is "not a term that can be defined once and for all time. It changes from year to year" (219).

The details of these juror debates remain private (not least, as Debbie Notkin points out, because the jurors are often discussing the work of colleagues [2005]). However, a number of past judges have published reflections on their experience of being on the jury, including the writers Suzy McKee Charnas, Mary Anne Mohanraj, writer/critic Larbalestier, and Debbie Notkin—chair of the first Tiptree jury and now chair of the "motherboard" of directors. Charnas was also a member of the very first panel in 1991 and has written of the kinds of questions they had to confront for the first—although by no means the last—time, such as: "what do *we* want this award to *do*?" or "Does the winning story have to say something new about gender, or can it say something old in a new way, or just really, really brilliantly?" (Charnas 2005: 95).

Charnas was a judge again in 2000 (since a custom had emerged to invite the previous year's winner(s) to be on the judging panel), providing a useful perspective for reflecting on developments in the processes and meaning of the award. As well as changes such as a vast increase in nominated works, the use of email for communication, and the broadening of the field of judges, Charnas observes that a certain number of ground rules and answers to earlier questions had evolved: "everyone now knew that this was an award for interesting and exciting fantasy and science fiction informed by a feminist awareness" (100). Yet, questions still arose, including, importantly, whether the Tiptree itself was still needed: "I think the questions of whether the award should continue must return with each year, given that this award is so vitally connected to an essential and constantly changing complex of ideas, values, and practices: the gender divide in human-kind" (102).

Despite the agreement on the inevitable fluidity of just what the Tiptree attempts to recognize, by the 1998 awards, enough "Tiptree texts" in the form of winners and short-listed works were behind the judges to enable clearer articulations of what gender bending was *not*. In her introductory comments to the 1998 panel, Candas Jane Dorsey stated:

> it's not enough to posit alien biology nor to imagine a differ-ent culture based on that biology—nor, I'd add, is it enough to tell a dystopian tale about how bad things are, nor use a cute premise to add interesting background, nor to posit future gender wars, biological mutations, genetic tamper-ing, utopias—if that's as far as the story or novel goes. The first condition of a Tiptreeable text for me is to show beings at the edge of change, transformation, challenge—on the boundary of questions (Dorsey, TAC 1998).[6]

For Dorsey, the presentation of "alternative [gender] orientations" was not sufficient to short-list a book:

> [T]he presence of diverse characters and relationships [are now] part of the normal range of possibilities when con-structing fiction in the present day. Therefore I came to be-lieve that they are—and should be, I think—background, not foreground, and therefore the presence of a gender-bending element was not the only thing which would move a story into eligibility for the final list. (TAC 1998)

This notion of how gender operates as a "background" or foreground element is a crucial one, to which I will return below.

A vital influence on the judging process and commentary is the of-ten unacknowledged impact of individual reader's contexts and the ef-fect this has on how one views "gender bending." That is, each judge

---

6   Tiptree Award commentary available at http://www.tiptree.org/index.php? see=award. For ease of reference, given the number of different attributions for comments, I refer to all the commentaries on the Tiptree Award site with the authors name, the abbreviation TAC, followed by the year of the award (for commentary on the winning text/s), and "SL" for comments about works on the short list. In some years comments were aggregated and individual authors not identified.

has a different reading history within sf, will have constructed differ-ent notions of what feminism and gender are, will be situating nomi-nated works within the context of often quite different sets of texts rather than a self-evident, neatly defined canon. These debates are also framed within the context of particular canons—for some, that classic body of overt feminist sf from the 1970s on, or, since the 1990s, the Tiptree-winning texts themselves.

Another key context is the individual's sociocultural positioning, since notions of gender are not approached as some isolated literary device or conceit but as central questions in society. Mohanraj makes this clear as she reflects on her experience of the 2002 discussions.

> We talked about gender, about what interested us about pre-vious Tiptree winners, about what questions about gender were interesting us today. An interesting nexus of interest developed—quite a few of us were fascinated by questions of masculinity; we felt that some of the most difficult gen-der problems confronting society today had to do with issues of maleness, and we hoped that we would see some work that addressed those concerns. (Mohanraj 2003)

Although expectations and assumptions amongst individuals vary, a common element in most jurors' expectations is that "expanding or exploring" seems to demand treatments that do something "new" with gender. To cite Mohanraj again:

> What was surprising to me, and somewhat disappointing, was that while many of the titles we read were well-written and interesting, and while lots and lots of them were quite feminist, few of them seemed to actually do much that was new or exciting with gender, per se. We read little that was actually gender-bending; most of what was sent to us seemed to be feminist stories, which sometimes raised interesting questions about feminism, but not so often about actually being female (at least to the extent that those two things can be divorced from each other). (2003)

Important questions are raised here about how connections be-tween gender bending and feminism are conceived by and within the feminist sf community, and whether a text could do something new with gender, yet *not* be feminist. This could be taken as a sign that feminism has on some level achieved a comfortable or less challenging position within sf—that is, a stage where feminist texts are published within the field without necessarily provoking challenges to or transformations in gender representation. (This is, of course, not a situation that would seem unusual within mainstream literary fiction, perhaps reflecting the unique complementarity of feminism as political project with sf's critical imperative in terms of extrapolation, cognitive dissonance, and utopian impulses.)

Yet one would expect that a text that is considered to best "explore and *expand* gender" would usually be classified as feminist in some form or other. This assumption does not seem to hold in the face of some recent winners. As Notkin observes,

> [o]ver the years, we've seen at least one award winner that many readers consider anti-feminist (Elizabeth Hand's *Waking the Moon*, a book that examines a rather bloodthirsty all-female society) ... Two years ago, the award (well, half of it) went to *Light* by M. John Harrison, a book which features a serial killer of women as a main character: can that overused and disturbing topic ever be a legitimate ground for exploring and expanding gender? (2005)

Clearly, the award winner is not always the most obviously or overtly feminist text under consideration each year. Indeed, the issue of whether or not the Tiptree is—or should be—an explicitly feminist award has been under debate from its beginning. Charnas remembers this as one of the questions faced by the first jury: "Are we going to call it a 'feminist award' outright? If we don't call it a 'feminist award,' is that just ducking the question (because, well, it *is*, isn't it?)" (2005: 95). Notkin has recently raised similar questions:

> Is the award really a feminist award in a vaguely transparent disguise? If it isn't, should it be? Does the science fiction world need a feminist award? Has the field changed enough—has the award helped the field change enough—in the last fourteen years to render the award irrelevant or passé? (2005)

For Notkin there is indeed a "distinction between feminism and gender," which in certain lights means it is incorrect to explicitly label the Tiptree a feminist award. This may well be a sensible political tactic if nothing else—responses to her article suggest that in the broader sf fan/reader community, "gender" provokes less discomfort than "feminism."[7] Given that Murphy and Fowler's initial inspiration for the award was specifically as a *women's* sf award, it is clear that both the nature and purpose of the award have shifted over time, as have the interests of sf feminisms.

The corollary to such developments in sf is how central gender continues to be for twenty-first century feminisms. A number of strands of contemporary and postmodern feminisms do not situate gender as the pre-eminent category of analysis or oppression. As I noted above, black and postcolonial feminists have of course long argued that gender must be considered as only a part of complex intersecting influences on identity and sociocultural position, equal — or even lesser to — race and other issues such as sexuality.

Gender and feminism: Tiptree taxonomies

The question of this slippery relation between gender and feminism can be examined more closely through the juror commentaries on Tiptree winners and short-listed works, which often explicitly address why — or why not — a work is considered "Tiptree worthy." A variety of identifiable and often repeated themes emerge, some of which are specific to sf, others of which are related to central concerns of the feminist movement/s. Approaches dominated by the latter tend to downplay the notion of gender bending and instead implicitly (and sometimes explicitly) invoke a relationship to feminism as the primary basis for judgment.

For many of the juries, an important facet of the award is the part it plays in the ongoing transformative relation of feminism and sf. Thus a number of works are identified as meriting short-listing because they constitute feminist reworkings of, or replies to, traditional sf tropes and themes. The 1991 jury, for example, posits both Karen Joy Fowler's *Sarah Canary* and Gwyneth Jones's *White Queen* as a "feminine reply" to the masculine endeavor of cyberpunk (TAC 1991, SL). Other examples emphasize the award's role in advancing feminist conversations in sf by acknowledging texts that build on earlier works. Tess Williams' story "And she was the Word," for example,

---

7   See the *Strange Horizons* bulletin board discussion of Notkin's article, available at http://www.strangehorizons.com/ubbthreads/showflat.php?Board=columns &Number=1353.

is read in terms of its connections to earlier works by authors such as Merril and Bradley. Le Guin's winning story, "The Matter of Seggri," is also marked as being part of a dialogue with earlier feminist texts: "The world of Seggri invites comparison with Gethen and While-away and Women's Country without being an imitation or a simple answer to any of them" (Attebery TAC 1994).

Other texts are singled out for the ways in which they reveal or deconstruct normative gender roles and, in particular, how this opposition has impacted notions of woman and female sexuality. A central theme running though feminist sf has been the challenge to the idea that the human is normatively represented by man, a theme identified in the 1993 winner, Nicola Griffith's *Ammonite*, about a "community of people, all of whom happen to be women" (Gomoll, TAC 1993). As Le Guin comments, "it answers the question 'when you eliminate one gender, what's left?' (a whole world, is the answer)" (Le Guin, TAC 1993). Other texts are recognized for their investigations of the role of reproduction and sexuality in the maintenance of normative gendered binaries. Thus Lisa Tuttle comments of Gwyneth Jones's "La Cenerentola":

> Reproduction and the consequent need for mothers and fathers clearly demarked has been the most consistent reason for forcing people into one of only two genders. Removing the link between sex and reproduction will inevitably change perceptions of gender—and this story begins to explore that area, way out on the frontier in Tiptree territory. (TAC 1998 SL)

Sexuality is of course central to feminist understandings of gender. A recurring issue in the juror comments is whether or not portrayal of non-heterosexual characters or even economies is enough to qualify as gender bending. Thus one year Gomoll questions whether Griffith's story "Touching Fire" qualifies: "does the fact that the lovers are lesbians make this gender-bending?" (TAC 1993 SL). Yet the following year, in the commentary on *Larque on the Wing* (joint winner), Susanna Sturgis notes that "Lesbian characters, erotic love between women: these are still out on the gender-bending frontier" (TAC 1994). Over a decade later, however, it would appear that the ground has shifted, with Notkin observing that,

[a] leading editor got very angry when a book from his list with a lesbian protagonist didn't get much attention from that year's jury. He ... seemed unable to understand the jury's response, which was that having a lesbian protagonist is no longer an exploratory or expansive auctorial decision. (Notkin 2005)

In contrast, reflecting Mohanraj's comment above, explorations of masculinity seem to be very Tiptree-worthy, featuring in winning texts such as John Kessel's "Stories for Men," Matt Ruff's *Set This House in Order*, and Harrison's *Light*. Michael Blumlein's "Fidelity: A Primer," for example, is recognized as being "one of the rare stores that explores gender issues by examining male body issues, and the choices they involve" (TAC 2000 SL). The joint winner of the 1996 award, Mary Doria Russell's *The Sparrow*, whilst not seen as Tiptree material by some, was chosen by that year's jury primarily for its approach to masculinity.

Central to *The Sparrow* is the examination of the importance of sexuality to gender identity, specifically masculinity. Can you be celibate and still be a man? At the same time the understandings of human masculinity and femininity that dominate the thinking of the Jesuit landing party make little sense in the face of the entirely different gender models of the two alien races. (Larbalestier, TAC 1996)

This last comment of Larbalestier's signals a central and recurring source of jurors' approval—the use of alien cultures and races to provide a distancing and oppositional perspective on contemporary gender norms. That is, where the social, cultural, and political systems mapped onto our normative gender system are exposed, often through parody, role-reversal, or exaggeration. Thus Eleanor Arnason's *Ring of Swords* is noted for creating "an alien race whose assumptions are just enough different than ours to bring ours into high relief" (McHugh TAC 1993 SL). Similarly, James Patrick Kelly's "Lovestory" is seen to provide a "wonderful example of how depicting an alien way of being 'normal' can make our own 'normal' society look weird" (Tuttle, TAC 1998 SL). This is the area where sf is seen to offer unique possibilities for re-examining gendered constructions, "by creating a society that has different assumptions than ours, thus forcing us to examine our own" (Murphy, TAC 1994). As Brian Attebery observes of Le Guin's winning story,

> "The Matter of Seggri" uses science fiction to map out social implications. It asks how gender enters into institutions like schools and marriages and how it might do so differently. It asks how power and love and justice might be redistributed along gender lines, and what the effect might be on individual lives. It asks what stake society has in enforcing models of femininity and masculinity and what happens to those who fail to follow the template. (TAC 1994)

Similar observations about the ways science fiction and alien cultures can be usefully employed to this effect were made in regard to Le Guin's 1996 winner, "Mountain Ways," a "story which suggests that every society's sexual norms and taboos are arbitrary" (Fowler, TAC 1996). For Larbalestier, in "Mountain Ways,"

> the alien is rendered knowable and familiar, and the taboos and normalities of our own worlds start to seem as "unnatural" as those within the story. Raising questions like why is marriage between two, and not three, four or five? Why is heterosexual union privileged over homosexual? Why formalise sexual relations at all? (TAC 1996)

Also part of this thread are those texts that disrupt the gendered order through an emphasis on the performativity of gendered roles and deconstruct binaries through a proliferation of gendered positions. Sylvia Kelso points to the connections between such texts and postmodern and queer readings of gender in her discussion of the 1998 winner, Raphael Carter's "Congenital Agenesis of Gender Ideation":

> It seems to me that although this story comes closest to overt deconstruction, even it has not completely mastered the intersection in "gender" between culture, performance, and biology…. That said, this is the closest to an overt and outright exploration of gender that I've seen so far. (TAC 1998)

Backgrounding gender, foregrounding…feminisms?

Some of the most insightful facets of the Tiptree Award dialogues are those points at which judges try and enunciate why short- or long-listed works didn't quite "make it." Often such nuances of judgment are framed in terms of the gender elements of the story being too much in the "background." That is, alternative notions or systems of gender or sexuality may be depicted, but are portrayed as being so accepted within the framework of the text that they are not explicitly situated as the main focus or drive of the narrative. A good example here is the commentary on Joan Slonczewski's (short-listed) *The Children Star*, which according to Candas Jane Dorsey does "a beautiful job of 'disappearing' gender, and is a strong and moving book, but it does not speak directly to Tiptree concerns" (TAC 1998 SL). Similarly, Kate Schaefer comments that,

> [g]ender really doesn't seem to be an issue for any of the sentient races in this book, and Slonczewski pulls this off as background. Deep enough background that I didn't notice it until I realized that she had portrayed two of the most powerful beings in her universe as lesbian lovers... Because it's done in deep background, gender is not explored nor expanded: it's resolved. The issues in the book are not gender issues, but issues of freedom, slavery, and sentience: extremely interesting issues, but not Tiptree Award concerns. (TAC 1998 SL)

Here, perceptions of Tiptree concerns are apparently restricted to overt examinations of gendered roles and how they are played out between individuals and within society; that is, how dominant sociocultural mores, economies, and institutions are gendered. On the one hand, the insistence that gender be at the foreground of Tiptree texts signals the variety and breadth of challenging work in this area evident in contemporary sf. On the other hand this focus also runs the danger of obscuring the gendered nature of other discourses—significantly, scientific discourses and constructions of nature. Such a position may fail to recognize the extent to which gender is imbricated in, and intersects with, other markers of difference: in particular race, but also class and sexuality. In my view, such assumptions about the need to foreground gender signals an important site of disjuncture between the sf feminisms played out through the Tiptree Award conversations and current developments in feminist theory, including postcolonial and queer feminisms, and feminist science studies.

To return to the example of Slonczewski's *Children Star*, what the above comments do not reveal is that the gender concerns of the novel are played out very consciously against the background of scientific narratives of biology. Indeed, Williams reads the book as a specifically feminist response to, and gendered critique of, evolutionary theories and discourse (Williams 2006). The lack of attention to this facet of the novel reiterates my argument in the last chapter about the continued disjuncture between sf feminism and feminist science studies. There have been rare exceptions in the Tiptree commentary, with a few jurors making explicit reference to the gendered nature of science or scientific discourses. One concerned the joint 1995 winner (and coincidently, the first male writer to win the Tiptree) Theodore Roszak's *The Memoirs of Elizabeth Frankenstein*:

> A powerful book about, among other things, the sexual politics of science, and the relationship between gender and knowledge — how gender may affect ways of knowing, ways of approaching and doing science, and affect our world views. It posits that the domination of "male" ways of knowing and doing science, lacking an understanding of, and sympathy for, the Earth and Nature itself, have resulted in a world being ravaged and destroyed in the name of progress and science. (Russo, TAC 1995)

A similar emphasis on the role of scientific discourse in normative gendered understanding is evident in Bill Clemente's description of Kim Stanley Robinson's "Sexual Dimorphism," which "offers a disturbing slant on the scientific method; the narrator's warped perspective demonstrates the power of persuasion to undermine analysis and to perpetuate myths concerning the biologically determined basis for gender differences" (TAC 1999 SL). Even more explicit connections between science and gender are made in Duchamp's comment on this story, "in which the author uses hard sf protocols to show how a reactionary, essentialist ideological agenda that naturalizes gender produces bad science" (TAC 1999 SL).

As I observed above, other seeming lacunae in many Tiptree conceptions of gender are the insights from postcolonial, black, and third-world feminist theories. This is not to say that concern with race is absent from either Tiptree texts or conversations; indeed Notkin's recent column evidences awareness of race and attempts to redress the continuing "white-washed" nature of sf, indicated, for example, by the fact that "the motherboard has made an effort to ensure that at least one person of color serves on each jury" (2005). However, the notion that it is *gender* that must be primary leads to some interesting statements about the relationship of gender to race. This is seen clearly in the annotation for Hopkinson's short-listed novel, *Midnight Robber*:

> A rollicking Caribbean feminist tale about a little girl turned outlaw, it is a blend of action-adventure, science fiction, allegory, and myth that offers a unique intersection of gender, race, and identity issues. While not overtly about gender, the ideas and concepts of gender are at its very heart. (TAC 2000 SL)

So whilst claiming that the novel is not "overtly" about gender, this comment acknowledges the interrelation of gender and race, and the fact that gender is "at its very heart"—but not foregrounded enough, presumably. Leaving aside the circumlocutory nature of these statements, such an interpretation missed the import of what Hopkinson's text does accomplish, in confronting and re-imagining a host of gendered and raced discourses central to science fiction. It sets out to rewrite the Anglophone tradition of the discourse of future science and sf, and reimagines the language and nomenclature of science and technology itself through a figure that is transgressive in both its race *and* gender: a black woman. Another quite different example of the potential color-blindness inherent in "foregrounding gender" is provided by Hopkinson as juror, commenting on *Cereus Blooms at Night*:

> My highest priority is this novel by Canadian Shani Mootoo. A Caribbean-based exploration of queerness, gender and preference written defiantly from within, given that in some Caribbean countries, being openly queer can invite societally condoned bashing. This novel is a radical act... A love story in which neither gender nor sexual preference are absolute. (TAC 1997 SL)

What Hopkinson makes clear is that judgments of how gender and sexuality are "expanded" must be considered within their own cultural and raced context, not just the default, normative position of Anglophone, colonialist, white cultures.

Appropriately enough, given the heightened awareness of race in the sf community over 2008-2009 (evidenced by debates at WisCon and also the ongoing online debates known as "RaceFail 09") one of the joint winners of the most recent Tiptree Award (awarded in 2009) was Nisi Shawl's *Filter House.*[8]

Tiptree in the twenty-first century

Most followers of the Tiptree would understand that the broadness and flexibility of the judging criteria and process mean that the text(s) chosen as winners will not always be what panel members thought was the best. Still, readers of sf, including myself, do tend to look to the Tiptree for guidance and inspiration, to provide a reading list of texts that feminist sf readers will probably enjoy. There is also a sense in which the award accomplishes a sort of benchmarking exercise, indexing the health of the state of sf feminisms or genderbending sf. Given this, it is inevitable that the award also provokes discussion about which texts have *not* won, and why. It is precisely in this space, between the "official dialogue" of Tiptree honors and the community reaction to such, that some of the fault-lines running through the debates around gender, feminism, and sexuality in the feminist sf community are most clearly exposed.

As Notkin noted, the early to mid-2000s saw a troubling trend to award books that many considered to be not feminist, and in at least one case perhaps anti-feminist (M. John Harrison's *Light*). For myself, at least, a number of these winners, whilst excellent books, offered little that was challenging, new, or particularly feminist in their approach to gender, for example Matt Ruff's *Set This House in Order*, Joe Haldeman's *Camouflage*, and Johanna Sinisalo's *Not Before Sundown*. A welcome change came in 2005 with the jury's choice of Geoff Ryman's *Air: Or, Have Not Have*, which, with its focus on a middle-aged woman in an imaginary third-world country, offered a fascinating interrogation of gender, race, and technology (although surprisingly, the issues of race, globalization, and postcolonialism were not highlighted in the juror's comments). Next, 2006 saw two

---

8 Consisting of a number of months of often fraught debate and argument, dispersed across the blogosphere, it is difficult to know how long many of the important postings of RaceFail09 will remain available. A timeline and summary can be found at the feminist sf wiki: http://wiki.feministsf.net/index.php?title=RaceFail_09.

inventive and very different gender-bending (and feminist) winners, although both are located at the edge of the sf/f field—Shelley Jackson's *Half Life* and Catherynne M. Valente's *The Orphan's Tales: In the Night Garden*. The 2007 winner, however, again provoked misgivings. Sarah Hall's *The Carhullan Army* was praised by the jury for its writing of "female aggression in a believable way" and exploration of "war, violence, and revolution" (TAC 2007), but some readers have found the depiction of a violent, separatist feminist revolution troubling. Cheryl Morgan sees similarities between Hall's book and Charnas's *Holdfast* series, but finds that unlike the process charted through Charnas's books, where "feminism grew from being a revolt against male rule, to a separatist movement, to a conquering empire, and finally back to a humanist movement.... *The Carhullan Army* looks awfully like a return to Riding Women politics" (http://www. cheryl-morgan.com/?page_id=1056). As it is always so tempting to do, Morgan points to books that she considered more Tiptree-worthy, including the short-listed *Dangerous Space* by Kelley Eskridge and Laurie Marks' *Water Logic,* as well as the absent *Illario* by Mary Gentle (all of which, I would agree, are much more radical in their treatment of gender, sexuality, and power).

Such second-guessing is, in the end, a futile exercise, but it is I think suggestive of a change in the relationship between feminist sf texts and the community, and also between and across generations. In a WisCon 30 panel on "Is Reading Feminist SF a Theory-Building Activity" Karen Joy Fowler got to the heart of the issue:

> I've been watching the Tiptree Award process for several years, and something has repeated itself several times. A fresh jury begins discussing the kind of book they want... Generally it turns out that they want to be reading *The Left Hand of Darkness* and want to be nineteen years old. That's what they're trying to create. Many, many months and books later, they begin to scale down their expectations and look for something more subtle that will have a less profound change in their thinking. I've seen this so many times that I've wondered: at our age, and with our reading histories, is it in fact possible to have that experience again? (Quilter 2007: 59)

Others responded that in fact what had shifted was the relation between the field and society—as another panel title asked, "Is Feminist

SF So Five Years Ago?" Morgan reports that "...to a certain extent we decided it was, because things have changed... We haven't won the war but we're now fighting in the trenches, not doing easy things" (Quilter 2007: 61).

So what, exactly, do Tiptree texts, the Tiptree Award, and its conversations have to say about feminism/s in sf? More than anything they reveal, I think, the complex and convoluted relation between feminism and gender, and most importantly, the historically contingent and changing nature of this relation. The Tiptree texts and commentary reveal a welcome turn to examining masculinity in sf, as a function of attention to gender that was obscured because of the overt masculinism of much sf. On a broader level, however, the award continues to reflect predominantly white western feminist concerns with gender—not surprisingly, given the constituency of the sf community and readership. While sexuality has always been to the fore, queer theory has not had as much impact as one would have expected. Issues to do with lesbianism are recognized, but not the ways in which texts might "queer" sexuality in actually challenging the hetero/homosexual dichotomy altogether.

In the last few years, some have indeed questioned whether gender alone is a sufficient focus for the award, and by implication, whether we are all in agreement about the meaning of the term. Notkin concluded a recent survey of the award by asking if it should reflect other social divisions such as race and class:

> What's so important about gender, that it has its own award? Should we be expanding our focus, becoming an "RCG" (...Race/ Class/Gender) award?
>
> No one on the Tiptree motherboard, and hardly anyone who's served on a jury, would deny that race and class are important questions that deserve comparable attention to gender. (2005)

One could argue that a more straightforward admission of feminist status might resolve such problems, as contemporary feminism/s moves away from the contradictions of claiming a coherent, universalizing identity for "woman" based on "gender" alone as basis for political movement and critique.

In coming to conclusions about these debates about the award, sf feminisms, and gender, it might be timely to revisit the original figure of inspiration for the award—the trickster Tiptree her/himself. What I think Tiptree's example should remind us of is that "feminism" is not *just* about gender. Indeed part of what I perceive as the changing terrain of feminist sf is exactly what Mohanraj started to adumbrate above—that studies of gender are not necessarily the same as feminism. Although whilst Mohanraj's opinion seems to be that (at least for the purposes of the award) the latter is in some ways less powerful or "new" than the former, I would argue the opposite: that if we are looking for new and radical sites of feminist theorizing and imagination in sf, then we do, in fact, need to look beyond gender alone.

If we are to take the contributions of women of color, and of postcolonial and queer theory seriously, then gender needs to be de-prioritized or perhaps, unseated altogether as the primary tool of feminist theory work. I do not think it is an accident that some of the most radical and exciting developments in critical sf feminisms and feminist theory in general—critical race theory, queer theory, and feminist science studies—all, in different ways, lead us away from, or beyond, gender.

Beyond gender

Gender is hard to let go of—for feminist critics as much as (if not more than) for readers—and as Pearson, Hollinger, and Gordon remind us, fiction is often ahead of critique in this regard. A useful example here is the series of Mars stories by Kelley Eskridge. Critics and readers spend enormous efforts on either overlooking the fact that Mars is genderless (and assigning a gender to per) or talking about how this non-assignment can be read in gendered terms (see for example, Merrick 1999). Yet much of this is to miss the point; in Eskridge's words, "It's not that Mars is genderless, but that gender isn't an issue in Mars's expression of self, or in the way that others respond to Mars. And Mars isn't meant to be a puzzle for readers to solve, but a space into which any reader can fit themselves" (Griffith and Eskridge 2008: 47). Mindful of the lessons Eskridge poses here for critic and reader alike, I want to consider another sf text that I think does similar work in terms of helping or forcing us to think of feminism, sex, and equality beyond or outside of the terms of the sex/gender system.

The 2005 novel *Life* by Gwyneth Jones is centrally concerned with the language and conception of sciences like biology and the way science underwrites and reflects the sex-gender order. The novel subjects scientific stories of "life" to a feminist interrogation of how such understandings intersect and conflict with our gendered social order. Set in a near-future Britain, the story of *Life* focuses on the biologist Anna Senoz, her career, relationships, and family. Woven through the narrative is also the story of her central scientific discovery (which ultimately brings her infamy)—the Transferred Y (TY) viroid. Extrapolated from real-world research into the "descent" of the Y Chromosome, TY describes a phenomenon whereby sections of the sex-determining region (SRY) of the Y chromosome are transferring over to the X chromosome, eventually producing men who are effectively XX males. Jones uses this imagined discovery to engage in detailed critiques of the sex-gender system, evolutionary biology, and the language and production of biological knowledge itself.

Jones experienced difficulty in getting *Life* published; many sf editors turned it down as being too mainstream, whilst as an sf author, Jones wasn't picked up by mainstream publishers.[9] Eight years after she started it, the book eventually found a home with the feminist sf publisher, Aqueduct Press. Even amongst the feminist sf community, *Life* received a surprisingly muted response. A number of reviews were ambivalently complimentary—praising the detailed depiction of a female scientist, but critical of the fact that Anna in particular was an "unlikable" and unsympathetic character. *Life* was nominated for the Tiptree Award but did not win. This is a crucial point. From my own perspective, *Life* was a more radical book by far, both in terms of its feminism and what it did with gender, than either of the two books awarded the Tiptree that year. Whilst mindful of the vagaries of consensus decision-making that inform such processes, the annotations from the Tiptree short list make clear that the jury did not concur with my reading.

There are, I think, two main reasons for the low-key response to *Life*; one has to do with the book's focus on science itself, and the other

---

9 As one reviewer perceptively notes: "you can't read this book and not reflect on the fact that had this been written by, say, Margaret Atwood, *Life* would be receiving more of the widespread attention it deserves... But Jones is a genre writer, the SFnal elements serve to underscore her themes, so instead of getting front page reviews on the Sunday *New York Times Book Review*, she has to settle for honorable mention in Gerald Jonas's ghetto column" (David Soyka, 2005, review of *Life*, SF Site http://www.sfsite.com/03a/li195.htm).

to do with the critical state of sf feminisms. Inspired by the transformative visions of the 1970s utopias, for many readers feminism
was meant to transform sf and its future visions, to show the way
across and beyond what Jones calls the "Great Divide" (when it wasn't
providing dystopian warnings and critique). Sf feminisms don't usually play out the way *Life* does, where the *deus ex machina* of the TY
phenomenon dissolves the Great Divide, but leaves us in the same
mess. So too, the lack of heroes (particularly female heroes), of con-
structive outcomes, of a triumph of (or over) gender won't appeal to
all feminist readers. Not surprisingly, the audience for feminist sf has
changed since the 1970s. Influenced by the steady increase of women
writers in the field and the growth of academic attention to the genre,
the audience has widened in terms of numbers and demographics. In
the process, however, there is a sense in which the oppositional nature
of sf feminism has been diluted as it has been incorporated: producing
what Jones refers to as "fem-sf."

> It's not that feminist analysis in an SF format is out of date.
> The story is as relevant as ever it was, and the books are still
> being written... But it's a niche market, a minority interest:
> whereas the kind of fem-sf reading that the popular audi-
> ence will read and buy has become practically indistinguish-
> able from mainstream feminine SF. Stories where "girls get
> to be guys," either on Space Patrol or with a swashbuckly
> sword and a feathery hat, will always be popular. Stories cel-
> ebrating feminine culture, even when men are [to] blame for
> everything evil, and women have been innocent bystanders
> for all the millennia, are also comfort fare. They're womanly.
> They offer no challenge to conventional, or hyper-conven-
> tional "separate development" views on gender roles.[10]

And even for those "minority readers," it is precisely Jones's radically feminist insistence on looking to, and learning from, science
(particularly when it comes to questions of gender) that I think trou-
bles the book's easy acceptance as feminist sf. For some readers, the
place of science in feminist sf such as *Life* is merely as prop or device through which to explore "proper" feminist concerns: "scientific

10 Jones, "Shora." Bold As Love. Blog entry, March 27, 2007. Unfortunately the post
   is no longer available as the blog archives at present only go back to Nov 2007.
   The essay is reprinted in Jones's collection, *Imagination/Space* (2009).

discussions work as metaphors for gender and sexual issues" (TAC 2004, SL). On the contrary (as I have argued elsewhere), the narrative of *Life* is as much about science itself—its cultures, practices, and knowledge—as it is "about" Anna, or the state of contemporary feminism (Merrick 2009).

More importantly, *Life* also actively engages biological theories and draws upon this science to reflect on that primary concern of feminist theory: the relation of sex and gender. Given sf's history, the lessons of sociobiology, and mainstream feminism's distrust of "essentialism," turning to biology as an answer to the "difference between the sexes" problem seems to go against the grain of sf feminisms. Indeed, the TY viroid challenges a number of normalized understandings about sex, biology, and gender from both scientific and non-scientific perspectives. As increasing numbers of men in the book are already shown to be XX males, the normative system coding sex chromosomes as biological markers of "sex-species" is rendered irrelevant. As Anna's friend, the "post-feminist" Ramone gleefully comments, "Men become women with dicks!" Anna replies: "Or women become men with tits. You can make the words do anything you like" (359). For Anna, this breakdown of the male-female distinction is not surprising, nor even very disturbing to her understanding of sexual difference.

> In nature, before any of this started, many people were sexual mosaics, whether they knew it or not. In time, TY may create a situation where there are no genetic traits exclusive to "men" or "women": when sexual difference is in the individual, not a case of belonging to one half of the species or the other. (362)

The separation of humans into two distinct "sexual species" does not predate and ordain the two-gendered social system but is itself structured by the assumption of the simple binary male/female. Such views are becoming commonplace in non-linear biology, as Myra Hird points out,

> "sex" is not dichotomous. It makes as much sense, biologically speaking, to talk about zero sexes (we are much more similar than we are different) or a thousand tiny sexes … That culture focuses on two sexes is, biologically speaking, arbitrary. (Hird 2004: 151)

Life thus fulfils the call from critics such as Haraway, Elizabeth Wilson, and Vicki Kirby for feminists to confront biological understandings. Like advocates of the new materialism such as Hird, *Life* reminds us that "while nature emphasizes diversity, culture emphasizes dichotomy," and illustrates why the use of biology "to reify sex dimorphism" should not deter feminists from seeing the natural sciences "as a useful site for critiques of this dichotomy" (2004, 152).

Life also alerts us to an emerging skepticism about the continuing political and epistemological salience of "gender" as the pre-eminent critical tool of feminist analysis. Anne Fausto-Sterling, for example has called for a reconsideration of "the 1970s theoretical account of sex and gender," which "assigned biological (especially reproductive) differences to the word sex and gave to gender all other differences" (Fausto-Sterling 2005: 1495, 1493). In Jones's case, this insight comes directly from her scientific research for the book:

> The idea that gender is all important could be simply wrong. Down among the chromosomes, the science is neutral. Every human body (right now, no fantasy intervention required) is a mosaic of male and female cells. The whole idea that humanity is divided into two halves could be a chimera. One day it could just vanish, like the Cold war, like the crystal spheres, like canals on Mars and jungles on Venus. (Jones 2008: 301)

Divorcing feminism from gender is a big ask, for feminist critics as much as for feminist sf readers. For me, reading books like *Life*, alongside critics like Haraway, Fausto-Sterling, Wilson, Kirby, and others leads to an inevitable questioning of the continuing value of feminist theory's useful category, gender. Texts like *Life* might help us think through how feminist theory and praxis can proceed in a world (and discourse) without gender. A world without gender like the one hinted at in *Life*: populated by men and women, and still troubled by "sex," rather than the genderless or androgynous utopias and/or dystopias this phrase has usually suggested for second-wave feminists. (The alternative might be uncomfortably close to the situation Jones describes in her Aleutian series: that of a "gender war—not wars between men and women, but between people who believe in gender and people who don't.")[11] Or as Haraway puts it, the "terribly contaminated" device of sex/gender theory suffers the serious problem of "misplaced concreteness," whereby "the analytical work was mistaken for the thing itself, and people truly believed, and believe, in sex and gender as things" (Haraway 2004b: 329-30). The ontologies built on sex/gender rely on a "contaminated philosophical tradition" of matter/form categories, rather than Haraway's preferred model of "getting at the world as a verb" where we are always thinking not in terms of nouns and things, but verbs, becomings, relationality and "worlds in the making" (330).

As I have argued in previous chapters, sf has long been a site where sex, sexuality, gender, and science have been invoked to produce alternative visions of such "worlds in the making." In particular, the insistent drive to emphasize materiality and corporeality in feminist sf and criticism is perfectly situated to think through and beyond the sex/gender system, in what is a potentially much more radical move than the drive toward the posthuman.

Future cabals

In her work on the production of the object feminist theory, Katie King calls attention to "how locations of publication are political, how they create specific audiences and identities, and how they constrain and construct possibilities for action" (2004: 121-2). My aim in this book has been twofold: to demonstrate how productions and publications from differing locations have constructed the shifting object "feminist sf" or "sf feminisms," and to show that such constructions are evidence of feminist cultural activity within, across, and sometimes in spite of, sf communities. My personal production of "sf feminisms" has emphasized its status as the product of a series of communities that variously intersect, compete, or complement each other. This documentation of fragments and moments of the debates and contests over and within feminism in sf communities confirms the vital and long-lived existence of sf feminisms, expressed not just through the texts written by feminist authors, but in the meta-textual conversations, exchanges, and amateur publications in the broader sf

---

11 Jones, Panel discussion: "Gwyneth Jones's *Life*: Feminist Challenge or Challenge to Today's Feminists?" WisCon 29, May 27-30, 2005, Madison; transcript available at http://coffeeandink.livejournal.com/459209.html.

community. It is this last facet of the operation of sf feminisms that necessitates the importance of acknowledging the field of sf as the context in which they have been articulated and produced. The feminist histories played out in this marginalized cultural arena are not only indicative of broader feminist relations, but in many ways offer salutatory lessons for the "mainstream," in particular in the close nexus between praxis and theory, and criticism and action typical of the sf feminist community.

My review of the various constructions and uses of feminist sf indicates that diverse sectors of the community of sf feminisms have their own approaches, uses for, and conclusions about the function of their particular formulation of or challenge to feminist sf. The differences within and between the canons constructed by each section of the community reveal, in microcosm, the continued dominance of hierarchical genealogies that help maintain boundaries such as that between genre and literature, feminist and non-feminist, or critic and fan. The hegemony of white, straight, middle-class, feminist taxonomies is also evident—most obviously in the formalized structures of feminist criticism focused on a body of texts produced in the main by "women of pallor." It is also, as I have indicated, similarly evident—but much more openly challenged—in the sf feminist community itself.

The mode of feminist cultural production manifested in sf presents a strong case for resisting the decontextualization of "community theorizing" (to paraphrase King) into published academic forms that "[mystify] their own processes of production" (K. King 1994: 147). My overview of the various sites of debate about feminist sf shows the wealth of opportunities for new forms of meaning-making, theorizing, reading, and production in the gaps and silences of my account. Each chapter could be seen as a preliminary survey, a potential nucleus for a myriad of other investigations into feminist cultural productions that could produce provocative reflections on mainstream (dare I say "mundane") feminist theory and criticism, as well as on the sf genre. So many untold stories beckon from the gaps of this book: histories of sf feminisms focused on alternative sexualities or the nexus of race and feminism; a detailed history of the women in fandom and their various communities; the transformation of the sf feminist "public sphere" through electronic communication; or the vital intersections between the ecofeminist movement and feminist sf.

Despite its many gaps and omissions, it is my hope that this book contributes to the continuing vitality and complexity of the "grand conversation" that is sf feminisms. My story also carries a less hopeful, albeit important sub-text: the ease with which our histories can be lost, rewritten, or, as Gomoll notes of the '70s, recast as boring and trivial. Attempts to incorporate or incapacitate feminisms in sf may work in more subtle ways now than in the pages of *Amazing Stories*, but the intent is much the same. As far back as 1978, Mary Kenny Badami was arguing against this sort of tactic: "Even as we take pride in the presence of achieving women in traditionally male enclaves, we know the difference between tokenism and equal representation" (Badami 1978: 10-11). I have argued that both women and feminists have been challenging sexism and tokenism in sf since the pulps. It is important to document both these (and later) challenges and the various ways they have been suppressed or forgotten in order to fully comprehend the nature of feminist interventions into sf. The more inclusive our "grand conversation," the better able we are to tell the feminist stories of our past and present—and to discover and sustain our storytellers of the future.

BIBLIOGRAPHY

Aab, Marjorie. 1973. Letter. *The Alien Critic* 2 (4), November: 47-48.

Adam, Alison. 2002. The Ethical Dimension of Cyberfeminism. In *Reload: Rethinking Women + Cyberculture*, eds. Mary Flanagan and Austin Booth, 158-74. Cambridge, MA: The MIT Press.

Agosin, Margaret, ed. 1992. *Secret Weavers: Stories of the Fantastic by Women of Argentina and Chile*. Fredonia, NY: White Pine Press.

Alaimo, Stacy. 1994. Cyborg and Ecofeminist Interventions: Challenges for an Environmental Feminism. *Feminist Studies* 20 (1): 133-52.

Aldiss, Brian. 1975. *Billion Year Spree: The History of Science Fiction*. London: Corgi.

Aldiss, Brian, and David Wingrove. 1988. *Trillion Year Spree: The History of Science Fiction*. London: Paladin.

Allen, Virginia, and Terri Paul. 1986. Science Fiction: Ways of Theorizing About Women. In *Erotic Universe: Sexuality and Fantastic Literature*, ed. Donald Palumbo, 165-83. New York: Greenwood.

Amis, Kingsley. 1962. *New Maps of Hell: A Survey of Science Fiction*. London: Victor Gollancz.

Among Our Members. 1938a. *Imagination* 1 (7), Apr.: 4.

Among Our Members. 1938b. *Imagination* 1 (9), June: 4.

Andermahr, Sonya. 1992. The Politics of Separatism and Lesbian Utopian Fiction. In *New Lesbian Criticism: Literary and Cultural Readings*, ed. Sally Munt, 133-52. Hemel Hempstead: Harvester Wheatsheaf.

Anderson, Jeffrey. 1973. What It's Not All About. *Riverside Quarterly* 5 (3): 232.

Anderson, Poul. 1956. Nice Girls on Mars. *Fantasy and Science Fiction* 10 (5), May: 47-52.

———. 1974. Reply to a Lady. *Vertex* 2 (2): 8, 99.

Annas, Pamela J. 1978. New Worlds, New Words: Androgyny in Feminist Science Fiction. *Science Fiction Studies #15* 5 (2): 143-56.

Anon. 1979. Letter. *Starship* 16 (2): 67.

Antell, Stephen. 1979. Letter. *Starship* 16 (2): 67.

Arditti, Rita, Renate Duelli Klein, and Shelly Minden, eds. 1984. *Test-Tube Women: What Future for Motherhood?* Boston, MA: Pandora.

Armstrong, Michael A. 1978. Letter. *Janus #12-13* 4 (2/3): 70.

Asimov, Isaac. 1939. Letter. *Astounding Science Fiction* 22 (5), Feb: 159-60.

———. 1982. The Feminization of Sci-Fi. *Vogue* Oct.: 608.

Atheling Jr., William. 1964. *The Issue at Hand.* Chicago, IL: Advent.

Attebery, Brian. 2002. *Decoding Gender in Science Fiction.* New York & London: Routledge.

———. 2003. The Magazine Era: 1926-1960. In *The Cambridge Companion to Science Fiction*, eds. Edward James and Farah Mendlesohn, 32-47. Cambridge, UK: Cambridge University Press.

Australian Spacemen Look into Space: Science Fiction Fans Are "Thinkers of Tomorrow." 1953. *The Australian Women's Weekly*, May 13, 16.

Bacon-Smith, Camille. 1992. *Enterprising Women: Television Fandom and the Creation of Popular Myth.* Philadelphia, PA: University of Pennsylvania Press.

———. 2000. *Science Fiction Culture.* Philadelphia, PA: University of Pennsylvania Press.

Badami, Mary Kenny. 1978. A Feminist Critique of Science Fiction. *Extrapolation* 18 (1): 6-19.

Baddock, Patricia. 1955. Letter: Femme(Fatale?). *Authentic Science Fiction* 57, May: 126.

Balsamo, Anne. 1996. *Technologies of the Gendered Body: Reading Cyborg Women.* Durham, NC, & London: Duke University Press.

Bammer, Angelika. 1991. *Partial Visions: Feminism and Utopianism in the 1970s.* New York & London: Routledge.

Bankier, Amanda. 1975. Editor Note. *WatCh* (3), Apr.: 42.

Bankier, Jennifer. 1974. "Women in Sf: Image and Reality": A Criticism. *WatCh* (2), Nov.: 10-14.

Barad, Karen. 2003. Posthumanist Performativity: Toward an Understanding of How Matter Comes to Matter. *Signs: Journal of Women in Culture and Society* 28 (3): 801-31.

Barr, Marleen S. 1982. Science Fiction and the Fact of Women's Repressed Creativity: Anne McCaffrey Portrays a Female Artist. *Extrapolation* 23 (1): 70-76.

———. 1984. Oh Well, Orwell – Big Sister Is Watching Herself: Feminist Science Fiction in 1984. *Women's Studies International Forum* 7 (2).

———. 1987. *Alien to Femininity: Speculative Fiction and Feminist Theory.* Westport, CT: Greenwood Press.

———. 1992. *Feminist Fabulation: Space/Postmodern Fiction.* Iowa City, IA: University of Iowa Press.

———, ed. 1981. *Future Females: A Critical Anthology.* Bowling Green, OH: Bowling Green State University Popular Press.

———, ed. 2000. *Future Females, the Next Generation: New Voices and Velocities in Feminist Science Fiction Criticism.* Lanham, MD: Rowman & Littlefield Publishers, Inc.

———, ed. 2008. *Afro-Future Females: Black Writers Chart Science Fiction's Newest New-Wave Trajectory,* Columbus, OH: Ohio State University Press.

Bartter, Martha A. 1992/1993. Science, Science Fiction and Women: A Language of (Tacit) Exclusion. *Etc* 49: 407-19.

Baruch, Elaine Hoffman, Amadeo F. D'Adamo Jr., and Joni Seager. 1988. *Embryos, Ethics, and Women's Rights: Exploring the New Reproductive Technologies*. New York: Harrington Park.

Ben-Tov, Sharona. 1995. *The Artificial Paradise: Science Fiction and American Reality*. Ann Arbor, MI: University of Michigan Press.

Benford, Gregory. 1979. Letter. *Starship* 16 (2): 67.

Benton, Jill. 1992. *Naomi Mitchison: A Biography*. London: Pandora.

Berger, Albert I. 1977. Science-Fiction Fans in Socio-Economic Perspective: Factors in the Social Consciousness of a Genre. *Science Fiction Studies* 4 (3): 232-46.

Bernabeu, Ednita P. 1957. Science Fiction: A New Mythos. *Psychoanalytic Quarterly* 26, October: 527-35.

Bethke, Bruce. 1983. Cyberpunk. *Amazing Stories* 57 (4), Nov.: 94-105.

Blackford, Russell, and Sean McMullen. 1998. Prophet and Pioneer: The Science Fiction of Norma Hemming. *Fantasy Annual* 2, Spring: 65-75.

Bleier, Ruth, ed. 1986. *Feminist Approaches to Science*. New York: Pergamon Press.

Bloch, Robert. 1979. Letter. *Starship* 16 (3): 81.

Bogstad, Janice. 1977. Editorial, the Science Fiction Connection: Readers and Writers in the Sf Community. *Janus #10* 3 (4): 4-8.

———. 1978/1979. Octavia E. Butler and Power Relationships. 4 (4): 28-31.

———. 1978/1979. Editorial. *Janus #14* 4 (4): 6-7.

———. 1981. Editorial. *New Moon: A Quarterly Journal of Feminist Issues in SF* 1 (2): 2-3, 17-19.

Bonner, Frances. 1994/1995. Review: Aliens and Others: Science Fiction, Feminism and Postmodernism. *Foundation* 62: 89-93.

Booth, Austin. 2002. Women's Cyberfiction: An Introduction. In *Reload: Rethinking Women + Cyberculture*, eds. Mary Flanagan and Austin Booth, 25-40. Cambridge, MA: The MIT Press.

Boothroyd, Irene. 1955. Letter: First. *Authentic Science Fiction* 54, Feb.: 138.

Bordo, Susan. 1990. Reading the Slender Body. In *Body/Politics: Women and the Discourses of Science*, eds. Mary Jacobus, Evelyn Fox Keller, and Sally Shuttleworth, 83-112.

Boston Women's Health Collective. 1969. *Our Bodies, Ourselves*. New York: Simon and Schuster.

Boucher, Anthony. 1963. Sf Books: 1960. In *The 6th Annual of the Year's Best S-F*, ed. Judith Merril. London: Mayflower. (Original edition, 1961.)

Bould, Mark. 2005. Cyberpunk. In *A Companion to Science Fiction*, ed. David Seed, 217-31. Malden, MA: Blackwell.

Bould, Mark, and Sherryl Vint. 2006. Learning from the Little Engines That Couldn't: Transported by Gernsback, Wells, and Latour. *Science Fiction Studies* 33 (1): 129-48.

Boulter, Amanda. 1995. Alice James Racoona Tiptree Sheldon Jr: Textual Personas in the Short Fiction of Alice Sheldon. *Foundation* 63: 5-31.

Bourdieu, Pierre. 1984. *Distinction: A Social Critique of the Judgement of Taste*. Translated by Richard Nice. Cambridge, MA: Harvard University Press.

Bradley, Marion Zimmer. 1951. Fan File: Marion Zimmer Bradley. *Quandry #13* 2 (1): 89.

———. 1954. Letter. *HodgePodge* 5, Jan.: 27.

———. 1975a. Letter. *WatCh* 3, April: 28-30.

———. 1975b. Letter. *WatCh* (4): 19-25.

———. 1977. An Evolution of Consciousness. *Science Fiction Review* 6 (3): 34-45.

———. 1977/1978. My Trip through Science Fiction. *Algol #30* 15 (1): 10-20.

———. 1978. *Darkover Landfall*. London: Arrow.

————. 1985. Fandom: Its Value to the Professional. In *Inside Outer Space: Science Fiction Professionals Look at Their Craft*, ed. Sharon Jarvis, 69-85. New York: Frederick Ungar.

————. 1988. One Woman's Experience in Science Fiction. In *Women of Vision: Essays by Women Writing Science Fiction*, ed. Denise Du Pont, 84-97. New York: St. Martin's Press.

Braidotti, Rosi. 2006. Posthuman, All Too Human: Towards a New Process Ontology. *Theory Culture Society* 23 (7-8): 197-208.

Bredehoft, Thomas A. 1997. Origin Stories: Feminist Science Fiction and C.L. Moore's "Shambleau." *Science Fiction Studies* 24 (3): 369-86.

Bretnor, Reginald, ed. 1953. *Modern Science Fiction: Its Meaning and Its Future*. New York: Coward-McCann.

Brizzi, Mary T. 1982. The Launching Pad. *Extrapolation* 23 (1): 3-4, 107.

Brown, Brian Earl. 1978. Letter. *Janus #12-13* 4 (2/3): 62.

brown, rich. 1994. Post-Sputnik Fandom (1957-1990). In *Science Fiction Fandom*, ed. Joe Sanders, 75-102. Westport, CT, & London: Greenwood Press.

Brown, Wendy. 1991. Feminist Hesitations, Postmodern Exposures. *differences* 3 (1): 63-84.

Broxon, Mildred D. 1974. Letter. *The Alien Critic #8* 3 (1): 22.

Bukatman, Scott. 1991. Postcards from the Posthuman Solar System. *Science Fiction Studies* 18 (3): 343-57.

————. 1993. *Terminal Identity: The Virtual Subject in Postmodern Science Fiction*. Durham, NC: Duke University Press.

Bulmer, Pamela. 1954. A Call to Arms. *Femizine* 2.

Burwell, Jennifer. 1997. *Notes on Nowhere: Feminism, Utopian Logic and Social Transformation*. Minneapolis, MN: University of Minnesota Press.

Bushyager, Linda. 1977. Fanzine Reviews. *Karass* (30), May: 11.

————. 1979. Letter. *Janus* 5 (1), Spring: 7.

Butler, Octavia E. 1988. *Dawn.* New York: Warner.

Byers, Mary. 1939. Letter. *Astounding Science Fiction* 22 (4), Dec.:
160-61.

Cadigan, Pat. 1990. Interview with Pat Cadigan. *Journal Wired*
Spring: 89-90.

———. 1993. Guest Editorial: Ten Years After. *Asimov's SF*
Magazine 17 (14): 4-9.

Cadora, Karen. 1995. Feminist Cyberpunk. *Science Fiction Studies* 22
(3): 357-72.

Campbell, Herbert J. 1955. Editorial Response to Letter: Femme
(Fatale?). *Authentic Science Fiction* (57), May: 126.

Carr, Helen, ed. 1989. *From My Guy to Sci-Fi: Genre and Women's*
Writing in the Postmodern World. London: Pandora Press.

Carr, Joan W. 1954. Editorial. *Femizine* 1, Summer: 2.

Carter, Paul A. 1977. *The Creation of Tomorrow: 50 Years of*
Magazine Science Fiction. New York: Columbia University
Press.

Chalmers, L.M. 1953. I Refugee: An Addict Confesses All. *Vertical*
Horizons 5, Oct.: 2-4.

Charnas, Suzy McKee. 2005. Judging the Tiptree. In *The James*
Tiptree Award Anthology 1, eds. Karen Joy Fowler, Pat Murphy,
Debbie Notkin, and Jeffrey D. Smith, 93-104. San Francisco, CA:
Tachyon Publications.

Chatelain, Julianne. 1984. Letter. *Janus #24* 9 (1): 7.

Chavey, Darrah. 1984. Evangeline Walton—Interpreter of Myths.
Janus #24 9 (1): 33-35.

Christian, Barbara. 1985. *Black Feminist Criticism: Perspectives on*
Black Women Writers. New York: Pergamon Press.

———. 1990. But What Do We Think We're Doing Anyway?: The
State of Black Feminist Criticism(s) or My Little Bit of History.
In *Changing Our Own Words: Essays on Criticism, Theory, and*

Writing by Black Women, ed. Cheryl A. Wall, 58-74. London: Routledge.

Clarke, Vin¢, and Joy Clarke. 1955. *Science Fantasy News*, Christmas.

Classified Page. 1954. *i: A magazine for Science Fiction Fans* 1 (3): back cover.

Cline, Cheryl. 1984. The Soul of Lillith: Nineteenth Century Fantastic Fiction by Women. *Janus #24* 9 (1), Summer: 26-29.

Clute, John, ed. 1995. *Science Fiction: The Illustrated Encyclopedia*. London: Dorling Kindersley.

Clute, John, and Peter Nicholls. 1993. *The Encyclopedia of Science Fiction*. London: Orbit.

Compendium. 1979. *Janus #16* 5 (2), Autumn: 24.

Coney, Michael. 1973. Letter. *The Alien Critic* 2 (3), August: 52-3.

———.1974. Letter. *The Alien Critic* 3 (1), February: 38.

Cook, Diane. 1985. Yes Virginia, There's Always Been Women's Science Fiction…Feminist, Even. In *Contrary Modes: Proceedings of the World Science Fiction Conference*, eds. Jenny Blackford, Russell Blackford, Lucy Sussex, and Norman Talbot, 133-45. Melbourne: Aussiecon 2.

Corea, Gena. 1985. *The Mother Machine: Reproductive Technologies from Artificial Insemination to Artificial Wombs*. New York: Harper & Row.

Cornea, Christine. 2005. Figurations of the Cyborg in Contemporary Science Fiction Novels and Film. In *A Companion to Science Fiction*, ed. David Seed, 275-87. Malden, MA: Blackwell.

Couch, Leigh. 1977. Letter. *Janus #9* 3 (3): 10.

Coulson, Juanita. 1994. Why Is a Fan? In *Science Fiction Fandom*, ed. Joe Sanders, 3-9. Westport, CT, & London: Greenwood Press.

Coward, Rosalind. 1986. Are Women's Novels Feminist Novels? In *The New Feminist Criticism: Essays on Women, Literature and Theory*, ed. Elaine Showalter, 225-39. London: Virago.

Cranny-Francis, Anne. 1990. *Feminist Fiction: Feminist Uses of Generic Fiction*. London: Polity & Basil Blackwell.

————. 1998. The "Science" of Science Fiction: A Sociocultural Analysis. In *Reading Science: Critical and Functional Perspectives on Discourses of Science*, eds. Jim R. Martin and Robert Veel, 63-80. London: Routledge.

Crimmins, Ann. 1978. Letter. *Janus #12-13* 4 (2/3): 70.

Crowder, Diane Griffin. 1993. Separatism and Feminist Utopian Fiction. In *Sexual Practice, Textual Theory: Lesbian Cultural Criticism*, eds. Susan J. Woolfe and Julia Penelope, 237-50. Cambridge, MA: Blackwell.

Csicsery-Ronay Jr., Istvan. 1991. Cyberpunk and Neuromanticism. In *Storming the Reality Studio: A Casebook of Cyberpunk and Postmodern Science Fiction*, ed. Larry McCaffery, 182-93. Durham, NC, & London: Duke University Press.

————. 1992a. Futuristic Flu, or, the Revenge of the Future. In *Fiction 2000: Cyberpunk and the Future of Narrative*, eds. George Slusser and Tom Shippey, 26-45. Athens, GA, & London: University of Georgia Press.

————. 1992b. Postmodern Technoculture, or the Gordian Knot Revisited. *Science Fiction Studies* 19 (3): 403-10.

D'Ammassa, Don. 1984. Appreciating Lee Killough. *Janus #24* 9 (1): 15-16, 36.

Davidson, Carolyn S. 1981. The Science Fiction of Octavia Butler. *Sagala* 2 (1): 35.

Davidson, Dan. 1979. Letter. *Starship* 16 (3): 81.

Davin, Eric Leif. 2003. Hidden from History: The Female Counter-Culture of the 1950-1960 *Science-Fiction Magazines*. *Fantasy Commentator X* (3&4): 138-91.

————. 2006. *Partners in Wonder: Women and the Birth of Science Fiction, 1926-1965*. Lanham, MD: Lexington Books.

Davis, Kathe Finney. 1994. Review of Marleen Barr, *Feminist Fabulation* and Robin Roberts, *a New Species*. *Extrapolation* 35 (1): 84-85.

———. 1995. Guest Editor's Pad: What About Us Grils? *Extrapolation* 36 (3): 177-80.

Day, Phyllis J., and Nora G. Day. 1983. Freaking the Mundane: A Sociological Look at Science Fiction Conventions and Vice Versa. In *Patterns of the Fantastic, (Academic Programming at Chicon IV)*, ed. Donald M. Hassler, 91-102. San Bernardino, CA: Borgo Press.

De Hart, H.O. 1928. Letter. *Amazing Stories* 3 (3), Jun.: 277.

de Lauretis, Teresa. 1990. Signs of W^a_onder. In *The Technological Imagination: Theories and Fictions*, eds. Teresa de Lauretis, Andreas Huyssen, and Kathleen Woodward, 159-74. Madison, WI: Wisconsin University Press.

deFord, Miriam Allen. 1956. News for Dr. Richardson. *Fantasy and Science Fiction* 10 (5), May: 53-157.

del Rey, Lester. 1960. Polygamy, Polyandry and the Future. *Amazing Stories* 34 (11): 99-106.

———. 1980. *The World of Science Fiction, 1926-1976: The History of a Subculture*. New York & London: Garland Publishing.

Delany, Samuel R. 1984. *Starboard Wine: More Notes on the Language of Science Fiction*. Pleasantville, NY: Dragon Press.

———. 1988. Is Cyberpunk a Good Thing or a Bad Thing? *Mississippi Review* 16 (1/2): 29.

Delany, Samuel R., and Carl Freedman. 2008. A Conversation with Samuel R. Delany About Sex, Gender, Race, Writing—and Science Fiction. In *Afro-Future Females: Black Writers Chart Science Fiction's Newest New-Wave Trajectory*, ed. Marleen S. Barr, 191-235. Columbus, OH: Ohio State University Press.

Delap, Richard. 1974. Tomorrow's Libido: Sex and Science Fiction. *The Alien Critic* 3 (1): 5-12.

Delhotel, Barbara. 1978. Letter. *Janus #12-13* 4 (2/3): 73.

Dery, Mark. 1996. *Escape Velocity: Cyberculture at the End of the Century*. New York: Grove Press.

Dick, Leslie. 1989. Feminism, Writing, Postmodernism. In *From My Guy to Sci-Fi: Genre and Women's Writing in the Postmodern World*, ed. Helen Carr, 204-14. London: Pandora Press.

Dick, Philip K. 1974. An Open Letter from Philip K. Dick. *Vertex* 2 (4): 99.

———. 1969. Replies to "A Questionnaire for Professional SF Writers and Editors." *The Double:Bill Symposium*; cited in *Worlds of If*, vol. 22, no. 5, #172, 1974, 106.

Donawerth, Jane. 1990. Utopian Science: Contemporary Feminist Science Theory and Science Fiction by Women. *NWSA Journal* 2 (4): 535-57.

———. 1994. Science Fiction by Women in the Early Pulps, 1926-1930. In *Utopian and Science Fiction by Women: Worlds of Difference*, eds. Jane Donawerth and Carol A. Kolmerton, 137-52. Liverpool, UK: Liverpool University Press.

———. 1997. *Frankenstein's Daughters: Women Writing Science Fiction*. Syracuse, NY: Syracuse University Press.

Donawerth, Jane, and Carol A. Kolmerton. 1994. *Utopian and Science Fiction by Women: Worlds of Difference*. Liverpool, UK: Liverpool University Press.

Downe, Kathleen. 1955. Why Not a Woman? *Authentic Science Fiction* 57: 101-02.

Drown, Eric. 2006. Business Girls and Beset Men in Pulp Science Fiction and Science Fiction Fandom. *Femspec* 7 (1): 5-35.

Dubey, Madhu. 2008. Becoming Animal in Black Women's Science Fiction. In *Afro-Future Females: Black Writers Chart Science Fiction's Newest New-Wave Trajectory*, ed. Marleen S. Barr, 31-51. Columbus, OH: Ohio State University Press.

Duchamp, L. Timmel. 2004a. The Cliché from Outerspace: Reflections on Reports of a Death Greatly Exaggerated. In *The Grand Conversation: Essays*, 21-38. Seattle, WA: Aqueduct Press.

————. 2004b. *The Grand Conversation: Essays.* Seattle, WA: Aqueduct Press.

————. 2006a. Joanna Russ's *We Who Are About To… New York Review of Science Fiction* 18 (6) 1, 4-6.

————. 2006b. Real Mothers, a Faggot Uncle, and the Name of the Father: Samuel R. Delany's Feminist Revisions of the Story of SF. Presented at *Samuel R. Delany: a critical symposium.* Buffalo, NY, March 23-24.

————. 2007. How to Do Things with Ideas. In *Scifi in the Mind's Eye: Reading Science through Science Fiction,* ed. Margret Grebowicz, 59-69. Peru, IL: Open Court Publishing.

————. 2008. Whose Romance? Whose Revolution? The Operations of Race and Gender in Panel Discourse at WisCon. In *The WisCon Chronicles, Volume 2: Provocative Essays on Feminism, Race, Revolution, and the Future,* eds. L. Timmel Duchamp and Eileen Gunn, 90-105. Seattle, WA: Aqueduct Press.

Duchamp, L. Timmel, and Samuel Delany. 2007. Sympathy and Power: L. Timmel Duchamp Asks Samuel R. Delany a Question. In *The WisCon Chronicles, Volume 1,* ed. L. Timmel Duchamp, 170-78. Seattle, WA: Aqueduct Press.

Duncker, Patricia. 1992. *Sisters and Strangers: An Introduction to Contemporary Feminist Fiction.* Oxford: Blackwell.

DuPlessis, Rachel Blau. 1979. The Feminist Apologues of Lessing, Piercy and Russ. *Frontiers: A Journal of Women's Studies* 4: 1-8.

————. 1985. *Writing Beyond the Ending: Narrative Strategies of Twentieth-Century Women Writers.* Bloomington, IN: Indiana University Press.

Easterbrook, Neil. 1992. The Arc of Our Destruction: Reversal and Erasure in Cyberpunk. *Science Fiction Studies* 19 (3): 378-94.

Editor. 1956. Note: Of Mars and Men. *Fantasy and Science Fiction* 10 (5), May: 47.

Elkins, Charles. 1990. The Uses of Science Fiction. *Science Fiction Studies* 17 (2): 269-72.

Ellison, Harlan. 1977. A Statement of Ethical Position by the Worldcon Guest of Honour. *Janus #10* 3 (4): 32-33.

———. 1978. Reply to Letter (Anne Crimmins). *Janus #12-13* 4 (2/3): 70.

———, ed. 1972. *Again, Dangerous Visions.* London: Millington. (New York: Doubleday.)

Eney, Richard H., and Jack Speer. 1959. Fancyclopedia II. Operation Crifanac. http://fanac.org/Fannish_Reference_Works/Fancyclopedia/.

Enrys, Barbara. 1984. Charlotte Perkins Gilman: Speculative Feminist. *Janus #24* 9 (1): 11-12.

Ernst, Henry. 1953. Romping through Fandom with the Little Woman. *Space Times* May: 14.

Evans, Frances. 1956. *Femizine* 9, May: 11.

Fanzines. 1954. *Authentic Science Fiction* 51: 137.

Faulkner, Wendy. 1995. Feminism, Science and Technology: Irreconcilable Streams? *Journal of Gender Studies* 4 (3): 341-7. 1995.

Fausto-Sterling, Anne. 1992. *Myths of Gender: Biological Theories About Women and Men.* New York: Basic Books.

———. 2005. The Bare Bones of Sex: Part 1—Sex and Gender. *Signs* 30 (2): 1491-527.

Fausto-Sterling, Anne, and Lydia English. 1986. Women and Minorities in Science: An Interdisciplinary Course. *Radical Teacher* 30.

Fawcett, Kris. 1974. Letter. *WatCh* (2), November.

Fee, Elizabeth. 1983. Women's Nature and Scientific Objectivity. In *Woman's Nature: Rationalizations of Inequality*, eds. Marian Lowe and Ruth Hubbard, 106-19. New York: Pergamon Press.

Fein, Adrienne. 1973. Letter. *Riverside Quarterly* 5 (4): 337-9.

———. 1977. Letter. *Janus #9* 3 (3): 50.

———. 1978. Letter. *Janus #12-13* 4 (2/3): 65.

———. 1978/79. Letter. *Janus #14* 4 (4): 49-50.

Felski, Rita. 1989. *Beyond Feminist Aesthetics: Feminist Literature and Social Change.* London: Hutchison Radius.

Firestone, Shulamith. 1979. *The Dialectic of Sex: The Case for Feminist Revolution.* London: Women's Press.

Fischlin, Daniel, Veronica Hollinger, and Andrew Taylor. 1992. "The Charisma Leak," a Conversation with William Gibson and Bruce Sterling. *Science Fiction Studies* 19 (1): 1-16.

Fitting, Peter. 1985. So We All Became Mothers: New Roles for Men in Recent Utopian Fiction. *Science Fiction Studies* 12 (2): 156-83.

———. 1990. The Lessons of Cyberpunk. In *Technoculture*, eds. Constance Penley and Andrew Ross, 295-315. Minneapolis, MN: University of Minnesota Press.

———. 1994. Beyond the Wasteland: A Feminist in Cyberspace. *Utopian Studies* 5 (2): 4-15.

Flanagan, Mary, and Austin Booth, eds. 2002. *Reload: Rethinking Women + Cyberculture.* Cambridge, MA: The MIT Press.

———. eds. 2007. *re:skin.* Cambridge, MA: MIT Press.

Flax, Jane. 1992. The End of Innocence. In *Feminists Theorize the Political*, eds. Judith Butler and Joan W. Scott, 445-63. New York & London: Routledge.

Fleming, Linda. 1977. The American Sf Subculture *Science Fiction Studies* 4 (3): 263-71.

Florence, Penny. 1990. The Liberation of Utopia or Is Science Fiction the Ideal Contemporary Women's Form. In *Plotting Change: Contemporary Women's Fiction*, ed. Linda Anderson, 64-83. London: Edward Arnold.

Foster, Frances Smith. 1982. Octavia Butler's Black Female Future Fiction. *Extrapolation* 23 (1): 37-49.

Foster, Thomas. 1993a. Incurably Informed: The Pleasures and Dangers of Cyberpunk. *Genders* 18: 1-10.

———. 1993b. Meat Puppets or Robopaths?: Cyberpunk and the Question of Embodiment. *Genders* 18: 11-31.

———. 2002. "The Postproduction of the Human Heart": Desire, Identification, and Virtual Embodiment in Feminist Narratives of Cyberspace. In *Reload: Rethinking Women + Cyberculture*, eds. Mary Flanagan and Austin Booth, 469-504. Cambridge, MA: The MIT Press.

Frank, Janrae, Jean Stine, and Forrest J. Ackerman, eds. 1994. *New Eves: Science Fiction About the Extraordinary Women of Today and Tomorrow*. Stamford, CT: Longmeadow.

Franke, Jackie. 1975. Letter. *Notes from the Chemistry Department* (10), March: 37.

Franklin, Sarah, and Maureen McNeil. 1988. Reproductive Futures: Recent Literature and Current Feminist Debates on Reproductive Technologies. *Feminist Studies* 14 (13): 545-66.

Frazier, Robert. 1984. The Poet Dreams: Sonya Dorman. *Janus #24* 9 (1): 19-20, 36.

Freedman, Carl Howard. 2000. *Critical Theory and Science Fiction*. Hanover, NH: Wesleyan University Press.

Friend, Beverly. 1972. Virgin Territory: Women and Sex in Science Fiction. *Extrapolation* 14 (1), Dec.: 49-58.

———. 1982. Time Travel as a Feminist Didactic in Works by Phyllis Eisenstein, Marlys Millhiser and Octavia Butler. *Extrapolation* 23 (1): 50-55.

Garey, Terry. 1978/1979. Letter. *Janus #14* 4 (4): 50.

Geis, Richard E. 1974. Letter. *The Alien Critic* 3 (1), February: 37.

———. 1975. Pardon Me, but Your Vagina Just Bit My Penis. *Science Fiction Review* 4 (2), May: 64-65.

Gernsback, Hugo. 1926a. Editorial: Editorially Speaking. *Amazing Stories* 1 (6), Sept.: 483.

———. 1926b. Editorial: Thank You. *Amazing Stories* 1 (2), May: 99.

———. 1930. Editorial Response to Letter: No Discrimination against Women. *Science Wonder Stories* 1 (8), Jan.: 765.

Gerrard, Nicci. 1989. *Into the Mainstream: How Feminism Has Changed Women's Writing.* London: Pandora Press.

Gilbert, Sandra M., and Susan Gubar. 1988. *No Man's Land: The Place of the Woman Writer in the Twentieth Century.* Vol. 1, The War of the Worlds. New Haven, CT, & London: Yale University Press.

Gilman, Sandra. 1985. *Difference and Pathology: Stereotypes of Sexuality, Race, and Madness.* Ithaca, NY: Cornell University Press.

Ginway, M. Elizabeth. 2004. *Brazilian Science Fiction: Cultural Myths and Nationhood in the Land of the Future.* Lewisburg, PA: Bucknell University Press.

Gomoll, Jeanne. 1976. Review: *More Women of Wonder. Janus #6* 2 (4): 35.

———. 1977. Happy Gays Are Here Again. *Janus #9* 3 (3): 21-22.

———. 1978. New Nurds. *Janus #12-13* 4 (2/3): 3.

———. 1978/1979a. New Nurds. *Janus #14* 4 (4): 2-5.

———. 1978/1979b. The View from Rapunzel's Tower. *Janus #14* 4 (4): 32-36.

———. 1980. Out of Context: Post-Holocaust Themes in Feminist Science Fiction. *Janus #18* 6 (2): 14-17.

———. 1986-87. An Open Letter to Joanna Russ. *Aurora #25* 10 (1): 7-10.

———. 2000. *GoH Speech, WisCon 24, May 26-29.* http://www.wiscon.info/downloads/gomoll.pdf.

———, ed. 1993. *Symposium: Women in Science Fiction, Khatru 3 & 4.* 2nd ed. Madison, WI: Corflu, SF3.

Gordon, Joan. 1990. Yin and Yang Duke It Out. *Science Fiction Eye #6* 2 (1): 37-39.

Gould, Stephen Jay. 1981. *The Mismeasure of Man*. New York: Norton.

Gray, Chris Hables, and Steven Mentor. 1995. The Cyborg Body Politic: Version 2.1. In *The Cyborg Handbook*, ed. Chris Hables Gray, 453-67. New York & London: Routledge.

Gray, Chris Hables, Steven Mentor, and Heidi J. Figueroa-Sarriera. 1995. Cyborgology: Constructing the Knowledge of Cybernetic Organisms. In *The Cyborg Handbook*, ed. Chris Hables Gray, 1-14. New York & London: Routledge.

Grebowicz, Margret. 2005. Consensus, Dissensus, and Democracy: What Is at Stake in Feminist Science Studies? *Philosophy of Science* 72 (5): 989-1000.

———. 2007. Introduction: Down to Earth. In *Scifi in the Mind's Eye: Reading Science through Science Fiction*, ed. Margret Grebowicz, xiii-xx. Peru, IL: Open Court Publishing.

Greene, Gayle. 1991. *Changing the Story: Feminist Fiction and the Tradition*. Bloomington & Indianapolis, IN: Indiana University Press.

Greenland, Colin. 1982/83. Redesigning the World: Science Fiction and Fandom. *Red Letters: Journal of Cultural Studies* 14: 39-45.

Griffith, Nicola. 1993. *Ammonite*. London: HarperCollins.

———. 1996. Writing from the Body. In *Women of Other Worlds: Excursions through Science Fiction and Feminism*, eds. Helen Merrick and Tess Williams, 247-60. Nedlands: University of Western Australia Press.

Griffith, Nicola, and Kelley Eskridge. 2008. War Machine, Time Machine. In *Queer Universes: Sexualities in Science Fiction*, eds. Wendy Gay Pearson, Veronica Hollinger, and Joan Gordon, 39-49. Liverpool, UK: Liverpool University Press.

Gubar, Susan. 1980. C.L. Moore and the Conventions of Women's Science Fiction. *Science Fiction Studies* 7 (1): 16-27.

Hall, Lesley. 2007. *Naomi Mitchison: A Profile of Her Life and Work* (Conversation Pieces #15). Seattle, WA: Aqueduct Press.

Hall, Stephanie A. 1989. "Reality Is a Crutch for People Who Can't Deal with Science Fiction": Slogan-Buttons among Science Fiction Fans. *Keystone Folklore* 4 (4): 19-31.

Halpin, Zuleyma Tang. 1989. Scientific Objectivity and the Concept of "the Other." *Women's Studies International Forum* 12 (3): 285-93.

Hansen, Rob. 1993. *Then.* http://fanac.org/Fan_Histories/Then/ (accessed 30th Dec 2008).

Haraway, Donna. 1986. Primatology Is Politics by Other Means. In *Feminist Approaches to Science*, ed. Ruth Bleier, 77-118. New York: Pergamon Press.

———. 1988. Situated Knowledges: The Science Question in Feminism and the Privilege of Partial Perspective. *Feminist Studies* 14 (3): 575-99.

———. 1989a. *Primate Visions: Gender, Race and Nature in the World of Modern Science.* New York & London: Routledge.

———. 1989b. The Biopolitics of Postmodern Bodies: Determinations of Self in Immune System Discourse. *differences* 1 (1): 3-43.

———. 1991. *Simians, Cyborgs and Women: The Reinvention of Nature.* New York & London: Routledge.

———. 1992. The Promises of Monsters: A Regenerative Politics for Inappropriate/d Others. In *Cultural Studies*, eds. Lawrence Grossberg, Cary Nelson, and Paula A. Treichler, 295-337. New York & London: Routledge.

———. 1997. *Modest_Witness@Second_Millenium.Femaleman©_Meets_Oncomouse™.* New York & London: Routledge.

———. 2004a. A Manifesto for Cyborgs: Science, Technology, and Socialist Feminism in the 1980s. In *The Haraway Reader*, 7-46. New York & London: Routledge. (Original edition, 1985.)

———. 2004b. *The Haraway Reader.* New York & London: Routledge.

——. 2008. *When Species Meet*. Minneapolis, MN: University of Minnesota Press.

Harding, Sandra. 1986. *The Science Question in Feminism*. Ithaca, NY, & London: Cornell University Press.

——. 1991. *Whose Science? Whose Knowledge?: Thinking from Women's Lives*. Milton Keynes, UK: Open University Press.

——. 1996. Rethinking Standpoint Epistemology: What Is "Strong Objectivity"? In *Feminism and Science*, eds. Evelyn Fox Keller and Helen E. Longino, 63-79. New York & Oxford: Oxford University Press.

——, ed. 2004. *The Feminist Standpoint Theory Reader: Intellectual and Political Controversies*. New York: Routledge.

Harper, Mary Catherine. 1995. Incurably Alien Other: A Case for Feminist Cyborg Writers. *Science Fiction Studies* 22 (3): 399-420.

Harrison, Rosalie G. 1980. Sci Fi Visions: An Interview with Octavia Butler. *Equal Opportunity Forum Magazine* 8: 30-4.

Hartouni, Valerie. 1997. *Cultural Conceptions: On Reproductive Technologies and the Remaking of Life*. Minneapolis, MN: University of Minnesota Press.

Hartwell, David. 1984. *Age of Wonders: Exploring the World of Science Fiction*. New York: Walker and Company.

Hauser, Eva. 1997. Men Are Burglars of Extraterrestrial Origin!: Women Writers and Science Fiction in the Czech Republic. In *Ana's Land: Sisterhood in Eastern Europe*, ed. Tanya Renne. Boulder, CO: Westview Press.

Hawkins, Jane. 1978. Letter. *Janus #12-13* 4 (2/3), Summer/ Autumn: 66.

Hawthorne, Susan, and Renate Duelli Klein, eds. 1991. *Angels of Power and Other Reproductive Creations*. West Melbourne: Spinifex.

Hayles, N. Katherine. 1992. The Materiality of Informatics. *Configurations* 1: 147-70.

———. 1993. The Life Cycle of Cyborgs: Writing the Posthuman. In *A Question of Identity: Women, Science, and Literature*, ed. Marina Benjamin. New Brunswick, NJ: Rutgers University Press.

———. 1999. *How We Became Posthuman: Virtual Bodies in Cybernetics, Literature, and Informatics*. Chicago, IL: University of Chicago Press.

———.2006. Unfinished Work—from Cyborg to Cognisphere. *Theory Culture & Society* 23 (7-8): 159-166.

Heilbrun, Carolyn. 1984. Why I Don't Read Science Fiction. *Women's Studies International Forum* 7 (2): 117-19.

Hekman, Susan J. 1990. *Gender and Knowledge: Elements of a Postmodern Feminism*. Boston, MA: Northeastern University Press.

Hellekson, Karen, and Kristina Busse, eds. 2006. *Fan Fiction and Fan Communities in the Age of the Internet: New Essays*. Jefferson, NC: McFarland.

Hemming, Norma. 1953. On the Trials and Tribulations of Being a Science Fiction Fan. *Vertical Horizons* 5, Oct.: 5-6.

Hemmings, Clare. 2005. Telling Feminist Stories. *Feminist Theory* 6 (2): 115-39.

Hicks, Heather. 2002. Striking Cyborgs: Reworking The "Human" In Marge Piercy's *He, She and It*. In *Reload: Rethinking Women + Cyberculture*, eds. Mary Flanagan and Austin Booth, 85-106. Cambridge, MA: The MIT Press.

Hine, Darlene Clark. 1989. *Black Women in White: Racial Conflict and Cooperation in the Nursing Profession, 1890-1950*. Bloomington, IN: Indiana University Press.

Hird, Myra. 2004. *Sex, Gender, and Science*. New York: Palgrave Macmillan.

Hogeland, Lisa Maria. 1998. *Feminism and Its Fictions: The Consciousness-Raising Novel and the Women's Liberation Movement*. Philadelphia, PA: University of Pennsylvania Press.

Hollinger, Veronica. 1989. Feminist Science Fiction: Construction and Deconstruction. *Science Fiction Studies* 16 (2): 223-27.

———. 1990a. Cybernetic Deconstructions: Cyberpunk and Postmodernism. *Mosaic* 23 (2): 29-44.

———. 1990b. Feminist Science Fiction: Breaking up the Subject. *Extrapolation* 31 (3): 229-39.

———. 1993. A New Alliance of Postmodernism and Feminist Speculative Fiction. *Science Fiction Studies* 20 (2): 272-76.

———. 1994. Utopianism, Science, Postmodernism and Feminism. *Science Fiction Studies* 21 (2): 232-37.

———. 1997. The Technobody and Its Discontents. *Science Fiction Studies* 24 (1): 124-32.

———. 1999. (Re)Reading Queerly: Science Fiction, Feminism, and the Defamiliarization of Gender. *Science Fiction Studies* 26 (1): 23-38.

———. 2008. "Something Like a Fiction": Speculative Intersections of Sexuality and Technology. In *Queer Universes: Sexualities in Science Fiction*, eds. Wendy Gay Pearson, Veronica Hollinger and Joan Gordon, 140-60. Liverpool, UK: Liverpool University Press.

Holloway, Karla F. C. 1992. *Moorings and Metaphors: Figures of Culture and Gender in Black Women's Literature.* New Brunswick, NJ: Rutgers University Press.

Hooper, Andrew. 1993. A Report from Confrancisco, the 51st World Science Fiction Convention. *Science Fiction Chronicle* 15 (2), Nov/Dec.: 40-45.

Hopkinson, Nalo, and Uppinder Mehan, eds. 2004. *So Long Been Dreaming: Postcolonial Science Fiction & Fantasy.* Vancouver, BC: Arsenal Pulp Press.

Hornig, Charles. 1939. Editorial Response to Letter: Five of a Kind. *Science Fiction* 1 (2), June: 121.

Hull, Gloria T., Patricia Bell Scott, and Barbara Smith, eds. 1981. *All the Women Are White, All the Blacks Are Men, but Some of Us Are Brave*. New York: Feminist Press.

Humm, Maggie. 1986. Feminist Literary Criticism in America and England. In *Women's Writing: A Challenge to Theory*, ed. Moira Monteith, 90-116. Sussex, UK: Harvester Press.

———. 1991. *Border Traffic: Strategies of Contemporary Women's Fiction*. Manchester, UK: Manchester University Press.

James, Edward. 1994. *Science Fiction in the 20th Century*. Oxford, UK: Oxford University Press.

———. 2009. Russ on Writing Science Fiction and Reviewing It. In *On Joanna Russ*, ed. Farah Mendlesohn, 19-30. Middletown, CT: Wesleyan University Press.

Jameson, Fredric. 1991. *Postmodernism, or the Cultural Logic of Late Capitalism*. London: Verso.

Jarvis, Sharon, ed. 1985. *Inside Outer Space: Science Fiction Professionals Look at Their Craft*. New York: Frederick Ungar.

Jenkins, Henry. 1992. *Textual Poachers: Television Fans and Participatory Culture*. London: Routledge.

Johnson, Lovina S. 1929. Letter. *Amazing Stories* 3 (12), March: 1140.

Johnston, Nancy. 2008. "Happy That It's Here": An Interview with Nalo Hopkinson. In *Queer Universes: Sexualities in Science Fiction*, eds. Wendy Gay Pearson, Veronica Hollinger, and Joan Gordon, 200-15. Liverpool, UK: Liverpool University Press.

Jones, Anne Hudson. 1982. Women in Science Fiction: An Annotated Secondary Bibliography. *Extrapolation* 23 (1): 83-90.

Jones, Gwyneth. 1988. In the Chinks of the World Machine. *Foundation* 43: 59-63.

———. 1993. *Khatru* Sex Symposium Revisited, 1993. In *Symposium: Women in Science Fiction, Khatru 3 & 4*, ed. Jeanne Gomoll. Madison, WI: Corflu, SF3.

———. 1997. The Metempsychosis of the Machine. *Science Fiction Studies* 24 (1): 1-10.

———. 1999. *Deconstructing the Starships: Science, Fiction and Reality*. Liverpool, UK: Liverpool University Press.

———. 2004. *Life*. Seattle, WA: Aqueduct Press.

———. 2008. True Life Science Fiction: Sexual Politics and the Lab Procedural. In *Tactical Biopolitics: Art, Activism, and Technoscience*, eds. Beatriz da Costa and Kavita Philip, 289-306. Cambridge MA: MIT Press.

———. 2009. *Imagination/Space Essays and Talks on Fiction, Feminism, Technology and Politics*. Seattle, WA: Aqueduct Press.

Jordan, Jean. 1973. Being Married to a Nonfan. *Girls' Own Fanzine* 1: 7-8.

Kadrey, Richard, and Larry McCaffery. 1991. Cyberpunk 101: A Schematic Guide to Storming the Reality Studio. In *Storming the Reality Studio: A Casebook of Cyberpunk and Postmodern Science Fiction*, ed. Larry McCaffery, 17-29. Durham, NC, & London: Duke University Press.

Kagan, Janet. 1991. *Mirabile*. New York: Tor.

Kaplan, Cora. 1989. Feminist Criticism Twenty Years On. In *From My Guy to Sci-Fi: Genre and Women's Writing in the Postmodern World*, ed. Helen Carr, 15-23. London: Pandora.

Katerinsky, Rhoda. 1976. Letter. *WatCh* (5+6): 25.

Keller, Evelyn Fox. 1983. *A Feeling for the Organism: The Life and Work of Barbara McClintock*. San Francisco, CA: Freeman.

———. 1985. *Reflections on Gender and Science*. New Haven, CT: Yale University Press.

———. 1992. *Secrets of Life, Secrets of Death: Essays on Language, Gender and Science*. New York & London: Routledge.

Keller, Evelyn Fox, and Helen E. Longino, eds. 1996. *Feminism and Science*. Oxford: Oxford University Press.

Kelso, Sylvia. 1996. Singularities: The Interaction of Feminism(s) and Two Strands of Popular American Fiction, 1968-89. PhD diss., James Cook University of Northern Queensland.

———. 2000. Third Person Peculiar: Reading between Acamenic and Sf-Community Positions in Feminist Sf. *Femspec* 2 (1): 74-82.

Kember, Sarah. 1996. Feminism, Technology and Representation. In *Cultural Studies and Communications*, eds. James Curran, David Morley, and Valerie Walkerdine, 229-47. London: Arnold.

Kenyon, Olga. 1991. *Writing Women: Contemporary Women Novelists*. London: Pluto Press.

Kessler, Carol Farley, ed. 1995. *Daring to Dream: Utopian Fiction by United States Women before 1950*. Syracuse, NY: Syracuse University Press.

Kidd, Virginia, ed. 1978. *Millennial Women*. New York: Delacorte Press.

King, Betty. 1984. *Women of the Future: The Female Main Character in Science Fiction*. Methuen, NJ, & London: The Scarecrow Press.

King, Katie. 1994. *Theory in Its Feminist Travels: Conversations in U.S. Women's Movements*. Bloomington & Indianapolis, IN: Indiana University Press.

Kirby, Vicki. 1999. Human Nature. *Australian Feminist Studies* 14: 19-29.

———. 2008. Subject to Natural Law: A Meditation on the "Two Cultures" Problem. *Australian Feminist Studies* 23 (55): 5-17.

Knight, Damon 1956. *In Search of Wonder*. Chicago, IL: Advent.

Kotani, Mari. 2007. Alien Spaces and Alien Bodies in Japanese Women's Science Fiction. In *Robot Ghosts and Wired Dreams: Japanese Science Fiction from Origins to Anime*, eds. Christopher Bolton Jr., Istvan Csicsery-Ronay, and Takayuki Tatsumi, 47-74. Minneapolis, MN: University of Minnesota Press.

Kress, Nancy. 2007. Ethics, Science, and Science Fiction. In *Scifi in the Mind's Eye: Reading Science through Science Fiction*, ed. Margret Grebowicz, 201-09. Peru, IL: Open Court Publishing.

Lambourne, Robert, Michael Shallis, and Michael Shortland. 1990. *Close Encounters? Science and Science Fiction*. Bristol: Adam Hilger.

Larbalestier, Justine. 2002. *The Battle of the Sexes in Science Fiction.* Middletown, CT: Wesleyan University Press.

———, ed. 2006. *Daughters of Earth: Feminist Science Fiction in the Twentieth Century.* Middletown, CT: Wesleyan University Press.

Latham, Rob. 1993. Cyberpunk = Gibson = Neuromancer. *Science Fiction Studies* 20 (2): 266-72.

———. 2005. The New Wave. In *A Companion to Science Fiction,* ed. David Seed, 202-16. Malden, MA: Blackwell.

———. 2006. Sextrapolation in New Wave Science Fiction. *Science Fiction Studies* 33: 251-74.

Laurence, Alice, ed. 1978. *Cassandra Rising.* New York: Doubleday.

Lauret, Maria. 1994. *Liberating Literature: Feminist Fiction in America.* London & New York: Routledge.

Lauter, Paul. 1991. Caste, Class and Canon. In *Feminisms: An Anthology of Literary Theory and Criticism,* eds. Robyn R. Warhol and Diane Price Herndl, 227-48. New Brunswick, NJ: Rutgers University Press.

Lawrence, Clinton. 2004. Interview: Karen Joy Fowler. *Strange Horizons,* 22 March. http://www.strangehorizons. com/2004/20040322/fowler.shtml

Le Guin, Ursula K. 1975. American Sf and the Other. *Science Fiction Studies* 2 (3): 208-10.

———. 1992a. A Citizen of Mondath. In *The Profession of Science Fiction: Sf Writers on Their Craft and Ideas,* eds. Maxim Jakubowski and Edward James, 73-77. Basingstoke & London: Macmillan.

———. 1992b. Is Gender Necessary? Redux. In *Dancing at the Edge of the World: Thoughts on Words, Women, Places,* 7-16. London: Paladin.

Lefanu, Sarah. 1988. *In the Chinks of the World Machine: Feminism and Science Fiction.* London: The Women's Press. (Original edition, Published in the U.S. as *Feminism and Science Fiction.* Bloomington, IN: Indiana University Press, 1989.)

Leith, Linda. 1980. Marion Zimmer Bradley and Darkover. *Science Fiction Studies* 7 (1): 28-35.

Lichtenberg, Jacqueline. 1975. Letter. *WatCh* (3): 28.

Lindsay, Ethel. 1956. *Femizine* 9: 10-11.

———. 1984. Letter. *Janus #24* 9 (1): 6.

Logan, Anne Laurie. 1978/1979. Letter. *Janus #14* 4 (4): 50-51.

———. 1980. Letter. *Janus #17* 6 (1): 34.

———. 1982/1983. Letter. *Janus #22* 8 (2): 5-6.

Longhurst, Derek, ed. 1989. *Gender, Genre and Narrative Pleasure.* London: Unwin Hyman.

Longino, Helen E. 1987. Can There Be a Feminist Science? *Hypatia* 1 (1): 51-64.

Lorraine, Lilith. 1930. Into the 28th Century. *Science Wonder Quarterly* 1 (2): 250-67, 76.

Lucas, Patty. 1981/1982. Evo-Systems. *Aurora #20* 7 (2): 22-25.

———. 1982. Review. *Aurora #21* 8 (1): 22-24.

Lucero, Judith A. 1978. Letter. *Janus #12-13* 4 (2/3): 69-70.

Luckhurst, Roger. 1991. Border Policing: Postmodernism and Science Fiction. *Science Fiction Studies #55* 18 (3): 358-66.

———. 2005. *Science Fiction.* Cambridge, UK, & Malden, MA: Polity.

———. 2006. Introduction (Technoculture and Science Fiction. Eds Luckhurst and Gill Partington). *Science Fiction Studies* 33 (1): 1-3.

Lunch and Talk with Suzy McKee Charnas, Amanda Bankier, Janice Bogstad, and Jeanne Gomoll. 1976. *Janus #6* 2 (4): 23-28.

Lundwall, Sam J. 1971. *Science Fiction: What It's All About.* New York: Ace.

Luttrell, Hank. 1994. The Science Fiction Convention Scene. In *Science Fiction Fandom*, ed. Joe Sanders, 149-59. Westport, CT, & London: Greenwood Press.

Lykke, Nina. 1996. Between Monsters, Goddesses and Cyborgs: Feminist Confrontations with Science. In *Between Monsters, Goddesses and Cyborgs: Feminist Confrontations with Science, Medicine and Cyberspace*, eds. Nina Lykke and Rosi Braidotti, 13-29. London & New Jersey: Zed Books.

Lykke, Nina, and Rosi Braidotti. 1996. Postface. In *Between Monsters, Goddesses and Cyborgs: Feminist Confrontations with Science, Medicine and Cyberspace*, eds. Nina Lykke and Rosi Braidotti, 242-49. London & Atlantic Highlands, NJ: Zed Books.

Lynn, Elizabeth A. 1977. Letter. *Janus #10* 3 (4): 26.

MacGregor, Loren. 1974. A Reply to a Chauvinist. *Notes From the Chemistry Department* 9, Nov.: 2-5.

Maciunas, Billie. 1992. Feminist Epistemology in Piercy's *Woman on the Edge of Time*. *Women's Studies* 20: 249-58.

MacLean, Katherine. 1981. The Expanding Mind. In *Fantastic Lives: Autobiographical Essays by Notable Science Fiction Writers*, ed. Martin H. Greenberg, 79-101. Carbondale, IL: Southern Illinois University Press.

Madle, Robert A. 1994. Fandom up to World War II. In *Science Fiction Fandom*, ed. Joe Sanders, 37-54. Westport, CT, & London: Greenwood press.

Maitland, Sara. 1989. Futures in Feminist Fiction. In *From My Guy to Sci-Fi: Genre and Women's Writing in the Postmodern World*, ed. Helen Carr, 193-203. London: Pandora Press.

Makinen, Merja. 2001. *Feminist Popular Fiction*. New York: Palgrave.

Marcus, Laura. 1992. Feminist Aesthetics and the New Realism. In *New Feminist Discourses: Critical Essays on Theories and Texts*, ed. Isobel Armstrong, 11-25. London & New York: Routledge.

Martin, Diane. 1992. Three Questions and Some Answers. In *The Bakery Men Don't See*, 2-3. Madison, Wisconsin: SF³.

Mason, Carol. 1995. Terminating Bodies: Toward a Cyborg History of Abortion. In *Posthuman Bodies*, eds. Judith Halberstam and Ira Livingstone, 225-43. Bloomington & Indianapolis, IN: Indiana University Press.

Mathur, Suchitra. 2004. Caught between the Goddess and the Cyborg: Third-World Women and the Politics of Science in Three Works of Indian Science Fiction. *The Journal of Commonwealth Literature* 39 (3): 119-38.

Mayberry, Maralee, Banu Subramaniam, and Lisa H. Weasel, eds. 2001. *Feminist Science Studies: A New Generation*. New York: Routledge.

McCaffery, Larry. 1991a. Introduction: The Desert of the Real. In *Storming the Reality Studio: A Casebook of Cyberpunk and Postmodern Science Fiction*, ed. Larry McCaffery, 1-16. Durham, NC, & London: Duke University Press.

———, ed. 1991b. *Storming the Reality Studio: A Casebook of Cyberpunk and Postmodern Science Fiction*. Durham, NC, & London: Duke University Press.

McCaffrey, Anne. 1974. Hitch Your Dragon to a Star: Romance and Glamour in Science Fiction. In *Science Fiction Today and Tomorrow*, ed. Reginold Bretnor, 278-92. New York: Harper and Row.

———. 1979. *The Ship Who Sang*. New York: Ballantine.

McCarron, Kevin. 1995. Corpses, Animals, Machines and Mannequins: The Body and Cyberpunk. In *Cyberspace/Cyberbodies/Cyberpunk: Cultures of Technological Embodiment*, eds. Mike Featherstone and Roger Burrows, 261-73. London: Sage.

McCaughey, Martha. 1993. Redirecting Feminist Critiques of Science. *Hypatia* 8 (4): 72-84.

McGowan, Christine. 1973. Reflections on Fannish Matrimony. *Girls' Own Fanzine* 1: 3-4.

McIntyre, Vonda N. 1973. Letter. *The Alien Critic* 2 (4), Nov.: 52.

———. 1974. Review of Darkover Landfall. *WatCh* (2), Nov.: 19-24.

McIntyre, Vonda N., and Susan J. Anderson. 1976. *Aurora: Beyond Equality*. Greenwich, CT: Fawcett.

McKenzie, Stuart. 1954. Letter. *Femizine* 2.

McNeil, Maureen, and Sarah Franklin. 1991. Science and Technology: Questions for Cultural Studies and Feminism. In *Off-Centre: Feminism and Cultural Studies*, eds. Sarah Franklin, Celia Lury, and Jackie Stacey, 129-46. London: HarperCollins.

McNeil, Maureen, Ian Varcoe, and Steven Yearley. 1990. *The New Reproductive Technologies*. London: Macmillan.

McRobbie, Angela. 1994. *Postmodernism and Popular Culture*. New York & London: Routledge.

Mengshoel, E. L. 1936. Letter. *Weird Tales* 27 (June).

Mercer, Archie, and Beryl Mercer. 1973. Letter. *Girl's Own Fanzine* 2: 26.

Merchant, Carolyn. 1980. *The Death of Nature: Women, Ecology, and the Scientific Revolution*. San Francisco, CA: Harper & Row.

Merrick, Helen. 1999. The Erotics of Gender Ambiguity: A Fem-Sf Symposium. In *Women of Other Worlds: Excursions through Science Fiction and Feminism*, eds. Helen Merrick and Tess Williams, 162-83. Perth: University of Western Australia Press.

———. 2009. Science stories, Life stories: engaging the sciences through feminist science fiction. *Women's Studies International Forum* forthcoming.

Merrick, Helen, and Tess Williams, eds. 1999. *Women of Other Worlds: Excursions through Science Fiction and Feminism*. Nedlands: University of Western Australia Press.

Merril, Judith. 1971. What Do You Mean: Science? Fiction? In *Sf—the Other Side of Realism: Essays on Modern Fantasy and Science Fiction*, ed. Thomas D. Clareson, 53-95. Bowling Green OH: Bowling Green University Popular Press. (Original edition, 1966.)

Merwin, Sam. 1950. Editorial: The Reader Speaks. *Thrilling Wonder Stories* 37 (2), Dec.: 6-7, 140.

Mines, Sam. 1953. Editorial Response to Letter. *Startling Stories* 28 (3), Jan.: 137.

Mitchell, Kaye. 2006. Bodies That Matter: Science Fiction, Technoculture, and the Gendered Body. *Science-Fiction Studies* 33 (1): 109-28.

Mitchison, Naomi. 1985. *Memoirs of a Spacewoman*. London: The Women's Press.

———. 1995. *Solution Three*. New York: The Feminist Press at The City University of New York. (Original edition, 1975.)

Mixon, Veronica. 1979. Futurist Woman: Octavia Butler. *Essence* 9, Apr.: 12-15.

Mohanraj, Mary Anne. 2003. The 2002 Tiptree: An Inside Look at a Juried Award. *Strange Horizons* April 7. http://www.strangehorizons.com/2003/20030407/tiptree.shtml.

Moi, Toril.1989. Feminist, Female, Feminine. In *The Feminist Reader: Essays in Gender and the Politics of Literary Criticism*, eds. Catherine Belsey and Jane Moore, 117-32. London: Macmillan.

Molesworth, Laura. 1953. Wanted: More Women Workers in Fandom. *Vertical Horizons* 5: 1.

Molesworth, Vol. 1994/1995. A History of Australian Fandom, 1935-1963. *Mentor* (82-87). (Reprint 2009. Burwood NSW: Graham Stone.)

Moore, C. L. 1995. No Woman Born. In *Women of Wonder: The Classic Years*, ed. Pamela Sargent, 21-64. New York: Harcourt Brace. (Original publication, *Astounding Science Fiction* 1944.)

Moraga, Cherríe, and Gloria Anzaldúa, eds. 1983. *This Bridge Called My Back: Radical Writings by Radical Women of Color*. New York: Kitchen Table Women of Color Press.

Morse, Lynne. 1978. Convention Reports. *Janus* #12-13 4 (2/3): 51-52.

Moskowitz, Sam. 1954. *The Immortal Storm: A History of Science Fiction Fandom*. Atlanta: The Atlanta Science Fiction Organization Press.

———. 1966. *Seekers of Tomorrow: Makers of Modern Science Fiction*. Westport, CT: Hyperion.

———. 1976. *Strange Horizons: The Spectrum of Science Fiction*. New York: Charles Scribner and Sons.

Moylan, Tom. 1986. *Demand the Impossible: Science Fiction and the Utopian Imagination*. New York & London: Methuen.

———. 1995. Global Economy, Local Texts: Utopian/Dystopian Tension in William Gibson's Cyberpunk Trilogy. *The Minnesota Review* 5: 182-97.

Mumford, Laura Stempel. 1995. *Love and Ideology in the Afternoon: Soap Opera, Women, and Television Genre*. Bloomington & Indianapolis, IN: Indiana University Press.

Munt, Sally. 1988. The Investigators: Lesbian Crime Fiction. In *Sweet Dreams: Sexuality, Gender and Popular Fiction*, ed. Susanna Radstone, 91-119. London: Lawrence and Wishart.

Murphy, Pat. 1991. Illusion and Expectation: A Rabble-Rousing Speech and Announcement by Pat Murphy Presented at WisCon 15, March 2, 1991. In *The Bakery Men Don't See* 6-9. Madison, WI: SF3.

Murphy, Pat, and Karen Joy Fowler. 2005. Introduction. In *The James Tiptree Award Anthology 1*, eds. Karen Joy Fowler, Pat Murphy, Debbie Notkin, and Jeffrey D. Smith, vii-xiii. San Francisco, CA: Tachyon Publications.

Nicholls, Peter, ed. 1979. *The Encyclopedia of Science Fiction*. London: Granada.

Nixon, Nicola. 1992a. Cyberpunk: Preparing the Ground for Revolution or Keeping the Boys Satisfied. *Science Fiction Studies* 19 (2): 219-35.

———. 1992b. In Response to John J. Pierce. *Science Fiction Studies* 19 (3): 440.

Notkin, Debbie. 2005. Call and Response. *Strange Horizons*, 14 February. http://www.strangehorizons.com/2005/20050214/notkin-c.shtml.

Notkin, Debbie, and the Secret Feminist Cabal, eds. 1998. *Flying Cups and Saucers: Gender Explorations in Science Fiction and Fantasy*. Cambridge, MA: Edgewood Press.

October 29th Group. 1989. The Oct 29th Group: Defining a Feminist Science. *Women's Studies International Forum* 12 (3): 253-59.

Oudshoorn, Nelly. 1996. A Natural Order of Things? Reproductive Sciences and the Politics of Othering. In *Futurenatural: Nature, Science, Culture*, ed. George Robertson et al., 122-32. New York & London: Routledge.

Palmer, Paulina. 1989. *Contemporary Women's Fiction: Narrative Practice and Feminist Theory*. Hemel Hempstead: Harvester Wheatsheaf.

———. 1993. *Contemporary Lesbian Writing: Dreams, Desire, Difference*. Buckingham & Bristol, UK: Open University Press.

Panshin, Alexei, and Corey Panshin. 1975. "Books" Column. *Magazine of Fantasy and Science Fiction*, August.

Parrinder, Patrick, ed. 1979. *Science Fiction: A Critical Guide*. London: Longman.

Pask, Kevin. 1995. Cyborg Economies: Desire and Labor in the Terminator Films. In *Postmodern Apocalypse: Theory and Cultural Practice at the End*, ed. Richard Dellamora, 182-98. Philadelphia, PA: University of Pennsylvania Press.

Pearlschtein, Karen. 1977. Letter. *Janus #10* 3 (4): 28.

Pearson, Carol. 1977. Women's Fantasies and Feminist Utopias. *Frontiers: A Journal of Women's Studies* 2 (3): 50-61.

———. 1981. Coming Home: Four Feminist Utopias and Patriarchal Experience. In *Future Females: A Critical Anthology*, ed. Marleen S. Barr, 63-70. Bowling Green, OH: Bowling Green State University Press.

Pearson, Wendy. 1999. Alien Cryptographies: The View from Queer. *Science Fiction Studies* 26: 1-22.

———. 2002. Sexuality and the Figure of the Hermaphrodite in Science Fiction; or, the Revenge of Herculine Barbin. In *Edging into the Future: Science Fiction and Contemporary Cultural Transformation*, eds. Veronica Hollinger and Joan Gordon, 108-23. Philadelphia, PA: University of Pennsylvania Press.

———. 2003. Science Fiction and Queer Theory. In *The Cambridge Companion to Science Fiction*, ed. Edward James and Farah Mendlsohn, 149-62. Cambridge, UK: Cambridge University Press.

Pearson, Wendy Gay, Veronica Hollinger, and Joan Gordon. 2008. Queer Universes. In *Queer Universes: Sexualities in Science Fiction*, eds. Wendy Gay Pearson, Veronica Hollinger, and Joan Gordon, 1-11. Liverpool, UK: Liverpool University Press.

Peck, Claudia. c.1980. Interview: Octavia Butler. *Skewed: The Magazine of Fantasy, Science Fiction, and Horror*, 1: 18-27.

Pei, Lowry. 1979. Poor Singletons: Definitions of Humanity in the Stories of James Tiptree Jr. *Science Fiction Studies* 6 (3): 271-80.

Penley, Constance. 1990. Brownian Motion: Women, Tactics, and Technology. In *Technoculture*, eds. Constance Penley and Andrew Ross, 135-61. Minneapolis, MN: University of Minnesota Press.

———. 1992. Feminism, Psychoanalysis, and the Study of Popular Culture. In *Cultural Studies*, eds. Lawrence Grosberg, Cary Nelson, and Paula A. Treichler, 479-520. New York & London: Routledge.

Pierce, John J. 1992. On Three Matters in Science Fiction Studies #57. *Science Fiction Studies* 19 (3): 440.

Piercy, Marge. 1991. *Woman on the Edge of Time*. London: The Woman's Press. (Original edition, 1978.)

———. 1992. *Body of Glass*. London: Penguin.

Plant, Sadie. 1995. The Future Looms: Weaving Women and Cybernetics. In *Cyberspace/Cyberbodies/Cyberpunk: Cultures of Technological Embodiment*, eds. Mike Featherstone and Roger Burrows, 45-64. London: Sage.

Platt, Charles. 1992. Letter. *Science Fiction Eye* 10, June: 6.

Plinlimmon, Judy. 1974. Letter. *The Alien Critic* 3 (2), May: 18.

Podojil, Catherine. 1978. Sisters, Daughters, and Aliens. In *Critical Encounters: Writers and Themes in Science Fiction*, ed. Dick Riley, 70-86. New York: Frederick Ungar.

Pournelle, Jerry. 1975. On What Standard? *Notes From the Chemistry Department* 11, Sept.: 4-9.

Pryse, Marjorie, and Hortense Spillers, eds. 1985. *Conjuring: Black Women's Fiction and Literary Tradition*. Bloomington, IN: Indiana University Press.

Quilter, Laura. 2007. Is Reading Feminist Sf a Theory-Building Activity? (Panel Transcript Notes). In *The WisCon Chronicles, Volume 1*, ed. L. Timmel Duchamp, 57-72. Seattle, WA: Aqueduct Press.

Quindlen, Ruthann. 1978. Letter. *Janus #12-13* 4 (2/3): 69.

Richardson, Robert S. 1955. The Day after We Land on Mars. *Fantasy and Science Fiction* 9 (6): 44-52.

Rieder, John. 2008. *Colonialism and the Emergence of Science Fiction*. Middletown, CT: Wesleyan University Press.

Roberts, Celia. 2000. Biological Behavior? Hormones, Psychology, and Sex. *NWSA Journal* 12 (3): 1-20.

Roberts, Robin. 1984. Katherine MacLean's Subtle Humor. *Janus #24* 9 (1): 13-14, 36.

———. 1993. *A New Species: Gender and Science in Science Fiction*. Urbana, IL: University of Illinois Press.

———. 1995. It's Still Science Fiction: Strategies of Feminist Science Fiction Criticism. *Extrapolation* 36 (3): 184-97.

Rogan, Alcena Madeline Davis. 2008. Tananarive Due and Nalo Hopkinson Revisit the Reproduction of Mothering: Legacies of the Past and Strategies for the Future. In *Afro-Future Females: Black Writers Chart Science Fiction's Newest New-Wave Trajectory*, ed. Marleen S. Barr, 75-99. Columbus, OH: Ohio State University Press.

Rose, Ellen Cronan. 1993. American Feminist Criticism of Contemporary Women's Fiction. *Signs* 18 (2): 346-75.

Rose, Hilary. 1983. Hand, Brain, and Heart: A Feminist Epistemology for the Natural Sciences. *Signs: Journal of Women in Culture and Society* 9 (1): 73-96.

———. 1986. Beyond Masculinist Realities: A Feminist Epistemology for the Sciences. In *Feminist Approaches to Science*, ed. Ruth Bleier, 57-76. New York: Pergamon Press.

———. 1994. *Love, Power, and Knowledge: Towards a Feminist Transformation of the Sciences*. Cambridge, UK: Polity Press.

———. 1996. My Enemy's Enemy Is – Only Perhaps – My Friend. In *Science Wars*, ed. Andrew Ross, 80-101. Durham, NC, & London: Duke University Press.

Rosinsky, Natalie M. 1982. A Female Man? The "Medusan" Humor of Joanna Russ. *Extrapolation* 23 (1): 31-36.

———. 1984. *Feminist Futures: Contemporary Women's Speculative Fiction*. Ann Arbor, MI: UMI Research Press.

Ross, Andrew. 1991. *Strange Weather: Culture, Science and Technology in the Age of Limits*. London: Verso.

Rosser, Sue V. 1987. Feminist Scholarship in the Sciences: Where Are We Now and When Can We Expect a Theoretical Breakthrough? *Hypatia* 1 (1): 5-17.

———. 1989. Ruth Bleier: A Passionate Vision for Feminism and Science. *Women's Studies International Forum* 12 (3): 249-52.

Rothschild, Joan. 1981. A Feminist Perspective on Technology and the Future. *Women's Studies International Quarterly* 4 (1): 65-74.

———. 1983. *Machina Ex Dea: Feminist Perspectives on Technology*. New York: Pergamon Press.

Round 2: Reactions to "Lunch and Talk." 1977. *Janus #8* 3 (2): 30-37.

Rowland, Robin. 1992. *Living Laboratories: Women and Reproductive Technologies*. Bloomington, IN: Indiana University Press.

Roy, Deboleena. 2004. "Feminist Theory in Science" Working toward a Practical Transformation. *Hypatia* 19 (1): 255-79.

Rubenstein, Robin. 1987. *Boundaries of the Self: Gender, Culture, Fiction*. Urbana & Chicago, IL: University of Illinois Press.

Russ, Joanna. 1972. What Can a Heroine Do? Or Why Women Can't Write. In *Images of Women in Fiction: Feminist Perspectives*, ed. Susan Koppelman Cornillon, 3-20. Bowling Green, OH: Bowling Green State University Popular Press.

———. 1974a. Letter. *The Alien Critic* 3 (1), February: 36-7.

———. 1974b. The Image of Women in Science Fiction. *Vertex* 1 (6): 53-57.

———. 1975a. Letter. *WatCh* 4: 15-18.

———. 1975b. Letter. *Notes from the Chemistry Department* (10), March: 38-39.

———. 1975c. Letter. *WatCh* (3), April: 26-7.

———. 1975d. Reflections on Science Fiction: An Interview with Joanna Russ. *Quest* 2 (1): 40-49.

———. 1976. A Letter to Marion Zimmer Bradley. *WatCh* 5&6: 9-13.

———. 1980. Amor Vincit Foeminam: The Battle of the Sexes in Science Fiction. *Science Fiction Studies* 7 (1): 2-15.

———. 1981. Recent Feminist Utopias. In *Future Females: A Critical Anthology*, ed. Marleen S. Barr, 71-85. Bowling Green, OH: Bowling Green State University Popular Press.

———. 1986. *The Female Man*. Boston, MA: Beacon.

———. 1987. *We Who Are About To...* London: The Women's Press. (Original edition, 1977.)

———. 2007. *The Country You Have Never Seen: Essays and Reviews*. Liverpool, UK: Liverpool University Press.

Salmonson, Jessica Amanda. 1977. Letter. *Janus #8* 3 (2): 19.

———. 1982/1983. Letter. *Janus #22* 8 (2): 6.

Sanderson, H. P. 1956. Jokers Wild. *Femizine* 9: 8.

Sandoval, Chela. 1991. U.S. Third World Feminism: The Theory and Method of Oppositional Consciousness in the Postmodern World. *Genders* 10, Spring: 1-24.

Sargent, Pamela. 1975. Women in Science Fiction. *Futures*, Oct.: 433-41.

———. 1976. *Cloned Lives*. New York: Fawcett Gold Medal.

———. 1978a. Introduction: Women in Science Fiction. In *Women of Wonder: Science Fiction Stories by Women About Women*, ed. Pamela Sargent, 11-51. Harmondsworth, UK: Penguin. (Original edition, New York: Vintage, 1974.)

———, ed. 1978b. *The New Women of Wonder: Recent Science Fiction Stories by Women about Women*. New York: Vintage.

———, ed. 1978c. *Women of Wonder: Sf Stories by Women about Women*. Harmondsworth, UK: Penguin. (Original edition, 1974.

———, ed. 1979. *More Women of Wonder: Science Fiction Novelettes by Women about Women*. Harmondsworth, UK: Penguin. (Original edition, New York: Vintage, 1976.)

———, ed. 1995a. *Women of Wonder: The Classic Years*. New York: Harcourt Brace.

———, ed. 1995b. *Women of Wonder: The Contemporary Years*. New York: Harcourt Brace.

Schiebinger, Londa. 2001. *Has Feminism Changed Science?* Cambridge, MA: Harvard University Press. Original edition, 1999.

Schlobin, Roger C. 1981. The Future Females: A Selected Checklist through 1979. In *Future Females: A Critical Anthology*, ed. Marleen S. Barr, 179-89. Bowling Green, OH: Bowling Green State University Press.

———. 1982. Farsighted Females: A Selective Checklist of Modern Women Writers of Science Fiction through 1980. *Extrapolation* 23 (1): 91-107.

Schneider, Joseph. 2005. *Donna Haraway: Live Theory*. London: Continuum.

Scholes, Robert, and Eric S. Rabkin. 1977. *Science Fiction: History, Science, Vision*. New York: Oxford University Press.

Schweickart, Patrocinio. 1983. What If…Science and Technology in Feminist Utopias. In *Machina Ex Dea: Feminist Perspectives on Technology*, ed. Joan Rothschild, 198-212. New York: Pergamon Press.

Scott, Melissa. 1992. *Dreamships*. New York: Tor.

Scutt, Jocelynne A., ed. 1988. *The Baby Machine: Commercialisation of Motherhood*. Carlton, Vic.: McCulloch Publishing.

Sedgewick, Christina. 1991. The Fork in the Road: Can Science Fiction Survive in Postmodern, Megacorporate America? *Science Fiction Studies* 18 (1): 11-52.

Severin, Laura, and Mary Wyer. 2000. The Science and Politics of the Search for Sex Differences: Editorial. *NWSA Journal* 12 (3): vii-xvi.

Shabot, Sara C. 2006. Grotesque Bodies: A Response to Disembodied Cyborgs. *Journal of Gender Studies* 15 (3): 223-35.

shahar, eluki bes. 1991. *Hellflower*. New York: Daw.

———. 1992. *Darktraders*. New York: Daw.

———. 1993. *Archangel Blues*. New York: Daw.

Sheldon, Alice. 1988. A Woman Writing Science Fiction and Fantasy. In *Women of Vision: Essays by Women Writing Science Fiction*, ed. Denise Du Pont, 43-58. New York: St. Martin's Press.

Sheldon, Racoona. 1975. Letter. *WatCh* (3): 26.

———. 1976. Letter. *WatCh* 5&6: 30.

Shiner, Lewis. 1991. Confessions of an Ex-Cyberpunk. *New York Times*, Jan. 7.

———. 1992. Inside the Movement: Past, Present, and Future. In *Fiction 2000: Cyberpunk and the Future of Narrative*, eds. George Slusser and Tom Shippey, 17-25. Athens, GA: University of Georgia Press.

Shorrock, Ina. 1954. A Call to Arms. *Femizine* 1: 17.

Short, Roger and Evan Balaban. 1960. *The Differences Between the Sexes.* Cambridge, UK: Cambridge University Press.

Siclari, Joe. 1994. Science Fiction Fandom: A Selected, Annotated Bibliography. In *Science Fiction Fandom*, ed. Joe Sanders, 245-63. Westport, CT, & London: Greenwood Press.

Silverberg, Robert. 1979. Letter. *(Random Factors) Starship* 16 (no. 3): 82.

Simmons, Rosemary. 1952. Editorial. *Vertical Horizons* 2, Nov.: 2.

Singer, Jon. 1979. Letter. *Janus* #15. 5 1 (16).

Slimmer, Naomi D. 1939. Letter: Five of a Kind. *Science Fiction* 1 (2): 118-21.

Slusser, George, and Tom Shippey, eds. 1992. *Fiction 2000: Cyberpunk and the Future of Narrative.* Athens, GA, & London: University of Georgia Press.

Smith, Barbara. 1985. Toward a Black Feminist Criticism. In *Feminist Criticism and Social Change*, eds. Judith Newton and Deborah Rosenfelt, 3-18. New York: Methuen. (Original publication, *Conditions II*, 1977,11: 25-44.

Smith, Catherine. 1956. Letter: Explanation Wanted. *Authentic Science Fiction* 66: 159.

Smith, Jeff (ed). 1975. Symposium: Women in Science Fiction. *Khatru* 3&4.

Smith, Stephanie A. 1993. Morphing, Materialism and the Marketing of *Xenogenesis. Genders* 18: 67-86.

Snow, C. P. 1965. *The Two Cultures, and a Second Look.* Cambridge, UK: Cambridge University Press.

Sobchak, Vivian. 1995. Beating the Meat/Surviving the Text. In *Cyberspace/Cyberbodies/Cyberpunk: Cultures of Technological Embodiment*, eds. Mike Featherstone and Roger Burrows, 205-14. London: Sage.

Sofia, Zoë. 1993. *Whose Second Self? Gender and (Ir)Rationality in Computer Culture.* Melbourne: Deakin University Press.

Spallone, Patricia, and Deborah Lynn Steinberg, eds. 1987. *Made to Order: The Myth of Reproductive and Genetic Progress*. Oxford and New York: Pergamon.

Sponsler, Claire. 1993. Beyond the Ruins: The Geopolitics of Urban Decay and Cybernetic Play. *Science Fiction Studies* 20 (2): 251-65.

Springer, Claudia. 1993. Sex, Memories, and Angry Women. In *Flame Wars: The Discourse of Cyberculture* ed. Mark Dery, 157-77.

———. 1996. *Electronic Eros: Bodies and Desire in the Postindustrial Age*. Austin, TX: University of Texas Press.

Squier, Susan and Melissa M. Littlefield. 2004. Feminist Theory and/of Science: Feminist Theory Special Issue. *Feminist Theory* 5 (2): 123-26.

Squier, Susan M. 1994. *Babies in Bottles: Twentieth-Century Visions of Reproductive Technology*. New Brunswick, NJ: Rutgers University Press.

———. 1995a. Afterword. In *Solution Three*, Naomi Mitchison, 161-83. New York: The Feminist Press at CUNY.

———. 1995b. Reproducing the Posthuman Body: Ectogenetic Fetus, Surrogate Mother, Pregnant Man. In *Posthuman Bodies*, eds. Judith Halberstam and Ira Livingstone, 113-32. Bloomington & Indianapolis, IN: Indiana University Press.

St. Clair, Margaret. 1981. Wight in Space: An Autobiographical Sketch. In *Fantastic Lives: Autobiographical Essays by Notable Science Fiction Writers*, ed. Martin H. Greenberg, 144-56. Carbondale, IL: Southern Illinois University Press.

Staicar, Tom, ed. 1982. *The Feminine Eye: Science Fiction and the Women Who Write It*. New York: Frederick Ungar.

Stallings, Fran. 1984. Free Radical: Miriam Allen DeFord. *Janus #24* 9 (1): 17-18, 21.

Stepan, Nancy Leys. 1986. Race and Gender: The Role of Analogy in Science. *Isis* 77: 261-77.

Sterling, Bruce. 1991. Cyberpunk in the Nineties. *Interzone* 48: 39-41.

———. 1994a. Preface. In *Mirrorshades: The Cyberpunk Anthology*, ed. Bruce Sterling, vii-xiv. London: HarperCollins.

———, ed. 1994b. *Mirrorshades: The Cyberpunk Anthology*. London: HarperCollins.

Stewart, Lula B. 1953. Letter: I Remember Mama. *Thrilling Wonder Stories* 42 (3), Nov.: 133-34.

Stocker, Laura J. 1989. Songs of Our Future: Feminist Representations of Technology in Science Fiction. *Media Information Australia* 54: 49-52.

Stone, Allucquére Rosanne. 1991. Will the Real Body Please Stand Up?: Boundary Stories about Virtual Cultures. In *Cyberspace: First Steps*, ed. Michael Benedikt, 82-118. Cambridge, MA: MIT Press.

Strachan, Alexander. 1979. Letter. *Starship* 16 (4): 65.

Strathern, Marilyn. 1992. *Reproducing the Future: Essays on Anthropology, Kinship, and the New Reproductive Technologies*. New York: Routledge.

Sturgis, Susanna J. 1989. Editorial: Memories and Visions, or Why Does a Bright Feminist Like You Read That Stuff Anyway? In *Memories and Visions: Women's Fantasy and Science Fiction*, ed. Susanna J. Sturgis, 1-9. Freedom, CA: The Crossing Press.

———, 1995. Inventing the Tiptrees: Reinventing an Agenda. *Feminist Bookstore News* 18 (1): 51-52.

Suvin, Darko. 1989. On Gibson and Cyberpunk Sf. *Foundation* 46: 40-51.

Swirsky, Rachel. 2007. Welcome Back to the Beginning. In *The WisCon Chronicles. Vol. 1*, ed. L. Timmel Duchamp, 19-21. Seattle, WA: Aqueduct Press.

Tatsumi, Takayuki. 1988. Some *Real* Mothers: An Interview with Samuel R. Delany. *Science Fiction Eye* 1 (3): 5-11.

Thomas, Sheree R., ed. 2000. *Dark Matter: A Century of Speculative Fiction from the African Diaspora*. New York: Warner books.

———, ed. 2004. *Dark Matter: Reading the Bones*. New York: Warner books.

Thompson, Sarah. 1978. Letter. *Janus #12-13* 4 (2/3): 67.

Thurston, Carol. 1987. *The Romance Revolution: Erotic Novels for Women and the Quest for a New Sexual Identity*. Urbana & Chicago, IL: University of Illinois Press.

Tiptree Jr., James. 1980. *Up the Walls of the World*. London: Pan.

———. 1990. The Girl Who Was Plugged In (1973). In *Her Smoke Rose up Forever*, 44-79. Sauk City. WI: Arkham House.

Traweek, Sharon. 1988. *Beamtimes and Lifetimes: The World of High-Energy Physics*. Cambridge, MA: Harvard University Press.

Tsai, K. Joyce. 2008. On the "Romance of the Revolution" Panel at WisCon 31. In *The WisCon Chronicles, Volume 2: Provocative Essays on Feminism, Race, Revolution, and the Future*, eds. L. Timmel Duchamp and Eileen Gunn, 61-68. Seattle, WA: Aqueduct Press.

Tuana, Nancy. 1987. Special Issue: Feminism and Science I. *Hypatia* 2 (3).

Tucker, Bob. 1976. *Neofan's Guide to Science Fiction Fandom*. 4 ed. Fond du Lac, WI: Mafia Press. Original edition, 1955.

Turnball, Donald G. 1938. Letter. *Astounding Science Fiction*, July: 162.

Tutihasi, Laurraine. 1978. Letter. *Janus #12-13* 4 (2/3): 73-74.

Vayne, Victoria. 1975. Letter. *Notes from the Chemistry Department* (10), March: 37-38.

———. 1978. Letter. *Janus #12-13* 4 (2/3): 65.

Vint, Sherryl. 2007. *Bodies of Tomorrow: Technology, Subjectivity, Science Fiction*. Toronto, ON: University of Toronto Press.

———. 2009. Science Studies. In *The Routledge Companion to Science Fiction*, eds. Mark Bould, Andrew Butler, Adam Roberts and Sherryl Vint, 801-21. London & New York: Routledge.

Wakely, Mark. 1978. Letter. *Janus #12-13* 4 (2/3): 71-72.

Walker, Nancy. 1990. *Feminist Alternatives: Irony and Fantasy in the Contemporary Novel by Women*. London & Jackson, MS: University of Mississippi Press.

Walker, Paul. 1975. Sexual Stereotypes: Whose Responsibility. *Notes from the Chemistry Department* 10: 9-11.

Warner Jr., Harry. 1969. *All Our Yesterdays: An Informal History of Sf Fandom in the Forties*. Chicago, IL: Advent.

———. 1977. *A Wealth of Fable* Vol. 3, *The History of Science Fiction Fandom in the 1950s*. Lighthouse Point: Fanhistorica Press.

———. 1994a. A History of Fanzines. In *Science Fiction Fandom*, ed. Joe Sanders, 175-80. Westport, CT: Greenwood Press.

———. 1994b. Fandom between World War II and Sputnik. In *Science Fiction Fandom*, ed. Joe Sanders, 65-73. Westport, CT: Greenwood Press.

Warren, Anne. 1974. Being Different. In *Tynecon II Programme Book*, 35-49. Newcastle, UK: TyneCon.

Watts, Carol. 1992. Releasing Possibility into Form: Cultural Choice and the Woman Writer. In *New Feminist Discourses: Critical Essays on Theories and Texts*, ed. Isobel Armstrong, 83-102. London & New York: Routledge.

Waugh, Patricia. 1989. *Feminine Fictions: Revisiting the Postmodern*. London: Routledge.

Wayne, Marta L. 2000. Walking a Tightrope: The Feminist Life of a *Drosophila* Biologist. *NWSA Journal* 12 (3): 139-50.

Weasel, Lisa H. 2001. Dismantling the Self/Other Dichotomy in Science: Towards a Feminist Model of the Immune System. *Hypatia* 16 (1): 27-44.

Weedman, Jane B., ed. 1985. *Women Worldwalkers: New Dimensions of Science Fiction and Fantasy*. Lubbock, TX: Texas Tech Press.

Westfahl, Gary. 1993. Superladies in Waiting: How the Female Hero Almost Emerges in Science Fiction. *Foundation* #58, Summer: 42-62.

———. 1998. *The Mechanics of Wonder: The Creation of the Idea of Science Fiction.* Liverpool, UK: Liverpool University Press.

———. 2005. Hard Science Fiction. In *A Companion to Science Fiction,* ed. David Seed, 195-98. Malden, MA: Blackwell.

Whalen, Terence. 1992. The Future of a Commodity: Notes Towards a Critique of Cyberpunk and the Information Age. *Science Fiction Studies* 19 (1): 75-88.

Whelehan, Imelda. 2005. *The Feminist Bestseller: From* Sex and the Single Girl *to* Sex and the City. New York & Basingstoke: Palgrave Macmillan.

White, Robin. 1968. Are Femme-Fans Human? *Algol* 13: 51-54.

Wild, Roberta. [1950s]. *Vagary* 7 (for *Ompa* 15): 13.

Wilhelm, Kate. 1975. Women Writers: A Letter from Kate Wilhelm. *WatCh* (3), April: 21-24.

Williams, Norma. 1952. Magazine Reviews. *Vertical Horizons* 2: 3-6.

Williams, Tess. 2006. Imagining Alternative Pathways of Biological Change and Co-Existence. *Foundation: The International Review of Science Fiction* 98: 99-115.

Willis, Connie. 1992. Guest Editorial: The Women Sf Doesn't See. *Asimov's SF Magazine* 16 (11): 4-8.

Willis, Martin. 2006. *Mesmerists, Monsters, and Machines: Science Fiction and the Cultures of Science in the Nineteenth Century.* Kent, OH: Kent State University Press.

Wilson, Elizabeth A. 1992. Is "Science" Feminism's Dark Continent? *Meanjin* 51 (1): 77-88.

———. 1999. Introduction, Somatic Compliance - Feminism, Biology and Science. *Australian Feminist Studies* 14 (29): 7-18.

Wilson, F. Paul. 1978. Letter. *Janus #12-13* 4 (2/3): 70.

Wisker, Gina, ed. 1994. *It's My Party: Reading Twentieth-Century Women's Writing.* London & Boulder, CO: Pluto Press.

Wolfe, Gary K. 1997. Reviews by Gary K. Wolfe. *Locus #432* 38 (1), Jan.: 17-18.

Wolmark, Jenny. 1986. Science Fiction and Feminism. *Foundation* 37, Autumn: 48-51.

———. 1993. *Aliens and Others: Science Fiction, Feminism and Postmodernism*. Hemel Hempstead, UK: Harvester Wheatsheaf.

———, ed. 1999. *Cybersexualities: A Reader on Feminist Theory, Cyborgs and Cyberspace*. Edinburgh: Edinburgh University Press.

Wood, Susan. 1977. Propellor Beanie. *Algol #28* 14 (2): 43-45, 68.

———. 1978. People's Programming (Guest Editorial). *Janus #11* 4 (1): 4-7, 13.

———. 1978/1979. Women and Science Fiction. *-Algol #33* 16 (1): 9-18.

Yaszek, Lisa. 2002. *The Self Wired: Technology and Subjectivity in Contemporary Narrative*. New York & London: Routledge.

———. 2008. *Galactic Suburbia: Recovering Women's Science Fiction*. Columbus, OH: Ohio State University Press.

Zettel, Sarah. 1997. *Fool's War*. New York: Warner.

Zimmerman, Bonnie. 1992. *The Safe Sea of Women: Lesbian Fiction 1969-1989*. London: Onlywomen Press.

Index

New from Aqueduct Press

Imagination/Space: Essays and Talks
  on Fiction, Feminism, Technology, and Politics
  by Gwyneth Jones

A collection of talks and essays on fiction, feminism, technology, and politics by Gwyneth Jones, the 2008 recipient of the Science Fiction Research Association's Pilgrim Award, conferred annually on science fiction's premiere critics for lifetime achievement. The contents of Imagination/Space range from Jones's acceptance speech for the Pilgrim Award to her detailed notes on shadowing a scientist in a lab in preparation for writing her Philip K. Dick Award-winning novel, Life, to her critical reconsideration of the feminist sf canon. Her sharp analyses and observations make this a must-read for anyone who cares about feminism, science fiction, or both.

Forthcoming

Narrative Power: Encounters, Celebrations, Struggles
  edited by L. Timmel Duchamp

Inspired by the WisCon 32 Narrative and Politics panel, which discussed how ideology infuses narrative and thus often blindsides writers, scholars, and intellectuals whose work expresses itself as narrative. In this volume, Samuel R. Delany, Lance Olsen, Andrea Hairston, Wendy Walker, Carolyn Ives Gilman, Eleanor Arnason, Rachel Swirsky, Claire Light, and other writers and scholars take a close look at narrative politics and the power of narrative.

The Universe of Things: Short Fiction
  by Gwyneth Jones

The stories in the *Universe of Things* span Jones's career, from "The Eastern Succession," first published in 1988, to the just-published "Collision." Each opens a window into a richly depicted culture in which its intelligent, resourceful characters struggle to make sense of the mysteries of their world.

Biography

Helen Merrick is a science fiction reader, fan, and critic. By day, she is Senior Lecturer in the School of Media, Culture and Creative Arts at Curtin University, Western Australia. She has published widely on feminism, science fiction, and science studies, including contributions to *The Cambridge Companion to Science Fiction* (2003), *Queer Universes: Sexualities in Science Fiction* (2008), and the *Routledge Companion to Science Fiction* (2009). She is the co-editor of *Women of Other Worlds: Excursions through science fiction and feminism* (University of Western Australia Press, 1999) and is on the editorial boards of *Extrapolation, Transformative Works and Cultures*, and *Paradoxa*. A co-authored book on Donna Haraway is forthcoming from Columbia University Press.

She shares her little slice of urban bushland with a partner, three children, and numerous wild and domesticated earth others.